Israel's Changing Society

Israel's Changing Society

Population, Ethnicity, and Development

SECOND EDITION

Calvin Goldscheider

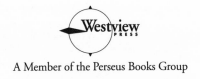

A Member of the Perseus Books Group

Copyright © 2002 by Westview Press, A Member of the Perseus Books Group

Westview Press books are available at special discounts for bulk purchases in the United States by corporations, institutions, and other organizations. For more information, please contact the Special Markets Department at The Perseus Books Group, 11 Cambridge Center, Cambridge MA 02142, or call (617) 252-5298.

Published in 2001 in the United States of America by Westview Press, 5500 Central Avenue, Boulder, Colorado 80301-2877, and in the United Kingdom by Westview Press, 12 Hid's Copse Road, Cumnor Hill, Oxford OX2 9JJ

Find us on the World Wide Web at www.westviewpress.com

Cataloging-in-Publication Data available from the Library of Congress.
ISBN 0-8133-3970-7 (hb) 0-8133-3917-0 (pb)

Map on page 2 used with courtesy of the University of Texas library (www.lib.utexas.edu).

The paper used in this publication meets the requirements of the American National Standard for Permanence of Paper for Printed Library Materials Z39.48–1984.

1   2   3   4   5   6   7   8   9   10—05   04   03   02

To
Dov Friedlander
and
Judah Matras

Contents

PART ONE
Demography, Development, and Ethnicity

PART TWO
The Formation of Israeli Communities

Tables and Figures

Tables

Figures

Preface and Acknowledgments

In this book I focus on the conjunction of population processes, ethnicity, and nation-building as the basis for understanding the changing society of Israel. These three themes provide important analytic handles in investigating the dynamics of change since the establishment of the state, and they are likely to be at the heart of changes in the future. To some extent, these factors in their actual and ideological guises have been at the foundation of thinking about Israel before it became a state; they are central to the formation of new states around the world. The arguments suggest an interplay between Israeli society as a unique sociopolitical entity emergent from its particular history and as a state that illustrates general social processes that are likely to characterize other states in other places. I have synthesized sociological and demographic materials, focusing on issues central to population studies, comparative development, and ethnic pluralism. In the process, I have identified linkages between the demographic transformations of the society and have delineated the importance of socioeconomic changes for ethnic group formation in Israel.

The volume is divided into several sections. In Part 1 I focus on population change and socioeconomic development in Israel's nation-building and relate ethnic diversity of the Jewish and Arab population to these societal perspectives. In Part 2 I detail the specifics of immigration patterns and policy as the basis for the formation of Israeli's society, and I review the emergence of the Arab population as a minority community. In Part 3 I examine processes of urbanization and focus on different community types, defined ecologically and ideologically (Kibbutzim, Moshavim, development towns, and urban centers). In Part 4 I then highlight three types of inequality based on the distribution of resources, gender roles, and death, focusing attention on the interrelationship of inequality and ethnic differentiation. In Part 5 I focus on issues of family and marriage and review the contexts of ethnic continuities and changes, with particular concern about the importance and meaning of interethnic marriages and the reduction of family size. Finally, I examine Israeli society in the context of relationships to two external communities—Jews in communities outside the state of Israel, and Palestinians, particularly those living in areas administered by Israel.

To clarify these changes and the intersections of the phenomena, I have taken a fresh look at the extensive data available and have reviewed the major social scientific studies of Israeli society. I have readily relied on the rich empirical and analytic frameworks that inform us about Israel, in particular, and societies, in

general. The research for the volume began as part of a series of studies that I conducted on the sociology and demography of Israel, beginning in the early 1970s.
This particular book grew out of my preparations for courses on Israeli society
that I have offered at Brown University and in lectures that I have given at confer-
ences and in universities throughout the United States. My goal was to provide an
up-to-date review and synthesis of materials on the connections between the demography and sociology of Israeli society, particularly its ethnic dimensions. As I
reexamined the issues, I discovered new and important linkages that had not been
systematically investigated in the past and that should form the basis of future
systemic research. It soon became clear to me that a reformulation and reanalysis
would be required, one that drew on the strengths of previous research and asked
new questions.

I offer a note about the substantive and political views that I have highlighted
in this book: No one who writes about Israeli society, from whatever perspective—social science or humanistic, political, economic, sociological, or demographic, Jewish or Arab, American or Israeli—can avoid the implications of language for conveying political biases and ideological commitments. I too am
biased, as a Jew, as an Israeli, as an American, as a sociologist and demographer,
and as a scholar of ethnicity and religion, comparative-historical demography,
and contemporary Jews and their communities. I have tried to present an analytic
picture, not a balanced one; thus, I have organized and offered a wide range of evidence and considerable empirical detail.

I do not intend to convey a political judgment, however, when I refer to a group
as "Moslem-Israelis" rather than as "Palestinians"; I do not necessarily want to
convey an ideological position by referring to the territories administered by the
state of Israel as the "West Bank" rather than Judea and Samaria. I refer to these
territories as administered not occupied; I do not refer to East Jerusalem as "occupied Palestine." I present and argue my viewpoint from, what seems to me, clear
evidence about trends and patterns. I have interpreted these trends, as well, utiliz-
ing a framework that is biased by the assumptions of social science rather than by
the ideologies of Zionism or Arab nationalism, or the biases of theology, psychology, or history. Although I cannot claim that I have succeeded (or that others have
succeeded) in being "fair" to all sides, and thereby fair to no one, I have made the
effort to be open about my values and clear about my biases. If my prose and categories convey more than that, it is inadvertent. If the analysis presented is
challenging, provocative, and interesting, then I am fully rewarded. I claim
personal allegiances to various ideologies and professional commitments to particular perspectives within social science that will become clear by an examination
of the themes I have selected to study and how I have selected to study them. I
hope that I have laid out the biases of my perspectives and the limitations of the
evidence so that others can interpret it in new and different ways, bring new types
of information, and redirect our thinking. I will have succeeded if others are stim-
ulated to do a better or different analysis based on my efforts.

As a final note on the data presented, in addition to my synthesizing the research reports of others and attempting to incorporate these as part of my analysis, I have relied extensively on the excellent data available from the Central Bureau of Statistics of Israel. All data not specifically referenced have been derived from that source, mostly from their statistical yearbooks. Wherever possible, I have included data from the early 1990s. My goal was to be up-to-date descriptively but not to review all the latest statistics and estimates for their own sake. The focus is on patterns and trends, processes and trajectories in understanding relationships. I was not aiming to replace the latest news reports or the monthly statistical adjustments of governmental statistical bureaus in Israel. These data are presented for description and analysis as well as for reference by the reader. It is likely that particular figures and measures will become more precise in the future and, of course, will change, but I am confident that the trends outlined and the processes reviewed are representative of what has characterized Israel's changing society. When I am not citing specific quantitative evidence and specific research studies, I am presenting conclusions from a variety of studies that I (jointly with others) have carried out. These interpretations should be viewed more appropriately as hypotheses to be tested rather than as firm conclusions.

Early versions of the book were first drafted in spring 1989, when I returned to the Hebrew University in Jerusalem as a visiting scholar in the Department of Sociology on leave from Brown University. I had lived in Israel from 1969 to 1985, working as professor of demography and sociology at the Hebrew University. Much of my more recent visit was organized by my colleague and friend Nachman Ben-Yehuda, who was generous with his time and unsparing in taking care of me and my family while we were in Jerusalem. Our stay in Jerusalem was made much more pleasant by his kindnesses.

Dov Friedlander, the doyen of demographers in Israel and chair extraordinaire of the Department of Demography at the Hebrew University, continues to bring me up to date on Israel's demography and share with me the results of his new research projects. He has been a good friend for a quarter of a century, and I miss the daily contacts we had when I lived in Jerusalem. Dov has challenged every idea I have had about Israeli society and, in the process, he has helped me sharpen my arguments. Judah Matras—of the Brookdale Institute in Jerusalem, Haifa University, and Carlton University in Ottawa, Ontario, Canada, former professor of sociology and demography at the Hebrew University—has been a colleague, friend, and confidant. His own research on Israeli society has always been innovative and challenging; after years of struggling with what I thought of as a new idea, I usually found it buried in his research. Both Dov and Judah were instrumental in bringing me to Jerusalem as a faculty member and were influential in my "absorption" in Israeli society and the university. I am forever indebted to them for changing my life.

No one who does research on Israeli society and its demography can proceed very far without taking advantage of the extensive data collected by the Central

Bureau of Statistics of Israel. Since the 1970s I have had access to its rich resources and to all those who are in research and administrative positions there.

My colleagues and some former students have been most generous with their critical advice, time, and insights, and they have fully shared the results of their own research. Moshe Sicron—the government statistician, director of the Central Bureau of Statistics, and a professor in the Department of Demography at the Hebrew University—has been my friend, colleague, and teacher for many years and has always been responsive to my requests for data and for sharing his broad insights into Israeli demography. Zvi Eisenbach is a dear friend and a former student who has been extraordinarily helpful in discussing with me his own work on Moslem fertility and his understanding of Arab-Israeli demography. I have benefited from his vast and detailed knowledge. I also appreciate the support and help provided by Eliahu Ben-Moshe, whose research on the internal migration of Jews is central to our understanding of the demographic consequences of immigration. Majid Al-Haj and Sammy Smooha, of Haifa University and occasionally affiliated with Brown University, have added depth to my understanding of ethnicity in Israel. Jon Anson of Ben-Gurion University and Dorit Tal, Eitan Sabatello, Hagit Weiss, Nurit Yaffe, and Julia Zemmel of the Central Bureau of Statistics have been helpful to me over the years, reminding me how important the view of Israel is from the inside.

The research that I cover in this volume has in recent years been supported fully by the Program in Judaic Studies, the Department of Sociology, and the Population Studies and Training Center at Brown University. My colleague Alan Zuckerman, of Brown University's Department of Political Science and a frequent visiting professor at Tel Aviv University, discussed with me many of the ideas and the details of this book. I share theory and research with him in studies of comparative Jewish communities, and he brings keen insight and critical understanding on Israeli politics and society. Ernie Frerichs, director of the Program in Judaic Studies at Brown University, has always understood my concern with Israel and has been generous and supportive far beyond my expectations.

The book was completed while I was basking in the sun (but not bungee jumping) in Santa Monica, California, at RAND, continuing my research affiliation with it for over a decade and enjoying part of a sabbatical year from Brown University. I am appreciative of the support that Peter Morrison and Jim Smith have extended to me over the years. The final revisions to this volume were made during my chairship of the Department of Sociology at Brown. I want to thank the provost of Brown, Frank Rothman, and the dean of the faculty, Bryan Shepp, for their support of me, my research, and the academic units that I am associated with and for assuring me that being chair is a short-term transition.

Over the past several years, I have benefited from discussions about ethnicity with my dear friend Edward Pryor, whose premature death in 1992 left a vacuum in the study of ethnicity in Canada and in our lives. Charles Hirschman of the University of Washington has always helped me understand the international dimensions of ethnicity and has been a dear and respected colleague.

Since the 1980s Frances K. Goldscheider has read everything I have written. She has helped me clarify my thinking and sharpen my presentation so that I can write what I mean. If the ideas in this book are interesting and clear, it is because of her insights and help. Her expertise as demographer and sociologist complements our increasing love for each other. She has given new meaning to my life.

I dedicate this book to Dov Friedlander and Judah Matras, who taught me about the sociology and demography of Israel in Jerusalem. They were instrumental in bringing me to Israel as a new immigrant and making me feel welcome, and they have become my friends and trusted colleagues. They shared the joys and conflicts associated with immigrant adjustment to Israeli society. Their research on Israel has been a model of scholarship and an inspiration to those who want to know about the transformation of Israeli society. I and all those who do research on Israeli society are in their debt. More than colleagues, they have always been there to help and to share in good times and bad; when I needed advice and support, they never hesitated. When I needed walls to build or dismantle, a meal, an idea, insight into the nature of Israeli society, or information on how to live with Israeli bureaucracies, or when I just needed to talk about family and children, I could always depend on them. There is nothing better than a good friend, and I have been most fortunate in having two in Jerusalem. I have dedicated this book to them as part of the expression of my continuing appreciation and recognition of their specialness to me.

My special thanks to Dean Birkenkamp of Westview Press, who has been supportive of publishing the results of my research for more than a decade and has encouraged in creative ways the development of important social science publications at Westview Press. Sabina A. Vanish copyedited the manuscript with great care and insight. I am grateful to her for sparing me the embarrassment of errors and inconsistencies. This book has taken me much longer to produce than others I have written, perhaps because of the personal attachments that I have to Israeli society and the difficulty of gaining a distance that permits a balanced social scientific analysis. I have gained time and distance from Israel, but the complexities remain. The changes that Israel has experienced since the mid-1980s have been enormous. If my nostalgia for Jerusalem's sunsets, sunrises, beauty, and inspiration shines through the often critical analyses of the challenges of inequality and nation-building that I describe in this book, I shall be pleased.

Calvin Goldscheider
Brown University

Preface to the Revised Edition

Israel has experienced many major changes since the first edition of this book was drafted in 1989. Prime Minister Yitzhak Rabin was assassinated by a Jewish extreme nationalist in 1995; Benjamin Netanyahu of the Likud party was elected prime minister in 1996; Ehud Barak (of the Labor party) defeated Netanyahu in 1999 and in turn was defeated by Ariel Sharon in direct elections in 2001. Optimism over reaching a political accord with the Palestinians to end the Israel-Arab conflict has been abandoned as new and continuous fighting has resulted in a newly defined *intifada*. Escalation of the fighting within the state of Israel and the territories it administers has replaced negotiations. Serious clashes continue between settlers of those territories and the Palestinian population. Attacks and counterattacks have bloodied the streets of Jerusalem and Jenin, Gaza and Netanya, Tel Aviv and Ramallah.

Also since the first edition, a large number of Russians have emigrated to Israel, adding well over a million persons to the population in the 1990s. The economy has moved into high tech, and new temporary workers from a variety of countries have entered Israel to take unskilled jobs, mainly to replace Palestinians. Israel has endured considerable internal religious conflict, some of it cultural and some political, among Jews. However, those conflicts have been put on temporary hold as attention has focused on clashes with the Palestinians. Many of the changes during the past decade have roots in the period before the 1990s. Continuities, as well as the continuous unfolding of changes, characterize Israel's changing society.

In preparing the revisions and updating the materials where appropriate, I have been struck by how the processes that were identified and reviewed continue to provide insight into contemporary Israeli society.

I have attempted to update all the empirical data in every chapter. No chapter has remained the same, although the fundamental analysis of population, ethnicity, and development still appears sound. I have extensively used the *Statistical Yearbook of Israel of 2000* to update most of the data, as well as other sources from the Central Bureau of Statistics of Israel; these sources are conveniently located on the bureau's Web site (cbs.gov.il). Only a few detailed pieces from the 1995 census in Israel have been released, and these have been incorporated. There is much research that can and will be carried out with the new extensive data, particularly comparisons with earlier data. But as I noted in the preface to the first edition, my goal is not simply to describe the latest report of the statistical bureaus, but to identify processes and trends. The update allows us to see the continuities as well as the changes. My colleague and friend Dov Friedlander has organized a pathbreaking, innovative project linking individuals in various censuses. These longitudinal files are a gold mine of data, and he has generously shared some of the preliminary findings with me. These matching files link information in a manner that allows for the analysis of ethnic differences in education and have important policy implications for redressing the ethnic gap. I am again grateful to him for permission to cite some of these findings.

As I prepared the update and revisions in the late summer of 2001, Israelis and Palestinians were locked in a new battle over control and their futures. The new *intifada* has raged on a daily basis for the last year, and peace does not seem to be on the horizon. I have reflected on that conflict and examined the roots and voices associated with that conflict in other publications. I have revised somewhat the last chapter of this book to reflect on this new/old crisis but have not in any way focused on it. I am committed to the principle that a focus on the contours of a society allows you to understand its problems better than a focus solely on the contours of the conflict itself. This conflict has had a major impact on the population, on development, and on ethnic relationships. I have no special insight into the resolution of the conflict, and you will find none in this book. I take no comfort in knowing that few others seem to have any insight or wisdom as well.

In preparing the revisions I have benefited from the assistance of Cathy Bueker, a doctoral student in sociology at Brown University. She saved me many hours of tedious labor in updating the statistical tables and the figures in the book. I am grateful to her for her patient and careful work, which she carried out in between her own doctoral research on the politics of American immigration and her trip to Thailand. I am also grateful to those who sent me positive comments and those who disagreed with some of my analysis in the first edition. I appreciated the positive feedback and tried to take into account some of the critical comments. I am grateful to Brown University, its administration, and the academic units with which I am affiliated for continuing to support my research.

There is no doubt that new data and new information will become available in the next several years. I am hopeful that the analysis presented will remain salient and interesting so that others can build on these foundations for future research.

Calvin Goldscheider
Brown University
September 2001

PART ONE

Demography, Development, and Ethnicity

Israel

- ——— International boundary
- —·—·— District (meḥoz) boundary
- ★ National capital
- ⊙ District (meḥoz) center
- ╫╫ Railroad
- ——— Divided highway
- ——— Other road

0   40 Kilometers
0   40 Miles
Lambert Conformal Conic Projection, SP 30N / 36N

Israel proclaimed Jerusalem as
its capital in 1950, but the US,
like nearly all other countries,
maintains its Embassy in Tel Aviv.

The West Bank and Gaza Strip
are Israeli-occupied with current
status subject to the Israeli-
Palestinian Interim Agreement –
permanent status to be determined through further negotiation.

LEBANON

UNDOF
Zone

Tyre

Qiryat
Shemona

As Qunaytirah

GOLAN
HEIGHTS
(Israeli-
occupied)

Nahariyya

SYRIA

'Akko

NORTHERN

Haifa

Tiberias

Lake
Tiberias

As Suwaydā'

HAIFA

Nazareth

Irbid

Daŕa

Busrá
ash Shām

Ḥadera

Jenin

Netanya

Ṭulkarm

Al
Mafraq

CENTRAL

Herzliyya

Nablus

Jarash

TEL AVIV

Tel Aviv-Yafo

WEST BANK

Bat Yam

1994
Treaty
Line

Az Zarqā'

Reḥovot

Ram
Allah

Amman

Ramla

Ashdod

Jericho

Mediterranean   Sea

Jerusalem

JERUSALEM

Mādabā

Ashqelon

Bethlehem

Gaza

Qiryat
Gat

Dead
Sea

GAZA STRIP

Hebron

1950
Armistice
Line

Khān Yūnis

1949 Armistice Line

Beersheba

Al Karak

Al Qaṭrānah

Al 'Arīsh

SOUTHERN

Dimona

Zefa'

Aş Şafi

JORDAN

Bi'r Lahfān

NEGEV

Zin

Abū
'Ujaylah

Mizpe
Ramon

'Ayn al
Quṣaymah

Bi'r Ḥasanah

Ma'ān

Al Jafr

EGYPT

SINAI

Al Kuntillah

Ra's an Naqb

An Nakhl

Yotvata

Elat

Tābā

Al 'Aqabah

*Gulf
of
Aqaba*

Al
Mudawwarah

**SAUDI
ARABIA**

Boundary representation is
not necessarily authoritative

Base 802833 (A00853) 9-01

1

Nation-Building, Population, and Development

The state of Israel is one of the oldest new societies to have been established in the post–World War II era. Its roots are embedded in the very distant past of the Hebrew Bible and in centuries of minority status and anti-Semitism in Christian and Moslem societies. Emerging politically out of the ashes of a European Jewry destroyed in the Holocaust, Israel was carved out of the nineteenth-century Ottoman Empire and was based on European ideologies of nationalism and ethnic politics. Built on Western foundations of justice, independence, and democracy, it has struggled continuously for political legitimacy among its neighbors, and its members have battled over its boundaries and territory, the distribution of its resources, and the treatment of its minorities. Committed to peace, it has been in warfare and ceaseless conflict. Though Israel is defined as a secular state and is dedicated to being an open, pluralistic, egalitarian society, religion has been an integral element of its politics and it is divided by ethnicity and religion. Fiercely independent, Israel remains the major recipient of economic and military aid from the United States and from Jews around the world. Designed as a haven for the remnants of world Jewry, it contains less than 40 percent of the world's Jewish population after more than five decades of statehood, immigration, and population growth.

Israeli society has integrated millions of Jewish immigrants from an enormous range of diverse countries, invigorated an ancient language to form a common basis of modern communication, and developed a rich culture of literature, theater, film, and scholarship. It has become one of the leaders in agricultural innovation and rural communal experiments, even as it is one of the most urban of contemporary societies. The deserts have bloomed, and modern technologies have flourished in Israel; major revolutions in the family have occurred, and extensive health care institutions have been organized. Israel has become a model state for many Third

World nations and a major source of identity for Jewish communities around the world. Characterized by heterogeneity and by intense and continuous change, Israel is a small state occupying a disproportionate share of the headlines and stories in the Western press. Indeed, contradictions and paradoxes seem to be some of the defining features of Israeli society, as does its complexity.

This book concerns these complex themes and is an attempt to understand Israel's changing society. I examine demographic processes and social-economic-political developments to describe the changes that Israel has experienced and to provide clues about the sources of these changes and their consequences. I focus on the linkages between nation-building and population growth and investigate the assimilation of immigrants from diverse societies and their mobilization into a coherent, pluralistic polity. I assess how resources are distributed and how external dependencies and internal conflicts are connected to clarify the basis of ethnic and other inequalities. To grasp the complexity of the everyday life of its citizens, I review normal, recurrent life events—births, marriages and family formations, sicknesses, and deaths. I investigate the communities where people live, the jobs they have, the children they love, their schooling, and their resources. I outline developments in culture, politics, and religion; minority inequalities and the creation of new communities, their distinctiveness and differential access to opportunities; the significance of gender roles and the sources of family values; and the relationship of Jews and Arab Palestinians in their diasporas to Israelis and their society. Together, these themes provide a portrait of contemporary Israeli society, an assessment of the historical roots of current patterns, and the basis for conjecture about the future.

To carry out the daunting goals of understanding this complex society, I use some overall theoretical maps to orient readers with the broadest images to fit the details into a coherent whole. I provide in this introductory chapter several points of entry into the complexities of understanding changes in Israeli society over the past several decades. Throughout, I emphasize the links among population processes, economic development, nation-building, and emergent ethnicity.

I make two core arguments about the patterns of nation-building in Israel: First, I argue that demographic transformations—changes in immigration, health and mortality, fertility and family structure, internal migration and residential concentration—have been critical in shaping nation-building and economic development in Israeli society and in that society's generational renewal. Second, I demonstrate how the sources of inequalities within Israel have changed over time and how new divisions among Jews and between Jews and Arabs are emerging. Demographic and social structural factors are at the core of these changing inequalities, transforming communities in the process of nation-building.

In my examination of Israel's changing society, I note the tensions between its uniqueness and its commonalities shared with other countries. Social patterns are emerging in Israel that are similar to other small, developing countries dependent on large and powerful nations for socioeconomic resources and political support.

At the same time, other processes reflect the specifics of the Jewish condition in recent history and the relationships between Israeli and non-Israeli Jews. Still other patterns in Israel can be understood only in light of Israel's particular history, related to its development and its role in the Middle East region. Israel is unique in the forces that have shaped its history; it is also a microcosm of population, development, and ethnic relationships. It is one country that comprises many communities—a political entity unified and organized, with official boundaries and administrative networks. Israeli society is an example of the processes of sociopolitical development, economic dependency, and ethnic pluralism; it is at the crossroads of East and West, where Western democracy, European socialism, and Jewish and Moslem fundamentalism blend with Middle East culture and society. [1]

It is difficult to generalize from the case of one small country to others in different areas of the world. The historical events that have been specific to the evolution of the Jewish state and the people who live there preclude any sweeping conclusions. Yet it is striking how the processes that have come to characterize Israeli society parallel those that have emerged elsewhere, in old and new states, in more- and less-developed nations, in Western and non-Western countries. The analyses that I present provide a basis for understanding one fascinating case study; my conclusions should be informative for comparative studies. The unique features of the Israeli case, as well as more general patterns of social change and social inequality, should emerge at the end.

Demographic Themes

Demography plays a powerful role in understanding the formation of Israeli society and the changes that it has experienced over time. Among the demographic themes are (1) the centrality of immigration in Israel's population growth, (2) the links between increases in population size and economic development, (3) the tie between the geographic distribution of Israelis and the political legitimacy of the state, and (4) the ways that residential patterns have created ethnic networks within a pluralistic society. There are other demographic themes. The relative size of Jewish and Arab populations has been of central political importance. Population processes are associated with social inequalities based on ethnic origins, religion, and gender. Family values and gender roles are linked to the changing size of families; differentials in health and death are connected to social inequalities. The centrality of demography is reflected in its core place within Zionism, the national ideology of Israel. And there are important cultural values about population issues. I expand on these themes throughout my analysis. Here, I outline five basic principles of population analysis.

First, there are only two sources of changes in population size—natural increase (the difference between births and deaths) and the net flow of migration. All social, economic, political, and cultural factors that affect the changing size of a population operate through these two sources. In turn, alterations in the social and economic composition of a population are influenced by the origins and selectivity of migrant flows and the differential reproduction of social groups. Entering and exiting processes indicated by fertility, migration, and mortality are the bases for understanding the changing demography of Israel's population.

Second, communities and families, like the populations of states, are shaped by these demographic processes. The number of children people have, where they live, who their neighbors are, and their own health and welfare are important for the generational renewal of society, as are the family roles of men and women, the networks that families sustain, and the values that they convey from generation to generation. Communities shape the national demographic profile, and families are the building blocks of communities. Thus, demographic analysis focuses on changes in population size and distribution for the country as a whole, as well as on families, communities, and groups.

Third, demographic processes are interrelated: Fertility, mortality, and migration (both internal and international) are linked to each other in dynamic ways. Changes in each process contribute to overall population-size changes and are likely to affect other processes. These population processes can be examined for their impact on demographic phenomena over time and in their different configurations. Each process influences the age and sex structure of populations and often the cohort changes in socioeconomic and ethnic composition. Together, these interrelated demographic processes form a population system.

Fourth, marriage and family formation are significant in a demographic context, since these processes bind families together, linking the generations to each other in a web of relationships. Community is defined as a pattern of interrelated networks. The tighter the networks and the larger the number of linkages between families through marriage, residence, jobs, and places of origin, the greater the community cohesion and the stronger the identification with the community. Demography shapes the shared intensities of interactions within and between generations; in turn, population processes are at the core of societal cohesiveness.

Fifth, demographic processes determine, and are determined by, social processes linked to families, households, and groups and are therefore fundamental social dimensions of communal life. It follows that as social changes occur, demographic processes will be affected; as demographic processes unfold, social changes are likely to follow. When we examine basic demographic processes and focus on population changes, we are confronted with the fundamentals of sociological analysis. Issues of family continuity and social inequality are critical parts of the generational issues highlighted by demography.

Demographic principles focus attention on the examination of how population processes are at the core of nation-building, development, and national political integration in Israel's changing society. They point to the need to investigate the linkages between population processes and group differences, including population changes among groups and demographic convergences among communities. They suggest the importance of population processes in the formation and transmission of social class concentration and the generational overlap of ethnicity and stratification. Studying demography in the contexts of nation-building, inequalities, and community provides a basis for understanding Israel's changing society.

Changing Demographic Snapshots

I begin empirically with a simple demographic profile of contemporary Israeli society. A snapshot, cross-sectional demographic view reveals a total population size in Israel in the year 2000 of 6.4 million and a rate of population growth of about 2.5 percent per year over the last 15 years.[2] Israel is an overwhelmingly urban society, with close to 90 percent of the population living in areas so designated. About 3 out of 10 Israelis are below the age of 15, and 10 percent are above the age of 65. During the decade between 1990 and 2000, almost 1 million immigrants arrived in Israel, over 90 percent from the former Soviet Union. Birth rates in the state of Israel (22 births per 1,000 population and a total fertility rate of about 2.9 births per woman, 1990–2000) were higher than in most industrialized Western countries and lower than in Third World countries. Death rates were among the lowest in the world (6 deaths per 1,000 population, an infant mortality rate of 6 deaths to children under age 1 per 1,000 births, and a life expectancy of almost 80 years.) The dominant ethnic-religious population in the state is Jewish, representing about 80 percent of the total, with a rather even split between those of European (Western) origins and those of Asian and African (Middle Eastern) origins. About 6 out of 10 Jews were born in Israel, and 28 percent of the Jewish population in 2000 were Israelis who were born of Israeli-born parents. The Arab population in Israel is largely Moslem (about 3 out of 4) and is concentrated in particular regions of the country.

Changes in the demographic portrait of Israeli society can be sketched in a preliminary way by examining these same elements about five decades earlier, when the state of Israel was established. At the end of 1948, there were 872,700 persons living in approximately the same land area in Israel, mostly Jews (82 percent), and there was a low rate of natural growth. During the first several months subsequent to statehood, there were very high rates of immigration and a potential for continuous Jewish immigration from a wide range of countries. At the same time, there was an exodus of Arab residents as war raged between Israel and neighboring Arab countries. Israel was established in part of the areas of Palestine, as territorial control switched from the British Mandate toward an emerging Jewish administration. There was a low level of industrial activity in 1948 but a high level of urban concentration. Israel was a country without a secure future, as war and political-economic uncertainty marked its birth; it had an unknown capacity then to economically and socially absorb large numbers of immigrants. The Arab population became a demographic, political, and social minority as Jews became the majority in the new state.

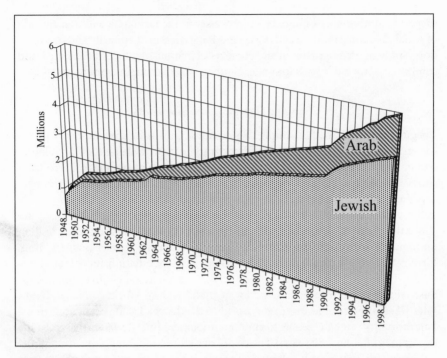

Figure 1.1 *Growth of Jewish and Arab Populations in Israel, 1948–1998*

The demographic snapshots begin to be sharpened when one reviews the pattern of population growth. The path of demographic growth in Israel has been rather uneven since the 1950s, even as the rate has been high. Data in Figure 1.1 dramatically show the increases in population size and the fluctuations since 1948 for both the Jewish and Arab populations. Starting with a base of 650,000 in mid-1948, the population surpassed its first million within the first year and doubled to 2 million within a decade. By the end of 1970, Israeli society had over 3 million people; by 1982 it had added another million to its population. Over 5 million people lived in Israel by the end of 1992, representing a sixfold increase in the Jewish and Arab populations in 45 years. In the year 2000 there were 6.4 million Israelis.

Much obviously happened over this five-decade period, transforming the fundamental characteristics of the society. Questions of war and economic uncertainty remain but are different than at an earlier time; the cultural, economic, and social integration of Israel's immigrant populations continue to be issues in the beginning of the twenty-first century, but the dimensions have radically changed. Israel's status as an independent state is largely unquestioned internationally and is increasingly accepted by its Arab neighbors, even as the boundaries that mark its political borders remain tentative and controversial.

So, while the snapshots sketch formal beginnings and the current demographic profile, they omit much that has happened in the society and miss the processes underlying these changes. Snapshots cannot adequately convey the nature of social and demographic change; the dynamics of change need to be examined directly in order to understand the society and fit the demography of Israel into a broader historical and comparative framework. When we place Israeli society in comparative demographic context, we begin to disentangle that which Israel shares with other countries and that which is unique to its development.

Are Israeli Demographic Patterns Unique?

The high rates of population growth reflect different combinations of demographic sources for Jews and Arabs. The Jewish population increased primarily as a result of immigration; natural increase accounted for most of the Arab population growth since 1948. These different sources of growth imply very different population trajectories and related social processes, even as the relative size of these populations has remained remarkably steady. The demographic transformations in Israeli society appear to recapitulate in compressed form the demographic transitions in Western, industrialized nations, historically and comparatively. They also seem to parallel the demographic processes unfolding in Third World countries over the past several decades. The general patterns are well known and include several conspicuous features:

1. Mortality levels have declined with improvements in public health services and have been extended to all sectors of the population.
2. There has been a transition to nuclear family structure, an increasing use of efficient contraception, and the emergence of small family size. Together, reductions in mortality and the shift from high to low fertility resulted in a period of rapid population growth, followed by a slowing of the population growth rate.
3. The population has become increasingly urban in concentration, and metropolitan areas have expanded as populations have moved to suburban areas.
4. Immigration and ethnic residential concentrations have characterized the society over time, and significant socioeconomic integration of populations from diverse countries of origin has taken place.
5. The population of Israel has become older—relatively and absolutely—as a result of the reduction of fertility and the extension of life. Welfare and health services have expanded to meet the changing needs of an aging population.
6. The state has become more involved in the formulation and implementation of a broad range of population and welfare policies.

These demographic changes in Israel (as in other countries) have been linked to the expansion of health services and economic opportunities, the changing roles of women, the growing diffusion of Western technology to developing nations, and the increasing political and economic dependencies of small periphery nations on a select number of large, powerful core countries. Israel's demographic uniqueness lies in the specifics of these processes, not in the transformations themselves. The demographic patterns in Israel compress in microcosm all of these transitions within the same society in a relatively short time span (see Berelson 1979; Friedlander and Goldscheider 1984). To take but one example: The transition to small family size that took over a century to unfold in Sweden's demographic history occurred within less than a generation among Israel's Asian-African population. Thus there are important generalizations to other places and times that emerge from an examination of the particular features of the demography of Israel, and there is much to learn about Israel from systematic comparisons to other countries.

Israeli demographic patterns also have distinctive features that reflect its unique population history, ideology, politics, and the complex social mosaic that has emerged there in the last generation. To unravel the complexities of Israeli demographic patterns, I consider the broader dimensions of social change common to developing countries as well as the specifics of Israel's internal demographic developments, the details of its changes over time, and the linkages between Israel and communities outside of Israel—in the Middle East and around the world, at the national level and at the ethnic-religious community levels. These features, in combination with the broader economic, technological, and political factors that have shaped demographic transitions over time, are the basis for interpreting Israel's demographic evolution.

Israel's Demography Among the Nations

To position Israel among nations and in history, I use a demographic classification scheme referred to as the theory of demographic transition. Descriptively, modern societies have been characterized by patterns of low population growth as a result of low fertility and mortality levels, since births and deaths increasingly come under individual and societal controls. The relative stability in population growth is also characteristic of premodern societies, but under reverse demographic conditions—fertility and mortality are not under the direct control of society and both are at high levels. The "transition" from high and uncontrolled fertility and mortality to low, controlled fertility and mortality—from one pattern of low population growth rates to another—is the demographic passage from premodern to postmodern societies. The period of transition is clearly exceptional since low growth rates are the result of temporary disruptions when mortality declines more rapidly than fertility. The length of this high population growth stage varies with the intensity and duration of mortality and fertility declines.

Although the initial formulation of the demographic stages was developed as a means of classifying countries, it has also been used as a basis for studying their historical evolution. The argument has been that the past of more economically developed nations resembles the current patterns of Third World countries, and the future of the Third World demographic patterns is presaged by the contemporary processes of Western societies. Without implying that demographic history is always recapitulative or that the pace of population change is identical, the scheme remains useful in classifying countries in terms of their population growth patterns. Thus contemporary demographic rates cluster around very low population growth levels in Western, modern, and European countries; often they do not replace their population generationally from natural increase. At the other end of the continuum are countries in which growth rates are fairly low because they still maintain high rates of fertility and mortality. These countries are diminishing in number, replaced by those in transition from their relatively high growth rates, due to increased levels of mortality and the retention of higher rates of fertility (see Goldscheider 1971; Matras 1977; Watkins 1990; Demeny and McNicoll 1998).

Where does Israel's demography fit in this classification scheme? It is not quite in the category of more economically developed nations of Europe and North America because of its higher-than-average fertility level. It is also not an area of high natural increase, as are Third World countries in Asia and Africa. On the whole, mortality rates in Israel are at a low level characteristic of more-developed Western nations, and fertility is at the higher end of more-developed Western nations but lower than the fertility of Third World countries. But it is not at all obvious how population growth rates relate to natural increase in Israel, since its recent demographic past has been influenced so strongly by a combination of immigration and natural increase among the various populations that make up its complex mosaic.

The importance of immigration in demographic growth rates is not unique to Israel, even as the rate of immigration (relative to the size of the receiving population) has at times been unprecedented. The demographic fascination with Israeli's society rests with examining the dramatic changes that have occurred in relatively short periods of time. For example, fertility reduction among Jews from Asian and African countries has taken place within the short span of a generation in a pro-natal normative context and without the use of modern contraception; mortality control has occurred within an even shorter period, indeed, noticeable in the period immediately subsequent to immigration. The entire range of demographic transitions can be identified and the entire spectrum of transition stages can be documented for major subpopulations living in the same society at the same time. The rich demographic heterogeneity is neutralized when the total society is examined, since the national "average" distorts the different processes.

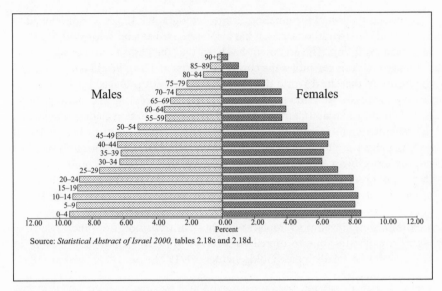

Figure 1.2   Age-Sex Pyramid, Israeli Jews, 1998

The age and sex structure of Israel's population is one of the clearest reflections of the demographic place of Israel among societies of the world. Population pyramids of Israel in the 1950s, when the state was growing rapidly through the immigration of high-fertility populations, closely resembled those of Third World countries, with a broad base to the pyramid and a slowly narrowing apex as age increases. In the late 1990s the population pyramid was becoming more like the European-American structure (see Figures 1.2 and 1.3). Some subpopulations in Israel retain the triangular structure of a Third World population (e.g., the Israeli Moslem population), but others have an inverted age structure (very narrow base and aging apex) since they are a disappearing segment (e.g., first-generation Jewish immigrants).[3]

What about the geographic distribution of Israel's population? A look at a map of Israel's population points to the major areas of residential density in Israel—the urban centers of Tel Aviv, Jerusalem, and Haifa. Since its founding as a state, Israel has been an urban society, more similar to the European, developed country model than the more heavily rural areas of Third World countries. Israel is small in population size and geographic spread and also in its sense of local community. In part, Israel's size makes it resemble a large extended community where each event has significance because of the connections among persons and families throughout the country. Israel, like other small states, has an intimate relationship with space.

Development and Nation-Building

There is an economic cost to high levels of continuous population growth if the economy does not expand. Israel could not sustain population growth rates,

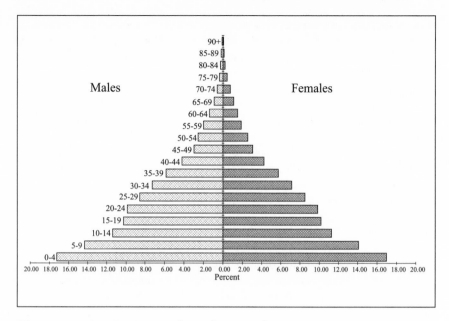

Figure 1.3   *Age-Sex Pyramid, Moslem Israelis, 1998*

retain the population, and continue to attract new immigrants without extensive economic growth. Indeed, the growth of Israel's economy has widened the opportunities of and generated increases in the standard of living for a growing number of people. In part, economic changes were brought about through the increase of population by way of immigration (the human capital and resources brought by the immigrants and their contributions to production and consumption) and the increased economic investments made in Israel from outside the country. Whether demographic changes generated the economic change or vice versa, both population size and economic production have increased over time.

The demographic transitions that I outlined occurred in the contexts of economic growth and an emerging national policy. Immigrants and their families were responsive to economic opportunities and affected economic change, as they operated in a new national political system. Immigrant economic integration in the short run and reduced ethnic-economic inequalities in the longer run are strongly related to the opportunities that were emerging for the new generation. Changes in the economy and in the distribution of resources between the generations are critical factors in understanding the changing linkages among population, nation-building, and ethnicity. Economic conditions in the country as a whole have improved. I want to clarify the sources of its economic development, internal growth versus external investments; identify the industries and economic sectors that have expanded; and examine the distribution of economic activities among ethnic and social class groups to study the connections between stratification and the emerging occupational hierarchies and their links to ethnic origin. Associated with economic growth are the transformations in the labor force and markets as the population becomes more educated, technology develops, and new sectors of the economy expand in a postindustrial world economy.

These complex issues are outlined below in broad strokes and are elaborated on as my analysis unfolds. I review several indicators of social and economic development in Israel over time. These show some dramatic changes that parallel the demographic revolutions that have occurred. At the same time, distortions may emerge when different patterns of socioeconomic change appear balanced at the national level. National indicators of economic growth can be misleading if the distribution of this growth is skewed in favor of some groups.

Overall Economic Measures

A range of economic indicators at the national level make it clear that Israel's economy has grown in terms of domestic production, technological developments, and labor force improvements. From 1950 through the mid-1970s, economic growth was quite high, apart from recessions in 1953 and 1966–1967 and stagnation in the mid-1970s (Plessner 1994). During the quarter century from 1950, the national product rose nine times, an average of 9 percent (Ginor 1986, p. 50). The sharp rise reflected an increase in capital stock (11 percent per year) and the number of employed (4 percent per year); hence, capital per employed increased 7 percent per year. The quality of the labor force increased dramatically after an initial decline (which reflected the ethnic and socioeconomic background of immigrants). Educational capital per employed declined by 7 percent in the first half of the 1950s, rose 22 percent in the period from 1961 to 1972, and continued to increase in the 1970s through the 1990s (Ginor, pp. 50–51). Gross domestic product (GDP) per capita at constant prices doubled between 1950 and 1965 and doubled again between 1965 and 1990. In the half-century from the establishment of the state, the GDP increased four-and-a-half-fold (Table 1.1).

The share of agriculture in the domestic product rose in the first years of the state, then declined steadily with a modest rise in the share of industry. The share of trade, finance, and personal services declined, and the share of public services rose, indicating the increased share in social services. The biggest rise in capital stock occurred in the shares of public services, transport, and communications, indicating the expansion of the infrastructure on a modernizing basis.[4]

In 1950 Israel's annual growth of per capita income was about one-fourth the level of that of the United States and was similar to the richer Latin American countries and Italy; it was well above Japan, but only half the level of Western Europe. From 1950 to 1970, per capita income grew more than 5 percent annually in Israel—similar to the high rates in Europe, Taiwan, and Korea—slowing considerably by the 1970s. The growth after 1950 led to an increase in Israel's relative

TABLE 1.1 Selected Socioeconomic Indicators in Israel, 1950–2000 [a]

			Gross Domestic Product	Years of Schooling (age 15 and over)			
			Per Capita Constant Prices	Jews		Arabs		Food in Consumption
				None	13+	None	13+	Expenditure
	NIS	Index		(%)	(%)	(%)	(%)	(%)
1950	2,736	100		–	–	–	–	39
1960	4,513	165		13	10	50	2	34
1970	7,474	273		9	13	36	2	31
1980	9,612	351		6	21	19	8	29
1990	11,045	404		4	29	13	9	26
2000	12,218	447		3	40	7	19	21

[a] Dates are approximate and are within one year.
Source: *Statistical Abstract of Israel,* various years.

real income to over half that of the United States by 1980 and to about 75 percent of the average level in Western Europe (Ben-Porath 1986b, table 2.1).

Economic growth in Israel is directly related to changes in population (Ben-Porath 1986a). In the quarter-century before 1948, the Jewish population increased eightfold, with the population doubling on average each decade. The total product of the Jewish economy in Palestine in the same period increased 25-fold, at an average annual rate of 13.7 percent; the total stock of capital increased fifteenfold. Total product increased elevenfold, and capital stock increased sixteenfold from 1950 to 1982, with a stronger growth during the first two decades. During the prestate and poststate periods, the correlation between the ratio of immigrants to mean Jewish population and the growth rates of gross national product (GNP) was high (0.72). High correlations have also been documented for the relationship between immigration and the growth rate of capital stock (Ben-Porath). After 1948, cycles in immigration tended to follow cycles in GNP. Immigration affected the economy by expanding the supply of labor and often the supply of capital; it generated surges in demand as well, increasing the working-age population and the labor supply. An examination of the direction of the relationship over time shows a stronger causality from immigration to economic growth in the prestate period, and overall from 1922 to 1982. For the period 1954 onward, immigration responded to the growth rate of per capita income and consumption (Ben-Porath).

TABLE 1.2 Israel's Employed Population: Economic Branch, and Occupation, 1955–2000[a]

				Economic Branch					
	Agr	Ind	Con	Com	Tra	Fin	Pub	Per	Total
1955	18	24	9	13	6	–	22	8	100
1960	17	25	9	12	6	–	22	8	99
1970	9	26	8	13	8	5	24	8	101
1975	6	26	8	12	7	7	27	6	99
1980	6	25	6	12	7	8	30	6	101
1985	6	24	5	13	6	10	30	7	101
1990	4	23	5	15	6	10	30	7	100
2000	2	19	6	16	6	14	31	6	100

Agr = Agriculture, forestry, fishing
Ind = Industry (mining, manufacturing, electricity and water)
Con = Construction (building and public works)
Com = Commerce, restaurants, and hotels (includes banking in 1955)
Tra = Transport, storage, and communication
Fin = Financing and business services
Pub = Public and community services
Per = Personal and other services

				Occupation					
	Sci	Pro	Mgr	Cle	Sal	Ser	Agr	Ski	Unsk	Total
1955	–	10	–	16	11	10	17	29	6	99
1960	–	11	–	14	9	13	17	31	5	100
1965	–	13	–	17	8	11	13	33	5	100
1970	–	16	–	17	8	12	8	32	5	98
1975	7	13	3	17	8	12	6	28	6	100
1980	8	15	4	19	8	11	6	26	4	101
1985	9	15	6	18	8	13	5	24	4	102
1990	9	17	5	17	9	13	4	24	3	101
2000	13	15	6	19	7	11	1	20	9	101

Sci = Scientific and academic workers
Pro = Professional and other technical workers
Mgr = Managers and administrators
Cle = Clerical and related workers
Sal = Sales workers
Ser = Service workers
Agr = Agricultural workers
Ski = Skilled workers in industry and elsewhere
Unsk = Unskilled workers

[a] The occupational and economic branch categories have changed somewhat over the years. The data should be viewed as approximate and the dates within one year.

Source: *Statistical Abstract of Israel,* various years.

Economic and Occupational Shifts

Economic shifts over time can be observed in the changing structure of economic branches and in occupations. The distribution of employed persons among economic branches reflects a combination of stability and change (Table 1.2). The most striking overall feature of the years between 1955 and 1990 is the relative stability of the employment distribution among various sectors. The industrial branch remained relatively steady (at about 25 percent of the employed) until 1990–2000. Commerce, transportation, and personal services have also remained steady over time. The major shifts in employment have been the decline in agriculture, from 18 percent to 2 percent, and in construction, from 9 percent to 5–6 percent. At the same time, there have been increases in employment in the finance sector (doubling to 10 percent from 1970 to 1990 and increasing to 14 percent in 2000) and in public community services (from 22 percent to 31 percent).

A complementary picture emerges from an examination of shifting occupational distribution over time in Israel (Table 1.2, bottom panel). There has been a clear and sharp decline in the proportion engaged in agriculture from the mid-1950s to 2000 (17 percent to 1 percent), modest declines in skilled laborers (from about 30 percent of the employed in the 1950s through the 1970s, to about 25 percent in the 1980s and 1990s and to 20 percent in 2000). Service and sales workers have remained at about the same level over time, declining somewhat in 1990–2000. The most conspicuous overall occupational shift has been the increase in the professional, scientific, and academic category (from 10 percent of the employed in 1955 to 28 percent by 2000).

Educational Changes

Along with these broad economic changes were improvements in the educational levels of the population. The median years of schooling for the total population in 1961 was 8 years; 9 percent of the population had 13 or more years of schooling. The median increased 2.5 years by 1980, and the proportion with higher education doubled to 19 percent. Average education in Israel in the beginning of the 1990s was 12 years. By 2000, fully 40 percent of the Jewish population had 13 or more years of schooling. These increases are even more impressive when the educational levels of Arab Israelis are examined. Fully half of the Arab population age 15 and over in 1961 had no formal education, and only 1.5 percent had 13 or more years; four decades later, over 90 percent of the Arab population had some formal education, and 19 percent had more than a high school education. Among Jews, the decline at the lower level of education was from 13 percent in 1961 to 3 percent in 2000, and the proportion at the higher educational level increased fourfold during the same period (Table 1.1).

These educational shifts have transformed the employed population and their educational quality (Table 1.3). In the early 1960s, 58 percent of the employed men in Israel had less than 8 years of education, and about 1 in 10 had more than a high school education. By 2000, only 1 out of 10 had less than 8 years, and 4 out of 10 had 13 or more years of education. In 2000, only 4 percent of the women employed in Israel had low levels of education, and over half had 13 or more years of education. This distribution reverses the patterns in the 1960s, when 45 percent of the employed women had less than 8 years of schooling and 15 percent had 13 or more years (see also Amir 1986).

Standard of Living

Other economic indicators reveal the increased standard of living and the improved quality of life among Israelis. For example, the percentage of food in consumption declined continuously from 39 percent in 1950 to 21 percent in 2000 (Table 1.1). Indicators of housing and crowding reveal the increase in the amount of household space available: In 1967, 85 percent of the Jewish population lived in households in which there was more than one person per room, compared to 58 percent in 1990; the proportion of households that had two persons or more per room declined from 31 percent to 8 percent. In 1999, only 27 percent of Jewish households had more than one person per room compared to 65 percent among the Arab population.

Increasing possession of consumer goods also indicates improvements in the standard of living and the quality of life among Israelis. In 1950 only 2 percent of the Israeli households had electric refrigerators, but one-half of the households had them in 1960, and virtually all had them by 1975. Seven percent of the households had washing machines in the mid-1950s, increasing to 43 percent in 1970 and to 80 percent in 1980. Only 4 percent of Israeli families owned a private car in 1960, 15 percent in 1970, 34 percent in 1980. These and related data reveal the overall increase in the standard of living, access to modern consumption items, and the diffusion of these to major sectors of the population.

Economic Dependency

As Israel's economy improved, there was also a growing dependency on external funds. In part, this is a direct result of the military burdens that Israel has experienced and the economic costs of building a modern defense system. Israel has devoted a considerable part of its economic capacity to defense, much higher per capita than in Western countries. Since World War II, the average rate of defense expenditures of Western countries has been below 10 percent; defense outlays in Israel averaged 25 percent per year from 1969 to 1981 (Berglas 1986, chap. 8). In 1970 total U.S. assistance to Israel was less than $100 million, and 85 percent was in the form of loans. A decade later the assistance had increased to over $2 billion, with half as loans. In 1985 Israel received $3.3 billion of military and economic assistance from the United States, all of it in the form of grants (Rabie 1988, table 14).

TABLE 1.3 Educational Level of Israel's Employed Persons, by Gender, 1963–2000[a]

Years of Schooling	Percent Employed				
	1963	*1971*	*1979*	*1990*	*2000*
Men					
0–8	58	50	34	20	10
9–12	30	35	43	50	48
13+	11	15	23	30	42
Total	100	100	100	100	100
Women					
0–8	45	34	21	11	4
9–12	40	43	46	48	41
13+	15	23	34	40	54
Total	100	100	100	100	100

[a] Dates are approximate and are within one year.

Source: *Statistical Abstract of Israel,* various years.

Israel has also received increasing support from the American Jewish community (as well as other Jewish communities around the world) and annual restitution payments from Germany (Halevi 1986). Estimates of external private and public support add up to over $8 billion annually, according to some, and considerably less on average, according to others (compare Rabie 1988 and Halevi). The important point is that Israel has increasingly become dependent on other states and on Jews living outside of the state for its continued growth. Israel's financial obligations abroad increased over threefold, to $3 billion during the 1970s and jumping to $21 billion in the 1980s. By the beginning of the 1990s these foreign obligations fluctuated at about $33 billion. Even though net export of goods from Israel increased from $211 million in 1960 to $5.3 billion in 1980 and to over $11 billion in the 1990s, net imports have increased even more sharply. These international flows are part of the economic dependency of a periphery country on a core country and have become an integral part of the economic structure of Israeli planning.

Overall economic, occupational, and educational shifts raise a number of questions about the distribution of these economic improvements among Jews and Arabs, among Jews of different ethnic origins and generations, and between women and men. These related economic development themes are analyzed in subsequent chapters when these macrolevel indicators are translated into measures of the quality of life in Israel's communities.

Zionism, Population, and Development

Zionism—a combination of national ideology, political movement, and established institutions—has had an important relationship with demographic issues and with development directions. Zionism has not been a monolithic ideology, nor has the Zionist movement established a singular set of institutions, goals, and policy commitments (see among others Avineri 1981; Halpern 1961; Hertzberg 1960; Vital 1975, 1982, 1987). Nevertheless, all of the Zionist variants have emphasized the centrality of Jewish immigration and the importance of building an autonomous Jewish community into an independent political unit. Zionism also had a vision of the Jewish condition as a minority community outside of the state and whether that minority status was problematic.

At various points in time, Zionism shaped the rate and sources of immigration, the development and support of institutions that encouraged maternal and child care, and the welfare system that provided benefits to children and families. Zionist institutions and underlying ideologies were instrumental in the development of agricultural enterprises and in subsidizing agricultural communities and new towns. Zionist institutions mobilized financial support for Israel among the Jewish communities outside of Israel, linking Jews together in supporting the state as a national Jewish homeland.

This is not to argue that the state of Israel is a direct outcome of Zionism as an ideology. The variety of Zionisms did not provide a clear directive to carry out any activity, nor was Zionist ideology a major determinant of the processes underlining immigration to the state. Similarly, it should not be assumed that ethnic inequalities among Jews and between Jews and Arabs are traceable directly to Zionist ideology or that economic, social, cultural, or religious developments are direct outcomes of Zionist ideological movements. As a combination of ideology, social movement, and a set of organizations, Zionism has been both a legitimating ideology and a source of financial support for the development of Israeli society. Phrased as a complex question, one can ask, How have ideological and organizational aspects of Zionism influenced different aspects of Israel's changing society? I consider this question throughout my analysis.

The National-Ethnic Connection

Israel has emerged as a national state, has developed and expanded its population and economy, and has articulated its commitment to national goals, institutions, symbols, and culture. Israelis have become integrated politically and economically into the emerging nation-state. At the same time that a national society has developed, there have been signs of internal divisions within the society. These divisions resulted from changes in the social and cultural construction of gender roles—for example, divisions by religious commitment, by type of residence in regions of the country, and by age and generational exposure to the country. These divisions are observable in Israel, as in many societies, and are not specific or unique to Israel's development. Their form varies among countries, and their particular nuance reflects the historical and cultural context of places.

There are also particular divisions within Israel that are more clearly a manifestation of local-regional contexts and specific historical circumstances. Two are obvious: divisions between Jews and Arabs and divisions among Jews by ethnic origins and generational status. These ethnic-religious divisions and their sources and intensities over time are reviewed in the next chapter in the contexts of population growth and economic development. In specifying the sources and sociocultural constructions of ethnicity, I focus on how population processes vary among ethnic communities and how economic growth is distributed among communities. I shall keep in mind the broader question of whether these divisions challenge the national integrity of Israeli society.

Notes

1. I shall use the convention Moslem, not Muslim, throughout this book.

2. I define the state of Israel within its formally recognized boundaries: Before 1967 it includes the state recognized internationally in 1948; after 1967 it includes the eastern part of Jerusalem. The territories added after 1967, the West Bank and Gaza, are defined as "administered territories," or those occupied by the state of Israel. In 1994 Gaza and Jericho on the West Bank were placed under Palestinian control. These political changes undoubtedly altered the demography of the state of Israel, but they cannot be assessed at this time. With minor exceptions, I do not use the Biblical names "Judea" and "Samaria" for these territories and do not include data for them, unless explicitly noted. All designations of these areas carry with them political significance and are social constructions. I do not want to convey a political statement or imply any judgment by my use of these designations. My goal is to be clear about the areas I am examining so that I can describe and analyze the processes occurring within them. I deal explicitly with these territories and their relationship to the state of Israel in Chapter 12.

3. Detailed pyramids of subpopulations illustrate the range of these age-sex population structures (Friedlander and Goldscheider 1984).

4. Demographers would also use mortality rate changes as an indicator of a rise in the standard of living; indeed, during this period, infant mortality rates declined and life expectancies at birth increased (see Chapter 9).

2

Ethnic Diversity: Jewish and Arab Populations of Israel

Population changes and political developments altered the emerging society in Israel by radically transforming its composition and redefining the basis of power. The Jewish community became the demographic majority and the source of political control. The transition from Yishuv (the Jewish settlement in Palestine) to Israeli society occurred in the context of a massive Jewish immigration from dozens of countries around the world, primarily from Eastern European and Middle Eastern countries. The Arabs in Palestine, devastated by war and depleted by mass and selective out-migration, became a minority in the emerging Jewish state. This recomposition of Jewish and Arab populations changed everything in the new state and created the diversity that characterizes contemporary Israeli society.

There are many forms of ethnic diversity within the complex society emerging in the state of Israel. Some of these forms are derived from the distinctive national origins of the population (countries and regions of the world); some are based on religious differentiation; still others are based on political constructions that have emerged in the new Israeli polity. The complex layers of ethnic differentiation are complicated further as some groups have assimilated and disappeared over several generations, though other ethnic-based sources of differentiation have emerged. My review of the changing meaning of ethnicity in Israel points to two central conclusions. First, no analysis of change and no investigation of differences within Israeli society can ignore the ethnic dimension since it is a major aspect of Israel's pluralism. Second, ethnic differentiation is a changing basis of distinctiveness and cannot be regarded solely as primordial or a constant of birth or of cultural heritage. It changes over the life course and is more salient in various contexts. I observe ethnicity in Israeli society over time, its changes, and its importance for different groups. As will become clear, the identification of types of ethnic distinctiveness is a first step toward understanding the structural and cultural bases of ethnicity.

National policy and cultural ideology favor the integration and total assimilation of Jews from diverse countries of origin in the Jewish state. Yet ethnic differences have characterized the social life and demographic changes in Israel. Paradoxically, the integration of groups has at times led to increased ethnic distinctiveness rather than to total assimilation. The tensions between ethnic change and continuity and between ethnic pluralism and an ethnic melting pot are powerful themes in our understanding of Israeli society. I examine how ethnicity emerged and how it is sustained over the generations, specifying the contexts that reinforce and sharpen ethnic distinctiveness and those that have reduced ethnic differences.

The primary objective of studying ethnic differentiation is not to examine ethnic differences per se but to identify how ethnicity is conveyed generationally. Throughout, I illustrate how ethnic differences have been translated into inequalities—the unequal access of groups to the rewards and opportunities within the society. I demonstrate how demographic factors—in particular the timing and selectivity of immigration and the continuing patterns of residential concentration—have been critical in shaping the emergence of the ethnic mosaic in Israel, and how they are central to the ways in which ethnicity has changed over the last half-century and are directly linked to the perpetuation of ethnic differentiation and inequality. I show how those ethnic differences, which are embedded in the structure of social life in Israel, tend to be perpetuated. At the same time, other ethnic differences that are primarily transfers from places of origins are rarely sustained and at best selectively reinforced. Hence, the sharp ethnic differences in fertility and mortality that characterized groups in the past have narrowed considerably as exposure to Israeli society has increased. These demographic factors are no longer the sources of ethnic distinctiveness and mainly reflect national origins and socioeconomic factors. In Israel, ethnicity emerges in new arenas. I set the stage by examining the construction of ethnic categories and describing the ethnic mosaic in Israel. These provide a basis for identifying the contexts of ethnic intensity and the basis of interpreting ethnic differences.

Ethnic Categories: Construction and Definitions

Included among the ethnic factors in Israel are both the internal ethnic divisions within and the differences between Jewish and Arab populations. Ethnicity captures an odd mixture of religion and ethnic-national origins in Israel and goes to the heart of who is a member of the society. Ethnic divisions within Jewish and Arab populations are social constructions, formed from very different sources, and are differentially linked to political, economic, and social factors. These differential sources of ethnicity have implications for their continuity.

Jewish Ethnicity

Jewish ethnic differentiation in Israel reflects a combination of social and cultural origins of immigrant groups and the effects of Israeli's social conditions. Ethnic divisions among Jews do not derive from Zionist ideological sources or explicit Israeli policies. To the contrary: The national ideology, Zionism, denies the salience of ethnicity as a continuing factor for the Israeli Jewish population. National origin differences among Jews are viewed as the product of the long-term dispersal of the Jewish people in the Diaspora; returning to the homeland, it is argued, will result in the emergence of a new Jew—untainted by the culture and psychology of the Diaspora and freed from the constraints and limitations of experiences in places of previous (non-Israel) residence (see Hertzberg 1960 for a review of different Zionist ideologies).

Zionism's construction of Jewish peoplehood, therefore, involves the assignment of ethnic origin to the minority experiences of Jews outside of Israel and, hence, requires its devaluation. Zionism rejected both the assimilation of Jews in communities outside of Israel and the retention of ethnic minority status as viable solutions to the position of Jews in modernizing societies. The long Jewish diaspora of 2,000 years is viewed simply as an empty interlude between the origin of a Jewish nation in the land of Israel and the return of Jews to their land of origin. Hence, Zionist ideology posits that Israel is the national origin of Jews. Their countries of "interlude," that is, their ethnicities, are not the source of their Jewish-national identity: Israel is. It follows that the recognition of ethnic origins as the country of ancestry would be, in part, a denial of the "return" home to Israel. To recognize the continuing salience of ethnicity would be to treat coming to Israel as immigration in the normal demographic sense, not as aliya, the imperative "ascent" to Israel of Zionist ideology. To deny "returning" to Israel would be ideologically and politically untenable, as would the acknowledgment of the value and salience of ethnic origins. The continuing distinctiveness of ethnicity among Jews in Israel is perceived, therefore, as temporary, reflecting the past, diminishing in the present, and expected to disappear in future generations. Zionist ideology as it is manifest in contemporary Israeli society constructs the obvious evidence of Jewish ethnic differences in Israel as transitional and largely irrelevant to the longer term goals of national Jewish integration and nation-building.

The consensus within Israel about the value of bringing Jews to Israel from diverse countries of origin and the resulting policies encouraging this "in-gathering" are consistent with Zionist ideology, as is the anticipated integration of immigrants with these diverse ethnic backgrounds into the national culture and polity. To hasten achieving this latter goal, explicit policies were designed and implemented to "absorb" Jewish immigrants into Israeli society.[1] Along with the deliberate policy of building the nation through immigration (see Chapter 3), the goal was to mitigate social splits along lines of national origin. These goals have been at the top of the

national agenda from Israel's earliest days. A great deal of effort and extensive resources were aimed at closing the gaps among Jews of different socioeconomic
backgrounds in the hope of achieving rapid integration and equalization. This social policy has been reflected in Israel's particular development as a welfare state and
its related economic system (Ben-Porath 1986; Doron and Kramer 1991).

Israeli policymakers fully expect the total assimilation of Jews from diverse
countries of origin as the third generation emerges, distant from ethnic origins,
socialized into the national polity and culture by exposure to educational institutions and the military, and raised by native-born Israeli parents. The ethnicity remaining among third-generation Israeli Jews is expected to be marginal, cultural
remnants of no economic or social significance celebrated in "Diaspora" muse-
ums as relics and curios of the past. Nation-building in the ideological and policy
contexts of Israeli society is expected to remove the diversity of ethnic origins, as
new forms of national Israeli loyalty emerge, focusing solely on Jewish peoplehood. Religious similarity, military service, and "collective consciousness" derived
from Israel's security situation, it is argued, operate to dilute ethnic differences
(Ben-Rafael 1986). Ethnic cleavage becomes a "problem to be solved," not a cultural trait or a source of generational socioeconomic inequality.

Nowhere is the ideology that denies the salience of Jewish ethnicity more
poignant symbolically than in the way ethnic origin is treated in official government statistical publications. Ethnic origin among the Jews in Israel is almost always
categorized in terms of the place of the person's birth (i.e., some "objective" fact
that is ascriptive and unchanging). For the Israeli born, place of parents' birth
(usually father) is obtained, also an unchanging characteristic. In that context,
ethnic origin is simply limited by time (until the third generation) and is descrip-
tive of the immediate past. Using this definition, generational distance from foreignness or exposure to Israeli society marks the progress toward the end of ethnicity
and ethnic self-identification (in the particularistic sense). The question of the
ethnic origins, or in the Western sense of the "ancestry," of the third generation
(the native born of native-born parents) has not so far been addressed by officials
in Israel. Indeed, to judge solely by the way official government bureaus in Israel
present their texts, this third generation has no differentiating ethnic origins of
significance—they are simply Israeli born of Israeli-born parents, with no need to
pursue retrospectively the origins of the generations.[2]

Information collected on specific country of origin is recategorized into broad
divisions by continents—Europe, America, and Asia-Africa (with a third category,
Israel born of Israeli-born parents). This ethnic categorization is unique historically among Jewish communities of the world and is constructed only for Jews living in the state of Israel. It clearly reflects a distinction between Jews of "Western"
and "Middle Eastern" origin. It is a rejection of the more widely used, and historically more complex, division between "Sephardic" and "Ashkenazic" Jewries, although there is some overlap. The latter distinction has been retained only to
identify the political designations of the two chief rabbis of Israel. The Rabbinate
is the only legitimate, governmentally recognized, and reinforced arena for Jewish

"ethnic" diversity. This designation is largely political and serves as a cultural division within the secular government of Israel.

Contemporary analysts portraying Jewish ethnic variations include a wide range of groups within the "ethnic" rubric. Some include Jewish ethnic subpopulations by specific countries of origin rather than by broad geocultural areas, and this has particularly characterized some anthropological analyses (see, among others, Goldberg 1977; Morag-Talmon 1989). As distance from immigrant origins increases and mixed ethnic parentage becomes more common, the boundaries defining and delimiting ethnic origins have become fuzzy. Who is in and who is out of the group has become variable over time, depending in part on how affiliation and group identification are defined, even among major ethnic categories. The fluidity of ethnic boundaries over time has also resulted in varying definitions among research studies and the resultant difficulties in comparing the same group, historically and among communities. Anthropologists argue on cultural grounds for the importance of distinguishing immigrants from Middle Eastern countries by specific places of origin (Goldberg; Morag-Talmon). Whether ethnic origin is rooted in specific countries (e.g., Poland or Yemen) or broad regions of origin (e.g., Eastern Europe or Asia), or whether new forms of ethnic categories are becoming salient in Israel (e.g., Europe-America or Asia-Africa) remain empirical questions.

Most of my review of materials on ethnic variations and ethnicity focuses primarily on the dichotomy between broad Western (European-American) and Middle Eastern (Asian-African) origins. Of course, I recognize variations within these groups, but my focus is on social demographic processes, not on the cultural variations in places of origin. My goal is to identify emergent values that are reflected in two (or three) major ethnic blocks or aggregates. I test the relative empirical salience of detailed country-of-origin differences in various arenas of social and demographic life (e.g., education, fertility, and mortality) versus broader divisions of Israeli-created ethnic categories.

Arab Ethnicity

The difference between Jews and Arabs is another basis of "ethnicity" in Israel. As constructed in government documents and in politics, these "ethnic" differences are based on religious affiliation, reflecting variations among Judaism, Islam, and Christianity. The core of Arab-Jewish differences is not viewed as based on national origins or ethnic characteristics, but religion. The distinction between "religion" and "ethnicity" as the basis of the Arab-Jewish differentiation in Israel lies centrally in the quagmire of a series of political and ideological debates: Are Jews a nation or a religion? What constitutes Arab nationalism? What is the relevance of commonalities among religiously diverse Arabs (Moslem, Christian, and Druze)? The treatment of Arabs in Israel in religious categories denies (symbolically) their ethnic national identity ("Palestinian") and their political relationships to Arabs (or Palestinians) elsewhere in the region.

The Arab-Jewish distinction is designated on the identity card carried by all adults in Israel and characterizes all transactions between Arabs and others in Israel. The Arab-Jewish distinction is therefore clearer publicly and socially than the more ambiguous ethnic differences among Jews. Arabs are often identified by the majority as the "other" and the category "non-Jew" is used explicitly in official government publications to reflect this otherness.[3] The formal designation of "minority" in Israel (along with government bureaus of minority affairs) is a category allocated to non-Jewish "religious" groups; their communities have their own "religious" organizational character, with appropriate religious leadership positions and institutions supported by government allocations.

Some might argue that the Arab-Jewish distinction is not another case of ethnic differentiation, because of the unique history and political status of Arabs in Israel, the particular forms of tensions that have long characterized Arab-Jewish relations, and the forms of residential segregation that have emerged (see Chapter 4). However, the Arab population within the state of Israel has citizenship rights without formal political constraints and with recognized rights enunciated in Israel's declaration of independence. The politics of the region, though, result in less than full rights of participation (e.g., in the military), limited political expression, geographic-regional concentration, and powerful informal rules about geographic mobility and residence, marriage, and social activities, and hence about access to economic opportunities, social integration, and quality education. Until 1966, Israeli Arabs lived under a military administration within Israel and were confined to specific geographic areas, resulting in their sharp differentiation from the Jewish population. In contrast to the political and institutional attempts to reduce ethnic origin diversity within the Jewish population, Arab-Jewish differences have not been a direct target of policy in Israel. Many of the developments within the Arab sector that have improved the welfare of that population have been an indirect consequence of changes in the Jewish sector (Ben-Porath 1986).

Although I document the different sources of ethnic formation among Israeli Jews and Arabs and their different ideological and social circumstances, I treat variation among Jews, among Arabs, and between Arabs and Jews under the rubric "ethnic." This allows me to make comparisons among the variety of groups in Israel, to identify important features that are unique for the groups within each category, and to generalize about what is shared among groups. I focus on the changing demographic processes underlying ethnic distinctiveness and ethnic inequalities in Israel, even as I recognize the unique culture and histories of particular groups and the specific economic, political, and social dimensions of their contemporary circumstances.

Ethnicity and the Life Course

Some have argued that ethnic categories should be treated as ascriptive—primordial, fixed at birth, and constant throughout the life course (Glazer and Moynihan

1975, among others). In the Israeli case it has been argued that ethnic encounters "take place on the basis of shared primordial historical and religious attachments that preserved the individual communities in their diaspora histories" but that ethnic convergences have tipped the scale in favor of "bridging gaps through a constant effort to draw on what is shared by all" (Morag-Talmon 1989, p. 37).

However, such an emphasis may be misleading, since it treats ethnicity as a "constant," unchanging over the life course of individuals and between generations; an ascriptive category that is "objective." In contrast, I treat the classification of persons into ethnic categories as a social construction that varies with who is categorizing, whom is categorized, and in what contexts these categories are applied during the life course. Thus, for example, Moslem Israelis may define themselves as Palestinians when joining those on the West Bank in political protest but as Israeli Arabs when they vote; they may be viewed by Israeli Jews as "Arabs" or categorized as "non-Jews." Similarly, third-generation Israeli Jews of Yemenite origins may be classified in Israeli government records as Israelis, born of Israeli-born parents (i.e., without ethnic origins). In a local community they may be classified as of "Middle Eastern" origins (or of Asian-African origins) or classified by family members as Yemenites of a particular regional origin. American Jews living in Israel may be referred to by some as westerners, European-Americans, Anglo-Saxons, or New Yorkers. When they are touring Europe or visiting family in the United States, they may be labeled "Israelis" (see Goldscheider 2001a).

These labels are neither correct nor incorrect but are constructions designed by different "others" in an attempt at social classification and definition. Ethnic categories designated formally or informally can, of course, change over time—in the historical sense of time and in its life-cycle meaning. Young adults living alone may be less likely to identify themselves ethnically, whereas families with young children may be linked to ethnic communities through networks, jobs, schools, friends, and neighborhoods. The salience of ethnic identification may increase as new families are formed or as transitions occur—marriage, childbearing, death—that link the generations. Ethnicity may be reinforced through family networking during particular seasons of the year, holidays, and celebrations. Since the boundaries dividing some ethnic groups tend to be flexible, people are able to shift between groups most commonly at particular points during the life course. Multiple social identities have emerged in modern pluralistic societies; the salience of any one identity varies with the particular context, of which life-course transitions are of special importance because of the link between the life course and family networks.

The life-course perspective emphasizes the treatment of ethnic classification as variable, focused on family networks and intergenerational connections, not as a fixed individual identity or a group ascriptive trait. As transitions occur in the life course—as persons marry and form new families, as they become ill or seek medical treatment, as they have children or when they die—issues of community and family support, of local institutions and networks based on ethnicity become more salient. In contrast, at points in the life course where there is an emphasis on independence and autonomy, or on broader national identity, ethnic networks are likely to be less valued.

Life-course transitions occur in a generational or a cohort context. Consider, for example, ethnic variation in terms of who has relatives and family available to be supportive in times of health care needs. The availability of these ethnic family members reflects the fertility and family history of the group, whether marriage has been interethnic, or intra-ethnic, its history of migration (who lives where and near whom, revealing degrees of generational family access), and the pattern of family structure and work (the extent of divorce and remarriage; the changing proportion of women working). An examination of different ethnic generations should reveal exposure to integration, distance from origins, and connections to cultures. Combined with the effects of particular time periods, the generational or cohort perspective is of particular importance in the study of ethnic differentiation over the life course.

A final point about terminology: I refer to ethnic categories, communities, and groups as a basis for the classification and categorization of individuals. I am also concerned about the intensity of the connection between the individual and the group. At times, ethnic categories do not capture the range of effects, because categories are static constructions and do not take into account the intensity of ethnic commitments and the variety of attachments within ethnic communities. Generation status or foreign-language usage are obvious bases for identifying greater ethnic intensity among some groups. The ethnic composition of neighborhoods or the participation in an ethnic economic enclave are other bases of ethnic intensity. I refer to these indicators of intensity as ethnicity, paralleling the examination of religiosity as the intensity of religious activities or commitments of members of religious groups.

The Changing Ethnic Mosaic in Israel

Despite the ideological and political denial of Jewish ethnicity in Israel and the concomitant reification of religion as the only basis of cleavage, there is significant ethnic differentiation (at one point in time) and ethnic stratification (over time, between the generations) within Jewish groups. Despite the categorization of diverse groups as "Arab" or "non-Jews," there is significant variation among Arab Israelis (see Chapter 4). Yet there is also substantial evidence of convergences among Jewish ethnic groups in some areas of social life. A central theme in the details that I examine in subsequent chapters is how some forms of ethnic differentiation diminish over time and how new forms of distinctiveness emerge for both Jewish and Arab ethnic communities. Underlying and reflecting these emergent ethnic patterns are complex and changing demographic processes.

As a prelude to investigating the demographic sources of ethnicity in Israel, I sketch the ethnic composition of the Israeli population and outline the major changes that have occurred. A snapshot, cross-sectional view of ethnicity in Israeli society reveals a complex mosaic of ethnic groups (Table 2.1). Out of a total pop-

TABLE 2.1 Ethnic and Religious Composition of the Population of Israel, 1948–1998

	Total Jewish Population (in thousands)	Foreign-born/ Jewish (%)	Europe-America origin/Jewish (%)	Jewish Total (%)	Moslem/ Arab (%)
1948	717	65	88	82	–
1961	1,932	62	56	89	69
1972	2,687	53	50	85	76
1983	3,350	42	50	83	77
1990	3,947	38	49	82	78
1998	4,785	38	43	79	81

Note: The ethnic data relate to the ethnic origin (father) of the native born of foreign-born parents and an estimate of the ethnic composition of the third generation, native born of native-born parents. There are no ethnic origin data and no data on the divisions among the Arab population in 1948; the data are estimates.

Sources: *Statistical Abstract of Israel 1991,* table 2.22; and *Statistical Abstract of Israel 2000,* tables 2.1, 2.24.

ulation size of over 6 million in 1998, Jews are the dominant subpopulation, representing 79 percent of the total, with a somewhat larger proportion of European-American origins than those of Asian-African origins. Among the first- and second-generation Jewish Israeli population in 1998, 20 percent were from Asia (of whom 35 percent were from Iraq, 21 percent from Yemen, and 19 percent from Iran), 24 percent from Africa (of whom 59 percent were from Morocco and 15 percent from Algeria and Tunisia), and 56 percent from Europe, the United States, and Oceania (of whom 49 percent were from the former Soviet Union, 12 percent from Poland, and 13 percent from Romania). The relative population size of the third generation (Israeli born of Israeli-born fathers) is increasing and was 27 percent of the Jewish population in 1998. Its ethnic origins can only be estimated, but given past immigration patterns, third-generation Israelis are currently dominated by Jews of Eastern European origin (see Chapter 3). When the state of Israel was established at the end of 1948, there were 716,700 Jews, representing about 82 percent of the total population within approximately the same land area. Most of these first Jewish citizens of the state were foreign born (65 percent) and of European origin (85 percent).

There were about 900,000 Moslems in the state of Israel at the end of 1998, almost all members of the Sunni branch of Islam. Moslem Israelis were 15 percent of the total of 6 million persons in Israel; 129,000 of the total population were

Christian (2.1%), most Greek Orthodox or Greek Catholic; and 99,000 (1.6%) were Druze. The Arab population has become more Moslem over time, increasing from less than 70 percent in 1948 to 81 percent 50 years later.

Snapshots that are years apart reveal some of the story about ethnic compositional changes but miss the processes underlying these changes. Thus, for example, there has been a rather stable Jewish-Arab population ratio for over half a century, despite the rapid population growth of both groups. This stable ratio reflects the growth of the Jewish population through immigration, combined with the indirect effects of the fertility of the immigrants; the growth of the Arab population has been largely by natural increase—the excess of births over deaths (Friedlander and Goldscheider 1984). How have demographic factors shaped the emergence of ethnic groups and the processes of ethnic group integration in the context of nation-building in Israel? Do these differential processes have important implications for the nature of political, social, and cultural change?

In the chapters that follow, I trace out the patterns of immigration, examine the processes of demographic and social assimilation of ethnic groups as the significance of ethnic origin in mortality and fertility has declined, and identify the sources of continuing ethnic differentiation. I focus on internal migration patterns that retain separate communities for some ethnic groups by reinforcing residential concentration and the resultant differential opportunities for social and economic mobility. Throughout, I focus on generational transmission of ethnic inequalities, not just the retention of cultural distinctiveness.

Contexts of Ethnic Differences: Methodological Considerations

Ethnic differences characterize social life in Israel, as in other pluralistic societies. The question is, What are the contexts that sharpen or diminish these differences generationally? Answering this contextual question requires addressing several sources of complexity in the examination of ethnic groups. First, ethnic differences vary over time, as the distinctiveness of groups changes and as differences among them in some areas of social life narrow or widen. Second, the importance of ethnic differentiation relative to other characteristics—for example, education, region, or occupation—changes over time as well and may be more pronounced among some groups. Third, convergences in ethnic differences in some areas of social life do not necessarily imply convergences in all areas. These features suggest that ethnic differentiation may be discontinuous over time and from one social dimension to another. In turn, the similarity among ethnic groups in the past or in one sphere of activity does not necessarily imply continued similarity under all conditions. Thus, the changing contexts of ethnic differences need to be explicitly considered.

Although general theories of ethnicity have not been fully specified, social scientists have suggested some historical, economic, political, and social factors that are important in the study of ethnic continuity and change in general. The identification of these factors becomes the first clue for understanding the changing contexts of Israeli ethnic patterns.

Of critical significance in studying the changing importance of ethnicity in society is to examine changes in socioeconomic opportunities and the differential access of ethnic groups to these opportunities. The concentration of ethnic groups in particular jobs, neighborhoods, industries, and schools implies at times socioeconomic disadvantage and inequalities. The ethnic-social class overlap almost always indicates more intensive interaction with members of the ethnic community than with those outside of the ethnic boundaries. The overlap of ethnic factors and social class connects to the importance of family and economic linkages. Social class combines with broad family-economic networks to establish bonds of community and generational continuities. Hence, the generational transmission of inequality becomes the key to understanding ethnicity over time. The importance of formal and informal, explicit or subtle forms of discrimination in jobs, housing, schools, and government allocations are among the primary factors that reinforce ethnic communities.

Changes in the generational reproduction of groups and their general demographic characteristics are also important in understanding the dynamics of ethnic group change. Population size, structure, and cohort succession are structural features that delimit ethnic marriage markets and family formation, childbearing, schooling, and the socialization of the next generation into the ethnic community. Migration (and for some groups, immigration) is of particular importance in the generational continuity of ethnic groups at the national and community levels.

Ethnic intensity is likely to be greater when the ethnic origins (and hence the intergenerational bonds) of a couple are the same. When ethnic family members live close to each other, when they attend the same schools, have similar jobs and leisure activities, marry within their ethnic groups, and are involved in ethnic social and political institutions, then ethnic attachments within groups are more intensive. Examining the intensities of ethnic attachments reinforces the notion that ethnic classification should be treated with movable boundaries over time; the degree of involvement in the ethnic community will vary over the life course.

In addition to the socioeconomic and demographic factors connected to ethnic groups, there is the important role that the state may play, including the development and implementation of ethnic-specific policies. The state may indirectly shape ethnic communities through policies affecting education, real estate and housing, business practices, jobs, public welfare, and health systems. The entitlement systems common in modern welfare states and their links to ethnic factors, therefore, influence ethnic continuities and change. These systems can encourage and reinforce ethnic political mobilization and may often become the basis for the institutional expressions of ethnic interests (see Glazer and Moynihan 1975).

These "external" contexts are often complemented by the reinforcing role that ethnic institutions play in sustaining continuity. Some of these are family based and others are political, social, and cultural institutions that create a more intense ethnic community. In the absence of economic discrimination or ethnic markers that distinguish groups in the eyes of others, ethnic institutions become the major constraint on the total assimilation of ethnic populations.

My investigation of the changing ethnic factor in Israel, therefore, disentangles cultural from social class linkages; separates factors that reflect attitudes from those that are primarily issues of access and availability; distinguishes technological factors from those embedded in the social, demographic, and economic structure; and analyzes those factors that reflect intergenerational continuities and those that are cohort specific. I separate as well individual-based factors of ethnic identify from those that relate to the family and household, the community, the state, and the broader society. Operating between the life course of individuals and the impact of the state on ethnicity are families and households, with their extensive patterns of exchanges that I refer to as community. Community and family factors are powerful and conspicuous bases of ethnic continuity, shaping the ways individuals identify themselves ethnically.

Ethnicity has often been assumed to diminish with time and exposure to the new place of destination. As generations exposed to places of destination increase, the impact of origins recedes in memory and diminishes in effect on the life of the group. As the third and fourth generations are socialized and integrated into the economy, are dispersed residentially and geographically, are exposed to the influences of educational institutions and mass media, and interact with others on a basis other than ethnic origin, they melt away—they are homogenized into the larger culture and become undifferentiated through intergroup marriages and broader national political identification. This view assumes the centrality of the past for the continuity of groups in the present and de-emphasizes the roles of family and community. When ethnicity is viewed primarily through the past, the driving questions are, How much of the past could be retained in the face of pressures toward integration and cultural homogenization? How long would it take before ethnicity becomes only "nostalgia" and hence difficult to transmit generationally?

This perspective appears to distort the questions that I address about the ethnic phenomenon. In contemporary Israeli society, ethnicity is constructed (or reconstructed) out of the present circumstances, shaped not simply by what was, but by what is, incorporating selectively from the past within the present. Ethnicity revolves around institutions, those that reduce and those that sustain ethnic communities. In the process, new ethnic forms appear, as different institutions develop to reflect these emergent cultural forms. Even when cultural differences weaken, institutions can be retained and can continue to shape communities. These institutions include family and kin, and social, economic, cultural, and political organizations. Ethnic groups that have retained, developed, and extended institutions have more cohesive communities compared to those whose search for individual identity or for cultural forms of the past take precedence over social institutions.

Interpreting Ethnic Differentiation: General Orientations

The identification of factors associated with ethnic groups and ethnicity is a starting point in my examination of Israeli society. To consider how these various themes fit together as a whole requires the presentation of some map or theoretical framework to organize how ethnic differences have been interpreted and to provide guidelines for the analysis of ethnic variation. The three types of interpretations that have been used to analyze ethnic variation are cultural, social class, and community networks—each emphasizing a different dimension of social organization and together providing a helpful orientation to studying ethnicity.[4]

Culture as Ethnicity

The first framework emphasizes the cultural aspects of ethnic groups and posits that ethnic variation reflects the culture or the values of groups. Ethnic differences are reduced over time as acculturation into the mainstream of society occurs. Becoming culturally similar to the dominant group proceeds through increased educational attainment and contacts with others in schools, neighborhoods, and on the job; through changes in the use of a foreign language; and through adopting local cultural values. The salience of ethnic distinctiveness recedes as groups of diverse cultural origins embrace similar values. Remaining ethnic differences reflect the legacy of the past that is temporary and transitional; or, differences are maintained by the state through multicultural policies.

This source of ethnic distinctiveness is more likely to characterize the foreign born and their immediate family members and those who speak a language other than the national language and those who have received most of their socialization elsewhere. The second and third generations, socialized formally in places of destination, are more distant from their cultural roots. Ethnic groups that are culturally closer to the native population (i.e., those whose values are from areas that most closely resemble their place of current residence) are most likely to lose their cultural distinctiveness compared to others whose cultural roots are more dissimilar.

Clearly, an emphasis on cultural themes focuses attention on indicators of values and foreignness and on closeness to the sources of ethnic cultural origins.

Social Class and Ethnicity

A second explanation treats ethnic distinctiveness as a reflection of the social class composition of ethnic groups. The association of ethnic differences with socioeconomic disadvantage and inequality has a long history in social science research. The argument is that ethnic differences—whether generated by discrimination and racism or by unequal access to opportunities, or whether fed by immigration and the lower occupational and educational origins of ethnic immigrant groups—reflect the disadvantaged socioeconomic status of the group as a whole and the inequalities in the overlap of social class and ethnic origin. Observed differences among ethnic groups are therefore primarily social class differences. Occupational mobility and education are the key processes that eliminate ethnic distinctiveness. Ethnic groups that are not concentrated generationally in particular social class categories and that no longer have a disadvantaged socioeconomic status become integrated and assimilated into the society. Ethnic continuity, therefore, implies generational inequality and persistent socioeconomic gaps between ethnic groups.

In its more extreme form, this social class argument views a focus on ethnic differences as distorting the underlying socioeconomic disadvantages of disenfranchised groups. The analysis of ethnic differences, it follows, should examine correlates of poverty and inequality and social class discrimination and competition. The reduction of economic discrimination—changing the overlap of social class and ethnic origin through equalized education and job opportunities and through residential mobility and generational discontinuities in socioeconomic characteristics—should diminish and eventually eliminate the basis of ethnic distinctiveness.

Both the cultural and social class perspectives tap important dimensions of the differences among ethnic groups in Israel. Ethnic differences become the combined consequence of cultural and social class factors; when social class factors are neutralized and discrimination minimized, the remaining ethnic differences are "only" cultural. These unmeasured, residual cultural factors are minor and tend to weaken generationally. Cultural factors are reinforced by the disadvantaged socioeconomic position of ethnic groups, which reflects discrimination, blocked opportunities, and economic origin (including the occupational skills and lower educational levels of the first generation acquired elsewhere). In more complex interactions, cultural forms of ethnicity are considered more intense among the less-educated, poorer social classes, since social mobility and the attainment of middle-class and higher status minimizes the salience of ethnic distinctiveness.

Both perspectives, in their own way, project the steady reduction of ethnic differences over time in Israel when cultural integration occurs, usually with the length of exposure to Israeli society. With linguistic homogeneity, educational equalization, and the reduction in ethnic job discrimination and residential segregation—and, in general, when social class factors are more equalized among groups—ethnic distinctiveness should be reduced or eliminated.

The cultural and social class perspectives assume that ethnic particularism and discrimination are likely to diminish over time because of the ideological and institutional commitments of the state toward the integration of groups into a political and economic system based on merit, achievement, and universalism. Hence, with political modernization, the social class basis of ethnic differentiation declines and cultural differences are homogenized. In short, the salience of group differences diminishes. Indeed, the Arab exception in Israel is often used to prove the rule. When discrimination blocks the integration of groups and their access to economic opportunities, continued inequality and distinctiveness are reinforced. When residential segregation and family patterns are reinforced by state policies, ethnic differentiation is likely to persist generationally. Political and social factors reinforce Arab cultural distinctiveness.

Ethnicity as Community Networks

An alternative and complementary view to the cultural and social class arguments, and the third framework, places emphasis on the structural networks and the power of a community and its institutions to reinforce ethnic distinctiveness and identity. The networks of ethnic communities may be extensive. They are often tied to places of residence, connected to families, linked to economic activities and enclaves, and expressed in political ties, cultural expressions, and lifestyles. These networks are reinforced by institutions and organizations that are ethnically based. The key element of this argument is that the cohesion of ethnic communities is based on institutions and networks. Hence, the intensity of community is facilitated by the intensity of social networks: the greater the social networks and the denser the institutions, the greater the cohesion of the ethnic community. Cohesion is reflected both in interaction patterns and in cultural expressions. The larger the number of spheres where interaction occurs within the ethnic community, the more cohesive the group; the greater the arenas of cultural particularities and activities, the higher the rate of ethnic attachments.[5]

According to this perspective, the basis of ethnic community is the extent of ethnic ties to the labor market over the life course, not simply the overlap of ethnicity and social class. Changing economic networks forge the greater interactions within ethnic communities, developing bonds of family and economic activities at different points during the life course. The support of kin and family and the concentration of ethnic groups in geographically defined areas become important bases of ethnic continuity. Whatever the values, common background, specific history, and unique culture are that may bind ethnic members together in a "primordial" sense, the key factors involved within this framework are structural—residence, jobs, schooling, and family. The cultural bases of ethnic groups reinforce and justify the cohesion of the community and are themselves variable, but they do not determine its continuity. Cultural distinctiveness and values occur in social contexts, and their construction changes over time as contexts change.

When networks and the communication within ethnic groups are strong, ethnic group attachments are more salient. Viewed in this way, ethnic distinctiveness is not limited to unacculturated immigrant groups or to ethnic groups that have experienced discrimination or are economically disadvantaged. Ethnic communities are sustained by informal institutions and networks, are often reinforced by local politics and policies, and are enhanced by extended family connections.

The network perspective emphasizes that national attachments do not necessarily imply the reduction of ethnic group distinctiveness, even when discrimination diminishes and social mobility occurs. Under some conditions, nation-building reinforces distinctiveness, particularly when there is increased socioeconomic competition among ethnic groups, intensified forms of economic concentration, and residential segregation. Often ethnicity is reinforced rather than diminished when acculturation takes place, when the values among ethnic groups become more similar, and when socioeconomic competition among groups becomes sharper. Ethnic social mobility through improvements in education and jobs may increase economic concentration at the upper levels of socioeconomic status, just as ethnicity was associated in the past with concentration at lower socioeconomic levels.

Under some conditions, nation-building results in the total assimilation of ethnic groups through the erosion of community and family based institutions, through residential integration and intergroup marriages, through open market forces and universal schooling, and through state policies that provide access to opportunities and that enforce nondiscrimination. But not always, not for all groups, and not as an inevitable by-product of urbanization, economic development, nationalism, and social mobility. The specific contexts must be studied to examine these patterns so as not to infer them from broad patterns of societal change.

Treating ethnicity as networks implies that ethnic groups may not necessarily be transitional or unimportant features of modern societies. Ethnicity may be embedded in the institutions, politics, and economy in ways that are likely to have a significant impact on the lives of people. The reinforcement of ethnic connections through continuous patterns of immigration ensures that ethnic origins remain important factors that distinguish communities for an even longer period of time. Community, not individual, identity is the most fruitful unit for an examination of ethnic expression in Israel. Therefore, I argue explicitly against those who would examine ethnicity among Jewish Israelis mainly as a reflection of transitional immigrant categories and individual ethnic identity.

Using community and networks as the framework, I emphasize in upcoming chapters how policies within Israel have reinforced generational continuities among some ethnic groups and study the role of external factors in ethnic communities (e.g., changing immigration patterns and the Israeli-Arab conflicts in the Middle East region). The documentation of continuing ethnic differences in a variety of social, economic, and political spheres and the estimation of ethnic convergences over time in other social and demographic arenas provide the basis for assessing ethnic communities in Israel.

Notes

1. The language used in Israel to describe Jewish immigrant integration into the society is "absorption" (*klita* in Hebrew). This is a rather unusual description of assimilation. The concept of assimilation is almost always used in Israel to designate the integration of Jews as a minority in communities outside of the state. From a Zionist ideological perspective, it

has negative connotation of "total" assimilation—the loss of community, continuity, and identity as Jews.

2. In the 1995 census, there were no provisions to directly ask ethnic ancestry. For many younger persons of the third generation who are Israeli born and living with their parents, ethnic identifiers are indirectly available only through place-of-origin data on their parents. For young adults of the third generation not living with their parents, no ethnic identifiers were collected.

3. The designation of Arab as "other" or "non-Jewish" precedes the establishment of the state. The Balfour Declaration of 1917 specifying the commitments of Britain to the establishment of a "national home for the Jewish People" in Palestine explicitly notes that the civil and religious rights of the "non-Jewish communities" should be safeguarded.

4. As in all generalizations, this is oversimplified, although it is useful for a broad orientation (see also Goldscheider and Zuckerman 1984; Smooha 1989).

5. For an application of this argument to the historical and comparative conditions of one ethnic-religious minority in Europe and America, see Goldscheider and Zuckerman 1984.

PART TWO

The Formation
of Israeli Communities

3

Immigration, Nation-Building,
and Ethnicity

Israeli society has been shaped by immigration patterns more than most other countries. Changes in the rates of immigration and in the characteristics of immigrants are critical for understanding each of the major themes that guide this analysis—population, ethnicity, and development. The ethnic mosaic and ethnic integration processes in Israeli society have been affected directly by fluctuations in the volume of immigration over time from different places of origin, as have all the major demographic transformations of the migrants and their children. Social, economic, cultural, and political developments in Israel and the internal conflicts among Jews and between Arabs and Jews are linked to the intensity of immigration and to the socioeconomic and demographic characteristics of those migrating. Moreover, immigration ideologies and policies have been at the core of Zionism and Zionist political movements and institutions for over a century, predating the establishment of the state and changing with its development. In this chapter, I outline the main contours of immigration patterns over time, their fluctuations and selectivity, and sketch some of the population, ethnic, and nation-building issues that will become the detailed foci of subsequent chapters.

Ideology and the Uniqueness of Immigration to Israel

Immigration has been a major strategy of nation-building in the state of Israel: The Zionist movement since the nineteenth century and the state of Israel from the time of its establishment have sought to gather together in one country those around the world who consider themselves Jewish by religion or ancestry. The processes, patterns, and policies of immigration have been unique. The conditions in Europe preceding and following the Holocaust and World War II, the emerging nationalism among Jews around the world, the conditions of Jews in Arab-Moslem countries, and the radical changes in the 1990s in Eastern Europe with the breakup of the Soviet Union have been among the most obvious external circumstances influencing the immigration of Jews from a wide range of countries to Israel. The emergence of a large and integrated American Jewish community that has not immigrated in substantial numbers to Israel is an additional factor in understanding the selectivity of Jewish migrations to Israel.

There are, of course, internal developments in Israel that have influenced the pace and selectivity of immigration. The demographic expansion of the Jewish community in prestate Palestine, the attractions of economic opportunity and Jewish political control, Israeli cultural developments, and religious activities have been important factors in decisions to immigrate. War and military victories have generated national commitments and euphoria that encouraged immigration (as in the post-1948 and post-1967 periods), but they have also caused fear and anxiety about living in uncertain and dangerous circumstances.

Immigration to Israel is also special because of the sociocultural diversity of the immigrants, their overwhelming importance in the formation and development of Israeli society, and the concentration of immigration in the first three years after the establishment of the state and in the 1990s. Immigration—in its ideological, policy, and behavioral forms—has symbolized the renewal of Jewish control over national developments and is an important value shared by Jews around the world. At the same, it has been one of the core symbols of the conflicts between Jews and Arabs in the Middle East (Al Haj 1992; Friedlander and Goldscheider 1979; Goldscheider 1990, 2001b; Smooha 1991).

Not surprisingly, immigration has been perceived very differently by Jewish and Arab populations in Israel (Al Haj 1992; Smooha 1991). The overwhelming majority of Israeli Jews are committed to the continuation of further Jewish immigration as an implementation of the Zionist agenda and a justification of their own national commitments. The Israeli Arab population views further Jewish immigration as part of the asymmetry between Jews and Palestinians, as a further diminution of their political power, and as a dilution of limited national economic resources. Immigration is central for understanding Israeli society because it shaped the ethnic composition of Israel's Jewish population and redefined the position of its Arab minority. Thus the immigration of Jews to a country of their own has been more than the process of moving people from one place to another. It has meant the building of a Jewish state and the reinforcing of an entire set of institutions and national goals. It has also meant converting the Arab population from a majority population before the establishment of the state to a minority group when the new boundaries of its population were drawn in 1948 (Al Haj 1987).

Yet the strategy of nation-building through immigration has been used by many countries (Alonso 1987). Both developing and rich nations have tried to restore to themselves through immigration, or at least through renewed allegiance, residents of other countries who share their identity. In one sense, therefore, immigration to Israel is similar to China courting overseas Chinese, particularly those with special skills, or to other developing nations trying to lure back those who left to seek special education or commercial sources. France and Spain have had active programs to support shared identity with former colonies and emigrant enclaves. These parallels with the role of immigration in other countries should not obscure the fact that immigration for Israel remains special because of the ideological centrality of immigration and its overwhelming importance in the formation and development of Israeli society, and the fact that Jews returning to the state of Israel had not lived there for almost 2,000 years.[1]

As it was for the United States at an earlier period of its history, immigration is Israeli history.[2] Understanding the basic contours of who immigrated to Israel, when and from which areas of the world they arrived, what happened to the immigrants in their integration into Israeli society, and what the connections are between places of origin and destination will go far in clarifying the changes in Israeli society over the past half-century. Pick any thread of social life in Israel— family, social mobility, residential patterns, politics, religion, stratification, culture— and the role of immigration will be important. Identify any social problem—Arab-Jewish relationships, inequality, economic dependencies, ethnic-religious conflict—and the continuing effects of immigration become clear. Much of the analysis in every chapter in this book surrounds some aspects of immigration and its consequences. Here, I document the basis of immigration patterns and sketch their importance in the economic development, demographic growth, and ethnic compositional changes of Israeli society. I begin with the historical context.

The Historical Context: Jewish Immigration to Palestine

Jewish immigration to Palestine and Israel has been rooted in theological aspects of Judaism for centuries and in secular Jewish nationalism, Zionism, since the middle of the nineteenth century. The beginnings of modern international immigration to Palestine, and subsequently to Israel, may be traced to the end of the nineteenth century, when organized groups of Jewish immigrants entered Palestine to build a national Jewish homeland. This migration was part of a much larger-scale immigration out of Eastern Europe, mainly in the direction of the United States and other Western, industrialized nations (Goldscheider and Zuckerman 1984). Ideological factors were central to the immigration of this small segment moving to Palestine, since social, economic, and political conditions in Palestine were not conducive to immigration. The migrants to Palestine were a small, select, relatively well-educated, secular, urban group entering a different cultural milieu, with the goal of working in agriculture to develop barren wastelands in order to create the basis of a new Jewish society (Horowitz and Lissak 1989a).

The First Waves

Two major waves of immigration occurred during the late-nineteenth and early-twentieth centuries (Friedlander and Goldscheider, 1979). First, from 1882 to 1903, an estimated 25,000 Jewish immigrants arrived, doubling the 1880 Jewish population in Palestine. During these years, the revolutionary migrants lacked funds and had little or no agricultural skills. They were rescued by outside capital, particularly from Jewish foreign investors. Over time, they hired Arab laborers and became administrators. Paternalism and inefficiency, along with disillusionment and emigration, became the dominant characteristics of these first settlers. The initial Jewish settlers were colonialists in their economic dependency on Jewish capitalistic interests outside of Palestine and in their relationship to local Arab labor. (See Figure 3.1 for patterns of Jewish immigration to Palestine, 1919–1948.)

A second wave of immigrants, estimated to number between 40,000 and 55,000, entered Palestine during the decade beginning in 1904 and built on the foundations of the first wave. Many had been part of the organized Zionist movement in Europe and had been active socialists in Russia. Their goal was to shape a new social order in Palestine based on socialist principles and Zionist ideology. The growing Zionist movement recruited, organized, and financed the immigrants, facilitating their migration and easing their economic accommodation and the purchase and development of land. The new immigrants in Palestine expanded existing agricultural settlements and founded new urban and industrial communities. They were educated, politically articulate, and organizationally skillful. The activities and principles of those immigrants in this second wave were at the heart of the social, cultural, political, and economic settlement of Jews in Palestine and subsequently the state of Israel (Goldscheider and Zuckerman 1984). The entry of these migrants into Palestine was opposed by the formal policies of the Ottoman government of Palestine (Mandel 1976). The opposition was ineffective, since the administrative apparatus to control and regulate immigration and to implement the formal policies was largely defective (Friedlander and Goldscheider 1979).

Thus, these two early waves of immigration to Palestine did not follow the established out-migration pattern in European modernization. The heavy reliance on outside capital, dependence on external economic and political support, shifts of urban workers into agriculture and rural residence, and the lack of conspicuous economic opportunity as pulls for immigration were exceptional features. Whereas most of those who emigrated from Eastern European countries were motivated by the relatively better economic opportunities available at their destinations and were moving into areas of urban industrial development, Jews immigrating to Palestine were guided by ideological commitments and political-nationalistic goals.

The British Mandate

Two major immigration policies dominated the British Mandate period in Palestine after World War I (Friedlander and Goldscheider 1979). Until 1936,

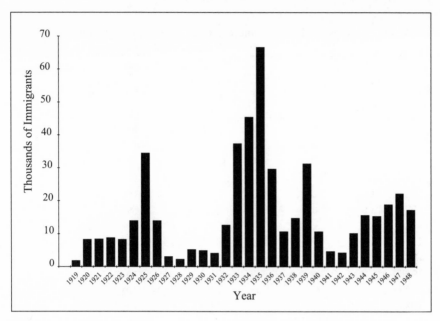

Figure 3.1   Jewish Immigrants by Year of Immigration to Palestine, 1919–1948

the guiding British policy was the regulation of selective types of immigration based in large part on economic criteria. The number of migrants subsidized by Zionist organizations was adjusted to what became defined as the "economic absorptive capacity" of the country. This regulation of immigration varied over the period but cumulatively allowed the entry of 300,000 Jewish immigrants, half of whom were subsidized and over 90 percent of whom were from European countries (Tables 3.1 and 3.2). Nothing in this British policy prevented wide annual fluctuations in the volume or composition of immigrants. Changes outside of Palestine—in particular, the changing quota restrictions on immigrant entry into the United States, political changes in Poland and later in Central Europe that directly affected Jews economically and culturally, and the economic depression in Europe—were major factors shaping the ebb and flow of migration.

The second period of the British Mandate, from 1937 to the declaration of statehood in 1948, was characterized by increasingly restrictive British immigration policies. These were directed toward greater British control over the total volume of Jewish immigration, using political and demographic criteria (the ratio of Jewish to Arab populations). During this period, 175,000 Jewish immigrants arrived in Palestine, the majority legally. British policy prevented an even larger number of immigrants from entering, particularly refugees from the Holocaust. Increasingly, toward the latter part of the period, British policy directly controlled the timing and volume of immigration. By the end of the British Mandate period,

TABLE 3.1 Number of Jewish Immigrants and Rate of Immigration to Palestine and Israel, by Year of Immigration, 1919–2000

	Palestine			State of Israel				
Year	Immigrants Number (000s)	Rate	Year	Immigrants Number (000s)	Rate	Year	Immigrants Number (000s)	Rate
1919	1.8	32	1948	101.8	229	1978	26.4	8
1920	8.2	135	1949	239.6	266	1979	37.2	12
1921	8.3	115	1950	170.2	154	1980	20.4	6
1922	8.7	106	1951	175.1	132	1981	12.6	4
1923	8.2	91	1952	24.4	17	1982	13.7	4
1924	13.9	146	1953	11.3	8	1983	16.9	5
1925	34.4	283	1954	18.4	12	1984	20.0	6
1926	13.9	93	1955	37.5	24	1985	10.6	3
1927	3.0	20	1956	56.2	35	1986	9.5	3
1928	2.2	14	1957	71.2	41	1987	13.0	4
1929	5.2	34	1958	27.1	15	1988	13.0	4
1930	4.9	30	1959	23.9	13	1989	24.1	7
1931	4.1	24	1960	24.5	13	1990	199.5	52
1932	12.6	69	1961	47.6	25	1991	176.1	43
1933	37.3	185	1962	61.3	30	1992	77.1	18
1934	45.3	177	1963	64.4	30	1993	76.8	18
1935	66.5	201	1964	54.7	25	1994	79.8	18
1936	29.6	80	1965	30.7	14	1995	76.4	17
1937	10.6	27	1966	15.7	7	1996	70.9	15
1938	14.7	32	1967	14.3	6	1997	66.2	14
1939	31.2	72	1968	20.5	8	1998	56.7	12
1940	10.6	23	1969	37.8	15	1999	76.8	16
1941	4.6	10	1970	36.8	14	2000	61.2	13
1942	4.2	9	1971	41.9	16			
1943	10.1	21	1972	55.9	21			
1944	15.6	29	1973	54.9	20			
1945	15.3	29	1974	32.0	11			
1946	18.8	33	1975	20.0	7			
1947	22.1	36	1976	19.8	7			
1948	17.2	72	1977	21.4	7			

Note: The rate of immigration is per 1,000 mean Jewish population; until May 14, 1948, immigration is to Palestine; after May 15, 1948, immigration is to Israel.
Sources: Friedlander and Goldscheider, 1979, table 2.6; *Statistical Abstract of Israel,* various years.

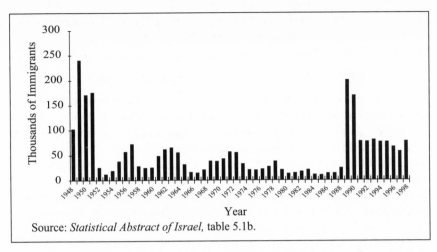

Source: *Statistical Abstract of Israel,* table 5.1b.

Figure 3.2   Jewish Immigrants by Year of Immigration to Israel, 1948– 1999

most Jewish immigrants entered Palestine illegally and became important symbols in the struggle for Jewish national independence.

Throughout the prestate period, there were ambiguous British political commitments to Jewish and Arab nationalisms. The emergence and the strengthening of the Zionist movement—with an emphasis on immigration, settlement, and development—occurred alongside the growing momentum of Arab nationalism. Improved economic conditions in Palestine, changes in immigration policy, and Zionist political ideology were not the main determinants of changing immigration patterns. Although ideological factors were clearly operative as important factors in the immigration of the early Zionists, it is incomplete to argue, as some have (Horowitz and Lissak 1989a), that the waves of Jewish immigration were ideologically motivated during the British period. Ideology played little direct role in the Polish and German migration of the 1920s and 1930s and was hardly the major factor through 1948. Instead, the deteriorating political situation of Jews in Europe after the rise of Hitler and Nazism in the 1930s was a major push factor. The absence of attractive (or available) alternative destinations in other countries facilitated the flow of Jewish immigrants to Palestine.

During the entire Mandate period, British policy was oriented toward the regulation and control of Jewish immigration. There were no clear policy guidelines on Arab immigration to Palestine. Arab migrants from neighboring areas were part of the movement of labor, often seasonal and temporary, in response to better short-term economic opportunities in Palestine. Most of the demographic growth of the Arab population in Palestine was through natural increase; immigration was the primary source of Jewish population growth (see the discussion in Kimmerling and Migdal 1993).

Jewish Immigration to the State of Israel: Four Major Streams—1948–1999

Between 1948 and 1999, almost 3 million Jewish immigrants entered the state of Israel, an average of over 60,000 per year. Of this total, over two-thirds were from European or Western countries and less than one-third from Middle Eastern (or Asian-African) countries. The proportion of immigrants from Asian-African countries shifted from over 70 percent in the period from 1952 to 1957 to less than 10 percent in the early 1970s and 1990s. Immigration during the late 1980s and 1990s was dominated by a large movement from Russia (and from the republics of the former Soviet Union). Of the 956,000 immigrants to Israel during the 1990s, about 90 percent were from Europe, most from Eastern Europe. (See Figure 3.2 for patterns of Jewish immigration to Israel, 1948–1999.)

New policies of immigration were implemented during the first period after the establishment of the state of Israel, contrasting sharply with the immigration restrictions enforced by the British. There was a conjunction of social and political pressures to open the gates of immigration widely to Jews in a variety of countries. As the highest priority, the state was to be a refuge for the Jewish survivors of the Holocaust. The movement of Jewish refugees to the new state was a critical part of the political rationale for its establishment, particularly since there were no alternative destinations for the thousands of stateless Jewish persons. Over time, Jewish communities in several neighboring Middle East countries and more distant Arab states became increasingly vulnerable as minority populations following the Arab-Israeli War of 1948. Jewish nationalist ideology gained international political strength and increased legitimacy from the potential for large-scale immigration from areas across Europe and the Middle East.

The formal context of Israel's immigration policy is contained in the Declaration of Independence (passed on May 14, 1948): "The State of Israel is open to Jewish immigration and the Ingathering of Exiles." This policy was combined with the first order enacted by the provisional Jewish government: to abolish the British restrictions on immigration and to define "illegal" Jewish immigrants retroactively as legal residents of the country. Together, these actions represented the foundation of Israel's immigration policy during the first two years subsequent to statehood. The Law of Return enacted July 5, 1950, granted to every Jew in the world the right to immigrate and settle in Israel, with minor exceptions related to health and security. These formal regulations do not convey the main thrust of Israel's policy, which was to actively encourage and subsidize the major phases associated with the immigration process (Friedlander and Goldscheider 1979).

From the establishment of the state of Israel in 1948 through the 1990s, the rates of immigration and the countries of origin of the immigrants have fluctuated significantly and can be divided roughly into four main periods (Table 3.2).

TABLE 3.2 Immigrants to Palestine and Israel, by Continent of Origin and
Period of Immigration, 1919–1999

	All Countries (000s)	Percent	Asia	Africa	Eastern Europe	Central Europe-Balkan	Other West
1919–1923	35.2	100	5	a	84	7	4
1924–1931	81.6	100	12	a	78	6	4
1932–1938	197.2	100	9	a	60	27	4
1939–1945	81.8	100	18	a	34	44	4
1946–1948	56.5	101	4	a	68	26	3
Mass immigration							
1948	101.8	100	5	9	54	29	3
1949	239.6	101	31	17	28	22	3
1950	170.2	100	34	15	45	4	2
1951	175.1	80	59	12	26	2	1
North African immigration							
1952–1954	54.1	101	25	51	12	5	8
1955–1957	164.9	100	6	62	23	6	3
1958–1960	75.5	100	18	18	56	2	6
1961–1964	228.0	99	9	51	32	1	6
1956–1968	81.3	100	19	31	37	2	11
Post–Six Day War							
1969–1971	116.5	99	17	10	41	2	29
1972–1974	142.8	100	4	5	71	1	19
1975–1979	124.8	100	10	5	60	1	24
1980–1984	83.6	101	8	19	43	1	30
1985–1989	70.2	101	12	13	42	1	33
New Russian immigrants							
1990–1994	609.3	100	1	5	91	0	3
1995–1999	347.0	100	11	4	79	0	6

Note: Eastern Europe includes USSR, Latvia, Poland, and Romania; Central
Europe includes Germany, Austria, Czechoslovakia, and Hungary; Balkans
includes Greece, Bulgaria, and Yugoslavia; Other West includes other European
countries, the United States, South Africa, and Oceania. The Asiatic
republics of the former USSR are included as part of Asia from 1996. The
percentages do not always add up to 100% due to incomplete information.
aCombined Asia and Africa; over 90 percent from Asian countries.
Sources: Friedlander and Goldscheider, 1979, table 2.6; *Statistical Abstract of
Israel,* various years.

Mass Immigration 1948–1951

The first and most dramatic immigrant stream occurred immediately after the establishment of the state and is referred to as the period of "mass" immigration. During the three years following the establishment of the state of Israel, in the contexts of war and the transition to national independence, a very high volume and rate of Jewish immigrants from diverse countries of origins arrived. The high rate of immigration doubled the size of the Jewish population—350,000 immigrants arrived in the first eighteen months after statehood and an additional 350,000 arrived during the following one and one-half years. It was a massive undertaking to provide the basics of settlement—housing, jobs, schooling, and health services—for immigrants who were not able to use the national language (Hebrew) and who often arrived from the depths of deprivation in postwar Europe. The immediate adjustment was complicated by the immigration of Jews from Middle Eastern countries, whose culture and language were significantly different from the European orientations of the emerging nation.

In the first period immediately subsequent to statehood, the immigrants were European in origin—Jewish refugees from the Holocaust coming to a predominantly European-origin society; in 1948, 85 percent of the 100,000 immigrants to Israel were of European origin. This pattern changed as Jewish immigrants from Middle Eastern countries joined this stream: In 1949 and 1950 only about half of the immigrants were from Europe; by 1951, over 70 percent of the immigrants were from Asian and North African countries, mainly Iraq, Iran, and Libya. The primary determinants of this migration were political and economic, with some elements of religious messianism among Jews from the traditional communities of the Middle East. The period of mass immigration established some of the basic contours of Israeli society—expanding major social, political, economic, and cultural institutions—and the development and extension of the welfare entitlement system.

North African Immigration

The second major stream of immigration to Israel occurred beginning in the mid-1950s, when over half the immigrants were from North African countries, particularly Morocco, Tunisia, and Egypt. Coming on the heels of mass immigration and the subsequent strains of nation-building and immigrant adjustment, 165,000 immigrants arrived between 1955 and 1957. The occupational skills and educational backgrounds of these immigrants differed significantly from the earlier European-origin streams. Immigrants arrived with fewer occupational skills and lower levels of education than earlier waves of European immigrants and were not easily integrated into the labor market. Selective immigration quotas and regulations to control the negative economic impact of large-scale migration were imposed by Israel during this period. Immigration continued slowly and picked up again in the early 1960s, when half of the 228,000 immigrants from 1961 to 1964 came from North African countries.

Soviet and Western Immigration, Post-1967

The third major immigration wave began after the 1967 war, mostly from Eastern Europe (the Soviet Union and Romania) and from Western countries, mainly the United States. These areas contained the largest Jewish populations outside of Israel; therefore, they were the major potential sources of Jewish immigration. Between 1972 and 1979, 267,582 immigrants arrived in Israel, 51 percent from the Soviet Union and 8 percent from the United States; of the 153,833 immigrants to Israel between 1980 and 1989, 65 percent were from Europe and the United States, 11 percent from Ethiopia, and 6 percent from Iran. Restrictions on the emigration of Jews from the Soviet Union and the option of alternative destinations (particularly the United States) reduced the flow of Russian immigrants to Israel until 1989. This third wave of immigrants entered Israel in the post-1967 period of economic growth and geographic extension, which was also characterized by a new national political and military self-confidence.

Higher standards of immigrant integration within the society emerged during this period. Attention to adequate housing, jobs, and provisions for university-level education for the children of immigrants contrasted with the elementary health care and minimum living accommodations provided to previous immigrant waves. The contrast between the subsidies offered to the new immigrants, particularly among those entering voluntarily from Western countries, and those available to the immigrants of the second period from Middle Eastern countries was conspicuous. The political challenge remained to provide resources in order to encourage new immigration and to ensure the immigrants' "absorption"; nevertheless, some immigrants of previous waves and their Israeli-born children remained disadvantaged.

Russians: The New Masses

The latest immigration stream to Israel began in 1989 and has continued into the twenty-first century. Significant numbers of Russian Jews emigrated from the former Soviet Union. (Immigration restrictions reduced the number of Russian Jews entering the United States during this period.) Of the 1 million Jewish immigrants who arrived in Israel during this period, the overwhelming majority were from areas of the former Soviet Union. The number of immigrants (although not the rate relative to the base population in Israel) was the largest since the period of mass immigration half a century earlier. This immigration stream is the largest ever to Israel from any one country during such a brief time period.

During the 1980s, 17,000 Ethiopian Jews were airlifted to Israel, and an additional 40,000 entered Israel from Ethiopia in the 1990s. Although small in number, these immigrants symbolize Israel's continuing commitment to be the political haven for refugee Jews from around the world. Ethiopian Jews have a significantly different cultural, religious, and economic background compared to other immigrants and to the native Israeli-born population, with a lower level of exposure to the educational, health, and welfare systems of Western nations and a lower level of formal education. They have occupational skills that need to be translated into the competitive postindustrial, service economy of Israel.

For the period of the 1990s, over 80 percent of the immigrants from Russia were defined as Jewish. The proportion of non-Jews entering Israel from the former Soviet Union increased to almost 50 percent in 1999–2000. The volume of Jewish immigration from Russia to Israel has declined, reflecting the reduced size of the Jewish population there and the increased Jewish activities re-emerging in Russia. On the other hand, conditions in Israel have also changed, as economic and political problems make immigration less attractive. There remains a significant number of Jews still living in Russia under uncertain economic and political conditions. They are the potential for future immigration to Israel. Labor demands in particular industries in Israel have resulted in the importation of temporary workers (non-Jewish) recruited from Romania, Thailand, and the Philippines who arrive on special work permits. These skilled and unskilled laborers have replaced the large pool of Palestinians from the administered territories who in 2000–2001 were no longer part of the commuting labor pool working within Israel.

The new immigration represents a continuing challenge to Israeli society. As in the past, serious short-term problems of housing and education have been generated by the volume of Russian immigration. It is likely that the descendants of previous waves of immigrants, particularly those who are disadvantaged economically, will have negative reactions to these newcomers and to the government subsidies they receive. Clearly the Arab Israeli population will continue to view the Russian immigration negatively and as competitors for government funds and benefits. Ethnic competition, if not ethnic conflict, is likely to result. Russian Jews who have arrived in Israel are well educated, with professional occupations and high socioeconomic aspirations for their children. They tend to be relatively uneducated in Jewish history, religion, and culture, having come from a secular society that had for decades denigrated the role of religion and limited the development of Jewish institutions. The experience of Russian immigrants with forms of political democracy has been weak and may lead them to greater vulnerability in the Israeli political system. However, for the first time in Israel's political history, one ethnic group has successfully organized to form powerful ethnic political parties as a basis for political mobilization and power sharing. Russian political parties have become the third largest bloc in Israel's political system. There is every reason to assume that the adjustment problems among this latest immigrant wave will be short term and transitional, as they have been for previous waves of immigrants.

In the year 2000, 61,000 immigrants moved to Israel compared to 77,000 in 1999. Given the choice of destinations, many Russian Jews in the past have turned to the United States. For those emigrating from the Soviet Union in the 1980s, well over half (and in the late 1980s, close to 90 percent) rejected immigration to Israel in favor of the United States. A comprehensive study of Russian immigrants concluded that had they had the choice of destination, about half would not have immigrated to Israel (Al Haj and Leshem 2000). Most would have selected the United States. Increasingly, significant numbers have moved to western European countries. The degree of economic and social integration Russian immigrants achieve will impact on their probability of remaining in Israel and whether their relatives will join them. A peaceful resolution of the Israeli-Arab conflict or continuation of the violence that began in 2000–2001 will affect the amount of further immigration and the possible return migration or forward migration of the Russians who have already arrived in Israel.

The lack of rapidly expanding economic opportunities to match the high educational and occupational skill levels of the new immigrants and their high socioeconomic aspirations for their children may result in selective remigration from Israel and a reduced flow of immigrants from Russia. Unlike those who arrived between 1948 and 1951, more recent immigrants from Russia were greeted by former residents of the Soviet Union who had arrived before them in the 1970s. This fourth wave was also met by a more developed set of institutions that were introduced in the established political regime to deal with their integration. In the longer run, the economic consequences of this immigration are likely to be positive, given the human capital and resources of the immigrants.

The movement to Israel from the former Soviet Union and from Ethiopia cannot be understood without attention to the conjunction of international crises and economic opportunities in Israel in the context of Zionist ideology encouraging immigration. In contrast, there has been a steady but small stream of immigrants to Israel from Western countries—particularly from the United States, the largest Jewish community in the world—that has not been tied to particular crises or to the relatively greater economic opportunities in Israel. This immigration can only be understood as reflecting the importance of ideology, secular and religious Zionism, in the context of some opportunity. Clearly, this migration is selective of the Jewish population of origin, disproportionately religiously and ethnically committed and of higher socioeconomic status (education and occupation) relative to Israel. The voluntary nature of this migration, along with the retention of family and friendship ties in places of origin, results in high rates of return movement back to the United States.

An interesting sidelight of this American immigration to the state of Israel is an analytic difficulty with standard frameworks of immigrant assimilation: What would the education and economic integration of Americans in Israel mean? If, on the one hand, integration means similar occupational and educational patterns among immigrants and native born, then a significant occupational and educational shift downward among American Israelis must take place, since on average these immigrants have rather high levels of education and occupation. On the other hand, immigrant assimilation might imply similar occupational returns to education rather than an identity of levels. But that, too, is problematic, because avenues of mobility that circumvent the educational system have been at play for years in Israel, and the economic opportunities there are significantly different than are those in the United States (see Chapter 7).

Moreover, the traditional immigrant-assimilation framework emphasizes the adjustments of immigrants in places of destination and misses the economic and social capital brought with them. Many immigrants to Israel from the United States bring financial support from family members remaining in their places of origin. A paradigm of immigrant integration needs to be developed to understand the integration of these high socioeconomic status immigrants in Israel who have options of returning to their places of origin. That model should include the socioeconomic and cultural selectivity of immigrants and their continuing ties to families and networks in their places of origins, for the second generation as well as for the immigrant generation. These factors, in somewhat modified form, also need to be taken into account to understand the integration of the more educated and occupationally skilled Russian immigrants of the 1990s.[3]

Although commitment to Jewish nationalism, Zionism, is among the determinants of immigration to Israel, ideological factors always operate in social, economic, and political contexts. Ideological changes do not account for the changes in the rates and sources of immigration over time. Similar to international migration elsewhere, economic factors have been critical in voluntary immigration to Israel; political factors have been central in refugee and nonvoluntary types of movement. Changes in the political condition of Jews in countries outside of Israel and the options available for migration to alternative destinations have shaped the fluctuating rates of migration to Israel and the changes in the national origins of immigrants. Having examined the relative rates of immigration from a variety of countries of origin, researchers have concluded that Zionist ideology is a necessary but not sufficient determinant of immigration. Those political and social factors that have been critical in determining immigration to Israel are mostly beyond the control of the Jewish polity, either in or outside of Israel (Dellapergola 1986; see also Friedlander and Goldscheider 1979; Al Haj and Leshem 2000). As such, policies in Israel are not likely to have a major impact on the rates and sources of Jewish immigration.

The Conspicuous Consequences of Immigration

Changes over time in the rate and composition of immigration to Israel have reverberated throughout the society, in terms of the integration of the immigrants themselves and their impact on previous immigrant streams as well as on the social and demographic structure of the society as a whole. Much of the discussions in subsequent chapters are related to the variety of the structural consequences of immigration to Israel in the process of nation-building. Here, I review several long-term demographic implications of these patterns, including the roles of immigration in national population growth and in the formation of ethnic communities in Israel.

Immigration and Population Growth

The most conspicuous and direct effect of immigration has been on the increase in the population size of the country. The size of Israel's population doubled between 1948 and 1951, and doubled again between 1951 and 1971, increasing to almost 5 million by the end of 1991 and to over 6 million by the end of 2000. The Jewish population component increased almost sixfold from 1948 to 1990, from 717,000 to almost 4 million; the number of Jews in Israel at the end of 2000 was close to 5 million, representing about 80 percent of the total population of Israel. Had there been no immigration, the size of the Jewish population of Israel in the 1970s would have been less than 1 million instead of 2.7 million, and the proportion of the Jewish population would have been 65 percent instead of 85 percent (Friedlander and Goldscheider 1979, table 7.6). In contrast, the Arab minority in Israel has grown by natural increase, since immigration has remained in large part restricted to the Jewish population. Almost half of the total growth of the Jewish population between 1948 and 2000 was a direct result of immigration, but 98 percent of the growth of the Arab population was due to natural increase.

Therefore, population growth and immigration are intimately and directly connected in the development of Israeli society. To the extent that population growth is linked to economic development, immigration has been indirectly associated with developmental processes (through its impact on population increase). Moreover, other indirect consequences of immigration for demographic growth are tied in to who immigrates and what demographic "baggage" (i.e., fertility, health, and mortality patterns) and social characteristics (family structure, educational level, and occupational skills) they bring. These more subtle effects are important in assessing the longer-term population growth implications of immigration. Some immigrants tend to come from high-fertility countries, and immigrant streams were in large part composed of young adults and families. Those arriving from more traditional Middle Eastern Jewish communities had higher fertility levels than those from European countries, which contributed disproportionately to Israel's population growth.

In subsequent analysis, I review the changes in the fertility patterns of immigrants as length of exposure to Israeli society increased (Chapter 11). I assess the economic integration of immigrants, the increasing levels of their education, and changes in the health and welfare of the first and subsequent generations. These factors are powerful indicators of whether fertility levels are translated into continuing large family size, which in turn sustained population growth over time and established the connection between immigration and social and economic differentiation among ethnic origin Jewish groups.

In addition to population growth, the changing volume of immigration, particularly mass immigration, had a ripple effect through the age structure of Israel at different periods of time—first, in the bunching up of births; several years later, in the schooling of children at younger and older ages; then in the enlarging of the number of men and women in their middle ages and in the workforce; and finally, in the increasing entrance of cohorts into the older ages (Ben-Porath 1986; Friedlander and Goldscheider 1979). This burst of age effects and its subsequent contraction has placed particular strains on a political and welfare system that attempts to address population needs and provide age-related services. The changing compositional effects of these age cohorts, particularly their ethnic origins and related socioeconomic correlates, exacerbate these strains.

Ethnic Composition and Demographic Change

In addition to issues of population growth and structure, immigration from a wide range of countries of origin has resulted in the ethnic diversity of the Jewish population of Israel. The ethnic composition shifted from an overwhelming Western-origin population to a more balanced composition of Western and Middle Eastern origins (see Chapter 2). Given the overlap of ethnic origin with social and economic resources, political orientations, and culture, the ethnic compositional shifts have had, and will continue to have, major implications for the social, economic, and demographic developments of Israeli society. I investigate the extent to which ethnicity in subsequent generations is associated with relative economic and educational status, differential access to economic opportunities and networks, and the generational transmission of ethnic stratification. I also explore whether ethnic differences among the third generation are linked to specific countries or to broad regional divisions of origin. And I review the evidence that identifies the economic, demographic, and cultural bases of contemporary ethnic differences in a wide range of social processes.

I expect that emergent Jewish ethnic communities in Israel are significantly different from those in places of origin, since the contexts of their lives and of their children's lives have been dramatically altered. For example, occupational patterns have become more diversified for all immigrant groups, educational levels have increased, mortality has declined, and family size has become smaller. Ethnic communities have experienced social mobility and occupational and educational transformations. Even as they are of diverse origins, Jews are united nationally by externals—their culture, history, and sense of peoplehood, as well as by their relationship to the Arab minorities in the state of Israel and in the territories administered by Israel (Goldscheider 1986; Smooha 1978). Ethnic immigration groups over the generations have been transformed and should not be treated simply as transplanted populations from countries of origin.

Indeed, the major changes that all immigrant groups have experienced have resulted in the emergence of new Israeli patterns, neither fully "Western" nor "Middle Eastern" (see Chapter 2). Although Jewish ethnic differences remain salient and distance from the immigrant generation continues to be an important factor in understanding social change in Israel, the critical question is whether there are structural features that continue to differentiate Israel's ethnic groups (Goldscheider and Zuckerman 1984). These features include the overlap of ethnic origin with educational attainment, residential concentration, and political orientation. Do higher levels of education and occupation continue to characterize European-origin populations of the third generation? Does ethnic residential concentration continue by region (e.g., living in a development town versus a major urban center) or by neighborhood that is linked, in turn, to job and educational opportunities? Are there continuing high rates of intra-ethnic marriages and ethnic self-identification? How do the children of mixed ethnic origins identify themselves? As in other pluralistic countries, we can assess whether an "Israeli" national identity has emerged, not only in myth but in fact, that negates the longer-term legitimacy and significance of ethnic origin or ancestry.

Ethnic pluralism has emerged in Israeli society as a result of immigration and its consequences. This pluralism is in tension with increasing Jewish national unity and integration among the diverse immigrant streams. Exposure to educational and military institutions has been an almost universal experience for the Jewish population and has served as an important mechanism of national integration. The Hebrew language has become a major integrative force nationally, linking Jews of different national origins and of diverse linguistic backgrounds to each other and to the emergent national culture as well as to past history. External hostilities and continuous wars with Arab countries have also resulted in the unification of the Jewish population of Israel and have linked Jews to Jewish communities around the world. Thus, there are tensions between ethnic integration and assimilation, on one hand, and a new form of ethnic stratification and distinctiveness on the other.

The occupational skills, educational background, and family and ethnic ties of the European immigrants facilitated their entry into Israeli society and their access to resources and opportunities. Europeans could build successfully on their connections to the European-dominated Israeli society and economy. Immigrants from Asian-African countries came from societies that were less-modern economically and demographically, and they were less able to compete initially with the European immigrants in Israel. The different timing of these immigrations and the cultural differences between groups in places of origin reinforced these structural factors. Immigration patterns created two new ethnic communities among Jews in Israel—"European-Americans" and "Asian-Africans"— and they have been sustained over the generations. The divisions have been marked by social class concentration and linkages to distinctive cultures. In part, these have been connected to places of origin and the ethnic networks that sustain them. However, most specific country-of-origin differences have declined in significance.

Immigration to Israel has resulted in the convergence of ethnic differences in some areas of social life, as well as ethnic continuities in others (see my discussions in subsequent chapters; see also Schmelz, Dellapergola, and Avner 1990). The question remains about the relative balance of these changes in current patterns, their implications for the next generation, and the factors that sustain ethnic distinctiveness. Commonalities and convergences in one dimension of social life do not necessarily imply commonality (and assimilation) in all areas. Thus, I explore whether convergences in some demographic characteristics result in the declining significance of ethnicity and ethnic communities in social behavior. Put analytically, I ask, Under what conditions do ethnic communities retain their salience, and what are the contexts that facilitate ethnic assimilation, particularly under a regime of converging demographic differentials?

Some new ethnic forms may be Israeli-made products, not simply the legacy of origins, background, and immigrant selectivity. It is therefore important to disentangle the ethnic variation that is the result of "origins" and the characteristics that immigrants brought with them from the factors that were shaped by their exposure to Israeli society. Although every ethnic group has been characterized by social mobility, the question remains whether the socioeconomic gap between ethnic groups has diminished. Inequalities may persist, even with rapid development and economic growth and the opening up of new opportunities within a relatively open stratification system. The questions raised by large-scale immigration in pluralistic societies are related to immigration's impact on overall societal growth and macroeconomic development as well as to the distribution of economic opportunities among groups and the access immigrants and subsequent generations have to economic mobility. The combination of country-of-origin differences plus those reinforced, institutionalized, or created by the state are the critical dimensions in the transition from immigrant to ethnic group. I investigate these factors in assessing the changing basis of ethnic divisions among Jews and between Jews and Arabs in Israel.

One final note about the salience of ethnicity relates to the links between religion (in this case Judaism) and ethnicity. Immigrants brought to Israel a variety of forms of Judaism from their different cultures of origin. Developments in Israeli society militated against the retention of forms of religious practices and customs. Some of these changes in religion may be considered under the rubric secularization. Nevertheless, new features of religious expression have emerged in Israel, building on the specific ethnic cultures of the past and redefining and transforming the nature of religious culture. Three aspects of these forms of Israeli Judaism will be discussed in subsequent chapters: (1) the role of the ultra-Orthodox or *haredi* groups in Israel and the singular power of the Orthodox rabbinate in issues of marriage, divorce, and Jewish identity in a secular society; (2) the organization of Sephardic, or Middle Eastern, Jews into a religious party (Shas) and its political, economic, and educational power; and (3) the role of religion among the Jewish settler population in the administered territories. These themes connect ethnicity and religion in Israel, reinforcing the ethnic cultural features of Judaism, the political and social context of religious expression, and the ways that the forms of Judaism result in ethnic and religious conflict. Just as the overlap of ethnicity and social class reinforces the salience of ethnic communities, so the overlap of ethnic origin and Judaic expression reinforces the diversity of Israeli Judaisms and their anchor in ethnic origins.

Emigration

For a long time, demographers have observed that all migrant streams have counter-streams (Goldscheider 1971). This is no less true for immigration to Israel, but it involves an ideological twist. In a society that has experienced massive and diverse immigration patterns and has fundamental ideological and policy commitments to immigration, it should not be surprising that emigration from the country is viewed negatively. Hence, whereas the Hebrew word used to describe Jewish immigration is *aliya*, or ascent, the word for emigration is *yerida*, or descent. To Israelis, the significance of these processes for loyalty to the state and to the values of the society is unambiguous, and the negative connotations of *yerida* are unmistakable. One would expect that the major streams of immigration to Israel would produce counterstreams of emigration, if not to the country of origin, then to areas of better economic opportunity. The concern expressed in Israel over emigration far exceeds the actual volume of out-migration and can only be understood in its deep-rooted ideological contexts (Lamdany 1982; Sobel 1986).

Ideological concerns spill over into definitional problems. When is someone who leaves a country to be treated as an emigrant? Although many countries define an emigrant as one who intends to remain abroad for over one year, such a declared intention in Israel violates the fundamental ideology of the state and the shared norms of the Jewish population. Given the stigma associated with emigration from Israel, that declaration cannot be the major basis for identifying emigrants. Indeed, over time the rate of emigration defined by declaration has declined and represents a negligible component (Lamdany 1982).

Estimates of emigration are based on the number of residents departing Israel, minus the number of arrivals during the year. This figure maximizes the estimate of emigration. At most, there were 340,000 emigrants from Israel between 1948 and 1979, an average annual rate of emigration of 4.6 residents per 1,000 residents, or 225 emigrants per 1,000 immigrants. Of these, 318,000 were estimated to be Jewish. The factors affecting Jewish and Arab emigration are different, and the magnitude and propensities of emigration differ over time for the two populations. A lower-bounded estimate of emigrants is the number of residents abroad for more than 10 years; by the end of 1979 that number was 145,000 (Lamdany 1982).[4]

Emigration is much more voluntary and individual compared to immigration. Employment opportunities outside of Israel and the potential for greater professional advancement, along with higher personal income and a better standard of living, are the critical factors shaping the migration from Israel (Lamdany 1982; Sobel 1986). The unusual military burden Israel has placed on its citizens on a continuous basis may have also influenced the decision to leave. Yet, it is likely that neither economic opportunity nor military concerns fully accounts for emigration, since few Israelis leave and since there has been a small, continuous stream of immigrants to Israel from Western countries. It is likely that family, social, and economic networks in Israel and the linkages between Israelis living in Israel and in other countries are important factors in accounting for emigration rates.

Variation in emigration rates from Israel are related empirically to changes over time in economic conditions, the security situation, and absorption of new immigrants. Changes in actual and expected standards of living affect the propensity to emigrate; emigration varies with changing levels of consumption per capita and follows the economic cycle, declining with prosperity and increasing during periods of economic stagnation. Economic factors are likely to affect the timing of emigration but not necessarily the decision whether to emigrate. Economic expectations, rather than economic conditions per se, have a strong effect on emigration. Aggregate data do not reveal much about who emigrates. Estimates are that young adults, single males, and immigrants from Western countries have higher rates of emigration (Lamdany 1982). Return migration to places of origin is more likely among immigrants to Israel from Western Europe and the United States. In general, it is likely that emigration rates are higher among those who moved voluntarily to Israel.

Some recent immigrants with no access to a passport other than from Israel often face waiting periods to acquire the right to leave Israel. They are often required to repay substantial loans or to secure cosigners to ensure the reimbursement for subsidized housing and mortgages. For example, immigrant Russians of the 1989 to 1992 migration period needed to wait several years for an exit visa or pay back housing loans or obtain cosigners. In all, however, the return rates and emigration (remigration) rates from Israel are relatively unimportant at the societal level and do not threaten the longer-term social demographic consequences of immigration. They challenge the ideological basis of one form of Zionism that negates the viability of Jewish communities outside of Israel. When native-born Israelis of the third generation emigrate, the ideological challenge intensifies.

Nation-Building, Zionism, and Immigrants

I have presented a view of Israel as a changing society of immigrants, shaped by ideology and altered by immigration from diverse sociopolitical and cultural areas of the world. As immigration helped form the nation and guided its development over time, it was and continues to be the basis of ethnic cleavages and conflicts. At the same time, immigration has drawn on communities outside of Israel and has resulted in enriching the social and cultural diversity that is at the core of Israeli society. Immigration has provided the basis for the formation of new communities in Israel and has helped Jews to forge linkages with communities outside of Israel that resulted in new economic and social dependencies and networks.

As the basis of Jewish population growth and the social construction of an Israeli Jewish identity, immigration has long been the symbol of the Jewish-Arab conflict. The Arab population in Israel views immigration as a continuing threat to the political and economic aspirations of its community and the Palestinian people. As in the past, this powerful symbol of Jewish nationalism is a source of tension and conflict with Palestinian and Arab nationalism.

There are different components to the Zionist imperative about immigration. First, there is the great success of the Zionist emphasis on immigration as the fundamental step in the nation-building process. Jews from dozens of countries around the world, many as refugees, immigrated to Israel to reestablish Jewish sovereignty and control there. But the Zionist movement has failed to bring all or even a majority of Jews to the new state, as millions of Jews voluntarily continue to reject this feature of Zionist ideology. The United States symbolizes the alternative community, where Jews live as a minority with full rights, open opportunities for social mobility, high levels of education, and diverse avenues of cultural and religious expressions. Although American Jews have rejected aliya as an imperative in their Jewish expression, they have articulated their sense of peoplehood and their culture in the form of common institutions and in their support of the Jewish state.

Some might argue from this analysis that a new Zionist ideology needs to take into account the realities of the beginning of the twenty-first century and the continuities of an assimilating community in the United States and in other places. Jews in Israel and in communities outside of Israel need to form new bonds and new ideologies that reinforce the symmetries between communities rather than the centrality of one over the other. This need may be more characteristic of Jewish communities in Western, democratic societies, where most Jews lived at the end of the twentieth century.

Another conclusion might point to the end of the ideological factors as part of the determinants of immigration to Israel. However, within the Western world there continues to be groups of people with religious and secular nationalistic ideologies that view Israel as central to their lives. If ideologies are always anchored in a context, as I have argued, then as contexts change, ideological changes would be expected. New ideologies are already developing that legitimate both types of Jewish communities in and outside the state of Israel and that posit a new basis for interrelationships that builds on the strengths of both.

My major questions about immigration do not revolve around the future estimates of immigration or speculations about the future of Jewish communities in areas outside of Israel (see Goldscheider 2002). Instead, my focus on immigration and its aftermath in Israeli society concerns: (1) its impact on differential demographic processes of mortality and fertility; (2) the residential concentration of immigrant communities and the geographical distribution of populations in the country; (3) patterns of marriage, family, gender roles, and interethnic interactions; and (4) the distribution of education, occupation, and income among ethnic groups over time. These themes of the transition from immigrant to ethnic groups are reviewed as I examine the lives of the foreign-born and later generations of Jews and begin to disentangle the effects of origins and the changing Israeli contexts on the lives of those living under its political and cultural auspices.

Notes

1. Some have argued that the long Judaic tradition emphasizing "return" to the Land of Israel makes the culture and the underlining ideology unique. Explicitly, they suggest that Israel is different from other new states that were established after World War II since Israel is not a new nation in an old society but rather a new state and a new society for an ancient people (Horowitz and Lissak 1989a). That may be the case; however, my focus is not the source of the ideology but the uniqueness of the immigration process.

2. When Oscar Handlin wrote the saga of American immigration, *The Uprooted*, he reported that he had set out to write the history of American immigration but had discovered that immigration was American history. A similar argument could be made for the history of Israel.

3. For a review of American immigration to Israel, see Avruch 1981; Dashefsky et. al 1992; Goldscheider 1974; Sobel 1986; Waxman 1989.

4. The numbers of emigrants do not include their children. From the point of view of the sending country (Israel), these are "losses"; the next generation is counted from the point of view of the "gains" to receiving countries.

4

Arab Israelis: Demography, Dependency, and Distinctiveness

Demographic issues were in the forefront of the conflict between Arabs and Jews in Palestine from the end of the nineteenth century until the establishment of the state. Subsequently, these issues have been controversial in Israeli society. In the prestate period, there were political conflicts over the number of Jews permitted to enter the country relative to economic opportunities and rates of Arab demographic growth. Since Israel was established, the economic and political implications of high fertility among Arabs and immigration among Jews have intensified. The relative size and growth rates of Arab and Jewish populations and their geographic distributions have been the most conspicuous demographic concerns under several political regimes and within different territorial configurations. Almost always, the focus has been on the society as a whole, whether in Palestine or in Israel, with a clear emphasis on the contrast and comparisons between Jewish and Arab populations. As a result, the analysis of Arab demographic patterns has generally been placed in the context of the Arab-Jewish conflict, rather than used as a basis for understanding Arab social structure.

In this chapter, I focus on a broad range of demographic issues associated with the distinctiveness of the Arab population in Israel, at both the society and the community levels of analysis. I outline the changing levels of inequality between Arabs and Jews in Israel, the role of fertility in reinforcing the position of women in the Arab community, and the centrality of residential segregation in sustaining the social, political, and economic dependency of Arab Israelis. These themes serve as a prelude to my subsequent, more detailed analysis. I demonstrate how demographic issues are integral to the understanding of the Arab community in Israeli society and identify the religious, social class, and regional heterogeneity within the Arab-Israeli population.

The dominant religious group among the Arab Israelis is Moslem, representing 81 percent of the Arab population of Israel at the end of the twentieth century, up from 69 percent in 1948. Christian Arabs in Israel are characterized by significantly different sociodemographic profiles than either Moslem or Druze Israelis. Christian Arabs have lower rates of mortality and fertility and are more urbanized and educated.

When not identified specifically, "Arab Israeli" or "Israeli Arab" will be treated as approximately equivalent to "Moslem Israeli" or "Palestinian Israeli." Each of these references has a political significance, as does the categorization of Arabs as "religious" (not national or ethnic) groups and their grouping as "non-Jewish" in official publications of the state (see Chapter 2).

As Israeli society has evolved, as state policies have altered, as the economy has developed, and as the sociopolitical conflict between Arabs and Jews have changed, Arab communities and their institutions have been transformed. Demography has been central to the unfolding of these changes in Arab Israeli communities, although the population issues of the 1990s are significantly different from those of earlier decades. An analysis of the relative growth patterns of minority and majority populations is a fundamental theme of ethnic demographic research in general (e.g., Blalock 1967; Lieberson 1980; Goldscheider 1995), and of Palestine-Israel demography (and related policy issues and political ideologies) in particular (e.g., Friedlander and Goldscheider 1979). Adding the perspective of Arab communities demonstrates how the "integration" of the Arab population into the Jewish-Israeli economy has resulted in the Arabs' increased dependency and continuing inequality. A key factor in this process has been the residential segregation of Israeli Arabs and the connection between segregation and limited economic opportunities.

The concept of dependency is used in the sociological sense, referring to the power exercised by the majority population and its control over the opportunities available to the minority population. I examine the sociodemographic underpinnings of the changing allocation of socioeconomic resources. Dependency does not necessarily reflect legal or political inequalities, but it does imply the continued distinctiveness of the Arab minority within Israel and the socioeconomic inequality. Issues of discrimination that result from dependency are structural and institutional, reflecting the particular location of the minority in the broader community. The structural sources of discrimination against Arab Israelis are reflected in the economic returns to education (i.e., the kind of jobs that Arabs can get with higher levels of education) and in the costs of residential segregation in limiting access to economic opportunity.

Five Arab-Israeli Demographic Issues

There are several major issues that highlight the centrality of demography for understanding Arab communities in Israel. Each is outlined below, in a conceptual and methodological framework that links changes in population processes to the social, economic, and political contexts of Arab communities in Israeli society. In turn, these demographic issues are linked to the changing economic dependency of Arab Israelis and to sources of structural discrimination and disadvantage.

Issue One

The issue that been at the core of the demographic history of Arab Israelis has been the changing Arab-Jewish population ratio in Israel. This often has been considered *the* demographic issue of the Arab-Israel conflict, with powerful political, economic, and ideological implications for the emerging Jewish state. The relative size and the implied growth rates of Jewish and Arab populations had been considered a key problem, recognized by all three political actors (Jews, Arabs, and the British) before the establishment of the state. It became a different, but no less critical, issue in the years following the mass Jewish immigration from 1948 to 1951 and in subsequent periods, when the volume and rate of Jewish immigration to Israel fluctuated. The problem of the Arab-Jewish population ratio emerged in more dramatic form after the 1967 war, with the inclusion of Arab areas and populations under Israeli administration and control (see extensive discussions and analyses in Friedlander and Goldscheider 1974, 1979, 1984).

The examination of Arab-Jewish population growth rates and the demographic sources of their differential growth rates tend to be viewed in the traditional framework of demographic transition theory (see Chapter 1). Some have argued that the Arab demographic pattern has reached the stage of "transition," with low levels of mortality and higher rates of fertility that only began to decline during the 1970s. In contrast, the Jewish demographic pattern has already reached a later evolutionary stage of low levels of both fertility and mortality rates—hence, low population growth rates due to natural increase. This pattern first characterized the European Jewish population in Israel and subsequently characterized second-generation Israeli Jews of Asian and African origin. Thus, although the younger cohorts of Jewish Israelis are moving toward zero population growth, the Arab Israeli population remains in the high population growth stage. It does not take much demographic orientation to imagine (and exaggerate) the sociopolitical consequences of a rapidly growing minority population and a relatively low-growth majority population.

The issue of the relative number and rate of growth of Israeli Jewish and Arab populations and the implied demographic threat of Israeli Arab population growth rates to the political control of the Jewish majority is a profound ideological construction but without a demographic basis. Since the establishment of Israel, the Arab proportion of the total population of the state has fluctuated around a narrow and low range, from 19 percent in 1948 to 20 percent in 1998.[1] No reasonable assumption of future demographic dynamics would lead to an Arab Israeli demographic threat to the Jewish majority, without the political incorporation of Arab populations currently not Israeli citizens—for example, those living in the West Bank—or the mass emigration of Jewish Israelis from the country. Focusing on Israeli Arabs, not on Palestinians living outside the state, and assuming that mass emigration of Jews from Israel or mass immigration of Arabs to Israel are very unlikely (and hence unpredictable) events, reveals unambiguously that, at the national level, the Arab population is likely to remain a permanent demographic minority in both the short and long run (Compare Tables 2.1 and 4.1).[2]

What about at the regional community level? Here, the evidence points in the opposite direction. There are regions within Israel that have a majority Arab population and areas within regions that have high levels of Arab population concentration and segregation (see Chapter 5). It is at the local, subnational level that changes in Arab population size shape the labor supply and demand in an economic market and set up the potential for local market expansion, as well as for the retention of some specialized skilled labor and professionals. The regional and community importance of Arab Israeli demography emerges from the differential growth rates of these populations, not the national Jewish-Arab population ratio or the demographic threat to the Jewish majority status.

Issue Two

The demographic growth of the Jewish Israeli population has been the direct result of immigration, combined with the indirect effects of the fertility of the immigrants, particularly those from high fertility Moslem countries. The high Jewish population growth rate has been balanced by the natural increase of the Arab population as a result of their higher rates of fertility than mortality (Friedlander and Goldscheider 1984). Higher Arab fertility was the counterweight to the higher Jewish immigration. Both populations have increased in size and have remained in approximately the same ratio to each other through these different demographic paths.

Several additional considerations are necessary to understanding these different demographic sources of growth. The first relates to the *selectivity* of post-state Arab populations relative to pre-state Palestine. The Arab population remaining in the newly established state in 1948 was different from the pre-state Arab population both in its smaller size and lower socioeconomic characteristics (Smooha 1989). This residual Arab population had a significantly higher level of fertility and mortality than the pre-state Arab population of Palestine. Hence, it had a subsequent demographic trajectory different from that of Palestinians living outside of the state. Some of the Arab demographic changes in Israel are the result of processes of population development and the transformation from a majority population to a demographic minority. Other changes resulted from the shift from an autonomous and somewhat diverse economic sectoral structure to a more homogeneous, agricultural, dependent sector under military administration in the larger Jewish economy (Al Haj 1987). The economic dependency of the Israeli Arab population emerges from the selectivity issue, as does its demographic minority status.

Declines in mortality and fertility were the key demographic changes influencing the size of the Arab population remaining in Israel. The decline in mortality began

TABLE 4.1 Arab Population Size and Percentage of Moslems in Israel,
1948–1998

	Total Number of Arabs (in thousands)	Moslems (%)
1948	156	–
1951	173	69
1954	192	69
1957	213	69
1960	239	69
1961	247	69
1964	286	71
1967	390	73
1970	440	75
1972	472	76
1973	493	77
1976	555	77
1979	618	77
1982	684	77
1983	706	77
1985	749	77
1988	818	78
1991	914	78
1995	1,005	81
1998	1,195	81

Note: After 1967 the Arab population of Israel includes the population
living in East Jerusalem (about 66,000 in 1967). Included are data for
the census years of 1961, 1972, 1983, and 1995.

Source: *Statistical Abstract of Israel,* various years.

before the establishment of the state and preceded the decline in fertility. The Arab
mortality decline was slower than that among Jewish Israelis, and infant mortality remains almost twice as high. Mortality levels are prime indicators of the changing life chances of Arabs in the context of their social situations. The relative inequality of Arabs and Jews in Israel and the disadvantaged status of Arab Israelis
becomes apparent when we examine the mortality gap between populations in the
same country. The mortality decline is significant because of the gap between Arab
and Jewish Israelis, despite improvements in both populations. The contribution of

mortality decline to the population growth issue takes second place to the broader implications of mortality differences for issues of inequality (see Chapter 9).

The fertility transition among Israeli Arabs was slower and later than mortality declines, resulting in rapid rates of population growth. Since the 1970s, lower levels of fertility among Moslem Israelis have been recorded. The decline in family size occurred earlier among Christian Israelis than among Moslem or Druze Israelis. Moslem women who married immediately before the establishment of the state (that is, between 1944 and 1948) had an average of over 9 children after 30 years of marriage. The total fertility rate in the 1960s (an estimate of average family size) was over 9 children; by the 1980s, it was less than 5 children. For the three years 1996–1998, the total fertility rate of Moslem Israelis was 4.6. Christian Arab women who were married before 1955 had an ideal family size of about 6 children and a total fertility rate in the 1960s of 4.5 children. The younger cohorts who married in the post-1967 period had an average ideal family size of 4 children. The total fertility rate for Christian Arabs in the late 1990s was 2.6 children, somewhat below the Jewish Israeli average (see Chapter 11).

Issue Three

The importance of differential Arab and Jewish fertility for population growth is unmistakable. Largely neglected, however, are issues associated with the costs of high fertility to the role of Arab women within their communities and families, and the costs of large family size to the socioeconomic opportunities available for the next generation of Arab Israelis. In large part, the traditional role of Arab women has almost always been treated as one of the determinants of sustained high fertility, following the argument that unless the status of women changes to nonchildbearing roles, there is little likelihood of significant changes in fertility.

One theoretical challenge is to understand why the role of Arab Israeli women did not change with the first indications of modernization and how family roles were reinforced by the absence of internal migrations and by state welfare policies (Friedlander, Eisenbach, and Goldscheider 1979, 1980). But the reverse causal connection operates over time—large family size sustains the family-oriented roles of Moslem women, and high Arab fertility reinforces women's childbearing roles. The disadvantages of high fertility are clearly present at the family and community levels. The value of sustained Arab fertility can be appreciated both from a demographic and a national perspective (as a balance to the high rates of Jewish immigration) and from the point of view of Arab males.

The third demographic theme revolves around the determinants and consequences of these Arab population processes. The determinants of mortality change involve the extension of health care and public health facilities in Arab communities. The significant remaining mortality differences between Arabs and Jews reflect, in part, their individual characteristics (for example, their educational levels and occupational concentrations) and, more important, the context of their communities. The distribution of health and related services to more iso-lated Arab communities in Israel and the differential access of Arabs to the more extensive health care facilities in Jewish areas are critical factors sustaining the higher Arab mortality. The Arab-Jewish mortality gap is clearly associated with, and a sensitive indicator of, social inequality in Israel.

Research on the determinants of Arab fertility has focused on the individual characteristics of women. As in other countries, studies have correlated the income, education, and labor force participation of women and have linked those individ-ual traits to fertility. A more thorough analysis places Arab fertility in the contexts of the economic and family structure of the Arab Israeli community, connecting economic networks, opportunities, and the role of women. Thus, household and community contexts are of primary importance for the understanding of Arab fertility and mortality. With rare exceptions (see Al Haj 1987), these contexts have not been extensively studied for Israeli Arabs.

The explanation of the decline in Moslem fertility since the 1970s illustrates the complexity of combining levels of analysis. First, the continuing declines in mor-tality and the low rates of infant deaths have had an impact on the goal of reducing family size. Second, there has been a continuing increase in the educational attain-ment of Moslem women. Moslem women who benefited from the Mandatory Edu-cation Act reached their childbearing period in the 1970s. Thus, less than 10 percent of the Arab women who were married between 1964 and 1968 had any formal edu-cation after the ninth grade, compared to about half of those who married in the early 1980s. A third factor in the decline of Arab fertility in Israel has been the in-creases in the participation of Arab women in the formal and informal labor force and the exceptional growth in the participation of educated Arab women.

These societal-level changes and individual-level factors combine with the links between Moslem families and their communities and the economic activities of those working outside of Arab residential areas. This is most conspicuous in the pat-tern of male employment and is tied into the economic "integration" of Arabs in the Jewish economy. There has been a continuous process of leaving agriculture to com-mute to jobs in the Jewish sector. Increases in the standard of living and education, along with the benefits from the welfare state and the increase in the opportunity structure, suggest that the economic futures of younger couples are more indepen-dent of the extended families. The past costs of high fertility among Moslem Israelis are not simply the relative proportion of the population in Israel that is Arab but the high internal costs for the role of women and for the economic future of the next generation of children. Thus, from the point of view of the Arab community, fertility levels are important, not because they are linked to population growth, but because fertility is part of family, which is part of community and the organization of society. Hence, fertility trends reveal, even more directly than do mortality changes, critical aspects of the social organization of communities and families.

Fertility patterns have had an impact on gender roles in households and on the hierarchy implied by the largely segregated roles of Moslem women. The distribution of household labor connects to both the circular movement of male Arab laborers in the Jewish sector of Israel and the substitute roles that Arab women have as unpaid laborers in agriculture. Thus, high fertility continues to bind Arab women to the household to take care of their families and places them in the control of the extended family and of neighbors. Arab women and young adults have increased their dependency on Israeli Jews.

The dependency role of young adults, particularly women, is further illustrated by the pattern of living arrangements. Moslem young adults generally live with their families until they marry and move from one family role (as child) to another (as spouse). Few unmarried Moslem Israelis live alone, compared to increasing proportions of Jewish Israeli adults (see Goldscheider and Fisher 1989). Therefore, Arab dependencies in Israeli society are manifested at the level of economic activities and the dependencies of Arabs on Israeli Jews. There are also gender dependencies of Arab women on Arab male control, and the younger generation's dependency on adults and extended families.

Issue Four

Most of the demographic studies of Arab Israelis have focused on the interrelationships of mortality and fertility issues and have ignored the role of internal migration and segregation. Our fourth issue focuses on internal migration patterns and the urbanization of the Israeli Arab population, as well as on the emergent forms of residential concentration, resulting in large part from political, economic, and demographic patterns. The overall political control over internal migration limited the voluntary movements of Arab Israelis through the mid-1960s; informal constraints continue to limit their internal migration. Nevertheless, some limited migration has occurred over time in selected areas, including urbanward movements and internal movements among Arab communities.

The major form of mobility, however, rarely captured and almost always underestimated by standard official migration data sources, is commuting—the daily movements of Arabs who work in Jewish areas. This circular or daily commuting pattern raises the theoretical question of whether the temporary migration of Arab Israelis substitutes for other, more permanent, migration forms. Hence, is this one factor slowing down changes that would have occurred under a different, more open internal migration policy? The absence of large-scale internal migration directly reinforces the dependency status of Arab women on Arab men, of Arab men on Israeli Jews, and of the younger generation on the extended family and the community. The regional concentration of the Arab Israeli population and the development of commuting as a substitute for internal migration exacerbate the economic dependency of Arabs on the Israeli Jewish population.

The residential concentration and segregation of Arab Israelis from Jewish Israelis is thorough. There are over 100 communities listed in the Israeli census; the proportion of Arabs in the 7 mixed localities ranges from 6 percent to 30 percent, and the others are either totally Arab (35 places) or totally Jewish (61 places). The high rates of residential segregation have been well documented (Semyonov and Tyree 1981). Segregation is only part of the story, since the nature of the places where Arabs are concentrated also implies a controlled and limited opportunity structure and the constrained access of Arabs to economic markets. In most of the Arab communities, job opportunities are scarce and economic and infrastructural developments are limited.

At the local level, studies of Haifa (Ben-Artzi and Shoshani 1986), Nazerith (Bar-Gal 1986), and Shefar'Am (Al Haj 1987) document the complexities of internal migration among Israeli Arabs. The growth of Haifa's Arab population, for example, was contained in segregated areas by the gradual evacuation by Jews through the 1970s. These areas became less mixed because Jews left and the growth of the Arab population through natural increase could be absorbed. With the absence of in-migration to the area, there was little geographic spread of the Arab population in the city. Until 1948, there were 62,000 Arabs living in Haifa, but only 3,566 remained after the establishment of the state and most were Christian. At the end of the military administration of the Arab population in Israel in the 1960s, there were 8,000 Arabs living in Haifa, reflecting growth based on unification of families and selected return migration to the city. In the areas where Arabs moved in Haifa, Jews moved away, thereby reinforcing Arab segregation.[3]

The geographic spread through this period was basically in the same area, since there was a sufficient number of housing units abandoned by Jews and available for occupancy. These units were densely overcrowded and poorly built, with a declining infrastructure and low levels of services. So as the new immigrants (Jews) left their first areas of settlement to move to better neighborhoods, the growing Arab population "reclaimed" Arab housing; Arab neighborhood concentration in the pre-1948 areas was continuous.

The results of the censuses show continuous growth of the Moslem population in the Haifa subdistrict. In 1961 there were 4,600 Moslems in this area, increasing to 7,400 in 1972, 10,300 in 1983, and 12,800 in 1995. Part of this growth was the result of high fertility, but a significant part, at least one-fourth, was the direct result of net internal migration to the city. The migration resembles rural to urban movements, in response to the pull of urban processes and opportunities. Later, I review the interrelated community elements of Shefar'Am in an attempt to assess the important and integral role of demographic processes on Arab social structure.

Issue Five

The fifth demographic issue focuses on the consequences of the residential concentration of Israeli Arabs. It is likely that the extent of health facilities, the nature of educational opportunities, and other social and economic infrastructural developments—combined with the patterns of geographic isolation in these places and their small size—conspire to affect the role of Arab women, their dependency on men, and the relative economic dependency of Arab men on the Jewish economic sector. Because Arab residential segregation has an impact on educational opportunities and the translation of educational levels into appropriate jobs, the potential for the next generation of young adults to improve their standard of living is constrained. This is particularly the case when options for out-migration are limited and there is an expanding population base.

The economic and labor force consequences of residential concentration for Arab men and women are critical, as are the effects of segregation on such infrastructural issues as education, job opportunities, and organizational and institutional developments. The dependency of Arab communities on the Jewish economic sector is a direct outcome of the state's segregation policies and the subsequent increased discrimination in the labor market. The lack of adequate schooling and, most important, the lack of independence and autonomy are linked to the residential constraints on Arab Israelis. These costs are part of the external Arab-Israeli conflict and are linked to internal ethnic tensions.

Research in one Arab community, Shefar'Am, demonstrates the changing political control associated with the ethnic composition of the town, its changing opportunity structure, the effects on the role of women, and the changing role of internal migrants (Arab refugees) on the community. Nowhere in Israel has the interrelationships of demographic, economic, social, and political processes been more clearly documented for Arab Israelis (Al Haj 1987). The economic move toward the Jewish sector was in the direction of increased dependency—internal colonialism in its extreme form (Zureik 1979). This shift toward dependency among Arab Israelis permeates the system of stratification among Arabs, influencing their status in the community, primarily their powerlessness. Patterns of dependency are an integral part of the educational system and the curricular orientation of Arab schools, of the Israeli values that inform Arab lives, of the national character of their communities, and of the general feeling that their communities are linked to an Israeli society that dismisses their culture as political and their independence as the basis for potential terrorism. Research systematically demonstrates how the dependence of the Arab population increased in direct relation to the rise in the standard of living in this Arab community (Al Haj).

From the point of view of the broader Israeli society, particularly the Jewish community and its political structure, the economic position of the Arab minority has been improving over time. At the same time, and less well appreciated, Arab economic dependency on the Jewish economic sector has become institutionalized. The changing economic relationships between Jewish and Arab Israelis have been the result of structural realignments of economic and population distribution patterns. Some aspects of kinship structure and control have increased among Israeli Arabs, at the same time that the specific economic roles of these kin groups have been substituted by the power exercised by Jewish control. These changes have resulted from pragmatic requirements and structural constraints rather than from ideological or cultural commitments.

Arabs and Jews compete for jobs in the "integrated" Israeli economic sector, and Arabs are less likely to succeed at obtaining employment. They are likely to pay a heavy price for occupational integration, since they will have to seek appropriate jobs outside their segregated sector in competition with better-educated and well-connected Jewish persons. It is reasonable to assume that, in the near term, Arabs will not be the advantaged group or equal in this competition. Unlike in the past, when educated Arabs were in demand in the Arab sector (replacing those who left the community in the 1948 war), more of the better-educated Arabs are now being pushed into the Jewish sector and into blue-collar work. Thus, through the early 1980s, there had been a nice fit between higher education and high-level white-collar work among Arabs. But a continuation of increased educational attainment without the expansion of high-level white-collar job opportunities in the Arab sector has resulted in a decline in the economic opportunities appropriate for the educational level attained by the younger generation. The lack of translation of education into jobs is one form of structural discrimination.

There may be economic benefits to residential concentration, since there is less direct discrimination in labor market terms when Arabs work in Arab communities instead of in Jewish economic sectors. Nevertheless, the increasing educational attainment of Arabs over time produces a new cohort of educated young men and women whose opportunities are constrained both by residential segregation and by their economic dependence on the Jewish sector. Even if segregation was beneficial for some in the past, it is likely to have more negative consequences when the increase in population size outstrips the available local economic opportunities. To the extent that a gradual reduction in economic dependency on the Jewish economic sector is desirable, an expansion of diverse economic opportunities in Arab communities will be required. Although such an investment may improve the occupational returns to education and increase the autonomy and independence of the population as a whole, it will likely reinforce the extended family's control over the lives of younger persons and limit the shift to more egalitarian gender roles. The trade-offs between increasing the economic independence and autonomy of the Arab population on the one hand, and the reentrenchment of gender inequalities on the other, pose the dilemma confronting the shapers of local and national policy.

Are Arab Israelis the American Blacks of Israeli Society?

One context for understanding the linkages between residential patterns and economic disadvantages, between dependency and demography, is to compare the long-term labor market costs of Arab population concentration with that of blacks in the United States (Massey 1990; Massey and Denton 1993; Wilson 1987). The answer to the question of whether Israeli Arabs are the American blacks of Israeli society (and by implication that Israeli Jews are the American whites) has often been no. In large part, this response has been based on an ideological rejection of the white American role for Israeli Jews and a stress on the uniqueness of the Arab-Israeli position (or the uniqueness of the slave background of African Americans and their exceptional family patterns). The analogy has also been rejected on the basis of a status attainment model of stratification and social class formation. It has been argued that similar factors affect the occupational achievement of Jews and Arabs in Israel; hence, there is no basis for isolating structural discrimination (Kraus and Hodge 1990). But the ideological objections are limited, and stratification based on status issues is only one of several social class contexts for understanding minority populations. Analogies are instructive, even when they are imperfect.

What can we learn about Israeli Arabs from the processes of segregation, disadvantage, and dependency that have been characteristic of American blacks? The changing nature of the economy in postindustrial America reduced the opportunity structure for blacks, particularly in cities; changed the employment pattern of black men and the prospects they had for jobs; and fed into the cycle of poverty, female-headed households, and continued discrimination.

The key factor in understanding these patterns is the extent of the segregation of blacks, which worsened considerably over time and therefore exacerbated the situation. Levels of racial segregation in large urban areas of the United States are high and show little signs of declining. As the educational and income levels of blacks have risen, the degree of segregation has not declined. The deteriorated economic condition of American blacks in the 1970s has been explained by a strong interaction between the level of segregation and changes in the structure of income distribution and economic opportunity. The concentration of poverty over time occurs even without taking into account the rates of middle class out-migration (i.e., the selectivity factor).

By analogy, two economic and demographic issues for Arab Israelis have appeared. First, in 1948, there was the out-migration of middle-class, more educated, and resource-rich Arabs (including the elite leadership), which left the Arab-Israeli communities in a disadvantaged status relative to where they were economically and socially before 1948. Second, there are patterns of residential segregation, regional concentration, and restriction of movement that have been imposed by the state, along with an increase in Arab population size. Complicating these processes are changing labor demands as Israel's economy has been transformed and the fact that, as with U.S. blacks, the Israeli Arabs' level of segregation has not declined with increases in their education or income.

The analogy is therefore not with the apartheid status of Arabs compared to blacks (see Smooha 1990) or the prejudice and discrimination against them in the context of status-based stratification, as has been argued (see Kraus and Hodge 1990). Instead, it is the similarity in the costs of residential segregation for both Arabs and blacks in the context of the changing economic structure, a segregated labor market, and increasing levels of education. All operate to the disadvantage of Arab Israelis, as they have for black Americans. The heart of the analogy does not concern the specifics of intergroup relations, the unique African-American background of slavery and race discrimination, or the broader Arab-Israeli conflict in the region. Instead, it is the striking parallels between the two minority populations in their structural relations between residential concentration and economic opportunity and the absence of reduced segregation that should come with increased income and higher levels of education.

Neither black Americans nor Arab Israelis can escape the broad-ranging, high costs of residential segregation and regional concentration. These costs are economic, social, and educational, and they include the poorer income returns to education and unmeasured social and psychological disadvantage. The new jobs that are opening in Israel demand more education, which further places Arabs in a disadvantaged position. So, increased educational levels actually *increase* disadvantage instead of reducing the capital returns gap. Vulnerability among Arab Israelis, as for black Americans, stems from the fact that segregation intensifies and magnifies any economic setback and builds deprivation structurally into the socioeconomic environment. The costs of segregation are exacerbated by the economic dependency of Arab Israelis.

The Arabs' residential concentration in Israel in this structural context, therefore, has resulted in their continuous economic powerlessness, leading to an Arab underclass. The expanded work opportunities that occurred in Israel in the post-1967 period did not change the status of Arab Israelis. Their increased segregation—resulting from their increased population growth and the limited expansion of the area where they could live—yielded increased levels of economic deprivation, hopelessness, and deterioration, precisely at the time when objective conditions were becoming better relative to what they had been. Residential segregation makes the Arab minority vulnerable and conspicuous—vulnerable in the sense that they are subject to economic changes, not to political harassment, and conspicuous because their distinctive lifestyle characterizes their communities and clearly identifies them as Arabs.

Policies that increased their level of educational attainment and the availability of some jobs in the market, as well as the Arabs' traditional supportive family structure, may have spared Arab Israelis some of the dire economic consequences of their residential segregation. The presence of West Bank and Gaza Palestinians in the labor market may have also reduced Israeli Arabs' level of disadvantage. Again, the consequences of segregation for the quality of life are as profound for Arab Israelis as they have been for black Americans, even though the reasons behind the residential concentrations are different. The longer-term disadvantages for Israeli Arabs may be as powerful as the "apartheid" residential situation that has been described for U.S. blacks.

Residential segregation is a structural condition, making deprived communities more likely; combined with social class disadvantage, racial segregation concentrates income deprivation in small areas and generates structural discrimination. The conclusion for American blacks that "segregation creates the structural niche within which a self-perpetuating cycle of minority poverty and deprivation can survive and flourish" (Massey 1990, p. 350) applies equally to Arab Israelis.

Some empirical evidence sustains such an interpretation. Data show that Arabs working in the Jewish economic sector suffer detrimental consequences in terms of both occupational and income inequalities (see the discussion in Chapter 7 and Semyonov 1988). Arabs working in Arab communities are occupationally advantaged, reflecting group competition in local labor markets. Although segregation into ethnic enclaves excludes minorities from equal access to broader opportunities and rewards, it provides temporary protection from discrimination generated by competition. Segregated Arabs who live and work in Arab communities are disadvantaged relative to Jews, but are advantaged relative to Arabs who live in Arab communities but work in the Jewish economic sector or Arabs who live and work in the several mixed residential areas of Israel. Working and living with Jews—that is, fuller residential and occupational integration—appears to be the worst case for Israeli Arabs. Working in their own communities and controlling their own occupational opportunities has the highest economic rewards.

There may be a need to develop greater pluralism within Israeli society in the short run, in the sense that Jews and Arabs develop opportunities in separate sectors. This reinforced segregation in Israel may be necessary, given the argument that there is a great deal of mistrust between the communities (Smooha 1991; Smooha and Hanf 1992). Greater segregation may work to the benefit of both Jewish and Arab communities. This may be viewed as a transition stage until greater trust between the communities develops. Such segregation must include greater symmetry between Jewish and Arab communities, with freedom of economic and political control internally and with important links to the central entitlement programs of the state.

The dependency of Arab Israelis does not operate only at the macrosocietal level, nor does it simply reflect an abstract economic position in a hierarchy. It is not solely a condition caused by socioeconomic stratification and the inequalities of politics and demography. Of course, it is all of these, but there is more. Dependency can and is often translated into the psyche of the individuals in the group. An Israeli Arab's description of the impact of dependency may resemble the image generated by black Americans about their own dependency: "We have a feeling that the authorities know everything about us anyway. They're the bosses, you know, the security agents, the state, the Ministry of Education, and it's as if they've already settled everything for us in advance. They've planned out our future, and all that's left for us is to toe the line. And we really toe it."[4]

Arab Israelis in Israeli Society and in Their Communities

What do the demographic, dependency, and distinctiveness patterns among Arab Israelis add up to? The examination of Arabs in Israel focuses our attention on the salience of ethnicity at the level of community. The ethnic cohesiveness of communities becomes the basis of analysis, incorporating the complex role of the state and its policies, including issues of entitlements, ideology, and discriminatory policies that shape demographic continuity and change in Arab communities. Arab "identity" emerges from the structural contexts of Israel's Arab communities, as it does from external factors. Ethnic identity is not constant but is variable over time. Its salience varies during the life course as it relates to economic and family transitions as well as to a variety of political contexts. The importance of Arab Israeli distinctiveness differs between cohorts and between stages of the life course within cohorts. It is clear that "culture," primordial identity, and an internally imposed or externally influenced political status and identity do not provide adequate orientations to the changing meaning of "Arab Israeliness." Since ethnicity is not only an intensity variable but also a categorical one, those who are more involved with the community are likely to be different from those who are less involved. Thus, an analysis needs to reflect this intensity dimension, at a minimum to test its salience in the Arab Israeli context.

An understanding of change and variation in Arab-Israeli communities must consider the embeddedness of population processes. The demographic structure of the Arab population and its changes reflect internal and external dynamics that are connected to patterns of economic development, to the meaning of internal dependency and the extent of discrimination, and to external social, economic, and political factors.

The story of the demographic development of the Arab-Israeli population has been told in large part from the point of view of Jewish-Israeli demography. The emphasis has almost always been placed on the relative Jewish-to-Arab population growth, which somehow is a threat to a continuing Jewish demographic dominance in the state—a theme that predates the formation of Israel. In addition, the high birth rate of the Moslem sector is viewed as an indicator of the frailty of Jewish demographic superiority—as are the "dangers" of a falling birth rate among Jews. Worst of all is the assumption inherent in the view of some that there is an Arab "mentality" or "culture" that reinforces the "backwardness" of Arab women, which results in their higher fertility—a condescending, ethnocentric Jewish view of the Arab population. The decline in Arab mortality has too often been viewed as an indicator of the extent of Jewish welfare largesse: Look at what Israeli Jews have done to take care of Israel's minority groups, in part despite the fact that Israel has been at war with the surrounding Arab states, which have much higher rates of mortality.

Although the demographic facts are hardly in dispute, the context within which these facts are presented almost always concerns the dominant themes of "integration" demographically, the Zionist ideology of a Jewish state, and the role of demographic statistics to underline political goals, policies, or programs. At the same time, Arab demographic studies have been equally distorting and biased in their interpretation, suggesting that the remaining demographic differentials between Arabs and Jews reflect the blatant discriminatory policies of the Israeli government.

These orientations unintentionally neglect the analysis of the impact of demography on the community of Israeli Arabs.

A conspicuous example is the neglect of research on the consequences of internal migration and residential segregation on the quality of life and opportunity structure of the Arab community in Israel. In particular, the linkage between Arabs' demographic behavior and the economic conditions of their lives has, with few notable exceptions, not been systematically discussed. In addition, the impact of the higher fertility rate of Arab-Israeli women on the lives of those women and their families and their responsibilities has rarely been studied.

It is necessary to change the focus and to emphasize Arab demographic patterns as processes linked to communities, not only at the national level and not only relative to the Jewish population. Such a reformulation of the analytic issues is necessary, even though there is as yet no solid empirical basis for answering these questions. To redress the increased tension between Jews and Arabs and reduce the dependency of Arabs on the Jewish sector, we must understand the structural bases of the Arab-Israeli community. If not, our understanding of the Arab-Israeli conflict will remain only ideological and idiosyncratic, cultural and personal, and political and abstract. It will generate defensive rather than ameliorating postures and policies.

A new generation of Arab Israelis is growing up, with higher levels of education, lower levels of occupational opportunities, and increasing Palestinian national identity. They are being socialized in smaller families, with higher levels of consumption and aspirations. But they have nowhere to go and little to do, with fewer outlets of social, cultural, and political expression. These generational changes and experiences clearly document that demographic changes are linked to quality of life issues and that demography is a major basis for understanding changes in the social, economic, and political structures of communities.

What is the picture of ethnic relations that emerges from a review of Arab Israelis? Clearly, it is different from that of Jewish ethnic groups, because of the source of their population increase (natural growth versus immigration) and their internal history of seclusion and control in the state. Arabs and Jews in Israel have a different relationship to the society and its national symbols. Arab Israelis also have a different relationship than do Jewish Israelis to the neighboring Arab countries and to Palestinians in the West Bank, the Gaza Strip, and elsewhere in their diaspora (see Chapter 12).

An interesting example of internal dynamics of an Arab community can be gained from the examination of one Arab town in Israel.[5] Shefar'Am was a central district serving twenty-two villages in the area. During the British period, the Christians were numerically dominant; Moslems were second in size, with a small Druze minority. In 1948, drastic changes occurred, partly because of the massive evacuations of local families, who became refugees in other countries, and partly because of the reshuffling of Arab populations within Israel's borders, creating internal refugees (Al Haj 1987). From a community point of view, the Arabs entering Shefar'Am were outsiders, not connected to sources of power and control that were internal to the community and certainly not linked to the former source of prestige and power—land ownership.

The shifting movement of the local population for the first several years after Israeli statehood and the disruptions of families that were organized by the Israeli government affected mainly the Moslem population. The influx of mostly Moslem internal refugees was significant numerically, constituting over one-fifth of the total population. These population shifts meant a major change in the demographic and religious composition of Shefar'Am. During the 1950s, one-third of its population was Moslem, and Christians constituted about half of the population. By the 1970s, the distribution was shared equally, with Moslems and Christians constituting about 40 percent each. Because of the differential fertility patterns—in particular, the significantly larger family size of Moslems compared to Christians—the Moslem population increased to 45 percent by the 1980s, with a Christian minority of 37 percent and 18 percent Druze. This close interrelationship of demographics, minority group factors, and sociopolitical control is seen in microcosm among the Arab communities in Israel.

The issues, of course, are not merely demographic, although demography has played a critical role in shaping the contexts within which the political, social, and cultural elements are expressed. There were class divisions within each of the communities, even during the British period (Al Haj 1985). The Christians were the dominant community in the economic as well as the demographic sense, possessing most of the land. They were the dominant group in trading and commerce in Shefar'Am and between Shefar'Am and the surrounding villages. Prior to the establishment of the state of Israel, all the merchants and owners of businesses were Christians. Large landowners were both Christians and Druze, but hired workers and poor agricultural laborers were almost all Moslems. The Moslem community was therefore dependent economically on the Christian and Druze communities. Moslems were the suppliers of unskilled labor. Regionally, the surrounding Arab villages were also dependent on Shefar'Am, with the dominant Christian community supplying services and trade.

This economic structure remained largely intact through the 1950s, but Shefar'Am was losing its dominance over the surrounding villages. In large part, the changes reflected shifts in the Jewish economy of Israel during the first years of statehood. As a result, the nature of the economic dependency of Shefar'Am changed, losing its former local economic base and developing no alternative base. From the point of view of the Jewish community of Israel, the economic position of the Arab minority was improving precisely at the same time that economic dependency on the Jewish economic sector was increasing. The first change within Shefar'Am occurring after the establishment of the state was the slow integration of the Arab refugee population that had been displaced from neighboring villages. Their integration was neither rapid nor complete, since the local population resisted full integration and since many Arabs expected to return to their former places of residence and their communities of origin. It took almost a decade for the refugee Arabs to plan for a more permanent settlement.

After 1948, the occupational structure of Arab communities in Shefar'Am changed to wage labor. The process of proletarianization was rapid and developed fully within a decade after the establishment of Israel, with a total economic and political dependency on the Jewish sector. The occupational structure fluctuated according to the economic conditions in the Jewish sector. In part, there were land confiscations that decreased the land available to the local Arab population; the internal migrants arriving landless contributed to the increasing search for wage labor outside of the town. In 1981, only about 10 percent of the labor force over age 15 was working in agriculture and 6 out of 10 people worked outside the town (Al Haj 1987, p. 43, table 2.4). None of the in-migrants to Shefar'Am and few of the Christians were working in agriculture.

The social class transformation under these conditions had significant implications for kinship and family structure, particularly for changing family relationships, the role of women, and the power of the Arab *Hamula*, or kinship system.[6] These changes were the result of structural realignments of economic and demographic patterns and the changing nature of dependency between the Arab community and the Jewish sector. The Arab kinship structure has not declined with modernization but, in some ways, has been reinforced since 1948. Some aspects of *Hamula* structure and control have increased at the same time that their specific economic roles and control have declined. The condition of the *Hamula* is a direct outcome of statehood and the position of the Arab community in Israeli society.

The *Hamula* system has become a key both to the local political system and to the marriage market. Sociodemographic changes resulted in the restructuring of kinship groups such that the rapid increase in kinship size reflected the growth due to natural increase and in-migration in the confined residential area. This combination of growth in limited geographical space resulted in the increased solidarity of kinship groups for social and political activities; group size and consolidation became powerful factors in local politics. Marriage markets, economic opportunities, and the residential housing market became severely constrained over time and were linked to the limitations imposed by the status of Arabs in Israeli society and their communities.

It is clear that under these conditions ethnic convergences between Jewish and Arab Israelis is not a likely outcome, given the residential concentration of Arab Israelis and their distinctive characteristics. Issues of convergence to the Jewish majority are also constrained in terms of standard of living and economic factors and the control exercised by the Jewish sector over the economy and over the opportunity structure. In contrast, issues of family, and perhaps women's, status are likely to have a local Arab (Moslem, Christian, or Druze) reference group.

Israeli Arabs in Democratic and Demographic Perspective

Israel has been described as an "ethnic democracy" in which the dominance of one ethnic group is institutionalized; this, in turn, has its own tensions and contradictions. Such a system extends political and civil liberties rights to the entire population but, at the same time, attaches a superior status to a particular segment of the population (Smooha and Hanf 1992). Israel is a state of and for Jews and is recognized as such internationally; Hebrew is the national language, and the use of Arabic is marginal in the public domain. All the state symbols and national institutions are Jewish (Smooha and Hanf), from the national anthem to national holidays, from the symbols around which national unity is organized to political symbols, flags, monuments, art, and literature.

The Arab-Israeli population was abandoned in Israel in 1948 as part of the Palestinian people and the vanquished Arab world; it was regarded by the Jews as a fifth column, as non-Jews in a Jewish state. Israeli Arabs were part of a residual community; they had lost their leaders, middle class, urban sector, and most of their institutions. Primarily, they had lost autonomy and control; that is, they became a minority. Hence, Arab Israelis were amenable to Jewish manipulation and discrimination, since assimilation into the Jewish majority culture and its institution was not possible. The Arab population in Israel has been granted civil rights and the status of a linguistic, religious, and cultural minority. Welfare services were extended, as were development funds. At the same time, it was also under military administration, largely exempt from military service. Large portions of Arab lands were confiscated (even though Arabs had also previously lost control of their urban sector). Israeli Arabs voted for Jewish political parties and protested minimally.

After 1967, their situation changed, as the overall military administration had been lifted. Palestinians in nearby territories were under Israeli occupation and increasingly worked in the state as day laborers. Israeli Arabs were more readily admitted to Jewish institutions and were encouraged to integrate into the working class of the Jewish economy. Their educational and occupational levels increased dramatically, as did their standard of living. At the same time that they developed a bilingual and bicultural Arab and Israeli orientation, they recaptured and enhanced their Palestinian identity when their contacts with those in the West Bank and Gaza increased. They developed a network of organizations, institutions, and leaders in their struggle for greater equality. But their leadership tended to be local—Israel has never had an Arab cabinet minister or even a director-general of a government office.

Palestinians and Israelis see Israeli Arabs as part of the state of Israel; hence, formal separation of Israeli Arabs as a regional or territorial independent unit is not an option. (In contrast, they argue that partition is the only likely way to handle the Israeli-Palestinian conflict because any permanent settlement must include

Palestinians outside of Palestine). The only legitimate political status for Israeli Arabs is as an integrated minority with some local autonomy but within the Jewish state. This political position must remain tenuous and conflicted, given the dependencies associated with this type of minority status.

Another perspective in understanding the role of Arab Israelis emphasizes their demographic context. One well-developed demographic argument has been that populations respond in a variety of ways to the pressures on resources generated by high population growth rates. Population growth itself is a major force in the reduction of fertility when the welfare of the family is threatened and there are no adequate outlets to relieve that pressure through out-migration, the expansion of territory, or through the more intensive use of land for production. In extreme form, when population size increases (e.g., through mortality reduction), the community may increase production on the land, may increase the intensity of land used for production, or may migrate to new areas, often in nonagricultural communities, that provide new economic opportunities. When population growth is the result of in-migration, there is a more immediate strain on the population-resource balance. The theory argues for the multiple responses of a population to the pressures of population (see Friedlander 1969; Goldscheider 1971).

The Arab-Israeli population has experienced these pressures from a combination of population growth generated by high fertility and declining mortality, with no outlet through out-migration. The family-oriented system of the Arab community of Israel militated against high rates of nonmarriage or childlessness. State welfare programs in Israel prevented a reduced standard of living, which would have resulted from these demographic processes. Welfare programs, combined with the commute to jobs outside of their communities, minimized the costs of high Arab population growth. But clearly, the crunch was delayed more than alleviated, particularly with the rising younger generation of more educated Arab Israelis who could find jobs in the Jewish economic sector, but not jobs that were commensurate with their educational levels. They could more readily and successfully compete with Palestinians from the administered territories working in Israel; they were and continue to be less successful when competing with Jewish Israelis in their labor market.

The combination of demographic and democratic tendencies requires a solution to the disadvantaged position of the Arab minority in Israel. If we take as our guide the value expressed by Israel's first president, Chaim Weizmann, that the quality of Israeli society will be judged by how it treats its minority communities, then Israel has a distance to go to improve the quality of life of its Arab minority and needs to set policies that diminish ethnic inequalities. At the same time, policies must recognize the powerful trade-offs between residential segregation and economic development, between cultural pluralism and national identity, and between the retention of a Jewish Israeli state and a tolerance (and supportive policies) for minority populations and pluralism. It is unlikely that the next generation of Arabs and Jews in Israel will experience minority integration. Whether Arab

Israelis continue to experience economic disadvantage and whether inequalities are reduced and sociocultural distinctiveness remains are open questions at the beginning of the twenty-first century.

Notes

1. There were 900,000 Moslems in the state of Israel at the end of 1998 out of a total population of just over 6 million persons; 107,000 Arab Christians, 22,000 other Christians, 99,000 Druze, and 129,000 persons not classified by religion.

2. Israel's inclusion of almost 1 million immigrant Jews since 1989 (see Chapter 3) and the virtual stability of the Arab-Jewish demographic ratio reinforces this point about the permanent demographic minority status of Israeli Arabs. See the population change data in Figure 1.1 in Chapter 1 and the ethnic-religious composition data in Table 2.1 in Chapter 2.

3. The analysis of these neighborhood migration-avoidance-replacement processes and their implications for intergroup relations in Israeli communities reads like the early "succession-invasion" human ecology literature of black and white neighborhood patterns in the United States. See the later discussion.

4. This is the way Mohammed Daroushe describes his feelings of dependency, as reported by David Grossman (1993, p. 2). Daroushe goes on to blame himself and his group for this situation, a not uncommon feeling among those who feel oppressed by dependency relationships.

5. I draw fully on the details presented in Al Haj 1985 and 1987.

6. The *Hamula* is a patrilineal and patriarchal system of social and biological relatedness that is more formal and extensive than the extended family system (see Al Haj 1987).

PART THREE

Ecology, Settlement, and the Development of Communities

5

Urbanization, Internal Migration, and Residential Integration

A dominant theme in Zionist literature has been the need for increasing the Jewish population in the national home to establish the basis of a total Jewish society and to solve the Jewish problems of disadvantage, anti-Semitism, and assimilation experienced in countries where Jews lived as a minority. Jewish population growth was expected to increase the base for economic production and establish a greater political presence. And there was an emphasis on the need to increase the size of the Jewish population relative to the Arabs to assure Jewish political legitimacy and control. These were fundamental demographic concerns in the articulation of a national ideology and in the development of population policies (Friedlander and Goldscheider 1979; see also the discussion in Chapter 1).

No less important were political, economic, social, and cultural concerns about the spatial distribution of the Jewish population living in Palestine and in the state of Israel. There were obvious needs to legitimate the Jewish presence in the areas defined as part of the Israeli state and a need to disperse the population to facilitate its economic development and national integration. Large-scale immigration, leading to rapid population increases, brought pressures to develop adequate housing, health care, education, jobs, and cultural activities in areas where immigrants settled. Population growth, economic development, and nation-building raised complex issues of immigrant integration, frontier settlement, and urban-rural concentration. Immigrants from diverse places of origin tended to settle together, leading to residential concentration of Jewish ethnic groups. Concomitantly, the territorial goals of the Jewish population brought questions of Arab population distribution to the forefront of policy and planning. Conflict over land and territory was a key element in the ideological and political battles between Jews and Arabs in Palestine and in Israel.

Ideological factors associated with elements of Zionism were in the background of these pressures for the territorial distribution of the population in Israel. Jews had been disproportionately concentrated in the urban places of their countries of origin (in Western and Eastern Europe), often residentially segregated as a minority (Gold-scheider and Zuckerman 1984). Their occupational patterns reflected these residential concentrations and the restrictions imposed on Jews in the societies where they lived. Some Zionist arguments emphasized that Jews should have a "normal" occupational distribution in their own state, a blend of rural and urban jobs spread throughout the areas of Jewish settlement in Palestine and Israel (Halpern 1961; Hertzberg 1960). Unlike in their places of origin, Jews should not be restricted in their residential choices in their national home. Many of the early Zionists in Palestine asserted the strategic and ideological value of a literal "return to the land" and argued for the deurbanization of the Jewish population. Immigrants to Palestine in the early years were the founders of the agricultural settlements and stressed the political and economic need to develop the land areas of Palestine.

This ideological and strategic emphasis on nonurban residential settlement and on a more balanced residential distribution in all regions of the country was reinforced after the establishment of the state by two pressing considerations: The defense needs of the emerging Jewish state and the goal of economically integrating large numbers of immigrants. Population dispersal was viewed as necessary to reduce the vulnerability to external military attacks and as a basis to defend the national borders. Settling the frontier areas was a statement about Jewish control over the whole country and became a strategic national goal. The emphases within Zionism on territorial control and on the settlement of frontier areas were used selectively to justify and rationalize this military defense position.

The influx of a large number of immigrants provided an opportunity to implement these Zionist goals and political objectives. Most of the immigrants in the first years of the state were dependent on government intervention and support for housing, health, education, welfare services, and jobs, at least in the first stages of their adjustment. Immigrants had to be integrated economically and residentially; their geographic location dictated the distribution of economic activities. They were more likely to be manipulated and "planned" for than were longer-term residents or those with more capital who were already settled in urban areas or had contacts there. Therefore, the dispersal of the population to nonurban areas and new towns on the periphery of the country developed as a policy. It was implemented as a national strategy to ease the economic and housing pressures in central urban places and to settle persons on the borders as a defense strategy.

The planned distribution policy was more feasible for Jewish immigrants from Middle Eastern countries, who arrived with fewer resources and less economic and social capital to be able to manage on their own. Their greater dependency on the state facilitated their shift to areas of settlement away from the urban centers. Jews from European countries had immigrated to Israel in the earlier period of national development, when urban housing was more available. More important, they arrived with urban occupational skills and had contacts with persons of European origin in longer-settled urban areas. They were less often directed to the peripheral areas of settlement; when they were settled in distant locations, their resources and their ethnic networks allowed them to migrate to urban central areas much faster than immigrants from the Middle East.

In general, the political and economic advantages of immigrant population dispersal were rationalized by the population distribution and occupational objectives of Zionist ideology. Population distribution policies were consistent with Zionism and were justified by invoking an appropriately constructed Zionist ideology, although they did not flow or derive directly from it. Population dispersal moved from the ideological arena to practical economic and political policies; it is among the clearest expressions of the links between nation-building processes and demography.

In this chapter I examine the actual population distribution in Israel over time, as a basis for assessing demographic developments in Israel and their economic and political ramifications. Moreover, I connect residential distribution changes to immigration in order to evaluate the longer-run costs and benefits of population distribution for the integration of ethnic groups. I assess how residential policies and patterns affect the Arab population of Israel and evaluate how residential concentration perpetuates ethnic generational continuity among Jews. In Chapter 6, I return to themes of residential patterns to specify the changing socioeconomic links to places of residence in different types of communities—Kibbutzim, Moshavim, development towns, and large urban areas.

Urbanization and Regional Population Distribution

I begin the larger picture by reviewing the extent of urban concentration of the population in Israel and the changing regional distribution of the population. Using the Israeli definition of urban localities, about 85 percent of the population resided in urban places in 1948, a level that was maintained through the 1960s; over 90 percent of the population was urban through the 1990s, a very high level of urban concentration by international standards.[1] The changes for the Arab-Israeli population were particularly dramatic, starting at a lower proportion of urban concentration in 1948 and increasing to the same level as the Jewish population in the 1990s. A look at the same picture from the point of view of the rural population reveals that between 1948 and 1998 the rural population in Israel more than tripled in size, but the percent of the total population that lived in rural areas declined. Population size was increasing in all areas but more rapidly in urban than in rural areas.

Another way to view the changing population distribution in Israel is to focus on different-size communities and the number of communities with large populations. The scale needs to be considered, given the size of the country and the relatively small size of its total population. There are no multimillion-person megacities in Israel, unlike in some industrialized and Third World countries. However, the four largest cities (Tel Aviv, Jerusalem, Haifa, and, more recently, Be'er Sheva) have dominated the social, economic, and demographic landscapes of the country.

TABLE 5.1 Population Distribution and Total Number of Areas by Size of
Locality in Israel, 1948–1998

| | Percentage of Population and Number of Settlements | | | | | |
Population	1948	1961	1972	1983	1991	1998
100,000+	31 (1)	34 (3)	36 (5)	45 (10)	45 (11)	44 (12)
50,000–100,000	22 (2)	7 (2)	15 (6)	9 (5)	9 (7)	11 (9)
20,000–50,000	3 (1)	22 (15)	16 (15)	17 (22)	19 (28)	17 (37)
10,000–20,000	10 (5)	8 (14)	11 (24)	9 (25)	9 (31)	8 (36)
1,000–10,000	22 (71)	18 (121)	13 (112)	12 (134)	11 (164)	10 (113)
<1,000	12 (362)	11 (718)	8 (743)	8 (895)	7 (929)	9 (983)
Total	100 (442)	100 (873)	100 (905)	100 (1,091)	100 (1,170)	100 (1,189)

Note: Settlements in parentheses.
Source: *Statistical Abstracts of Israel,* various years.

Examining the number of large cities and their population sizes since 1948 (Table 5.1) shows the increase from one city with 100,000 people in 1948 to 12 cities with that number in 1998; from a population concentration in these large cities of 31 percent in 1948 to 45 percent in the 1980s and 1990s. Although about the same proportion of the country's total population lived in cities of 50,000 people or more in both 1948 and 1998 (53 to 55 percent), a sharp decline occurred in the proportion of those people who lived in places of 50,000 to 100,000 people (22 percent in 1948 to 10 percent in 1980s and 1990s). The relative balance of the population in the largest cities (100,000 people and over) compared to the next smaller-size cities (50,000 to 100,000 people) increased. The number of places in the 20,000 to 50,000 population size range also increased. These middle-sized urban areas increased from 1 place to 37 places from 1948 to 1998, and from 3 percent to 17 percent of the total population. As a result of these changes over time, the proportion living in areas with less than 10,000 people declined considerably. One-third of the population lived in these small-size places in 1948, but only 19 percent lived in areas of this size in 1998. This pattern occurred despite the more than doubling of the number of places of small size (from 433 places in 1948 to 1,096 places in 1998).

Thus, in the context of countries around the world, taking into account the overall smallness of its size geographically and demographically, Israel was a fully

TABLE 5.2 Number and Percentage of Rural and Urban Dwellers in Israel,
1961–1998 (selected cities)

Selected Cities	1961 (000s)		1972 (000s)		1983 (000s)		1991 (000s)		1998 (000s)	
Jerusalem	167	(8)	314	(10)	429	(13)	544	(11)	634	(10)
Tel Aviv-Yafo	386	(18)	364	(12)	327	(8)	353	(7)	349	(6)
Haifa	183	(8)	220	(7)	226	(6)	251	(5)	264	(4)
Total Urban	1,838	(84)	2,789	(89)	3,616	(90)	4,575	(90)	5,487	(90)
Total Rural	342	(16)	359	(11)	422	(10)	484	(10)	561	(9)
Total	2,180	(100)	3,148	(100)	4,038	(100)	5,059	(100)	6,041	(100)

Note: Percentage of population in parentheses.

Sources: *Statistical Abstract of Israel 1992*, table 2.12; *Statistical Abstract of Israel 2000*, table 2.6.

urbanized society when it was established, and it has remained so. It is clear that the early ideological emphasis on the returns to agriculture and the antiurban bias of the founders of the Jewish settlements in Palestine and Israel have had little effect on the forces that generate urban concentration (Cohen 1977). The causes of increasing urbanization in Israel are likely to be similar to those in other countries, including economic concentration and specialization, industrial production, availability of amenities, technology, and state investments.

Complementary to and interrelated with the overall process of urbanization, there has been a decline in some of the core areas in urban places as housing and neighborhoods have deteriorated, and new areas have developed on the suburban periphery of urban locations. Thus metropolitanization has proceeded almost from the beginning. The relative population size of urban Tel Aviv-Yafo declined from 386,000 in 1961 to 327,000 in 1983, although it increased to 349,000 in 1998 (Table 5.2). During the same period, the proportion of the population living in this large urban area declined from 18 percent to 6 percent. A similar process occurred in Haifa. The major urban population growth is taking place in the suburbs of urban areas and in large, but not the largest, urban areas. As in other industrial and Western nations around the world, suburbanization and metropolitanization have characterized Israeli society, with a clear decline in the population of the urban core of the largest areas and a growth of the peripheral dormitory suburbs around major metropolitan areas.

Jerusalem, Israel's capital, is special because of the inclusion of its eastern part into Israel after 1967, along with its Arab population. In the Israeli-controlled part of Jerusalem there were only about 2,400 non-Jews in 1961; the 1967 reunification

TABLE 5.3 Israel's Population Distribution by District and Ethnicity, 1948–
1998 (selected years)

District and Ethnicity	1948	1961	1972	1983	1991	1998
Total population (in thousands)						
Tel Aviv	306 (36)	699 (32)	907 (29)	1,000 (25)	1,132 (22)	1,139 (19)
Central	122 (14)	407 (19)	580 (18)	831 (21)	1,078 (21)	1,358 (23)
Northern	144 (17)	337 (16)	474 (15)	656 (16)	856 (17)	1,027 (17)
Haifa	175 (21)	370 (17)	484 (15)	575 (14)	681 (14)	789 (13)
Southern	21 (3)	174 (8)	354 (11)	479 (12)	618 (12)	840 (14)
Jerusalem	87 (10)	192 (9)	347 (11)	473 (12)	601 (12)	717 (12)
Jewish Population (in thousands)						
Tel Aviv	302 (43)	693 (36)	900 (34)	989 (30)	1,112 (27)	1,097 (23)
Central	106 (15)	380 (20)	535 (20)	764 (23)	989 (24)	1,224 (26)
Northern	53 (8)	194 (10)	256 (10)	327 (10)	431 (10)	490 (10)
Haifa	148 (21)	322 (17)	409 (15)	465 (14)	537 (13)	596 (13)
Southern	6 (1)	155 (8)	324 (12)	434 (13)	537 (13)	701 (15)
Jerusalem	84 (12)	188 (10)	261 (10)	347 (10)	444 (11)	509 (11)
Moslem Population (in thousands)						
Tel Aviv	4 (2)	3 (2)	4 (1)	6 (1)	8 (1)	10 (1)
Central	16 (10)	25 (14)	42 (12)	62 (12)	82 (12)	104 (12)
Northern	91 (58)	89 (52)	145 (41)	220 (42)	288 (41)	364 (40)
Haifa	27 (18)	34 (20)	56 (16)	84 (16)	108 (15)	132 (15)
Southern	15 (10)	18 (10)	30 (9)	43 (8)	74 (11)	103 (11)
Jerusalem	3 (2)	2 (1)	74 (21)	112 (21)	141 (20)	186 (21)
Christian population (in thousands)						
Tel Aviv	–	3 (6)	3 (4)	5 (5)	11 (8)	7 (6)
Central	–	2 (4)	2 (3)	4 (4)	7 (6)	6 (5)
Northern	–	36 (71)	46 (64)	57 (61)	70 (55)	78 (60)
Haifa	–	8 (15)	9 (13)	13 (14)	19 (15)	19 (15)
Southern	–	0.4 (1)	0.3 (1)	2 (2)	6 (5)	4 (3)
Jerusalem	–	2 (3)	12 (16)	14 (15)	15 (12)	14 (11)
Druze population (and others) (in thousands)						
Northern	–	18 (68)	27 (73)	52 (79)	67 (79)	79 (80)
Haifa	–	7 (26)	10 (26)	14 (21)	17 (20)	19 (19)

Note: The data for 1948 are for the total non-Jewish population. The figures in parentheses
are percent distributions.
Sources: *Statistical Abstract of Israel 1992*, table 2.7; *Statistical Abstract 2000*, table 2.7.

led to a dramatic increase in its non-Jewish population size and its continued growth—83,500 in 1972, 122,400 in 1983, and 151,300 in 1991. The growth of the Jewish population of Jerusalem has been impressive as well—from 165,000 in 1961 (even less than Haifa with a Jewish population of 173,600) to 230,300 in 1972, and 306,300 in 1983. Jerusalem became the city with the largest urban population of Israel in the mid-1980s. In 1998, Jerusalem had a Jewish population of 440,000 within a total population of 634,000 (69 percent).

Jerusalem is also undergoing rapid suburbanization, extending into new areas away from the urban core. The population expansion in Jerusalem is a result of a combination of new immigrant settlement and internal migration, along with higher-than-average fertility. The growth of Jerusalem is clearly among the top priorities of government policy in Israel. Whatever the specific combination of demographic sources, the rapid growth of Jerusalem's population demands new housing, a transportation infrastructure, and more intensive use of larger land areas surrounding the city. At the same time, the growth of the Jewish population has generated conflict and tension with the Arab communities, which have also increased since 1967 in the expanded areas of Jerusalem. The conflict is basically political, but there are complex economic, infrastructural, and social dimensions associated with the emerging political realities of the socially, culturally, and residentially divided city, which is both economically integrated and politically controlled by Israel.

Urban distributional changes are linked to regional changes over time, which have been influenced by population growth, particularly by immigration and economic and political development patterns (Table 5.3). There have been increases in the population size in all six regions,[2] reflecting both overall population growth and the powerful impact of immigration, particularly in the aftermath of statehood through 1951 and in the post-1967 period. The Tel Aviv district dominated the country in population size in 1948, and together with the Haifa district, covered 57 percent of the total state population. There were only 108,000 people living in the combined southern and Jerusalem districts when the state was established, about one-third the number of people living in the Tel Aviv district.

Over the half-century since 1948, the distribution of the population among the six districts has become more equal. The population in the Tel Aviv district declined relative to the total population from 36 percent to 19 percent; the population in the Haifa district declined from 21 percent to 13 percent. These relative declines occurred despite sharp population increases in these two districts—each almost quadrupling in size between 1948 and 1991—from 306,000 to 1,139,000 in Tel Aviv and from 175,000 to 789,000 in Haifa. The central district increased from 14 percent to 23 percent; the population in the southern district increased from 21,000 to 840,000 and from 3 percent to 14 percent of the total population. The combined results of these differential regional population growth patterns over time has been an increasing balance among districts: The Tel Aviv district dominated the other districts demographically in 1948, with a relative population 11 times larger than the smallest district and 40 percent larger than the next size district; in 1998 the population of the largest and smaller districts varied by less than 50 percent.

Changes in these regional distribution patterns become clearer when we subdivide the population into four groups by religion and ethnicity. The regional changes in the distribution of the Jewish population parallel those of the total population, given Jewish demographic dominance throughout the state. The one striking difference is the very sharp increase in the southern district: The Jewish population increased from 6,000 to 701,000 and from 1 percent to 15 percent of the total Jewish population of the state from 1948 to 1998. The reduction in the dominance of the Tel Aviv district in the Jewish geographic distribution is also sharper, as the Jewish population declined from 43 percent of the total in 1948 to 23 percent in 1998.

Moslem and Christian populations increased disproportionately in the Jerusalem district when they were incorporated within the territory of Israel following the 1967 war. These political changes resulted in their decreased concentration in the northern region. The distribution of Moslems, like the Jewish population, has become increasingly balanced across regions as a result, declining from 58 percent living in the northern region in 1948 to 40 percent in 1998. The regional distribution of Arab Israelis remains significantly different from that of the Jewish pattern, but this is the result of Arab population concentration and the incorporation of some Palestinians after 1967, not Arab immigration or internal migration. In contrast to the Jewish population's concentration in the southern district, the northern district remains the regional area of concentration of the Moslem and the Christian populations. There is less dispersal of the Druze population, with an increase over time in their relative concentration in the northern district. In part, this reflects the incorporation of the Golan Heights and the inclusion of its Druze population in Israel after 1967. The impact of the 1967 boundary changes on Jewish and Arab populations of the northern and the southern regions emerges clearly.

The increasing balance among districts and the changes over time toward greater residential dispersal has resulted in the evolution of a national, urbanized Israeli society. Urbanization and population distributional changes, along with centralized state planning, have linked Israelis into one national community politically, socially, demographically, and geographically. Population dispersal reduces the sense of local, relative to national, identity, even as the character of the older urban places, along with their economic and sociopolitical functions, has remained distinctive (see Chapter 6). The existence of this national community implies that even those on the periphery and in rural areas are part of the urbanized society and are likely to be influenced and dominated by urban values and structures. The links between population dispersal and nation-building have been clearly forged.

The third theme of this analysis needs to be addressed directly: Have these changing urban geographic patterns resulted in the residential integration of immigrant populations from diverse areas of origin? I turn to a consideration of the residential dispersion of ethnic populations as another basis for assessing the connections between population, nation-building, and ethnic continuity.

Ethnic Urban Patterns

As cities expanded in population size and as new areas were developed in Israel, what happened to the residential concentration of the immigrants? Rapid and intense immigration would be expected to result in their short-term residential segregation; hence, my focus extends to the residential integration of their children. Did the regional balances involve the redistribution of Israelis of Middle Eastern origin with those of Western origin? Did Jews and Arabs become more integrated residentially? What are the residential patterns of the children of immigrants who attended local schools, developed local ethnic friendships and family ties, served in the military, and started new families? In short, the question of ethnic residential concentration in Israel needs to be investigated as part of the analysis of nation-building and demographic change. The evidence from studies in the early 1960s through the 1990s points to an initial segregation by place of origin and time of immigration among the foreign born and a continuing segregation by broader ethnic categories among their children.

Paradoxically, both residential segregation and integration have characterized Israeli cities in the 1990s. There has been a general decline in the level of segregation of the European-American-origin population as upwardly mobile Asian- and African-origin families have moved into the higher status core areas of cities. At the same time, small clusters of what had been exclusively European-American-origin population in new garden suburban neighborhoods have been joined by Jews of Asian and African origin. Nevertheless, high levels of European-American concentration remain in the wealthier suburbs of cities and in veteran areas of settlement (Kirschenbaum 1992). Further, although some Israelis of Middle Eastern origin are integrating with Israelis of Western origin, this process has been limited to some geographic areas. Many other Jews of Asian and African origin have become increasingly segregated, often in neighborhoods that are pockets of poverty. Those who have been left behind in the social mobility process have become a hard-core disadvantaged group with a high level of separation from the Western-origin population and from the upwardly mobile second generation Asian and African population (Gonen 1985; Kirschenbaum; Klaff 1977).

The overall pattern of continuing ethnic residential segregation is not only associated with poverty in large urban areas but has also become a major source of ethnic continuity for all groups. This is reflected in the regional variation in ethnic Jewish composition, with high levels of continuous Asian-African concentration in development towns and Moshavim and in some neighborhoods within cities (see Chapter 6). Thus, both ethnic residential segregation and ethnic integration are occurring in Israel's major cities, with cultural and communal costs associated with ethnic integration and socioeconomic and political costs associated with ethnic segregation.

The volume and concentration of immigration from the former Soviet Union in the 1990s has resulted in the development of strong ethnic-based Russian-speaking neighborhoods and communities. Government-subsidized housing and work-related projects in and around the major cities have resulted in new forms of ethnic residential segregation (Leshem and Sicron 1999; Gitelman 1995).

One way to document these complex ethnic residential concentration patterns is to show the relative proportion of persons from particular ethnic backgrounds who reside in various geographic areas of the country. High levels of concentration in particular areas are revealed when the percentage of those of Western (or Middle Eastern) origin are significantly higher than they are nationally. An analysis of the 1983 Israeli census shows the extent of geographic underrepresentation of Jews originating from Western countries (Gonen 1993). When we divide the geographic distribution of places in Israel into four types of areas, a clear pattern of residential concentration (or underrepresentation) emerges. On the national periphery, areas of new (or development) towns in the north and south of the country reveal some extreme cases of ethnic residential concentration. For example, only about 5 percent to 6 percent of the population in Bet She'an in the Northeast and Ofaqim and Netivot in the south are of Western origin, compared to 40 percent nationally.

A second area of residential concentration of Asian-African-origin Jews emerged on the periphery of older towns (i.e., those that were established before 1948), since housing projects were developed there for new immigrants in the 1950s and 1960s. These immigrant housing projects gradually deteriorated; with selective out-migration, these became areas of low socioeconomic status with poor-quality housing. Initially, new immigrants, primarily of Middle Eastern origin, settled in these projects. Over time, they became areas of even greater ethnic residential concentration, as the smaller group of immigrants from Western countries who arrived during that period moved to new, more affluent areas. Families of Western origin arriving later were not attracted to the housing available in these neighborhoods. In contrast, Middle Eastern–origin Jews were often attracted to these areas by the presence of relatives and others who shared community and culture. As a result, these housing projects became neighborhoods of residential concentration almost exclusively for those of Middle Eastern origin. Around Jerusalem and in the metropolitan area of Tel Aviv, neighborhoods with few Western Jews abound.

Some towns in the urban areas have also maintained their ethnic character. Rosh Ha'Ayin, for example, originated in 1948 as a Yemenite camp on the outskirts of Petah Tiqwa and has remained largely a Yemenite ethnic community. It doubled in population from 6,000 in 1950 to 12,000 in the 1980s to 33,000 in 1998. Over 80 percent of the residents of Rosh Ha'Ayin are of Yemenite origin, and fewer than 5 percent are of Western origin. This is clearly an extreme, but it illustrates the power of ethnic and family networks and continuity in the context of ethnic residential concentration. It should be noted that there are no legal barriers to internal migration among Jewish Israelis and few informal ones as well, although there are clearly economic constraints. The retention of residential clustering among some ethnic communities is a positive statement about the value of family, economic, and neighborhood networks.

Did ethnic residential concentration only result in new peripheral areas as a result of waves of immigrants arriving from particular countries? The evidence points to ethnic residential concentration in the old urban core as well, mainly of long-term settlers of both Western and Middle Eastern origin. These older areas were characterized by specific country-of-origin ethnic enclaves in 1948. These specific urban neighborhoods were linked to ethnic economic enterprises and had not disappeared by the 1980s. Gonen (1993) identifies several "Oriental territories" in the older urban core areas of Jerusalem and Tel Aviv-Yafo, as well as in the urban areas of middle-size towns. European enclaves can also be identified. These neighborhoods combine specific ethnic origin and low socioeconomic status. The out-migration of young, successful, and upwardly mobile second-generation Israelis has left behind the poorly connected, poorly educated, and hence economically poor ethnic populations. Selective migration has further reinforced the avoidance of these areas by new immigrants of Western origin and those who are upwardly mobile. But the boundaries between these older urban neighborhoods are fuzzy, and many are becoming more homogeneous by social class rather than by ethnic origin.

Immediately after the establishment of the state and the out-migration of local Arab residents, former Arab neighborhoods in Jewish areas were occupied by the influx of immigrants during the period of mass immigration. Over time, many, but not all, of these neighborhoods became areas of deteriorated housing and overcrowding, again in part because of the out-migration patterns of those who were more easily integrated (i.e., primarily the first generation of Western origin and some of Asian and African origin). By the 1980s, Western-origin Jews left these areas in the cities of Jerusalem, Tel Aviv, and Haifa, and immigrants from Middle Eastern countries moved in, creating new neighborhoods of ethnic residential segregation.

The "gentrification" of some of these places may have occurred in the late 1980s and in the 1990s, although the upgrading and renewal of places does not necessarily imply changes in the overlap of ethnic origin and socioeconomic characteristics. These trends are just emerging, as third-generation Israelis move through the life course and as urban areas continue to be renewed. As new immigrants from Russia are integrated economically and residentially, they too will experience social and geographic mobility, and new areas of residential clustering and ethnic concentration are likely to be formed. As of the 1990s, however, there are unmistakable signs that social mobility has been more selective of the Western-origin population, and differential geographic mobility has followed. Although many of the second generation of Middle Eastern origin have also moved up socially and changed their residence geographically (see Chapter 7), the residual population has become more distant and segregated geographically and socially from the Western-origin population and from their Middle Eastern cousins who have prospered socially and economically.[3]

Thus, the overlap of neighborhood and ethnic origin is not a feature limited to the immigrant generations or their children and is not confined to areas of initial settlement. Ethnic residential concentration appears to be pervasive nationally, even as some types of integration are also extensive and neighborhood boundaries are increasingly blurred. There continues to be residential enclaves of ethnic groups throughout the country, some stronger and some weaker. The immigration from the former Soviet Union and from Ethiopia is not likely to break this pattern, since there is a strong economic component to this ethnic residential clustering. Whatever their sources, patterns of ethnic segregation have consequences for the socialization of the next generation. Growing up in ethnic families and neighborhoods, attending local schools with disproportionate numbers of students from similar ethnic backgrounds, marrying persons and joining families of similar ethnic origins, and working with and spending leisure time with family and friends who share similar ethnic cultures reinforces the cohesion of ethnic communities. In the context of the ethnic continuity question (Chapter 2), my assessment is that residential segregation reinforces ethnic generational continuity—when it occurs, ethnic cohesion is stronger; when it is less pervasive, ethnic cohesiveness is weaker.

One feature of the ethnic residential map is that it has become more complex over the last several decades. The overlap between ethnicity and poverty is a clear and national concern. Ethnic segregation in development towns has had, and continues to have, negative economic consequences for some ethnic groups. Segregation increases the socioeconomic gap in Israel through the differential availability of local educational institutions, jobs, and access to the other institutions of society (Lipshitz 1991; Spilerman and Habib 1976). The dispersion of immigrants to the national periphery of Israel in the 1950s tended to more evenly spread the population spatially, but it resulted in increased polarization in the distribution of development (Lipshitz 1991; see my discussion in Chapter 6).

A final comment about residential patterns relates to changes in the substantive meaning of ethnic community in Israel. The initial settlement of immigrant groups occurred among those from specific places of origin, and pockets remain of second and later generations from particular countries who have maintained ethnic residential enclaves. These enclaves tend to be composed of the larger ethnic groups (e.g., from Morocco) and located in select areas in Israel. Over time, particular locations in Israel have become less concentrated in terms of people's specific country of origin but characterized more by the concentration of persons in broader ethnic categories. Where ethnic residential concentration is maintained, new ethnic combinations have developed. In the 1990s, residents of neighborhoods or towns in Israel were less likely to be referred to as being from particular countries and more likely to be characterized as being of "Western,"

"Asian-African," or Middle Eastern" origin.[4] These are constructed ethnic categories that have been shaped by both economic and residential changes in Israel. They are Israel-made ethnic products that are unlikely to disappear generationally, since the third generation has already been socialized in their ethnic families and in neighborhoods that are ethnically concentrated. In this sense, the reduction of the social class and ethnic overlap is but one of the several types of generational connections that foster ethnic continuity in its newer forms in Israel. The residents of the new ethnic enclaves that were formed as a result of the immigration of the 1990s are more likely than not to reinforce these ethnic divisions. The internal ethnic variation among immigrants from the former Soviet Union are likely to form a new ethnic community as "Russian-Israelis" than to retain specific place-of-origin identification. This will be most conspicuous among the second generation.

Internal Migration

The streams of people moving to central urban places and to various districts of Israel are the primary sources of urbanization. Their movement results in changes in the regional distribution of the population. Internal migration tends to be selective of those who are more likely to respond to educational and job opportunities and housing availability, and who are less tied to local communities and places of origin. Young adults and those who are searching for ways to translate educational attainment into jobs and those who are in transitional stages of life course (getting married or dissolving a marriage, having children, joining or leaving the labor force) are the most likely to change residences. The educational background of Western-origin Jews makes them more receptive to opportunities in new locations, and hence they are more geographically mobile. Ethnic and family networks may play an important role in providing information and support to potential migrants. Relocation is tied in with other social changes, which are linked to changes in fertility, health, and family structure. In Israel, the links between immigration and internal migration are strong, and both are intimately connected to the process of nation-building and ethnic change.[5]

Internal migration of Jews in Israel is not constrained by direct government policies, despite the subsidies, housing, and jobs that the state has provided to those who live in some areas (e.g., development towns) or to those who live in new territories developed by Israel after the 1967 war (e.g., the West Bank, the Gaza area, and the parts of Jerusalem annexed to the state). The primary determinants of internal migration for Israeli Jews have been market economic forces and the educational and occupational opportunities that vary among areas; housing availability and cost figure prominently among the factors shaping residential mobility. Along with family life-course changes—marriage, family formation, and dissolution—these are the key variables separating migrants from nonmigrants. Ethnic factors, net of these economic, demographic, and social factors, influence migration to a much lesser extent, although ethnic differentials in migration patterns operate through these factors. Since some opportunities (e.g., housing, jobs, and schools) are provided by government subsidies, government policies indirectly influence and shape migration. The availability of jobs, housing, education, and transportation combine with individual resources (money, education, and networks) to shape migration patterns in Israel.

Consistent with the regional and areal data, there has been a tendency for internal migration to be in a direction away from the large cities and large towns toward urban localities of smaller size (below 50,000 population and particularly below 10,000). There have been cases, however, in which relocations have been substantial in both directions. Nevertheless, net gains from internal migration have been documented for rural localities.[6] Population exchanges—low net rates and high population mobility—characterize all six districts. Although the number of internal migrants has increased over the last quarter-century, the rate of movement has fluctuated and has decreased overall (from 56.8 per 1,000 population in 1965 to 34.9 per 1,000 in 1980 and to 41 per 1,000 in 1998). The source of the differential growth of areas thus owes more to internal migration than to the role of immigrant settlement and differential natural increase (Ben-Moshe 1989).

Net migration patterns show very strong out-migration from development towns on the periphery of the society, growth through in-migration to suburban areas around Tel Aviv, and declines in central city areas, except Jerusalem. The ethnic and social class composition of the towns and the relative economic opportunities and services available at the local level are critical in understanding community development in Israel. Internal migration has often been selective of those groups that have been economically mobile and less tied into ethnic networks. The smallness of the country, the constraints on housing turnover, and the local socioethnic patterns mitigate against major internal mobility not associated with economic opportunities or with family life-cycle changes.

These population exchanges among places over time apply to the internal migration of Jews and to the basic "voluntary" nature of that migration. It does not apply to the Arab-Israelis, who in the past have been formally restricted in their housing and economic choices and who have been informally confined to their own communities and residential areas.

Arab Residential Concentration

Unlike for Jewish Israelis, political control limited the voluntary internal movements of Arab Israelis through the mid-1960s. Informal constraints—including lack of accessible housing, limited economic networks, and discrimination—continue to limit their internal migration. Nevertheless, a small amount of Arab relocation has occurred over time in selected areas, including urbanward movements and some residential mobility among Arab communities. One type of mobility underestimated by standard official migration sources is commuting—the daily movements of Arabs who work in Jewish areas. This circular or daily commuting pattern has substituted for other, more permanent, migration forms and has been one factor slowing down changes that would have occurred under a more open internal migration policy (see Chapter 4). The absence of Arab relocation has re- inforced Arabs' local ties and the powerful influences of kinship and family net- works. Arab population growth without migration or territorial expansion as outlets has had major economic and social consequences, particularly since there are pressures on the opportunities available in local areas because of the increas- ing numbers. The regional concentration of the Arab-Israeli population exacer- bates Arabs' economic dependency on Jewish employers and on jobs in economic sectors controlled by Jews.

The Arab-Israeli population has become a fully urbanized sector of Israeli so- ciety, with over 90 percent living in urban localities. Arabs have taken urban jobs as they have shifted from their heavy concentration in agriculture and in rural areas. Much of this shift was the result of changes in the land accessible to Arab Israelis after 1948 and the heavy state investments in, and control over, agricul- tural production and markets. These controls flowed from both the political and the economic interests of Israel and the commitment of Labor party govern- ments to the support of rural Jewish agricultural enterprises. The increase in the proportion that is urban among Israeli Arabs, however, has not resulted from their geographic movement from rural to urban areas but from the reclassifica- tion of rural communities as urban when these have grown in population size through natural increase. The administrative designation of areas as urban with- out migration or changes of residence, therefore, has resulted in urban concen- tration in a statistical, but not necessarily a sociological, sense. Clearly, the eco- nomic, political, and social meanings of urbanization for Israeli Arabs and Jews are significantly different.

Over 90 percent of both Jews and Arabs live in places defined as urban, but in their detail, these places differ sharply. Using data for the end of 1998, about half of the Arab population live in urban places of less than 20,000 (compared to 11 percent of the Jewish population); 29 percent of the Arab population live in urban places with less than 10,000 people (compared to 6 percent of the Jews). Of the 21 percent of the Arab population in the three largest cities (with over 200,000 pop- ulation) 85 percent live in Jerusalem; of the 21 percent of Jews living in these large cities, almost 60 percent live in Tel Aviv or Haifa. Almost 40 percent of the Jews live in urban localities of medium population size (50,000 to 200,000 people), compared to only 8 percent of the Arab population. I have already noted that the residential segregation of Arab Israelis is thorough (Chapter 4). Viewing concen- tration among regions in Israel demonstrates that in 1998, 40 percent of the Moslems, 60 percent of the Christians, and 80 percent of the Druze lived in the northern region, compared to 10 percent of the Jewish population (Table 5.3). The high levels of residential segregation means that 85 percent of the Arab Is- raelis reside in village communities, towns, and urban neighborhoods where

Arabs are the only residents (Al Haj 1995; Lewin-Epstein and Semyonov 1993; Semyonov and Tyree 1981).

The geographic location of Arabs creates differential and disadvantaged opportunity structures and limits their access to economic markets (Lewin-Epstein and Semyonov 1993). Most Arab communities are small, semi-urban places, where economic opportunities are scarce and economic development and infrastructure are limited. Health facilities, educational opportunities, and other key elements of social and economic infrastructure are significantly weaker in Arab communities, and the state has disproportionately invested in areas with Jewish populations. The geographic isolation, small community size, and residential separation, combined with lower state investments, conspire to impoverish the everyday lives of Arab Israelis as well as to increase their powerlessness. The reduced aspirations of the young, their poorer education, the restricted role of women that results from increased dependency on men, and the relative economic dependency of the men on the Jewish economic sector are major consequences of this residential concentration (see Al Haj and Rosenfeld 1990; Lewin-Epstein and Semyonov 1993).

The evidence suggests that the economic dependence of the Arab population has increased in direct relation to the rise in the standard of living within Arab communities (Al Haj 1995). The residential clustering of Arab Israelis reinforces separate spheres of development between them and the Jewish majority. In turn, Arab segregation has an impact on the Jewish population, since contacts between Arabs and Jews are limited in large part to asymmetrical work relations, with separate local networks and kinship relationships.

These residential patterns and their economic and demographic implications have complex sources. First, there is the historical context. The out-migration of Arabs from the newly established state in 1948 was selective of the middle classes, who were more educated and urban, and the wealthier Arab leadership. This migration (whatever the political sources and whether voluntary or the consequences of Israeli military activities) left Arab-Israeli communities disadvantaged relative to where they had been economically and socially in the pre-1948 period. Second, the state has reinforced the historical separation of the Jewish and Arab populations. The relative residential segregation, regional concentration, and restriction of movement imposed by the state, combined with a growth of Arab population size through natural increase (declining mortality and high levels of fertility) put enormous pressures on Arab communities. Added to these circumstances are changing labor opportunities as Israel's economy has been transformed and the fact that the Arab-Israeli level of residential segregation has not declined with increases in their education or income. Finally, the state welfare system has often discriminated against those who have not served in the military and as a result excludes or reduces benefits to the Arab population.

The economic and labor force consequences of residential concentration for Arab men and women have been critical in maintaining their disadvantaged economic status through location-specific distribution of educational institutions, employment opportunities, and organizational and institutional developments. The dependency of the Arab communities on the Jewish economic sector is a direct outcome of state policies and the increased discrimination in the labor market. The lack of adequate schooling can be linked directly to the residential stability and geographic segregation of Arab Israelis, since residential changes were so restrictive. These patterns are clearly part of the Arab-Israeli conflict in the region and are related to the internal ethnic tensions in the state of Israel. They are as well reflective of the sources of the demographic growth differences between Arabs and Jews in Israeli society (immigration primarily of the Jewish population and out-migration of the Arabs from Palestine before, or immediately subsequent to, the establishment of the state) and the nation-building patterns of the Jewish state.

There are those who have noted that some economic benefits may accrue to the Arab population because of residential segregation, since there is less direct labor market discrimination within Arab communities than there is for Arabs working in the Jewish economic sector (see Chapter 4). Nevertheless, the increasing educational attainment of the Arabs over time has created a young cohort of men and women whose opportunities are constrained both by residential segregation and by economic dependence on the Jewish sector. Even if residential segregation has been beneficial for some in the past, it is more likely than not to have negative consequences when the increase in population size outstrips available local economic opportunities. There are high social, demographic, and economic costs to the state and to the Arab community of these forms of residential segregation. Although residential segregation is seen as a necessary short-run response to the Arab-Jewish conflict, it is also a political statement about national Jewish legitimacy over the land areas of the state, and it serves as a defense against external Arab attacks.

The exercise of political control by the Jewish majority has generated long-term costs, including the continuous economic powerlessness of Arab Israelis and the creation of an Arab underclass. The expanded work opportunities that occurred in Israel in the post-1967 period did not change the status of Arab Israelis. Their increased segregation, which resulted from increased population growth and limited expansion of the area where they could live, led to greater economic deprivation, hopelessness, and deterioration, precisely at the time when objective conditions were becoming better relative to where they had been.

The generally held view that there is no significant internal migration among Arabs in Israel is challenged by the analysis of the immediate post-1948 internal movements and some recent, modest moves of Arabs to mixed Arab-Jewish cities. The post-1948 movement was of displaced Israeli Arabs to other Arab communities. This movement was the result of state land policies and national political control and was characterized by displacement, not by migratory choices. Although some of this internal movement resulted in a changed Arab occupational structure and had the appearance of a rural-to-town movement, there were profound negative economic and social consequences to the Arab migrants, who were internal refugees in their places of destination (Al Haj 1987).

Some internal migration among Israeli Arabs has occurred in the recent period, but it has not resulted in a decrease in overall levels of residential segregation. Local community studies (Bar-Gal 1986; Ben-Artzi and Shoshani 1986) indicate continuous residential segregation of the Arab population in mixed Arab-Jewish areas. The small changes that occurred during the 1980s led to Arab succession, as some Jewish neighborhoods emptied out and became Arab as a result of in-migration. Neighborhood deterioration and Jewish residential mobility to new neighborhoods have provided some opportunities for Arab Israelis to move and have increased their opportunities for employment and education. But Arab residential segregation continues. The growth and spread of the Arab population and the options to move to new areas may encourage further Arab migration to cities. These movements are modest when examined against the background of socially restricted movements for most Arab Israelis. Migration may generate tensions with the majority Jewish population living in these areas, particularly if demands are made for equal municipal services (education, religious, welfare, and health) and if competition over limited jobs and educational opportunities occur. It also may raise the expectations of the younger generation, whose aspirations are likely to be blocked in the Jewish sector of the economy.

Residential location for Arab Israelis, as for Jews, reveals important dimensions of community life. Where people live in relation to jobs and amenities, educational opportunities and services, ethnic and economic networks informs us about the lifestyle, life chances, and quality of life experienced by different communities. The history of immigration patterns for Jews and the Arab-Israeli integration as a minority in the state have in the past shaped the distribution of the population and have influenced the expansion and composition of neighborhoods. Several generations of Jews and Arabs have experienced these living patterns. Their children have been socialized under these circumstances. Their identities as ethnic and religious communities have been shaped by their areas of settlement and the institutions that characterize different locations. Because of the power of place, it is unlikely that local communities will lose their influence in the nationally integrated Israeli society of the twenty-first century.

Notes

1. As a basis for comparison, the United Nations estimates that 47 percent of the world's population lived in urban places in 2000; 76 percent of those in more-developed nations and 40 percent of those in less-developed nations lived in places defined as urban. Israel's urban population level is therefore at the high end of the more-developed nations.

2. These six broad geographic divisions are defined in terms of districts based on official administrative divisions of the country. More detailed analysis could be presented by subdistricts and by natural regions, by conurbation and their internal structure. These areas are defined in official publications and are reviewed in the statistical yearbooks of Israel. The smaller areal units show the same basic trends.

3. It is difficult to calculate the precise proportion of third-generation Israelis who combine social and geographic mobility. In large part, data on the ethnicity of the third generation are not collected (see Chapter 2), and the connections between intergenerational social mobility and residential concentration have not been specified. The details of the 1995 census, when fully released, will be useful in investigating these changes. My best estimate is that between one-third and one-half of the third-generation Israelis live in areas of high ethnic residential concentration.

4. These people also live in neighborhoods or areas that are defined as "religious" or ultra-orthodox (*haredi*, in Hebrew). These areas are typified by some neighborhoods of Jerusalem (e.g., Me'a She'arim, Bayit V'gan, Qiryat Matisdorf, among others) and B'nai B'rak. They contain large populations of Jews who are observant of religious rituals, wear distinctive clothing that is defined as religiously modest, vote disproportionately for non-Zionist religious political parties, and have larger-than-average families. There are extensive religious institutions in these areas—synagogues, religious academies, religious charities, and ritual bathhouses. There is a connection between these religious communities and people's ethnic origin, since many of these neighborhoods are composed of Jews of European origin. There are other neighborhoods that have significant numbers of Sephardic Jewish residents where there are also religious institutions and welfare-related agencies.

5. See the systematic analysis of internal migration in Israel by Ben-Moshe 1989a.

6. There is obviously a greater amount of mobility than these net patterns indicate. In 1998, as one extreme example, 35,300 persons moved into the central district and 35,200 moved out, for a net loss of 100 persons over the year as a result of the movement of 70,500 persons! The Tel Aviv district had a net mobility loss of 19,000 persons as a result of the movement of 116,800 persons in 1998. For details, see the *Statistical Abstract of Israel 2000*, table 2.16.

6

Communities: Kibbutzim, Moshavim, Development Towns, and Cities

As in other societies, social life in Israel occurs in communities. These are often based on families and kinship groups and incorporate ethnic networks, religious groups, and political, economic, and social organizations. A few of these communities are characterized by ideological and cultural particularities associated with Israeli society, Zionism, and Judaism. All of them take place in geographic-ecological settings and social contexts that shape how communities develop, who shares them, what amenities and institutions are available to improve the quality of daily life, and the values and norms that set them apart from others. I compare the socioeconomic and demographic characteristics of these communities to clarify the variation in the contexts that shape the lives of Israeli residents. These profiles provide a basis for a comparative assessment of the impact of place on the Israeli population.

I review several very different locales and social contexts in Israel, some rural and some urban:[1]

1. Kibbutzim—the plural form of the Hebrew word "Kibbutz"—are settlements located primarily in rural areas, with a collective system of production, marketing, and consumption. These communal settlements have been of major interest in the study of the evolution of Israeli society.

2. Moshavim—plural of Moshav—are rural agricultural settlements where marketing and purchasing are collective and consumption and production are private. Unlike Kibbutzim, Moshavim have been economically, not ideologically, committed to collective organization. (When only consumption is private, the settlement is officially referred to as a "collective Moshav.")

3. Development towns are a heterogeneous categorization of relatively small urban places, mostly established after 1948 and located on the geographic periphery of Israeli society or in distinctive neighborhoods in metropolitan areas. These mostly began as residential communities, heavily subsidized by the government to attract newly arrived immigrants, and they expanded rapidly in the 1950s.

4. Large cities—Tel Aviv, Haifa, and Jerusalem—are where the majority of the population lives. These cities have spread to encompass areas in their metropolitan peripheries as their urban cores have declined.

5. Administered Territories are new settlements on the periphery of Israeli society located in Judea, Samaria, and Gaza, and settled by Jews since the 1967 Six Day War. They are located in what I have referred to as territories "administered" by the state of Israel. The Jewish population living in these settlements are Israeli citizens, surrounded by a large majority of Palestinian Arab residents. The Gaza area (along with the city of Jericho) was given over to Palestinian control in Summer 1994. Jewish settlements around Gaza have remained. Their future remains unclear as they have become part of the contested issues in the broader Arab-Israel conflict.

Kibbutzim: Origins, Developments, and National Influence

The image of the Kibbutz community has been among the most engaging conjured up by Israeli society. Small, simple, and egalitarian, Kibbutz life projects the image of people committed to the basics of hard work and communal sharing—selfless and dedicated to the highest ideals. This representation of life on these communal settlements borders on the idyllic. For those living in and outside of Israel, the Kibbutz image has sometimes been taken as synonymous with the historical reality of the state as a whole or at least of its ideals. The ideological construction of Israel as a new society finds its clearest expression in the ideals of Kibbutz life.

A Kibbutz is a relatively small, demographically limited community in Israel. Its image needs to be examined relative to its reality and to other types of settlements in Israel. How is life on Kibbutzim different? How does Kibbutz life reflect the ongoing transformations experienced by the society as a whole? Who lives in Kibbutzim, and how do they recruit the next generation? What are the values of these communities, and how have they changed over time? I review these themes by assessing changes in the ethnic composition of the Kibbutzim and their place in Israel's nation-building. I start with some historical context.

The Kibbutz movement in Palestine and in Israel has been a continuing experiment in collective economic, political, cultural, and social life for over three-quarters of a century. Each settlement is small; when taken together, they comprise only a few percent of the Israeli population. Nevertheless, the movement had a disproportionate influence on the formation of the Jewish community of

Palestine. As such, the Kibbutz movement remains a fascinating subject for social and historical analysis. Its origin may be traced to the first two decades of the twentieth century, when the movement's economic and ideological bases were developing, when Kibbutzim were expanding and consolidating, and when members of Zionist youth movements were being recruited to populate rural collective settlements. The organizational structure of the Kibbutz evolved in the context of a broader set of political controversies, economic fluctuations, demographic growth, and geographic expansion in the changing political and economic milieu of Palestine (see Near 1992; Rayman 1981; Talmon-Garber 1972). In its origin and development, the Kibbutz was an integral part of the larger Yishuv (the Jewish community in pre-state Palestine) and the broader society.

There were powerful European intellectual sources of Kibbutz ideology, which were central to developments in the Yishuv and later in the state. Socialism and nationalism were core themes in Kibbutz ideology. The balance of religion (Judaism) and ethnicity (Jewish national secular culture) in defining Jewishness and Zionism were continuing sources of controversy in nearly every Kibbutz; and the importance of agricultural activity, socioeconomic and gender equality, Jewish cultural renaissance, and the collective basis of responsibility were debated endlessly. Kibbutz activities were often viewed suspiciously and competitively, often with curiosity, and sometimes with hostility by other residents of Palestine—the Arabs, the orthodox Jews of the old Yishuv, the urban residents, and the colonial British. Kibbutzim were financially dependent on the Palestinian Jewish community and on external Zionist funds, and at times they relied on Arab labor and markets. These dependencies had implications for economic activities within the Kibbutz, for ideological variations among them, and for institutions that were developing within the Kibbutz movement. Kibbutz responses to the problem of generational renewal (the demographic challenge of replacing older members and expanding production to accommodate increasing numbers) occurred initially by recruiting young members of Zionist youth movements and Jewish immigrants to Palestine. These sources of demographic growth meant weaker family and kinship-based networks in the Kibbutz. The persistence of traditional gender roles and family life and the connections between these and work allocations directly challenged an ideology emphasizing gender equality and minimizing family autonomy.

The Kibbutz movement is an expression of the values of labor Zionism that developed in the nineteenth and twentieth centuries, rather than those derived from "Jewish" social traditions as some have argued (for example, Near 1992). The spirit of the small Jewish town (shtetl) of Eastern Europe and the values of biblical Judaism had little to do with the formation of the Kibbutz, even though both were used selectively and imaginatively as sources for its legitimacy. The Kibbutz movement constructed its ideological views most directly from the currents of European, not Jewish, thought. Developments in the Kibbutz, its economic, political, and demographic successes and failures, were the result of the financial and institutional support provided by Jewish communities in Palestine and elsewhere. They were not the direct result of the power of Kibbutz ideology or the salience of its lifestyle (see Goldscheider and Zuckerman 1984, chapter 12).

No one who has studied Israeli society, the history of Zionism, or the emergence of utopian movements escapes the powerful images that the Kibbutz evokes. Social scientists who have raised general questions about gender equality, the family and its future, and the possibility of a return to agriculture in urbanized societies via a collective rural community have often used the Kibbutz as part of the metaphors informing their analyses. The Kibbutz in Israel symbolizes the ideals of the secular Zionist dream: a return to the land, equality of gender roles in the family, and social class equality in the distribution of goods and consumption patterns, energized by pioneering and communal-collective commitments. Few would have expected the Kibbutz movement to have carried out all these revolutionary changes or to be able to sustain them generationally. Nevertheless, it is remarkable that the Kibbutz has been among the most successful of the communal utopian movements, as the second and third generations have carried on some of the major ideological imperatives of the movement and have generated new ones (Krausz 1983; Spiro 1979; Talmon-Garber 1972).

There has been a dynamic interaction between the Kibbutz movement and Israeli society. As part of the society, Kibbutzim were shaped by what was happening in Palestine and, for the past several decades, in Israel. They were an integral part of the Yishuv and the state and were not isolated communities with minimal national economic, political, military, social, and cultural roles. Indeed, the Kibbutz influenced Israeli society far beyond its small size, as it was influenced by the state. A disproportionate number of Kibbutz members have been active in party and national politics, becoming political and ideological leaders of Israel, prominent in the Knesset (Israel's Parliament), and overrepresented as officers in the Israeli armed services. Kibbutz ideals include the quintessential symbols of national Zionist values. The Kibbutz movement has been studied extensively, but primarily as an esoteric social movement or as an influence on various facets of the Israeli economy, society, polity, and culture. My interests in this chapter focus on how the demographic and ethnic transformations in Israeli society have influenced changes in the Kibbutz.

Clearly, Kibbutzim have changed over time, and some have shifted their emphasis away from collective family activities and from communal ownership toward the nuclear family, greater privacy, and individualism. There have been difficulties incorporating the second and third generations. At the same time, new members have been continuously attracted to them. There have been difficulties, demographically, with the processes of entering and exiting Kibbutzim, as well as with changes in their population size, age structure, and ethnic composition. The economic and political support Kibbutzim have received from the national government has also varied considerably, faring better when the Labor party was in power (from 1948 until 1977) and more poorly under the Likud party regime. The economic structure of the Kibbutz has changed in response to economic and demographic developments in Israeli society and shifts in political administrations and their priorities.

The relationship of the Kibbutz to ethnic issues mirrors some of the conflicts in Israeli society. Kibbutz ideology has always stressed equality among groups and the irrelevance of ethnic origins as a legitimate basis of differentiation or generational stratification. Although Kibbutzim have always been "Jewish" communities, they were often seen as supporting the equal status of the Arab minority and the need to develop symmetrical relations with local Arab communities. Yet the ethnic composition of the Kibbutz has been overwhelmingly "Western" or European in origin.

Residents of Kibbutzim competed with Arab agriculture, used former Arab lands for their own agricultural development, and have occasionally employed Arab laborers. Some of them expressed and supported a left-liberal social, political, and economic ideology that was welcoming and accepting of Middle Eastern Jews and Arab Palestinians. At the same time, Kibbutzim benefited from government controls and regulations that have affected the distribution of land and the production and distribution of goods and resources. Central government policies were supportive of Kibbutz institutions while being detrimental to Arab populations and to Jewish immigrants from Middle Eastern countries. In all, the ideals of equality sustain the Kibbutzim, and although people often view them as special, the reality falls somewhat short of that.

To be sure, not all Kibbutzim are the same, since they are linked economically and organizationally to different federation and supraorganizational structures, which are tied to political organizations and parties and guided by different political and economic ideologies. There are secular, antireligious Kibbutzim, and religious Kibbutzim that are hostile to secular lifestyles; there are Kibbutzim that are primarily agricultural, and others that specialize in the manufacturing of industrial products; some are involved in the production of goods for local Israeli consumption, while others are organized for the export market; there are Kibbutzim of different size populations, some newly established and others that are veteran areas of settlement. Some Kibbutzim maintain maximum community control over children, collectively raising and educating them; others are much more individual and nuclear family based. Many of the Kibbutzim are egalitarian in ideology, although some have become more capitalistic. As a result of this diversity and of the changes over time in Kibbutz life, it is difficult to make generalizations. My focus is to place the Kibbutz in the context of a changing Israeli society, to note its demographic transformation generationally, its migration and fertility patterns, and its changing ethnic composition.

Kibbutzim: Population and Ethnicity in the Countryside

The ideological underpinnings of the Kibbutz movement, its egalitarian ideals, its collectivist lifestyle, and its organizational structure are revealed by the formal

TABLE 6.1 Number and Regional Distribution of Population in Israel's
Kibbutzim and Moshavim, 1998

District	*Kibbutzim*		*Moshavim*	
	Number	*Population (in thousands)*	*Number*	*Population (in thousands)*
Northern	130	57.9	117	43.9
Southern	65	23.7	111	41.9
Central	31	16.9	130	73.1
Haifa	23	11.5	22	9.9
Jerusalem	8	3.3	41	17.0
Tel Aviv	1	0.3	1	0.5
Other	9	1.9	32	8.3
TOTAL	267	115.5	454	194.6

Note: "Other" is the area composed of what are referred to as Judea, Samaria, and Gaza; I have referred to it as the Administered Territories.

Source: *Statistical Abstract of Israel 2000,* table 2.9.

structure of Kibbutz organizations. There are five major groups of Kibbutzim. The largest group is affiliated with the United Kibbutz Movement (60 percent of all Kibbutzim). Next in size are those associated with the political group Hashomer Hatzair—which was founded in 1913 and which adopted Marxism in the 1920s—and thus part of HaKibbutz HaArzi (30 percent of all Kibbutzim). Religious Zionists have their own Kibbutz organization—HaKibbutz HaDati (17, or 6 percent, of all Kibbutzim). Two smaller organizations are HaOved HaZiyoni, the Zionist worker organization (5 Kibbutzim and 2,000 persons), and Po'ale Agudat Yisrael, representing the ultra-Orthodox, who are opposed to Zionism in its secular form (2 Kibbutzim and 1,700 persons). Kibbutzim are located in all six regional districts of the state. Most are in the northern district (130 Kibbutzim with a population of 57,900); 65 Kibbutzim are in the southern region, and 31 are in the central district (Table 6.1).

When the state of Israel was established in 1948, there were 177 Kibbutzim with a total population of 54,200, representing 7.6 percent of the Jewish population (Table 6.2). The rapid Jewish population growth through immigration and the settlement of most of the newcomers in urban places resulted in a decline in the proportion of Jews living in Kibbutzim to less than 3 percent in 1998. This decline occurred in the context of the doubling of the Kibbutz population to 115,500 within 50 years after the establishment of the state and the addition of almost 100 new Kibbutzim in five decades. Kibbutz populations have grown, and the number of settlements has increased over time, but from the perspective of

TABLE 6.2 Jewish Population of Israel's Kibbutzim and Moshavim, 1948-1998

| | Kibbutzim | | | Moshavim | | |
Year	Population	Number	Jewish Population (%)	Population	Number	Jewish Population (%)
1948	54,200	177	7.6	30,100	104	4.2
1961	77,000	228	4.0	124,200	366	6.4
1972	89,500	233	3.3	130,400	386	4.8
1983	114,800	267	3.4	149,900	448	4.5
1991	129,300	270	3.1	168,500	456	4.0
1998	115,500	267	2.6	194,600	454	4.3

Sources: *Statistical Abstract of Israel,* various years; data for 1948 are from Bachi 1977, p. 43.

the society, their relative demographic importance has always been small and has declined over time.

The population structure of Kibbutzim in the past tended toward the younger ages; the average (median) age of persons living in Kibbutzim was 26.2 years in 1991, about two years younger than the Jewish population as a whole, and almost three years younger than the Jewish population in urban localities. About 10 percent of those living in Kibbutzim in 1991 were over age 65, and 30 percent were below age 15. However, the population structure of the Kibbutzim has aged considerably—the percentage that is 65 years old and over has more than doubled from 1970 to 1991. By 1998, the proportion of older persons in the Kibbutzim in Israel closely resembled the proportions among the urban Jewish population (around 12 percent). This aging has increased the economic strains of having sufficient workers, paying health costs, and finding jobs for older members of the labor force. Aging within this type of communal setting has social consequences as well, including the increased collective responsibility necessary to care for the elderly and the problem of incorporating multigenerational units within collective decision making. It also involves shaping new socioeconomic and cultural priorities for an increasingly top-heavy age pyramid. The generational aging pattern is exacerbated by the out-migration of younger family members and young adults.

Kibbutzim have struggled to retain their young adult population generationally and to incorporate new members who have been socialized elsewhere, in or out of the country. In 1971, 7,800 persons entered Kibbutzim as internal migrants and 6,600 left for a net gain of 1,200 (an entering rate of 62 per 1,000 population and an exiting rate of 53 per 1,000, resulting in net in-migration of 9.1 per 1,000). These net changes have fluctuated over time. In 1998, Kibbutzim lost population through net migration (4,200 entered and 8,000 left, yielding a loss of 3,700 persons or 31.5 per 1,000 population).

The rates of migration only tell the "net" demographic story: The net loss to Kibbutzim of 3,700 persons in 1998 was the result of the movement in and out of over 12,000 persons. Each decade, the movement of several tens of thousands of people in and out of Kibbutzim points to important labor force turnover and social integration problems in terms of commitments to the collective.[2] As a small ideologically oriented community, a Kibbutz relies on a core of continuous residents to sustain its uniqueness, even as new members are socialized and return movers are resocialized. Work and social relationships disrupted by out-migration need to be repaired and readjusted. Indeed, in- and out-migratory flows require adjustments by those leaving as well as those remaining in a Kibbutz. The proportion of the Israeli population who have had some Kibbutz experience is thus much larger than those currently residing in them. Migration to and from a Kibbutz is therefore one of the sources of the integration of Kibbutzim in the broader urban society of Israel, where economic and human resources flow in both directions. Kibbutzim and Israeli society impact one another through these migratory exchanges.

Unlike the ethnic compositional shifts in the society as a whole that changed as a result of immigration from Asian and African countries, the ethnic makeup of Kibbutzim has remained highly skewed. In 1961, about 85 percent of Kibbutz residents were of Western origin, similar to the percentage of Western-origin population living in the country as a whole in 1948. In the 1972 census, 87 percent of the population living in Kibbutzim were born in either Europe or the United States or were born in Israel of parents of Western origin.[3] An even higher proportion (89 percent) of those living in veteran Kibbutzim (those established before 1948) were of Western origin. Thus, a quarter-century after the establishment of the state, after mass immigration had occurred and the children of immigrants had reached adulthood, when immigrants and their children from Middle Eastern countries were altering the composition of the Israeli population, the ethnic composition of Kibbutzim remained close to their European sources.

For those of non-Western origins, with different economic experiences and ideological commitments, Kibbutz life was less attractive than that of urban places with their greater economic diversity and opportunities to establish different types of communities. By the 1980s, there had been some increase in the proportion of persons of Middle Eastern origin living in Kibbutzim, but the dominant ethnic origins remained Western—in 1983 this was 82 percent of the ethnically identified population (Bachi 1977, table 18.4; Keysar 1990, table 5.2). These proportions are unlikely to have altered significantly in the 1990s.

Jews of Middle East origins living on Kibbutzim have significantly higher levels of education than their Middle Eastern cousins living in urban places. In 1983, fully one-third of those born in Asian or African countries and living in Kibbutzim had 13 or more years of education (an overall average of 12.5 years), compared to only 10 percent of Asian- or African-born population living in Israeli cities (who had an overall average of 3 years less) (Keysar 1990, table 5.4). More-educated Middle Eastern–origin Jews are therefore more likely to reside in places where Western-origin Jews live, reinforcing the connections between education and ethnicity at the community level.[4]

Until the early 1950s, the Kibbutz community had somewhat lower fertility rates and smaller family size than the Israeli Jewish population as a whole. In part, this reflected the European origins of the Kibbutz population and the economic struggles that people in Kibbutzim faced. Children were economic burdens to the whole community because they were reared collectively. With improvements in the Kibbutz economy, raising children began to occupy a more central place, and larger families became important sources of continuity and generational survival. Care during pregnancy and the subsequent costs of parenthood and education are a collective, not an individual, responsibility in Kibbutzim, and children are not a direct economic burden on the family. In the 1960s, fertility levels increased somewhat in the Kibbutzim, higher than in urban areas, and fluctuated around a family size of three children (Friedlander and Goldscheider 1979).

An analysis comparing the fertility of Israelis living on Kibbutzim and in urban environments in the 1980s documented that average family size continues to be somewhat larger in both secular and religious Kibbutzim than in cities.[5] Kibbutz women have different birth spacing patterns than urban Jewish women—at the birth of their first child, Kibbutz women are older than urban women, and they are older than urban women when they gave birth to their last child as well. Family planning practices are strikingly different in the two types of communities: Overall, 70 percent of Kibbutz women use efficient birth control, compared to 40 percent of urban women; 85 percent of Kibbutz women use birth control before their first pregnancy, compared to 40 percent of the urban women; and twice as many Kibbutz women as urban Jewish women used efficient contraceptive methods between their first and second pregnancies. Trial marriage or cohabitation is much more common in Kibbutzim than in urban Israel (three-fourths of Kibbutz women lived in sexual unions before they married, in contrast to 19 percent of secular urban women). The evidence also points to higher levels of sexual activity and more equal relationships between young men and women in the Kibbutz (Keysar 1990). Fertility and family planning differences between Kibbutz and non-Kibbutz communities are smaller among the more religious and the educated.[6]

The evidence about changes in the distinctive lifestyle in Kibbutzim, therefore, reveals an increasing convergence in some areas with the urban Jewish population. Migratory exchanges between the city and the Kibbutz facilitate the diffusion of lifestyles among places. Although the key differentiator of Kibbutzim has been their collective agricultural economic activities and family patterns, these too are changing as some Kibbutzim have moved away from agriculture and have switched to a more family-centered lifestyle. As in urban Jewish communities, ethnic concentration and religiosity are major factors that differentiate the various Kibbutzim.

Moshavim: Cooperative Agriculture

Immigrants to Israel from Middle Eastern countries were not, in large part, channeled to Kibbutzim but were directed to small, newly established cooperative farming villages called Moshavim. These villages were designed for the settlement of some of the massive number of immigrants arriving immediately after the establishment of the state; they were modeled after the *moshav ovdim* (rural worker collectives) that had been in Palestine. These agricultural settlements were part of the organizational structure of the Moshav movement. As a result of the government's settlement policies, by the mid-1960s, the Moshav became the dominant form of rural agricultural settlement in Israel (Klayman 1970; Weintraub, Lissak, and Azmon 1969). During the early years of statehood, the Israeli government created hundreds of new agricultural villages and populated them with immigrants of diverse social and cultural background, the overwhelming majority of whom did not have farm background or experience (Weintraub et al. 1971).

Unlike the Kibbutz, where the collective was the unit of production, consumption, and socialization, the Moshav was a cooperative community of individual households of working family farms. Typically, the Moshav was made up of a small community of about 100 family units, sharing responsibility for communal welfare and networks of economic resources (agricultural, credit, supply, and marketing). Moshavim were developed to solve a series of immediate problems in the new state: (1) integrating diverse immigrant populations; (2) settling rural lands and increasing agricultural production by Jews, to replace displaced Arab farm laborers; (3) population dispersal, decentralization, and political legitimacy over sparsely inhabited border areas; and (4) the provision of immediate employment—all within the context of national ideals exemplified by the Kibbutz movement. Between 1949 and 1958, 251 new Moshavim were established, settling 11,350 households (Weintraub et al. 1971, table 1; Klayman 1970).

Developing a rural agricultural population as a basis for integrating large numbers of immigrants was a limited experiment. Moshavim (as Kibbutzim in an earlier period) never attracted the majority of new immigrants. Agricultural development was ideologically and politically salient but was not viable economically in an urbanized society. Further, this method of creating communities and integrating immigrants of diverse backgrounds often failed even when economic conditions were favorable. As a result, during a ten-year period, over one-third of all those settled in Moshavim migrated away from their communities, primarily to urban areas (Weintraub et al. 1969, table 26). Families remaining on the Moshavim often turned to part-time rather than full-time farming; inequalities within Moshavim emerged that weakened the spirit of cooperativeness and violated the organizational goals of cooperative farming. Some of these difficulties stemmed from poor infrastructural developments, lack of needed economic supports, and planning difficulties at the central level. Other problems were generated by the absence of agricultural skills and the poor training of the new immigrants.

Systematic research has shown that these external constraints were only part of the difficulties. Social structural factors internal to the Moshav community and linked to the integration of immigrants into these new types of communities represented the crucial axes around which Moshavim's relative success varied. For example, demographic variation among households (in size and family structure) conflicted with the policy of standardized and equally divided agricultural units and production needs; the agricultural, commercial, financial, and managerial skills often required background or training that new immigrants lacked and that conflicted with kinship networks and relationships. Pluralism among households was not matched by diversity in management. Kinship relationships and family structure appeared to be key elements in the transfer of managerial control to the younger generation (Weintraub et al. 1971).

The Moshav met the government's commitment to greater population dispersal, particularly away from city centers and distant from their high levels of population density, crowding, and housing shortages. Israel's establishment of Moshavim was also consistent with the rural emphasis of Zionism and moved the new immigrant population from areas that were then characterized by a slow rate of industrial production. Over time, immigrants were directed instead to new towns, as the rural areas and the various collective agricultural settlements—Kibbutzim and Moshavim—were unable to attract immigrants or to receive the necessary financial investments to make the economy of these rural places viable. The urban population was not attracted at all to the Moshavim (unlike to the Kibbutzim),[7] nor were economic opportunities sufficiently rapid to compete with urban developments, or at least the potential for economic advancement in the city. It was therefore difficult both to integrate new immigrant families into the rural areas and their economies and to attract veteran urban residents there. The small community structure may have had the potential to ease the immigrant absorption process for some in the short run, but it also became a basis of intense generational conflict, dependency on government supports, and reduced social and economic mobility. Those who wanted increased educational and employment opportunities had to seek them in the cities.

The number of Moshavim increased from 104 in 1948 to 324 in 1954, and their populations increased almost fourfold during this period, from 30,100 to 112,500. Unlike the domination of the Western-origin population in Kibbutzim, by 1972, only 34 percent of the population of Moshavim were of Western origin; only 22 percent of the residents of Moshavim established after 1948 were of Western origin. The Moshav population increased fivefold between 1948 and 1991, yet the proportion of Jews living in Moshavim declined from 6.4 percent to 4.0 percent from 1961 to 1991, and most were of Asian-African origin. At the end of 1998, there were 454

Moshavim in Israel, with a total population of 194,600, about equally distributed among the central, northern, and southern regions (Table 6.1). The most significant growth during the last decade of the twentieth century was the addition of several Moshavim in the administered territories.

The contrasting ethnic composition of Moshavim and Kibbutzim, Asian-African versus European-American, respectively, underlines the fact that ethnic residential concentration has become entrenched even for rural agricultural areas (compare the discussion in Chapter 5). Indeed these ethnic divisions were reinforced by the settlement strategies of the national government, even though these policies reaffirmed the ideal of Israel as an ethnic melting pot. Although ethnic differences were rooted originally in places of origin, Israeli policies embedded new forms of ethnicity in the communities they created and supported. The policies designed for the socioeconomic absorption of immigrants from diverse places of origin resulted in the formation of ethnic enclaves. Community and residential segregation of ethnic immigrant populations shaped the overlap of ethnic origins and socioeconomic status and perpetuated this conjunction for the next several generations. The emergent ethnic pattern is ubiquitous, since it encompasses veteran and newly established areas, ideologically egalitarian and ethnically neutral communities, and third and later generations growing up in Israeli society at the end of the twentieth century. Areas of ethnic concentration were reinforced by the selective movement to Moshavim of new immigrants of particular ethnic origins, the selectivity over time of immigration by country of origin, government policies associated with immigrant settlement and rural investments, and selective out-migration of ethnic groups from Moshavim to urban locations.

Development Towns and Small Urban Areas

By the mid-1950s, the rural areas of settlement were inadequate to absorb the flow of new immigrants and the larger metropolitan areas were already densely populated. It became clear that a different solution for locating the great waves of arrivals from Asian and African countries was needed. New urban areas, referred to as "development towns," were planned—partly to complement the rural strategy of immigrant settlement, with similar goals of economic development and the dispersal of population to border areas in order to meet political and military needs. These new towns were located in sparsely settled regions, particularly near the borders of the state, to reduce original territorial imbalances. They were designed as middle-size cities to absorb immigrants and would serve as a solution to regional population concentration (see Berler 1970; Kellerman 1993; an earlier analysis of the importance of these new urban frontiers is reviewed by Matras 1973).

The number of areas designated as development towns in Israel increased fourfold, from 4 in 1948 to 16 in 1950, doubling again in the next decade (Table 6.3). Most of these development towns are located in either the northern or southern regions of the country. Several development towns located in the more-developed

TABLE 6.3 Population and Percentage of Jews in Development Towns
in Israel, 1948–1990

Year	Number	Population (in thousands)	Jewish Population (%)
1948	4	11.3	1.5
1950	16	85.4	7.1
1955	26	180.6	11.4
1960	32	303.1	15.9
1965	34	448.9	19.5
1970	30	447.2	17.3
1975	29	597.6	17.9
1980	29	692.9	18.4
1985	29	646.0	18.4
1990	29	702.5	18.5

Sources: Adapted from Kellerman 1993, tables 3.3, 3.4, and figures 3.1, 3.3;
1990 data are my estimates based on information for specific towns in the
Statistical Abstract of Israel 1991.

central region of the country (e.g., Rosh Ha'Ayin, Ramla, Lod, Or Yehuda, Or
Akiva, Yehud, Yavne) lost their designation as development towns during the
1960s (Kellerman 1993, figure 3.1). The number of development towns has remained constant since the 1970s. The population living in these towns increased
dramatically between 1948 and 1965 and then growth rates slowed down. Starting
with only 11,300 persons in 1948 and representing 1.5 percent of the Jewish population, the development towns grew almost eightfold, to 85,400 in 1950 (7.1 percent of the Jewish population), and then to 180,600 in 1955 (11.4 percent of the
Jewish population). In 1961, the percentage of the Jewish population living in development towns surpassed that of rural communities. Their relative population
growth peaked by the mid-1960s, reaching almost 20 percent of the total Jewish
population, and fluctuated thereafter to about 18.5 percent in the 1980s and
1990s. Unlike in the Kibbutzim and Moshavim, population growth in development towns has roughly followed the pattern of Jewish population growth. The
proportion living in development towns is more than twice the combined proportion in Kibbutzim and Moshavim. The steady growth in the number of Jews
living in development towns reflects a considerably higher fertility rate, balanced
by continuous net out-migration from many of these towns.

   The population in development towns has been and continues to be disadvantaged socioeconomically. The third generation growing up in them are largely of

Asian and African origins, less educated, in lower-ranked occupations, and with lower incomes and fewer resources than the Jewish population as a whole or than their ethnic cousins in more central urban places. Research based on the 1961 census, at the peak of the expansion of development towns, documented the extensive ethnic residential concentration in these areas for people from specific countries of origin and the tendency for their labor forces to be concentrated in specialized industries (Spilerman and Habib 1976). There was little industrial diversity among development towns, partly reflecting the small size of their labor force and the pattern of central government investments in particular industries. For example, the labor force in Dimona and Qiryat Shemona was heavily concentrated in textile manufacturing; in Yeroham, mineral and chemical processing; and in Bet Shemesh, the manufacturing of transportation equipment. Over-representation of particular ethnic groups in specific industries followed from this community pattern: Yemenites were concentrated in textiles, Moroccans in mining, Libyans in cement products, and Algerians and Tunisians in wood product industries.

Patterns of ethnic-based enterprises connected to development towns continued through the 1980s. Most important, the educational and occupational disadvantages of ethnic groups were exacerbated by their community-level residential concentration. Out-migration of the more ambitious and successful young adults searching for better educational and occupational opportunities in the larger metropolitan areas left the residual ethnic population in development towns in an even more disadvantaged socioeconomic position, with even higher levels of ethnic occupational concentration.

In classic fashion, the low level of economic development in these towns and their distance from a metropolis had negative effects on their power of attraction (Berler 1970). Development towns do not compete with each other but with the larger cities and older, established urban places. Residents of development towns who move are likely to go to a city or an established town rather than to another development area. Out-migrants from development towns do not leave when they are poor but when they are doing better and the opportunities for further advancement are blocked. Hence, development towns that have increased economic growth are paradoxically more likely to be characterized by extensive out-migration. At the same time that moving away from the development towns enhances the social and economic mobility of the migrants, the socioeconomic disadvantage of the town increases. Indeed, development towns that are more prosperous and attractive to investments and sufficiently attractive to stabilize the population and prevent further out-migration need to sustain a major expansion of economic opportunities so as not to generate aspirations of young adults that cannot be met (Berler).

"Development town" is an official designation that carries with it government subsidies. Other urban places also have economic and ethnic concentrations. In general, an analysis of the Jewish population in districts and subdistricts (*nafot*, in Hebrew) based on census-related official data from 1961 to 1983 shows that in the more urban districts (Tel Aviv, Petah Tiqwa, Rehovot, Ramat

TABLE 6.4 Selected Socioeconomic and Demographic Characteristics of the Jewish Population of Israel by Town and Ethnic Origin

Town	Pop. Size 1988 (000's)	Migration per 1,000 Pop.	Asian-African (%)	Asian-African Ages 0–14 (%)	15–64	65+	European-American Ages 0–14 (%)	15–64	65+
Dimona	24	-34.6	84	32	63	5	28	53	19
Qiryat Shemona	15	-16.1	75	28	66	6	20	68	12
Ramla	37	- 9.1	65	22	72	6	20	62	17
Qiryat Gat	28	- 2.9	66	28	66	5	21	61	18
Giv' Atayim	46	- 7.2	25	13	79	8	6	66	18
Nazerat Illit	22	- 2.7	30	28	67	5	22	62	16
Qiryat Bialik	33	3.7	28	23	73	5	16	69	15
Qiryat Motzkin	29	9.0	26	23	73	4	14	68	18
Tel Aviv	307	- 7.3	33	13	75	12	7	58	35
Jerusalem	350	5.9	37	20	73	7	21	64	15
Haifa	201	- 8.9	24	17	75	8	9	63	28
Be'er Sheva	113	-10.0	57	25	70	5	21	66	19

Town	High Level of Education Age 25–29 1961 (%)	1983	High Level of Occupation Age 20–64 1961 (%)	1983	Women in Labor Force Age 35–44 1961 (%)	1983	Earnings Upper Decile (%)
Dimona	5	18	7	23	33	46	7.3
Qiryat Shemona	5	22	11	22	30	59	3.9
Ramla	3	11	9	13	16	46	6.2
Qiryat Gat	7	23	14	20	31	56	3.6
Giv' Atayim	14	46	26	34	30	71	17.5
Nazerat Illit	8	30	10	23	51	71	5.3
Qiryat Bialik	10	41	36	35	23	68	14.9
Qiryat Motzkin	15	40	19	33	29	66	12.6
Tel Aviv	12	41	22	31	28	62	11.8
Jerusalem	20	43	22	36	36	57	8.5
Haifa	14	50	24	38	29	65	15.2
Be'er Sheva	10	35	32	34	27	58	9.2

Note: High- level of education is 13 or more years; high-level of occupation includes professionals and managers.
Sources: Adapted from data presented in Friedlander, Ben-Moshe, Schelkens, and Feldman 1990.

Hasharon, Haifa, and Jerusalem), the level of education is higher, the proportion of European origin population is higher, fertility is lower, and life expectancy and in-migration rates are higher. The reverse characterizes less-urban districts. Two-thirds of Israel's Jewish population live in the six largest urban districts, and this division has not changed much from 1961 to 1983 (Friedlander, Ben-Moshe, and Schellekens 1989; Friedlander et al. 1990). It remained the pattern throughout the 1990s.

A comparison of different places shows the range of heterogeneity in demographic socioeconomic indicators and their general connection to ethnic residential concentration (Table 6.4). Dimona, Qiryat Shemona, and Qiryat Gat are development towns in the southern, northern, and southeastern regions, respectively. Ramla, in the central region, had been a development town until the 1960s. The next grouping of four urban places shows significantly lower proportions of Asian-African-origin Jews and, except for Nazerat Illit, are established urban areas that are more properly considered part of the Tel Aviv or Haifa metropolitan area. They compare in population size to development towns but are significantly different in other ways. The four largest cities of Israel are included for comparisons and are reviewed here. The highlights of these community differences include:

1. Dimona and Qiryat Shemona are development towns with very high rates of net out-migration, in large part as a response to the lack of local employment opportunities. Out-migration also characterizes other development towns like Qiryat Gat and Ramla (the latter is no longer defined as a development town but is clearly disadvantaged socioeconomically). In contrast, Qiryat Bialik and Qiryat Motzkin in the north are examples of urban places with higher rates of stability, and they have gained in population because their socioeconomic levels have been high along a variety of dimensions.

2. There is a clear association of out-migration in towns with a high proportion of Jews of Asian and African origin. Even more significant is the very high level of ethnic residential segregation evidenced by these data. The proportion of Asian- and African-origin population ranges from 84 percent in Dimona to 25 percent in Giv'Atayim and clearly distinguishes the first four from the second four town groupings.

3. The age distributions of the specific towns (presented separately by ethnic origin) reflect the higher fertility of Middle Eastern populations, particularly those in development towns, and the aging of the population of Western origin. These data also show the aging of the Western-origin population everywhere—in development towns and established areas. The proportion of older persons (over age 65) among the Western-origin population is two to four times higher than that for the Middle Eastern–origin population. A Middle Eastern–origin person living in a town with a large Western-origin population is very unlikely to be over

age 65 (e.g., 4 percent of Asian-African–origin Jews in Qiryat Motzkin are over age 65 compared to 18 percent of the Western-origin population); a Western-origin person living in a development town is two to three times more likely than a Middle Eastern person to be over the age of 65 (e.g., 19 percent of the European-American–origin population in Dimona are over age 65, compared to 5 percent of the Asian-African population).

4. The variation in ethnic origin and age structure among towns is connected to socioeconomic differences. Data in the lower panels of Table 6.4 show that the proportion with more than thirteen years of education and in professional-managerial occupations is significantly lower in places with dominant Middle Eastern populations than in those where Western-origin populations are more numerous. The proportion of those with high levels of education was two to three times higher in urban places with a Western-origin population than in places with high proportion of persons from Asian and African countries. These differences occur in the context of sharp increases in the levels of education in all towns since 1961. Differences in occupational levels are in the same direction but are less striking; an examination of detailed occupations (not only the categories of professionals and managers) would likely reveal sharper differences. Labor force participation of women is higher in the Western-origin towns than in development towns, as is the percentage in the upper decile of earnings.

We can translate these aggregate figures into real terms by describing, in the limited context of these crude indicators, what it implies to live in these urban places. For heuristic purposes, I contrast Dimona (a development town) and Qiryat Motzkin (an urban town in close proximity to Haifa). At the end of 1998, these two urban places had about the same size populations (the former had a population of 33,400 and the latter 36,700). The populations of both places were fully Jewish, with no Arab populations living there.

Living in Dimona means residing in a place where many persons are moving out every year, largely young adults looking for work and perhaps for educational opportunities. Most of your Dimona friends and neighbors are of Middle Eastern origin and very likely segregated by specific countries of origin. There are a large number of children living at home and few older persons; indeed, six times as many persons are below age 15 than are over age 65. Most young adults have less than a high school education, and very few of the older generation have attained even that educational level. Few people work as professionals or managers, and most women in their middle ages do not work outside of the home. Only a very selected few in Dimona earn a lot of money.

Living in Qiryat Motzkin means living in a community that has expanded from a population of 4,000 in the 1950s to over 30,000 by the end of the 1980s. It is a community that continues to attract new residents, primarily from the urban center of Haifa; most of those who migrate are of Western origin. An increasing number of the residents are older; more are over age 65 than are below age 15. Young adults have high levels of education and are concentrated in professional and managerial occupations in increasing numbers. Two out of three women are working, and many families are well-off and have ample financial resources available to them. If obtaining an education after high school is rare in Dimona, not continuing beyond high school is unusual in Qiryat Motzkin.

The key to understanding this contrast is not in these specific differences but the implications of these differences for lifestyle and life chances in both the economic and demographic senses. The overlap of ethnic origin with socio-economic characteristics in these places is profound, and the consequences for the education and employment opportunities of the next generation are clear. It is not conceivable, except with a radical change in the society as a whole, that ethnic origin will not remain salient for economic advantage and lifestyle, for the opportunities, and for the quality of life of the next generation of young adults in Dimona and Qiryat Motzkin. Ethnicity, economic opportunity, and residential concentration reinforce each other, not just as symbols of the distribution of resources within the society, but also in terms of the quality of social life for future generations.

The Largest Cities

Most of the Jewish population lives in the metropolitan areas surrounding the largest cities: Tel Aviv, Jerusalem, and Haifa. I have already noted some of the demographic patterns of these large urban places (Chapter 5) and have suggested that there are neighborhoods within these cities that are ethnically segregated. Data in Table 6.4 show similarities among the three cities, in which all are ethnically of Western origins, and show their contrast with Be'er Sheva' (still designated as a development town), the largest city of the Negev, with a predominately Asian- and African-origin population.

These data show general out-migration from these large cities, except for Jerusalem. Annual migration data from the late 1990s show net out-migration from Jerusalem as well. Unlike the out-migration from development towns, migration from the largest cities is almost always to other parts of the metropolitan community. Three-fourths of the Jewish population living in the city of Haifa is of Western-origin, as is two-thirds of the Jewish population of Tel Aviv and six of ten of the Jewish residents of Jerusalem. These figures contrast with Be'er Sheva', where 57 percent of the Jewish population is of Middle Eastern origins. More of the Western-origin Jewish population of Tel Aviv and Haifa are older (35 percent and 28 percent, respectively, are over the age of 65) compared to that of Jerusalem or Be'er Sheva' or other urban areas.

Educational attainment is higher in Haifa, Tel Aviv, and Jerusalem than in Be'er Sheva'. There are fewer differences among the large cities in the proportion of people in professional and managerial jobs, although the development towns are clearly disadvantaged in this regard. Women in Haifa and in Tel Aviv are more likely to work than are women in other large urban areas, and the proportion with high earnings is particularly high in Haifa, compared to other large cities.

A general comparison of the two largest cities in Israel, Tel Aviv and Jerusalem, illustrates the potential impact of place on the next generation. Separated by about 40 miles and connected by expressways, these cities dominate the country. Their metropolitan areas have spread geographically to accommodate their growing populations, but their urban cores have declined. Metropolitan Tel Aviv, consisting of 41 municipalities, has a population of almost 2 million; Jerusalem has a metropolitan population of 500,000 in only one municipality. Many of the suburbs of Jerusalem, more so than in Tel Aviv, have spilled over into the surrounding administered territories and are part of Judea and Samaria. Including these broader areas raises the population of a constructed "metropolitan" Jerusalem to almost 1 million (Kellerman 1993).

Jerusalem is characterized by government activities, public bureaucracies, and by cultural, educational, and religious institutions. This capital, with its ancient and historical roots, has been redeveloped. Jerusalem has been the spiritual center of Jews for centuries, and for Christians and Moslems as well; and it is a newly rebuilt metropolis. After 1948 and before 1967, Jerusalem was on the Jordanian border and hence geographically marginalized. Since 1967, the city has expanded and incorporated newly rebuilt Jewish areas and has included large Moslem and Christian populations. As the historical core, Jerusalem exhibits an ethnic and religious pluralism and has become a symbolic center for many religious groups. Jewish religious groups scramble for power in Jerusalem and represent heterogeneous and institutionally divided communities that are often ethnically segregated as well. Conservative Judaism, known in Israel as Masorti, and Reform Judaism have institutions and constituencies in Jerusalem. Both chief rabbinates (representing Sephardic, mostly Middle Eastern, and Ashkenazic, mostly European, religious traditions) are located there, as well as local *haredi* rabbinical courts and institutions that deny the legitimacy of the chief rabbis. There are other non-Orthodox Judaisms there as well that are also not recognized by the Orthodox rabbinates.

Tel Aviv is the commercial, industrial, and financial center of Israel. It is a more diffuse city, structurally and geographically. It is newer than Jerusalem, established in 1909 by secular Zionists, shifting away from its Yafo neighbor, and is the political and secular center of the country (even though Israel's political institutions and formal parliament, the Knesset, are located in Jerusalem). Some have described the conflicts in Jerusalem as those between secular and religious, Arab and Jew, the political right and left, Western- and Middle Eastern–origin Jews, and the old and the new. In contrast to Jerusalem, secular struggles characterize Tel Aviv—the struggle for status, property, and material success (Kellerman 1993). Tel Aviv has its roots in secular Zionism and its institutions; Jerusalem draws its inspiration from traditional Judaic texts and is identified with history and spirituality. The images of Tel Aviv are of beaches, cafes, and nightlife—the excitement of city life. Located in the hills, Jerusalem generates images of the quarters of the old city, archaeological sights, and people praying at the western wall. Jerusalem, with its religious pluralism and contested history, is a core arena of conflict between Israelis and Palestinians.

Tel Aviv is the leading center of Israel's postindustrial economy, facilitating the shift to high technology industries and producer services. In many ways, Tel Aviv is the center of contemporary Jewish Israel, the focus of urban technological, economic, and cultural innovations. Jerusalem is the spiritual and bureaucratic center of the country, its administrative core, and historical-institutional center. Together, Jerusalem and Tel Aviv reflect the major themes of Israel's changing society.[8]

Administered Territories: Judea, Samaria, and Gaza

The territories and populations living in the eastern parts of Jerusalem that were under Jordanian control between 1948 and 1967 were incorporated into Israel after the Six Day War; the area of the Golan Heights was formally annexed in 1981. Israel also took political and administrative control of large territorial expanses and populations in the West Bank, Gaza, and Sinai. The Sinai Peninsula was returned to Egypt as part of the peace treaty initiated by the leaders of Israel, Egypt, and the United States. Gaza and the city of Jericho were transferred to Palestinian administration in mid-1994. The controversial issues of population and territory center on the West Bank and Gaza and the large Arab Palestinian population living there. I examine some of the demographic and political questions about these areas in Chapter 12. Here, I review briefly the Jewish population growth and settlement in the West Bank and in the Gaza area, which occurred under the auspices of, and with financial subsidies from, the Israeli government.[9]

There are a variety of views about the legitimacy of Jewish Israelis settling in these areas. Some Israelis, associated in large part with Gush Emunim—Bloc of the Faithful—have advocated the full annexation of the West Bank and Gaza to Israel; a smaller Jewish minority have argued for the annexation of these areas but not the Palestinian population living there.[10] A small number of Jews with Israeli citizenship, many of whom commute to jobs in the state of Israel, have settled in the administered territories. They are of considerable symbolic importance and a powerful demographic and political presence. Most Israeli Arabs, and probably all of the Arab Palestinians living in these territories, view the Israeli Jewish presence in the West Bank as a foreign settlement in their territory. Jewish settlers here receive financial support from the Israeli government, as do their institutions. Their areas of settlement have developed ecologically and economically with Israeli government planning and support. They receive the full protection of the Israeli military.

Settlement of these areas may be viewed in part as the next phase in the Zionist territorial reconstruction of the land of Israel. These new Jewish settlements evolved as part of the continuous policies of the Zionist movement and Israeli governments to populate land areas in order to establish political legitimacy and control. Starting with the Kibbutz settlements in the first decades of the twentieth century, the first new form of Jewish resettlement in the modern era, Israeli governments continued to subsidize the settlement of Jewish immigrants in rural Moshavim and then in development towns located in peripheral border areas. In the post-1967 period, new Jewish settlements were supported politically and economically in parts of reconstructed West Bank and Gaza areas, the previously defined area of Palestine.

Counted formally in the 1972 census were 1,500 Jewish residents of the administered territories—Judea, Samaria, and Gaza—located in 15 settlements. At the next census in 1983, there were 22,800 Jews living in 76 settlements in Judea-Samaria and 900 living in 5 settlements in the Gaza area. By 1991, these areas and the Jewish population living there increased—to 90,300 in Judea-Samaria in 120 settlements, and to 3,800 in 13 settlements in the Gaza area. Of these 133 places, 10 were defined as urban locations, 9 of which had less than 10,000 Jews counted in their population. Of the 123 rural locations, 30 were Moshavim, 10 were Kibbutzim, and 83 were other rural settlements. There were 173,000 Jews in these territories at the end of 1998, representing 3.5 percent of the Jewish population of Israel.

More than half of the Jews in the administered territories live in urban localities. Many of the others are in urban occupations and commute to their privately owned suburban residences. Economic and ecological linkages have been forged between the largest of the Jewish settlements and the metropolitan areas of Israel, since a significant proportion of the population in these settlements lives in close proximity to Tel Aviv and Jerusalem. These settlements broaden the narrow area in the center of the country that became the state of Israel in 1948 and expand the area around Jerusalem that had been divided between 1948 and 1967. The urban-suburban character of most of these settlements contrasts with the relative regional and urban isolation of development towns and the rural character of the Moshavim and Kibbutzim.

Three-fourths of the Jewish population in these territories in 1998 were born in Israel. Half of the foreign born arrived in Israel during the 1990s and half of those born in Israel were at least second generation. The ethnic origin of the settlers was predominately European-American (60 percent); the overwhelming majority (80 percent) of the Asian-African settlers are at least second generation; the majority (51 percent) of the European-American-origin settlers were born abroad and most of those (60 percent) arrived in Israel in the 1990s.[11]

The establishment of new Jewish settlements as a basis for territorial legitimacy had been a long-established feature of Zionism. At the same time, the settlers, often religious and messianic, have not been ideologically "correct" in the context of socialist and secular Zionism. Their urban lifestyles and their private ownership of property were inconsistent with the older, rural Zionist ideology of a return to agriculture. Their settlements were not always planned by the government and sometimes were in conflict with formal policies, although they rarely, if ever, were built without government infrastructural and economic supports. The Jewish settlers' conflicts were not with an external government, as with the British at an earlier point in prestate Palestine, and often not with the local Arab population (even as their activities inflamed the Arab-Israeli conflict and exacerbated the tensions between Israel and Arab neighboring countries; see Chapter 12), but with the Jewish government of the state of Israel and with the Israel Defense Forces.

The areas designated as Judea, Samaria, and Gaza under the administrative control of Israel had one of the highest Jewish growth rates of any place in Israel in the 1990s and one of the highest positive rates of internal migration per 1,000 population. In many ways, the Jewish population in these areas is small relative to the majority Palestinian population and relative to the Jewish population in the state of Israel. Nevertheless, the settlers living there tend to be highly motivated persons, with strong Zionist and pioneering ideologies; many are religiously committed to the settlement of the whole land of Israel. They represent the interests of the right wing of political parties and their commitments to settle in these areas, but they have been subsidized by diverse central governments in Israel.

Each of the territories or ecological settings I have reviewed played its particular role in the evolution of Israeli society and was consistent with some form of Zionist (and, in turn, Jewish) ideology. Each of these place types was an attempt to deal with a changing conception of territory and population that was informed by external and internal events. Each settlement was planned to create political facts and to establish a Jewish presence on the outer reaches of the borders that were defined as part of the resettlement of the historic land of Israel. Surely these areas were variously defined at different times in the history of Palestine and Israel, and each in its turn and for different reasons, generated conflict and debates among friends and foes inside and outside of the state. These territories also required enormous government investments and financial and political supports to sustain their developments and to insure their survival. And, at least to some extent, each was viewed as a critical part of the Zionist pioneering effort to rebuild and settle the land, fulfilling some utopian or messianic imperative. These areas generated a reaction on the part of the Arab residents, since each settlement was threatening to them symbolically and culturally, as well as demographically, politically, and economically. In turn, each was only partially successful in solving the problems of territorial and demographic politics.

The Role of Place in Israeli Society

I have described Israel as a small, nationally integrated state that is subdivided ecologically and socially by a complex grouping of areas. Some of the divisions are common in most societies—rural, town, city, and metropolitan area; others are uniquely Israeli, fitting in with the history and culture of the society—Kibbutzim, Moshavim, development towns, and the small Jewish settlements in Judea, Samaria, and Gaza. These geographic and ecological settings are important for understanding Israeli society because they are associated with lifestyles and values and with the social, political, and economic characteristics that differentiate Israel's population and affect its future generations, who are socialized there and have access to its institutions. These ecological settings often reinforce economic and social inequality. Areal differences are overlaid with ethnic patterns and institutions that relate to current residents and that shape the ethnic commitments and distinctiveness of their children. Community-based differences in resources, economy, and ethnicity, along with ideologically motivated settlements, are likely to continue for the next decades.

I have documented how place matters for lifestyle and life chances. Residential segregation among Jews of different ethnic origins occurs in urban and rural areas, in new and old settlements in the West Bank, in the rich suburbs of Tel Aviv, and in the poor development towns on the northern and southern borders of the state. All of these areas have been influenced by when and by whom they were settled and by how much economic support and investments have been given to them by the central government. Beyond the esoteric, experimental, and ideological interests of the uniquely Israeli settlements, there is the conjunction of social class, economic opportunities, ethnic origins, and religion that matters in these places.

In a society that continues to value the freedom of internal movement—where people have choices about where to live and where to raise their families—differences among areas in economic opportunities, educational possibilities, and housing availability are of enormous importance. The characteristics of individuals and their families shape how these areal differences are translated into settlement responses. The choice of where to live is not abstract but embedded in social class, kinship, and ethnic resources and networks. As well, it is the state and its policies that selectively and differentially support these settlements and areas. Those who do least well are those with fewer resources and weaker economic networks. Areas that provide few educational or occupational opportunities—those local and central governments that do not follow through economically on their ideological and political commitments—reinforce differentiation and convert the unequal distribution of resources into the generational perpetuation of inequality.

Where people live influences their social and economic lives in profound ways; most importantly, in the extension to their children of the conditions of the contemporary generation. It is the dynamic, long-term, and continuous impact of ecological space on future opportunities and institutions that makes the examination of social and geographic settings necessary and complex. These communities reflect the evolution of Israel as a society; they are likely to shape its future politics, economy, and culture.

Notes

1. I have relied on the detailed official definitions of these areas for my data, which are included in the introduction to the *Statistical Abstract of Israel*. Although there is increasing diversity within these categories, I emphasize their broader outlines. The official designation "development towns" remains somewhat ambiguous.

2. Many of those who are moving in and out of Kibbutzim may actually be return or repeat migrants. Some are volunteers who only spend short periods of time in a Kibbutz for the "experience" or as national service. The net figures mask these various types of migrations. There are no systematic studies of the different types of movements or the selectivity factors of remaining in or leaving a Kibbutz; that is, there are no socioeconomic or demographic data concerning characteristics of those who enter or leave a Kibbutz.

3. No official data are available on the ethnic origins of the third generation. It is reasonable to assume that about 90 percent of the third-generation Jews living in the Kibbutzim were of Western origin. See the discussion of the ethnicity of the third generation in Chapter 2.

4. A similar trade-off between education and ethnicity appears to occur in interethnic marriages (see Chapter 10).

5. In 1983, Kibbutz fertility was higher than urban fertility by 0.5 children per women, on average, the same as that estimated for the 1970s. Compare Keysar 1990, p. 4, and Friedlander and Goldscheider 1979, pp. 149–153. Over time, fertility convergences between comparable populations in Kibbutzim and in urban areas have occurred (Keysar, table 5.6). The findings on fertility and contraceptive use for the 1980s, reviewed later, are based on the data reported in Keysar 1990; see also Peritz and Baras 1992.

6. See Keysar 1990, for more details on fertility and family planning in Kibbutzim; see Friedlander and Feldman 1993, Kupinsky 1992, and Peritz and Baras 1992 for more general analyses of Israeli Jewish fertility. The highlights of these studies are reviewed in Chapter 11. The review of gender issues in Chapter 8 examines the myth and reality of gender equality in Kibbutzim.

7. Individuals could move to a Kibbutz, since family connections were de-emphasized; however, Moshav living was almost always family based, with a strong kinship structure already in place. Individual migrants from urban places seeking a different lifestyle would either join a Kibbutz or would find a way to set up a new Moshav, a daunting task.

8. Although these descriptions of Tel Aviv and Jerusalem are crude and somewhat stereotypical, they are reflective of some part of the differences between these two large urban places.

9. The focus on the minority Jewish population in the West Bank and Gaza follows from the fact that Israel subsidizes these settlements, and the Jewish population has rights and obligations of citizenship (including military obligations) and the educational benefits and welfare entitlements of Israeli society. Unlike the Palestinian population in these areas, they are fully part of Israeli society, except that they are living in areas administered by the state of Israel and not formally or legally part of Israel.

10. For an analysis of the ideological and religious roots of Gush Emunim, see Aran 1990 and Waxman 1991. On the political governmental and nongovernmental organizations involved in Jewish settlements in the West Bank, see Peretz 1986.

11. I do not know of systematic studies of the ethnic origins of the Jewish population of the administered territories. My guess is that in the large areas around Jerusalem and Tel Aviv, there is a rather even split between those of European and those of Asian-African origin, reflecting the ethnic composition of third-generation Israelis. In smaller places, particularly in areas of more nationalistic, ideological, and religious settlement, the proportion of Jews of Western origin is likely to be higher. The median age of the Jewish population in these areas is by far the youngest among all areas (18.9 years), several years younger than the national Jewish average.

PART FOUR

Forms of Inequality:
Social Class, Gender, and Death

7

Resources and Inequality:
Education, Occupation, and Income

In my exploration of Israel's changing society, I have linked population processes and ethnicity in the context of nation-building. Underlying these connections are major transformations in economic development that have characterized Israeli society over the past several decades, including the growth in some sectors of the economy, the expansion of export markets, and the extension of higher levels of living and increased consumption to its diverse population. As Israeli's economy expanded and institutions were established to maintain continuous growth, new forms of stratification and inequality emerged. These forms revolve around the transmission of social class position and other inequalities from one generation to the next and around how available resources are distributed.

In this chapter, I address basic questions about social class resources and ethnic inequality. What is the changing structure of inequality in Israel? How does the social class hierarchy overlap with ethnicity, and do social class differences among ethnic groups persist generationally? What are the trajectories of change in the social class gap among groups: In other words, are socioeconomic differences converging? How are the sources of stratification connected to population processes and immigration? The answers to the persistence, convergence, and explanations of stratification will help us better understand how Israeli society and its policies have altered the bases of resource distribution and ethnic inequalities.

I separate stratification from differentiation by looking at the dynamics of generational change.[1] In all societies, there is an educational-occupational distribution, and there are differences in the way economic resources and income are allocated. When these differences are transmitted generationally and reinforced institutionally, the resultant hierarchy is referred to as social stratification. Similarly, social class differences among immigrants are expected, since these differences are the direct outcome of their historical circumstances in places of origin prior to coming to Israel, of the differential resources they brought with them, and of the economic condition in Israel when they arrived. My focus is on generational changes in ethnic inequalities that have emerged over time, in particular the transmission of social class inequalities among those born in Israel. The analysis of stratification differences among second and later generations addresses issues of the persistence of inequalities and ethnic convergences.

I have already outlined the increase over time in educational levels, the different economic resources brought by immigration, the occupational changes of immigrants, and the general changes in consumption and dependency patterns (Chapter 1). I have also reviewed the diverse ethnic origins of immigrants and their continuing residential concentration in Israel and have noted how government policies have reinforced these patterns (Chapters 3, 5, and 6). I now investigate the implications of these changes for the distribution of resources and for the changing overlap of ethnic origins and social class.

The Educational Dimension of Inequality

As the state of Israel grew demographically and economically, educational levels of the population increased, networks of schools expanded, new academies were established, and opportunities for attending school were extended to (indeed, required of) all citizens. Public elementary and high schools, colleges, and universities developed to accommodate the needs of an increasing population, to educate the next generation in the political goals of the state, and to address the economic demands of an expanding and more diversified labor market. The values placed on educational attainment and the emphasis on learning in Israeli culture were expressed in the development and location of educational institutions and in the provision of resources for educational developments. Educated individuals were often highly valued in Jewish culture, and the transfer of status from "religious" to "secular" education was relatively straightforward among most Israelis who were committed to secular values. No less important, high levels of educational attainment provided entry into better jobs and access to higher incomes and were a powerful basis for intergenerational social mobility. The expansion of educational opportunities and increases in educational levels were matched by growth in the availability of jobs demanding higher educational attainment. Job opportunities expanded and industries developed to meet the increasing number of people participating in the labor force (where the ethnic composition was changing) as well as in the broader economic goals of the state. Educational and occupational opportunities developed in new geographic areas where immigrants and their families lived; those opportunities changed in the growing metropolitan areas.

The ethnic origins of families and the ethnic composition of communities of residence are key contexts that shaped opportunities for schooling and access to jobs. The educational and occupational background of parents and their resources are important determinants of the amount and type of schooling of children. The location of educational institutions, the quality of teachers, and the orientation of their curricula are factors linking education to jobs. These sources of educational stratification are complex and involve family and personal background characteristics, institutional location, and school personnel quality. Their systematic analysis requires documentation of the changing levels of educational attainment, occupational achievement, and distribution of income; they point toward the exploration of changes in the education and occupation of parents, the translation of education into jobs, and the community contexts where educational and occupational opportunities vary. My main focus in this chapter will be on whether these broader socialization factors are translated into greater inequality among ethnic groups within the Jewish population.[2] Throughout, I emphasize the links between indicators of stratification and ethnicity in the context of Israel's changing society and population.

Educational attainment is a fundamental basis for social stratification. The average number of years of schooling completed provides the first clues about the complexities of ethnicity, generation, and stratification. Three findings emerge from an examination of schooling in Israel (Table 7.1). First, Jews from Western countries (Europe-America) have higher average levels of education than those from Asian and African countries. Among the foreign born, the difference averages 1.6 years; among the Israel born, the average difference is smaller (1.4 years). Second, the average educational gap has narrowed between ethnic groups because educational levels have increased for both groups, but somewhat more sharply for the Asian-African origin group. The third finding makes the education story more complex because it focuses on a fuller educational distribution and shows the potential distortion when we only examine average levels of education. Examining the upper end of the educational distribution, those with 13 to 15 years and those with 16 or more years of schooling, reveals small generational changes for both ethnic categories and the retention of higher levels of post–high school education among the Western-origin population. Almost twice as many European-American Jews had 13 to 15 years of education than did Asian-African Jews, and three times as many had more than a college education. These ratios are almost the same for the foreign- and Israel-born generations. At the upper levels of education, therefore, the ethnic gap in the 1990s is about the same for the first and second generations. Data not shown reveal that the same pattern prevailed in the early 1990s, although all groups increased their average levels of education during the decade.

To what extent do these 1999 cross-sectional generational data reveal changes over time? Data organized from the 1961, 1972, and 1983 censuses of Israel (Nahon 1987) show sharp increases over time in the educational attainment of Israelis and a continuing variation by ethnicity (Table 7.2). Without exception, each religious-ethnic gender group experienced an increase in the average level of education from 1961 to 1983. Educational levels for Jewish males increased from an average of 8.6 years of

TABLE 7.1 Years of Schooling of Israel's Population, by Ethnicity, Age 15 and
over, Standardized by Age, 1999

	Average (Median) Years of Education	Percentage with 13–15 Years of Education	16+ Years of Education
Jews	12.5	23	18
Foreign born			
European-American	13.2	29	22
Asian-African	11.6	15	7
Israel born	12.6	23	18
European-American	13.5	27	27
Asian-African	12.1	17	8
Israel born	12.8	23	22
Arabs	10.8	11	8

Source: *Statistical Abstract of Israel 2000,* tables 22.1 and 22.2.

education in 1961 to 10.8 years in 1983; for Jewish women the increase was from 7.2 years to 9.8 years of school. Average educational levels increased for Arab Israelis as well: For men from 4.1 years to 7.3 years of schooling, and for women from less than 2 years, on average, to 4.5 years of schooling. Comparisons between the data for 1999 and for these census years show consistent increases over almost four decades in the educational level of the population. Thus, these data reinforce the conclusion that increases in educational attainment have not been limited to specific subpopulations and are a ubiquitous feature of Israeli society.

At the same time, an ethnic hierarchy clearly emerges in these data: Jews have higher levels of education than Arabs; Jews of European ancestry have higher levels of schooling than non-European Jews; and Christians have higher educational levels than Moslems within Arab population. Time has not eliminated the ethnic divisions among Jews despite educational increases for all groups. European-American Jews maintain higher levels of schooling than Asian-African Jews, even as the second generation of both Jewish ethnic groups has experienced increasingly higher levels of schooling.

What about changes in the ethnic gap in educational attainment over time? The average gap in educational level between European-American and Asian-African Jews declined over time for both men and women. The ethnic-educational gap among foreign-born men was reduced by one year (from a difference of 3.6 years to 2.6 years from 1961 to 1983) and among foreign-born women by 1.8 years

TABLE 7.2   Average Educational Level of Israel's Population by Ethnicity, Religion, and Gender, Age 25 and Older, 1961–1983

Religion and Ethnicity	*Average Number of Years of Education*					
	Males			*Females*		
	1961	*1972*	*1983*	*1961*	*1972*	*1983*
Jews						
Total	8.6	9.3	10.8	7.2	8.0	9.8
Foreign born						
European-American	9.7	10.2	11.3	8.9	9.4	10.5
Asian-African	6.1	7.1	8.7	3.3	4.8	6.7
Difference	3.6	3.1	2.6	5.6	4.6	3.8
Israel born						
European-American	11.7	13.0	13.7	11.1	12.4	13.5
Asian-African	8.3	9.6	10.8	7.1	8.9	10.8
Difference	3.4	3.4	2.9	4.0	3.5	2.7
Israel	10.2	11.3	12.2	7.2	10.0	11.8
Arabs						
Total	4.1	4.7	7.3	1.6	2.0	4.5
Jews and Arabs						
Difference	4.5	4.6	3.5	5.6	6.0	5.3
Christians	6.5	7.6	9.5	4.6	6.2	7.9
Moslems	3.2	4.3	6.3	0.4	1.4	3.7
Christian and Moslem						
Difference	4.3	3.3	3.2	4.2	4.8	4.2
Druze	3.3	7.1	6.9	0.8	4.6	3.2

Source: Derived from Nahon 1987, Appendix table 1.

(from a difference of 5.6 years to 3.8 years). The native born have higher average educational levels than the foreign born, without exception within ethnic categories, and the average ethnic gap has diminished over time. Although full equalization in educational level among those of different ethnic origins has not occurred, educational convergences seem to be occurring on average.

The educational level of the Israeli born of Israeli parents cannot be disentangled by ethnic origin. Given the immigration and settlement history of Israeli society, the third generation is heavily concentrated in the European origins group (Chapter 2). Their educational level is below that of Europeans of the second generation and higher than that of the Asian-Africans. These data suggest that time alone or generations of exposure to Israeli society are not the only factors that need to be considered in understanding ethnic changes in educational levels.

Consistent with this series of cross-sectional findings over time is research using the 1974 Israeli Mobility Study to examine the changing ethnic-educational connection (Shavit and Kraus 1990). Detailed data document that the overall process of educational stratification remained remarkably stable despite the profound changes in Israel during the 1950s and 1960s. In an attempt to reduce the school dropout rate among Asian- and African-origin Israelis, the government expanded vocational education at the secondary level, extended the number of years of compulsory education, and introduced compensatory education at the primary level. As a result, the effect of ethnicity on the transition from primary to secondary education declined. But there were no significant changes in the factors that governed access to higher levels of education, and ethnic origin remained a powerful differentiator of attaining and completing college-level schooling. As a growing proportion of the population completed more years of schooling, educational credentials began to lose their value as a discriminating factor in attaining jobs; new cohorts needed to attain even higher levels of education to compete for the best jobs.

What about Israeli Arabs? There are fewer consistent patterns over time, except for the increase among Arabs in educational level noted earlier. Educational levels for Christian Arabs increased about three years for both men and women (from 6.5 years to 9.5 years for men and 4.6 years to 7.9 years for women). At 3.2 years of schooling, Moslems had very low levels of education in 1961; in 1983, this figure more than doubled to 6.3 years among men, and increased from 0.4 years to 3.7 years among women. The Druze pattern followed that of the Moslems, although the improvement among Druze women has been slower and their educational levels lower.

By the 1990s, the Jewish-Arab educational gap had narrowed slowly, but there remained a two-year difference among men and three years among women. The Christian-Moslem difference has narrowed for men but not for women. Both Christians and Moslems continue to exhibit a wide gender gap, with only modest indications of reduction.

Research in the 1990s, based on detailed linked data from the 1995 and earlier censuses, reveals that the increase in higher education among all groups has resulted in a widening gap between Jewish and Arab Israelis. Gaps among all groups remain in the probabilities of moving from high school exposure to the *bagrut* (a high school certification required for entrance to universities) and in the transition to higher educational levels. This comprehensive study shows stability over birth cohorts in the ranking of overall educational attainment among ethnic and

TABLE 7.3 Percentage of Israelis with Advanced Academic Degrees by
Ethnicity, Age, and Gender, 1983

Ethnicity	Males		Females	
	Age 30–34	Age 60–64	Age 30–34	Age 60–64
Jews				
Asian-African				
Socialized in Israel	6.1	2.5	3.4	1.3
Immigrated age 17+	19.4	2.7	12.0	0.7
European-American				
Socialized in Israel	28.3	10.2	23.3	6.8
Immigrated age 17+	37.7	10.7	33.6	5.5
Arabs				
Moslems	7.3	0.7	0.0	0.4
Christians	19.4	9.6	7.3	3.3
Druze	3.5	0.0	0.0	0.0

Source: Adapted from Nahon 1987, tables 3a and 3b.

religious groups in Israel. In descending rank order of educational achievement are the following: the European Jewish group, Christian Arabs, Jews of Asian origin, Jews of African origin, Druze, and Moslems (Friedlander et al. 1998).

Going beyond the average number of years of schooling, we can refine the educational analysis by investigating three issues in depth: (1) educational attainment at the upper levels of the distribution; (2) detailed country-of-origin differences in educational trajectories to clarify the changing importance of specific places of origin; and (3) changing transitions by grade level among ethnic communities.

Education at the Upper Levels

An examination of changes over time at upper educational levels shows a sharp increase by age in the proportion of men and women of all ethnic origins with higher academic degrees and the significantly higher levels of education among European-American-origin Jews than other groups (Table 7.3). Differences between those socialized in Israel and those immigrating to Israel at age 17 or over (i.e., receiving their education in countries of origin) are striking. Immigrants arriving after age 17 have higher levels of education than their age cohorts and gender counterparts socialized in Israel. Significantly lower proportions of Asian-Africans socialized in Israel have attained advanced academic degrees than those who migrated to Israel after age 17, but their numbers are lower than that of European-Americans, whether socialized in Israel or immigrating as adults. The proportion of younger Asian-African Jewish males socialized in Israel who have advanced academic degrees (6.1 percent) is significantly below that of Christians (19.4 percent) and even below that of Moslems (7.3 percent).

These results are a powerful test of the ethnic convergence issue, since they reflect the educational inequalities that have been generated and reinforced by the expansion of schooling opportunities for Jews of different ethnic origins in Israel. The expansion of educational opportunities increased the average level of education for all groups. In part, this reflects the enactment and implementation of government policies mandating minimum education for all. Only Arab women have not experienced the full impact of the law, and only among Moslem and Druze women. The educational increase has reduced major intragroup variations among some groups (women, Arabs, and Asian-Africans). Asian-African Jews socialized in Israel have moved toward a high school level of education; the educational level of the European-American Jews has increased to a post–high school level. At the same time, these changes have not eliminated the educational gap among different ethnic origin populations. Educational inequalities have persisted in the face of the Israeli policy committed to reduce (if not eliminate) ethnic educational gaps. Again, data from the 1995 census confirm these patterns at the upper end of the educational distribution.

It should be noted that in the absence of an educational policy to reduce inequalities among Jews and between Jews and Arabs, the educational gap would likely have been substantially greater. The question of educational inequality must be considered not only relative to an ideal of perfect equality but also relative to an alternative of no policy or a weaker policy. The measure of comparison must as well take into account initial educational differences among immigrants in places of origin and levels of education among minority populations when the state was established.[3]

Israeli Ethnicity Versus Country of Origin

A second set of issues relates to the nature of the categorization of ethnic populations in Israel. The construction of ethnic groups into two categories (European-American and Asian-African origin) appears somewhat artificial, since there are dozens of specific countries of origin that make up these groups, and there appear to be wide cultural and social-demographic differences within these ethnic categories (Chapter 2). One way to investigate whether the ethnic dichotomy so often used to characterize Jewish ethnic origins in Israel captures the complexity of ethnic divisions is to examine empirically the educational transformation of each of the detailed groups.

Studies have documented that sharper educational differentiation between the broad groups designated as Asian-African and European-American has emerged over time that has altered the degree of educational variation within each of these Israeli-created ethnic groups. Using 1983 census information, research has shown that there was significant educational variation within the older (age 60 to 64) Asian-African group born abroad. An examination of three countries illustrates the range: Older Israeli Jews born in Egypt had an average of 10 years of formal education; those born in Iraq had 8.5 years; and those born in Yemen had only 4.0 years. Thus, some Asian-African immigrants (e.g., those from Egypt) had levels of education as high as some immigrants born in Europe (e.g., Poland and Romania).

The second generation from these specific countries of origin (those ages 30 to 34, who were raised in Israel) had almost identical educational levels. Israelis of Egyptian origin had 11.3 years of education; Israelis of Iraqi origin had 10.8 years, and those of Yemenite origins had 11.0 years. Thus, the educational levels of younger cohorts of Israelis of Asian-African origin, when divided by specific countries of origin, were much more similar to each other than to that of their parents, who were educated outside of Israel. More important, their educational levels had become increasingly different from the second generation of Jews of European origin. Although the children of Romanians and Poles attained levels of education similar to better-educated European-Americans, the children of better-educated Asian-African immigrants attained levels similar to the less-educated Asian-Africans. The educational level of most Israeli-born Asian-African groups was about three years lower than the average among the various European-American groups. Ethnic polarization in the educational level of the dichotomous ethnic groups (European-Americans and Asian-Africans) emerges in the second generation, and differences among specific country-of-origin groups of an earlier generation have been reduced to insignificance.[4] While the gap in the average level of educational attainment among ethnic Jewish groups had been reduced by the 1990s, the rank order of ethnic differentiation at higher levels of education remains among the second and third generations.

One conclusion from this exercise is that an examination of the educational patterns of the socially constructed dichotomous ethnic categories is fully justifiable. Analytically, these findings are consistent with the argument that ethnic differences among the second and later generations are not simply a carryover from places of origin but are the result of an Israeli-generated stratification system, reinforced by a complex combination of people and institutions—schools, teachers, family, and neighbors. The ethnic groups designated "Asian-Africans" and "European-Americans" are Israeli ethnic constructions, based on the ethnic origins of groups but reflecting the contexts of Israeli society. The evidence available is clearly not consistent with the view that educational and other distinctions among ethnic groups are primarily the result of cultural distinctiveness and proximity to the cultures of places of origin (see Goldberg 1977; Morag-Talmon 1989).

What factors account for the emerging dichotomy among Jewish ethnic groups? One part of the explanation for the growing similarity in the educational level attained by the diverse ethnic origin groups within the Asian-African group relates to their treatment in educational and related institutions. These diverse groups were often lumped together by the European-dominated systems as if they were an undifferentiated and a socioeconomically deprived segment. This "labeling" occurred despite the wide range of levels of educational attainment in countries of origin and the negative socioeconomic selectivity of immigration to Israel.[5] Children of Asian-African-origin Jewish immigrants tended to be labeled *t'unei tepuach*, educationally deprived children requiring remedial assistance. In addition, the larger-than-average family size of Jews from Asia and Africa generally reduced the available capital they needed to invest in the education of their children (particularly at upper levels of education). Ethnic discrimination in the school setting, combined with larger family size, contrasts with the greater economic control and more extensive networks of veteran European-origin Jewish populations whose family size was smaller and socioeconomic resources greater.

Educational Transitions and Tracking

We can further specify these ethnic-educational gaps by examining the transitions between types of educational institutions (Nahon 1987, tables 5 and 6). The probabilities of educational transitions among Asian-African-origin Jewish males ages 25 to 29 (in the 1983 census) are lower than among European-American-origin Jews at each transition above eighth grade. Even the transition from grade 8 to grade 9 is lower among children of Asian-African Jews (0.85) than it is among European-American Jews (0.98). The discrepancies become more pronounced at the higher grades: The transition from grades 12 to 13 is 0.38 for Asian-Africans and 0.62 for European-Americans. The low transitional probability among Asian-Africans from grades 12 to 13 is even lower than it is for Arabs (0.58). These contrasts derive from a greater high school dropout rate among Jews of Asian-African origin, since 75 percent of Asian-Africans begin high school compared to 36 percent of Moslems. These different transitions have changed during the 1990s and shifted to the upper levels of education. Ethnic differences in the transition to post–high school education remain, despite narrowing somewhat over time (Friedlander et al. 1998).

An additional part of the educational picture in Israel relates to the type of school attended by members of these ethnic groups: Asian-African-origin Jews had been more concentrated in vocational schools, European-American-origin Jews are in academic schools, and Arabs are almost all enrolled in academic schools since there are few vocational schools accessible to them (Nahon 1987; Shavit 1984, 1989, 1990, 1993). Research using the 1954 cohort of young Israeli men shows that there is a higher dropout rate in vocational schools. Most of the vocational schools do not encourage or allow the attainment of a *bagrut*; this, therefore, prevents or discourages the attainment of a college- or university-level education. Again, these patterns have changed somewhat during the 1990s, but significant ethnic differences remain in the shift to academic-oriented high schools and to post–high school education.

There are also economic constraints that affect the high school dropout rate among Asian-Africans, such as direct costs of continuing in school and wages lost through delayed employment, particularly among those with lower educational levels (see the studies by Shavit 1984, 1989, 1990, 1993). These findings may not apply to more recent groups, who have been exposed to greater schooling continuation rates among those attending vocational schools. However, the role of the economic crunch following the *intifada* in the late 1980s, the increase in tuition costs and the deterioration of general educational quality that seems to have occurred at that time (see Ben-Yehuda 1989), and the increased competition from the large number of East European immigrants in the early 1990s do not point in the direction of greater equalization of educational outcomes among ethnic groups.

These tracking patterns reinforce the observation that the educational system and its institutions have shaped the ethnic educational distinctiveness for the generation of the 1990s, beyond differences among ethnic origin groups in "ability" and family background. Moreover, normative expectations result in greater tracking of Israelis of Asian-African origins into nonacademic institutions and their continued educational distinctiveness. This educational distinctiveness is translated into socioeconomic disadvantage. Administrators and teachers are likely to play important roles in continuing this type of tracking. There is some indication that they tend to reinforce the lower expectations of Asian-African-origin Jewish students (see the review in Nahon 1987). Over time, therefore, as the educational system in Israel expanded, ethnic differences were reinforced and reestablished even as overall levels of education increased.[6] One conspicuous ethnic difference in educational levels connects to the role of place (Friedlander et al. 2000). Jews living in development towns (see Chapter 6) are the most disadvantaged educationally and have been the least successful in completing high school and going beyond. In turn, this has led to the continuing socioeconomic disadvantage of the population living in development towns. The concentration of the Asian-African-origin population in development towns results in the continuation of the ethnic gap in education among third-generation Israelis.

Occupational Opportunities

One of the consequences of reinforced educational distinctiveness among ethnic groups relates to the linkages between schooling and jobs. Educational experiences are intimately related to access to jobs and, in turn, to socioeconomic status and its correlates. As educational levels on the whole increased and as the labor market continues to demand higher levels of education to carry out more techni-cally based jobs, the rarity (in the statistical sense) of completing higher levels of education gets transformed into a new normative expectation. Ethnic educational distinctiveness leads to occupational distinctiveness and, in turn, to ethnic in-equalities in occupations.

What are the occupational distribution patterns among ethnic groups? Occu-pational differences among ethnic origin groups remained significant through the end of the 1990s (Table 7.4). About one out of four Jewish males are in jobs classi-fied as academic or professional occupations. When these types of occupations among foreign-born European-American-origin Jews are combined, the propor-tion is 31 percent; the level is even higher among immigrants from Europe arriv-ing 1975–1989 (47 percent). In sharp contrast, only 16 percent of the foreign-born Asian-African Jews are in these two types of high-level jobs.

There are also large ethnic differences in the age profile of participation in the labor force. Jews of Asian-African ethnicity enter and retire from the labor force earlier than do European-American-origin Jews, reflecting differences in length of time spent in school and variations in labor market opportunities, as well as the effects of public and family support systems. As with education, ethnic differences reflect the educational and occupational conditions of Jews in countries of origin and the selectivity of immigration to Israel. The critical question about ethnic group occupational distinctiveness is the extent to which there is a carryover be-yond initial occupational differentiation to stratification in the younger genera-tion raised and educated in Israel.

About one-third of the Israeli born of European origin males can be classified in high-level white-collar jobs, a slight increase from their parents' generation. In sharp contrast, only 18 percent of the Israelis of Asian-African origins are in these high-level jobs. An examination of the lower end of the occupational distribution confirms the generational transmission of occupational level among ethnic groups. Among the foreign born, 33 percent of the European-American-origin Jews and 36 percent of the Asian-African origin work in jobs classified as skilled laborers. By the next generation, the percentage of Israel-born Jews of European origin who held these lower-level occupations dropped to 19 percent, but the level among Asian-African-origin Israelis remained about the same (37 percent).

In my review of the changing occupational distinctiveness of ethnic groups in Israel, I underlined the occupational concentration of ethnic groups in particular sectors of the economy and the links between jobs and schooling. The expansion of the occupational structure in Israel in the 1980s and 1990s reduced the oppor-tunities for those with only a high school education who were more likely to ob-tain blue-collar work. The great expansion of educational opportunities for Asian-Africans and their attainment of high school levels of education did not in the aggregate improve their access to the expanding occupational structure. Their vocational training was more likely to lead to blue-collar work. Comparing the older and younger generations of Asian-African-origin Jews shows that despite the increase in the number of years of schooling among the younger generation,

TABLE 7.4 Occupation of Israel's Employed Persons, by Religion, Ethnicity, and Gender, 1999

Ethnicity	Occupation (%)								
	Aca	Pro	Mgr	Cle	Sal	Ser	Agr	Ski	Unsk
Males									
Jews	13	12	10	9	9	8	33	0	7
Foreign born European-American	18	13	7	7	5	6	2	33	10
Asian-African	7	9	8	10	8	8	3	37	9
Israel born	12	12	12	10	11	8	4	27	6
European-American	19	14	17	9	9	5	4	19	3
Asian-African	8	10	8	10	11	10	3	37	7
Israel	15	14	11	10	11	8	5	20	7
Arabs	7	9	2	8	6	8	2	43	14
Jews	Females								
Foreign born	13	20	4	29	6	16	1	5	8
European-American	16	18	3	19	7	16	1	9	12
Asian-African	5	17	2	22	5	29	1	5	14
Israel born	14	21	4	34	6	13	1	3	4
European-American	22	24	6	30	5	9	1	2	2
Asian-African	8	18	4	39	5	17	1	3	6
Israel	14	24	4	32	5	15	1	2	3

Note: Aca = Academic professionals
        Pro = Associate professional and technicians
        Mgr = Managers and administrators
        Cle = Clerical and related workers
        Sal = Sales workers
        Ser = Service workers
        Agr = Agricultural workers
        Ski = Skilled workers in industry and elsewhere
     Unsk = Unskilled workers

These are rounded estimates based on a new occupational classification.
Source: *Statistical Abstract of Israel 2000,* tables 12.14, 12.15.

their occupational structure reproduced that of their parents' generation. These ethnic generational contrasts result in an increase in the occupational gap between the younger Israeli-born generation of Asian-African and European-American Jews. The continued concentration of second-generation Israelis of Asian-African origins in blue-collar jobs, combined with the decline in the status of these jobs, has meant that generational occupational stability has been translated into the declining occupational status of the less-advantaged group.

In contrast to Asian-African-origin Jews, Arabs with higher levels of education have better jobs and even better opportunities to move into white-collar, particularly high-level white-collar, jobs in their own communities. As the rate of higher education increased among Arab Israelis and with less expansion of the high-level white-collar job opportunities in the Arab sector, the more-educated Arabs have had to seek job opportunities in the Jewish sector and compete with better-educated Jews. It is reasonable to assume that in this competition, Arabs are not likely to be the advantaged or the equal group (see Chapter 4). At the end of the twentieth century, the Arab population was significantly more concentrated than Jewish Israelis at the lower end of the occupational structure.

Occupational Prestige

I have been reviewing the concentration of ethnic groups in Israel in different parts of the occupational hierarchy. Another view of the occupational distribution emphasizes the relative prestige of detailed occupations, modeling in the factors determining rank. There has been a long and distinguished history of using occupational differences as an indicator of "prestige" in Israel (see Kraus and Hodge 1990). Most of the occupational studies of Israeli society have argued that occupational prestige differences among the various ethnic groups reflect differences in educational attainment. The first studies of the stratification process focused on a period of time after the establishment of the country, the economic absorption of mass immigration, rapid economic growth, and the crystallization of economic, social, and political institutions. The major changes in the stratification system identified in these studies have been the social mobility associated with increasing educational attainment, particularly the expansion of post-elementary and high school education, increases in the occupational skill levels of the Israeli-born population, and the development of alternative avenues of social mobility that were not necessarily based on formal education (Kraus and Hodge; Nahon 1987, 1989; Shavit 1990; Yuchtman-Yaar 1986).

Hence, the major transformation has been from stratification based on ethnic origin toward one based on universalism and achievement. It is generally argued that the critical factor in the lower occupation prestige of Asian-African Jews is their lower educational attainment and, only indirectly, their socioeconomic origins. At similar educational levels, it is argued, Asian-African-origin Israelis are able to convert their education into status and income (Kraus and Hodge 1990). But as I have documented, educational inequalities among ethnic groups have persisted through the 1990s.

Part of the increasing merit-based (educationally driven) stratification system has been the policy of the state to generate greater ethnic equality through equal access to educational institutions. As in Western nations, the commitment to the expansion of the educational enterprise as a basis for reducing ethnic inequality has only partially been successful in Israel. Too often the expansion of the educational system has resulted in the "reproduction" of the existing class structure and its legitimation. Indeed, the expansion of educational and occupational opportunities in Israel seems to have duplicated the ethnic gap and moved it from lower to higher levels. Increasing the educational levels reduces the value of average educational attainment as a basis for particular openings, because when everybody must obtain a high-level education to qualify for a job, other criteria need to be invoked for job selection. The dominant group (European-American-origin Jews) tends to be favored when educational levels are equalized; networks and connections are invoked as deciding factors in employment. Even in the merit-based system, it is often who you know—that is, the connections and networks that you have—rather than your credentials that determines the occupational returns to education.

Together, these factors have resulted in the differential exploitation of job opportunities among the different ethnic groups in Israel. Occupational inequalities have been retained among the Israeli born in conjunction with educational expansion, since the educational and occupational systems carry their own institutional biases toward European-American Jews. These biases combine with differences in parental resources to invest in the next generation, the negative labeling of Asian-African Jews, and the more-valuable economic networks of Europeans Jews.

The disadvantageous occupational patterns and educational levels of the younger generation of Asian-African Jews are exacerbated by location and ecological factors. Geography combines with government policy to set limits on where job opportunities are located and where related institutions were developed to promote educational mobility. Both job and educational opportunities have been more concentrated in the urban centers of Israel and not in the periphery. Government policy defined where resources were allocated and where investments were made geographically. Initially, these policies attempted to redirect industries and people away from concentrated and densely settled urban centers toward development towns and then toward territories administered by Israel, where Jews were settling. These subsidized economic activities encouraged selective immigrant streams to move toward these areas and, over time, resulted in the reinforcement of economically disadvantaged ethnic populations. Ethnic origin often interacts with location to increase ethnic economic inequalities (see Chapter 6 for a review of these communities).

Self-Employment in Israel

Are there alternative paths to social mobility that are less reliant on educational attainment beyond high school or on an achievement-based hierarchy? Are there social mobility tracks that circumvent the educational disadvantages of ethnic groups? One such path for ethnic social mobility may be by way of ethnic economic networks that operate through self-employment or family-economic connections. There are important aspects of self-employment that connect to ethnic continuity. First, self-employment means greater direct control over one's own job and, indirectly, greater reliance on family for resources and connections. Working in a family business or being self-employed may also involve power over resources to be distributed to others, and where appropriate, to co-ethnics. It often implies the formation of networks and contacts with others in similar positions. My question is whether there are ethnic differences in self-employment and whether working for oneself (or more broadly for one's family) is an alternative avenue for social mobility that is less connected to educational attainment. Self-employment would be a form of ethnic entrepreneurship that reinforces ethnic distinctiveness and at the same time reduces ethnic economic disadvantage.

In Israel, there is a small proportion of the employed who work for themselves; they have a higher rate of income than those who work for others but have lower levels of education. Given that the income returns to self-employment are greater than that obtained by working for others and that educational levels are lower, self-employment appears to be a potential source of social mobility for some ethnic communities outside of the educational system. Since a major source of the lower socioeconomic position of Israelis of Asian and African origins is their continuing lower level of education and the occupation gap, the question of substitute paths to social mobility, circumventing the educational system, takes on particular importance.

As in other countries, there have been steady declines over time in self-employment in Israel. The proportion of self-employed declined from 21 percent in 1961 to 13 percent in 1970 and to 7 percent in 1999. Among Jewish men of European-American origin the decline was sharper. Self-employment has remained relatively steady among Asian-African-origin Jewish men. Indeed, the percentage of self-employment among men age 25 and over in 1983 was about the same for European-American Jews, Asian-African Jews, and Arabs (Nahon 1989).

Are these self-employment patterns characteristic of the dichotomous constructed Jewish ethnic groups (Asian-Africans and European-Americans), or are there internal country-of-origin differences that are masked by these divisions? Overall, there is not a clear European-American and Asian-African origin dichotomy, since the proportion of self-employed Iranian and Iraqi Jews is significantly higher than among Yemenite and Moroccan Jews but is closer to Russian and Bulgarian-Greek Jews. A more detailed look at the self-employed who are employers splits more dichotomously into the two broader ethnic groups, with greater homogeneity within these two broad groups than between them (Nahon 1989, Appendix table 3).

Self-employment patterns need to be further refined by categorizing occupational level, since the different meaning of self-employment for carpenters and for physicians is substantial. This is particularly the case when we focus on the social mobility and stratification implications of self-employment. In the 1980s, with only minor exceptions, Asian-African-origin Jewish males had higher self-employment levels than did European-American-origin Jewish males in every job category that was blue-collar, and they had lower levels of self-employment in every high-level white-collar job category. Thus, the occupational inequality between ethnic groups in overall occupational distribution extends to job concentration and self-employment. Most importantly, ethnic occupational inequality characterizes the youngest age groups of the Israeli born.

When the linkage between education and occupation is added to the self-employment equation, the evidence becomes even sharper: The correlation between educational level and occupation is weaker among the self-employed than among the employed. Although education remains an important factor among the determinants of occupation even among the self-employed, it is less significant than among those who work for others. The ethnic gap in self-employment increased between 1961 and 1983 and among those young adults socialized in Israel, but somewhat less so than among those who work for others (Nahon 1989). More recent data from the 1995 census have not yet been available to confirm these patterns for the 1990s.

An intergenerational finding of importance documents that the economic success of the Jews of Asian-African origins who are self-employed is translated into the educational achievement of their children. There is some intergenerational inheritance of self-employment, for both Asian-Africans and European-Americans. Research carried out in the late 1980s showed that Asian-African-origin Jews who were self-employed in partnership with others were more likely than European-American-origin Jews to prefer to be partners with their brothers, even after controlling for the number of brothers (Nahon 1989). Thus, self-employed European-American-origin Jews exhibit a wider economic network that is nonfamilial than do self-employed Asian-African-origin Jews. The connection between education and self-employment appears to be weaker at the individual level but stronger intergenerationally—educational attainment does not appear to strongly affect the likelihood of higher education of the next generation. As the labor force structure of Israel's economy changes and self-employment levels are reduced even further, the major impact of self-employment as an avenue for ethnic social mobility has to be through the educational system.

Income and Consumption

When one examines the economic mobility patterns of Asian-African- and European-American-origin Jews, it is clear that those who came from European countries started with an initial advantage with their concentration in professional, managerial, and clerical occupations. Evaluated by relative earnings, the Jews of European-American origin and their children continue their economic advantage over those of Asian-African origin (Ben-Porath 1986). As a result of the exposure to Israeli society, Asian-African Jews were transformed twice: First, they were directed into agriculture, and the relative earnings gap between Asian-African and European-American Jews became larger in Israel than in their countries of origin. In the 1960s and 1970s, the exit of Asian-African Jews from agriculture and entry into blue-collar and some white-collar occupations occurred, but European-American Jews entered into white-collar occupations, abandoning all others. The economic gap in the second generation grew even larger than that of their parents, so that upward mobility was more marked in the group that was more advanced to begin with (Ben-Porath).

Consistent with my findings regarding self-employment, the convergence in earnings among ethnic groups was faster than it was in occupational and educational levels. A review of earnings and income differentials by ethnic origin, based on an income survey conducted by the Central Bureau of Statistics, shows that ethnic origin–related income differences have narrowed over time (Ben-Porath 1986). Income differences by country of origin appeared in the late 1960s to stem almost entirely from educational differences (Ginor 1986). These reflected the background of immigrants and the differential exposure of the second generation to educational opportunities in Israel. But the continuing ethnic educational differences among the Israeli-born Jews have implications for perpetuating the economic disadvantages of Asian-African-origin Jews, even as some small proportion may circumvent the education-occupation connection through self-employment. The process of finding alternative avenues to the educational system as a means of increasing income will result in a reinforcement of ethnic distinctiveness, although not necessarily in conspicuous earnings differences or in standards of living. The differences may be in the emphasis on educational attainment of the next generation or the cultural values associated with higher levels of education. Although we should not expect major differences in consumption patterns among ethnic groups, we should expect continued ethnic differences in lifestyles and values.

Measures of consumption patterns among ethnic groups point in the direction of greater equalization. The ethnic gap in purchases of consumer durables in basic commodities declined in the 1960s (e.g., refrigerators and washing machines); in the 1970s, the ethnic gap declined in purchases of cars, telephones, and entertainment equipment, and differences in housing density declined as well. However, government policies to fully close the ethnic gap among Jews in the standard of living and in human capital—such as health and education and housing and income redistribution, through taxes and transfers—confronted other forces that were operating to preserve and increase the gap and perpetuate it generationally. Some of these forces are embedded in family and households, in different locations within the country, and in the differential endowments with which workers enter the labor force (school and family). The extension of universal education in Israel in the 1950s and the subsequent expansion of vocational training helped close the gap at the base of the occupational pyramid, but this was countered by expansion at the upper end of the educational system, largely serving the European-American-origin Jewish population. The provision of public employment to women was more beneficial to European-American-origin Jewish women than it was to others. In the transfer system, the emergence of the elderly population of Jews of European-American origin and the decline in the fertility of Asian-African-origin Jewish women offset part of the effects on the ethnic gap of child allowances. The advantages of the early arrival of immigrants involved the priority in employment and the accumulation of skills by origin, and also capital gains from the early acquisition of real estate. The massive involvement of the government in housing was designed to partly offset this, but it had a restricted redistributive effect (Ben-Porath 1986).

Concluding Observations

Intergenerational mobility has not fully closed the educational or occupational gap between immigrant Jewish groups and their children. Although every ethnic group has been characterized by social mobility, the ethnic gap has not fully diminished and, at times, it has even widened. Thus, inequalities have persisted, even with rapid development and economic growth and the development of new opportunities in a relatively open stratification system (Kraus and Hodge 1990). Ethnic differences in economic, social, cultural, and political spheres extend to the second and third generations born in Israel. Social inequality can be only partially explained by the different socioeconomic backgrounds of these ethnic groups. Exposure to Israeli society has led to social mobility but has also reinforced disadvantage among some as the economy has changed and the demands for a more educated labor force have increased. The economic integration of immigrant populations in Israel resulted in continuing forms of ethnic distinctiveness; social mobility did not necessarily result in greater equality or in the elimination of the socioeconomic gap between groups. Ethnic residential concentration among areas and within large metropolitan areas are central to the perpetuation of Israel as an ethnically divided society. This conclusion applies to the ethnic divisions among the Jewish population and clearly characterizes the Arab-Jewish distinction. The immigration of a large number of Russian immigrants in the 1990s with high levels of education and occupational experience is likely to result in the perpetuation of the ethnic gap that disadvantages those from Asian and African origins. This may be particularly the case among the children of the Russian immigrants who are likely to attain higher levels of education and become more prepared for Israel's expanding technological sectors.

Socioeconomic differences are not the only manifestations of ethnic inequality. I consider questions of ethnic differences in mortality and health to examine how socioeconomic differences are translated into "life chances." Moreover, ethnicity and gender are often intertwined and form an additional basis of inequality. In the Israeli context, gender differences interact with ethnic origin and reinforce ethnic distinctiveness at the family-household levels. I turn to a consideration of these forms of inequality in the next two chapters.

Notes

1. A similar distinction is made in my review of ethnic differences in sociodemographic process (Chapter 2).

2. A review of gender factors and stratification is presented in greater detail in Chapter 8; demographic inequalities are reviewed in Chapter 9.

3. I make a similar argument in Chapter 9, in the context of inequality as indicated by mortality levels among ethnic populations in Israel.

4. For more detailed statistical evidence, see Nahon 1987, table 4. Compare similar patterns for mortality and fertility differentials by ethnic origin and generations in Chapters 9 and 11.

5. See Inbar and Adler 1977 on the higher levels of educational attainment of Moroccan brothers who immigrated to France compared to those who immigrated to Israel.

6. Among Asian-African-origin girls, the rate of enrollment in academic institutions is twice as high as that of boys (Shavit 1984). This gender difference has implications for ethnic intermarriages and the nature of the marriage market for Asian-African Jewish women (see Chapter 10.).

8

Changing Roles of Israeli
Women and Men

Socioeconomic differences among ethnic groups are clear indicators of inequality, particularly when there is evidence of the generational persistence of social classes and when ethnic socioeconomic distinctiveness means economic disadvantage. Another source of inequality involves gender roles and statuses. Differences between men and women in access to resources and in translating resources into jobs and income are key aspects of disadvantage. Gender differentials in autonomy and control, in independence and decision making, are conspicuous signs of how distinctive spheres of activity become disadvantageous. The extent to which power in the workplace, within households, and in political and cultural institutions is shared equally between men and women represents the treatment of gender as a difference unattached to disadvantage.

Gender and Inequality: Theory and Mixed Expectations

Changes in gender roles have been part of the revolutionary shifts associated with the modernization of industrialized societies. Along with the transitions toward nuclear family structure and living arrangements that are not family based, there have been major transformations in the roles of women inside and outside of families and the beginning of changes in the roles of men (among others, see Goldscheider and Waite 1991). How are gender changes related to the revolutionary socioeconomic developments that have characterized Israeli society? How are they linked to changes in the family, in ethnic distinctiveness, and in population processes? How are gender differences connected to social and economic inequalities and to political and religious institutions in Israel?

Parallel to changes in socioeconomic inequality in Israel, there are indications that greater equality between men and women is emerging in some spheres in Israel and that the empowerment of women has increased. At the same time, evidence abounds documenting the continuation of traditional gender differences in everyday life and the discrimination against women in key economic, political, and cultural institutions of the society. My focus is on the differences between women and men that can be understood as indicating gender inequality.

The issues associated with the status of women and changing gender roles can be understood in the contexts that have informed this analysis of Israel's changing society. In the context of modernization and westernization, we would expect that increased educational attainment and participation in the paid labor force would broaden the scope of women's activities, provide access to better jobs, and increase their control over their own lives. As Israel's population and economy expanded and diversified, some of the constraints on women's activities should have decreased and new opportunities should have opened for sharing equally with men. As universalistic criteria of achievement and merit filter through the society, women should have equal access to societal rewards and compete more equally with men.

Similarly, the emergence of the nuclear family, the reduction in family size, and the control over reproduction that have come to characterize Israeli society should have led to a reduction in the domestic roles of women, creating greater access to work opportunities outside the home and thereby expanding women's roles beyond mothering, child care, and housework. Combined with later ages at marriage and an elaborate welfare system to care for parents and older relatives, women should increasingly have time within the life course to better take advantage of outside work opportunities and convert their educational advances into good paying jobs. In turn, the monetary rewards and the greater economic autonomy associated with these activities should reduce the economic dependency of women on men. In general, increasing affluence and changing domestic technology should result in lessening the time women spend on household care; life course changes (e.g., increase in the time spent in school, later age at marriage, and decreasing family size) should increase the time available for nonfamily roles, particularly for work in the formal economy.

Education, money, technology, and the changing opportunity structure in the labor market set the stage for alterations in women's nonfamily roles. They combine with changing values emphasizing autonomy and independence to shift the status of women away from family activities and tip the balance toward more equal sharing between spouses. Although there has been a shift toward individualism, Israel remains a family-oriented society with high priorities placed on gender-segregated family roles. Working outside the home and having a small family size do not automatically extricate women from the control of their families, husbands, or fathers. When women work in part-time jobs, in gender-segregated occupations, and retain responsibilities for household activities, working outside the home may extend gender inequality and result in a "double burden" on women, rather than their empowerment and increased independence from the control of men and their dependency on families. This double burden may be exacerbated if women are unable to translate their years of schooling into jobs comparable to men and when they cannot successfully compete in outside employment because they lack access to primary sources of power.

Educational attainment, occupational concentration, and economic discrimination are all part of the puzzle in understanding the role of gender in Israeli society. There are other facets related to this issue that are institutional and cultural. How do political and religious institutions deal with issues of gender? Are there forms of ideological commitments or legal discrimination against women that shape and reflect how Israeli society reinforces gender differences? Are there values and attitudes that are shared by significant sectors of the population that define women's and men's roles as different and are used to justify discrimination, inequality, and continued subordination? How have the various political transitions in nation-building and the shifts in the centrality of the military affected gender roles? The answers to these questions focus attention on the ways that specific institutional features of Israeli society may have shaped gender inequalities.

Cutting across issues of gender stratification, institutional structures related to gender, and attitudes and values about the roles of men and women is the changing ethnic and religious composition of Israeli society. This is a particular feature of Israeli society that has an important role in shaping gender issues. The differing ethnic origins of the Jewish population represents different exposures to the openness of their societies of origin to women's employment, status, and roles in society and the family. Ethnicity is connected to different levels of education and to jobs, to resources people have and to how they are used. Those from Western and European societies have been exposed for a longer period of time to greater gender equality and to values and attitudes that were more open to a wide range of roles for women. Israelis of Western origin were socialized in their homes and in schools with images of women who had access to the world outside of families and whose commitments to gender equality and independence were valued.

In contrast, Israelis from Middle Eastern societies originated from communities characterized by high levels of gender segregation. They were more likely to have been socialized in families emphasizing the centrality of the place of women in the domestic economy, their responsibilities as mothers and wives, and their subordination to male power. In general, among Jews of Middle Eastern origin, women were more dependent on men and subordinate to them, and women's roles were located in separate spheres of activities. Ethnic divisions among Jews may be associated with gender differences in the extent of employment outside the home, in levels of education, and in different levels of commitment to family values. The critical questions are whether socialization and educational exposure in Israeli society results in greater equality between men and women in diverse spheres of activity and whether there is a tendency toward convergence in gender differences among the Israelis born of different ethnic origins.

In this chapter, I follow these mixed theoretical orientations and sketch in broad strokes the different contexts in which gender matters in Israel. I assess how changes in Israeli society have resulted in patterns of greater gender equality in different social activities. First, I review issues of education, labor force, and occupational concentration. I then turn to gender factors in military, political, and religious institutions and the role of women in contraception and abortion decisions as indicators of the relative independence of women from families and from men. Together, these pieces of the puzzle provide clues about the relative autonomy of women of various backgrounds in Israel and the trajectory of gender role changes. These changes fit into the broader themes of demographic and ethnic changes in the context of nation-building.[1]

Three cautions need to be highlighted as a backdrop to this assessment of gender inequalities in Israel. First, the pace of change in gender relationships is expected to vary among ethnic groups and is linked to length of exposure to Israeli society. The diversity of Israel's population has implications for understanding the dynamics of change in the society as a whole. The study of the intersection of gender and ethnicity becomes critical in assessing the direction and intensity of changes. Second, the reduction and elimination of the gender gap in one area—e.g., education—does not necessarily imply the absence of gender differences in other areas of social life; vice versa, gender discrimination in one area does not mean discrimination in all areas. Each of the major areas needs to be examined directly rather than by inference. As with indicators of socioeconomic inequality, variation in the extent of gender inequality is expected among the spheres of social life. Third, the reduction in the gender gap in any area cannot always be linked directly to the emergence of new egalitarian norms. Legal and behavioral equalities between men and women do not automatically correlate with norms of gender equality or the empowerment of women. Similarly, differences between men and women do not necessarily imply structural discrimination, state policies, or intentionality. My focus is on forms of gender differentiation and the gender dependencies that have emerged in Israel that are both the legacies of societies of origin and that are sustained by Israeli society.

The Narrowing Gender Gap in Education

Increases in educational attainment have been among the most powerful changes that have characterized Israeli society since the 1950s (Chapter 7). Have these increases been spread equally among men and women? There is clear empirical confirmation of the narrowing of gender differences over time in educational attainment. Overall, in the late 1990s, the median years of schooling for Israelis was the same for men and women (12.2 years); 19 percent of the men and 22 percent of the women had 13 to 15 years of education, and a larger proportion of men than women had 16 or more years of schooling (17 percent and 15 percent, respectively). Most of the gender differences in educational attainment are characteristic of older cohorts, with smaller gender differences for Jews than for Arabs. For example, the median levels of education for Jewish men and women are the same for ages below 55; only for those age 55 and over (and mainly among persons exposed to educational systems outside of Israel) do men have higher educational levels than women.

Although the general level of education among Arabs in Israel is lower than that among Jews (see the discussion in Chapters 4 and 7), the gender gap in years of schooling among Arabs ages 15 to 35 has been largely eliminated: Arab men and women in these age groups have the same average number of years of schooling. At each age over 35, Arab men have higher average levels of education than Arab women. The largest gender difference is among the oldest age group: Almost six out of 10 Arab women over age 65 and four out of 10 ages 55 to 65 had no formal education, compared to 29 percent and 7 percent of the Arab men.[2]

These data point to the conclusion that the gender gap in educational attainment has narrowed for all groups in Israel. Moreover, and not unexpectedly, there remains sharper gender differences among Arabs than among Jews, given the greater gender-segregated lives characterizing Arab Israelis. Inferred from the cross-sectional patterns is the different timing of the closing of the gender gap, which is earlier among Jews than among Arabs. The narrowed educational gap has been influenced in large measure by Israel's educational policy that opened schooling opportunities to both boys and girls. One direct consequence of these policies is that there are no gender differences in years of schooling attained among young Jews and Arabs in the last decade of the twentieth century.

Educational changes for men and women measured for three census years—1961, 1972, and 1983—confirm these conclusions for detailed ethnic origin Jewish populations and among Arabs, and they help to pinpoint the timing of the gender convergence in educational attainment (Table 8.1). Examining gender differences in the number of years of schooling attained reveals a reduction in the gender difference in education for Jews (from 1.4 years in 1961 to 1.0 years in 1983). The gender gap in years of schooling among foreign-born Jews is largely confined to and accentuated among those from Asian and African countries; but the gender gap in years of schooling has declined among them as well. By the 1980s, there was a very small gender gap among the Israeli-born Jewish population. From these data, fewer signs of change in the gender gap may be discerned among Moslems and Druze, but there is a small shift toward a reduced gender gap in years of education starting in the 1970s, consistent with the broader changes that were occurring among Moslems in that decade (see Chapter 4). By the 1990s, trends are discernible toward greater similarity in numbers of years of schooling attained by young Israeli Moslem men and women.

A recent detailed analysis of cohort changes in education documents what it refers to as "the spectacular change" in educational attainment among Arab women. The study documents the substantial transition to completing high school (and the *bagrut*) and the increased participation of Arab women in post-secondary education. This reflects the opportunity structure among Arab Israelis and the large demand for teachers for the expanding Arab Israeli population of children, particularly when significant numbers of the teachers at the elementary school level are women. The general reduction in gender differences in various dimensions of the educational experience among Israeli Arabs does not characterize the transition to post-secondary education that remains relatively low among Arab women (Friedlander et al. 2000). In 1999, 23 percent of Arab Israeli women completed 13 or more years of education, identical to the proportion among Arab men. In contrast, over half of the Jewish Israelis in that age group completed at least 13 years of education. Thus, at the same time that the gender gap in educational attainment within these two ethnic categories has been largely eliminated, the ethnic gap within gender categories has remained very wide. The level of educational attainment at the upper end of the educational distribution is more than twice as high among Jews than Arabs for both men and women.

Are these changing gender gaps in education an indication of a reduction in gender differences in other areas, and do they point to a move toward egalitarian relationships in Israel, as in other more industrialized nations? Tendencies toward similar educational levels by gender are likely to have implications for spheres of both work and family. I now examine several related areas to document whether gender differences have converged and to identify the contexts of greatest change in the gender gap. I begin with changes in the participation of women in the paid labor force.

Working Women: Juggling Part-Time Employment and Families

One of the direct implications of the closing gender gap in education is the connection to the quality of labor market; in particular, how educational attainment is converted into employment for men and for women. At the simplest level, we can document the increasing educational levels of employed women over time and the relative education of employed women and men. Data presented earlier (Chapter 1, Table 1.3) showed that the educational level of employed persons increased between the 1960s and the end of the 1990s. The percentage of employed women with higher levels of education (defined as more than 13 years of schooling) increased from 15 percent in 1963 to 54 percent in 2000; the proportion with less than an eighth-grade education who were employed declined from 45 percent to 4 percent. As of the 1970s, employed Israeli women had a higher level of education than employed men, suggesting that employment may be more selective of women (the more educated) than of men. Fewer women than men who were in the labor force had low levels of education, and more had higher levels. Increased educational level

TABLE 8.1 Gender Differences in Number of Years of Schooling Attained by
Israel's Population, Age 25 and over, 1961, 1972, and 1983, by
Religion and Ethnicity

Religion and Ethnicity	Educational Gap Between Males and Females (in years)		
	1961	*1972*	*1983*
Jews			
Total	1.4	1.3	1.0
Foreign born			
European-American	0.8	0.8	0.8
Asian-African	2.8	2.3	2.0
Israel born			
European-American	0.6	0.7	0.2
Asian-African	1.2	0.7	0.0
Israel born			
Arabs	3.0	1.3	0.4
Total	2.5	2.7	2.8
Christians	1.9	1.4	1.6
Moslems	2.8	2.9	2.6
Druze	2.5	2.5	3.7

Note: The basis of the data in this table may be found in Table 7.2.
Source: Derived from Nahon 1987, Appendix table 1.

raises the quality of the women's labor force and poses directly the question of
whether the labor force participation rate of women has increased.

Indeed, the evidence is clear that there has been a dramatic increase in the
labor force participation of women in Israel from less than 30 percent overall
until the 1970s to 47 percent in 1999 (Table 8.2). The increase reflects the increased levels of education of women, the changing labor market structure in Israel, the changing ethnic composition of the population, and family size
changes. The increase has been most striking in the working patterns of mothers,
the opening up of opportunities for part-time employment, mainly in the service sector, and the greater availability of child care facilities. In earlier cohorts,
women entered the labor force before marriage and before bearing children,
withdrew as they were raising their young children, and reentered when their
children grew up and were in school. Life-course employment patterns of Israeli

TABLE 8.2 Percentage of Israeli Women Participating in the Labor Force, by
Age, 1955–1999

	1955	1965	1970	1975	1980	1985	1990	1999
All women	27	29	29	32	36	38	41	47
Ages								
14–17	32	27	18	11	11	9	9	8
18–34	32	38	39	42	47	48	51	56
35–54	26	31	33	39	46	52	60	69
55–65	17	23	22	22	26	25	30	35
65+	5	6	5	6	7	6	7	5

Source: *Statistical Abstract of Israel,* various years.

women resembled an M-shaped pattern, with changes and variations due to the
timing of marriage, childbearing, and child rearing. Replacing the M pattern was
an emergent inverted U-shaped pattern—women entered and remained in the
labor force through children, preschool, and schooling of children, exiting from
the labor force, like men at retirement. The first signs of the transformation from
an M to an inverted U was among Israelis of European-American origin; more
recently, the switch-over has characterized Israelis of Asian-African origin. Labor
force participation rates of Arab women remain significantly below that of Jewish women (see also the review in Ben-Porath 1986).

Features of the increased labor force participation of Israeli women over time
may be summarized as follows (see Tables 8.2 and 8.3):

1. The proportion of Israeli women in the labor force was 27 percent in
   1955, and it increased to 47 percent in 1999. The increase was sharper for
   women ages 35 to 54: 7 out of 10 were in the labor force in 1999, more
   than 2.5 times the participation rate in 1955.
2. As the number of children age 14 and under in the household increases,
   the proportion of Jewish women in the labor force decreases; as their children get older, the proportion of women in the labor force increases. Over
   60 percent of the women with their youngest child below age 1 worked,
   compared to 80 percent with children ages 10 to 14.
3. Israeli women of Asian and African origins are less likely to be in the labor
   force than those of European-American origins, reflecting differences in
   family formation and educational background and different priorities
   about the balance of family and work, particularly among mothers with
   young children. Israeli women of all ethnic origins with the same number

TABLE 8.3 Percentage of Married Israeli Women Participating in the Labor Force, by Selected Characteristics, 1999

	In Labor Force (%)	Children at Home (None)	(Some)	Age of Youngest Child 0–1	3–9	10–14
All married women	55	41	73	62	78	80
Age						
15–34	71	79	69	63	78	79
35–44	78	83	77	62	80	84
45+	39	34	72	–	70	75
Place of birth						
Asian-African	38	29	65	51	70	71
European-American	46	36	76	58	80	85
Israel	71	65	73	64	79	79
Years of Schooling						
0–8	15	12	40	28	37	50
9–12	55	43	67	53	72	76
13+	70	59	82	71	87	88
Employ household help						
None	53	40	70	58	75	78
Some	64	46	86	80	90	88
Less than 15 hours	65	50	85	75	88	89
16 or more hours	66	33	89	89	93	–

Source: *Statistical Abstract of Israel 2000,* table 12.6.

of children at home and the same level of education have more similar labor force participation rates.

4. The different levels of education that characterized the women of these different ethnic groups and the resultant higher rate of labor force participation of Israeli women of Western origin indicate that Asian-African-origin Jewish women contribute less financially to the household. Hence, household income of Israelis of Middle Eastern origin is lower than those of Western origin, even when husbands have the same occupations.

5. The more years of schooling completed, the higher the rate of labor force participation. The differences are quite impressive: from a labor force participation rate of 15 percent among married women with low educational levels to 70 percent among those with 13 or more years of schooling. The

pattern is no less characteristic of those with and without young children at home. Among those with infants at home, 28 percent of the least-educated women work, compared to 71 percent of the most-educated women.

6. Having household help at home enhances the labor force participation of Israeli women. Though 53 percent of the women without help at home work in the labor force, 66 percent of those with 16 or more hours of help work outside the home. Having help is a reflection both of educational level and of resources available and does not include family assistance. The causal direction of this association is not clear, since women work because they have access to and are able to afford child care assistance, and women develop child care assistance because they work outside of the home.

7. Women are considerably more likely to work part-time than are men. From the 1980s to the early 1990s, about 15 percent of Israel's civilian male labor was working part-time. During the same period, the percentage of women engaged in part-time work was closer to 40 percent, over 2.5 times higher than that of men. There has been a trend, although not linear, toward an increase over time in the proportion of working women who work part-time from about 30 percent in the 1950s and 1960s, to 35 percent in the 1970s, and to 40 percent in the 1980s and 1990s. At the same time that the percentage of women participating in the labor force has increased, the proportion working part-time has increased as well.

Occupational Concentration, Feminization, and Discrimination

The increase in the labor force participation of Israel's women clearly documented in these official data reflects the expansion of the Israeli economy and the demand for more educated workers, particularly in the public sector and in financial and business services.[3] At the same time that an increase in the participation of women in the formal labor force has occurred, an almost complete feminization of certain occupations has also taken place (Ben-Porath 1986; studies cited in Azmon and Izraeli 1993). This pattern appears in the detailed specific occupation categories, not in the crude occupational distributions. This highly gender-segregated job structure can be documented in a variety of ways. In 1990, for example, three-fourths of the female labor force was employed in only 3 of the 9 major occupation categories, and one-half was concentrated in only 8 of 90 occupations (Azmon and Izraeli 1993).

There are, therefore, three interrelated dimensions of the labor discrimination against women in Israel: (1) men and women in the same job are differentially treated; that is, women with similar characteristics and skills as men are promoted less and rewarded less for similar jobs; (2) there is a concentration of women in particular jobs; that is, a process of feminization of particular occupations has occurred, in which the fringe benefits of particular jobs are less when they are occupied by women; and (3) part-time workers have significantly fewer benefits than do full-time workers, and women are more likely than men to have part-time jobs.

Even in those industries in which the criteria of promotion and salary are presumably based on merit and achievement, gender factors seem to operate. In one study of scientists in one large Israeli industry, research demonstrated that Israeli men and women experienced differential rates of promotion to the detriment of women. Although there was no direct discrimination in the wages of men and women scientists, women professional employees experienced salary discrimination. Since promotional practices affect wages, discrimination in promotional employment practices resulted in gender discrimination in wages (Shenhav and Haberfeld 1993). The number of women on a career track in academic jobs is small and concentrated in the lower echelons of the academic scale. There is little pay difference within the scale, but the different jobs of men and women result in a discriminatory pattern (see Toren 1993).

Research comparing women located in jobs dominated by women and those more equally shared by men (and the reverse as well—men in female- and in male-dominated occupations) shows the high level of discrimination against women, measured in terms of income, particularly for women in women-dominated occupations (Moore 1993). Relative to Israeli men, Israeli women, in general, have lower-paying jobs, with lower levels of seniority and authority in occupations or industries, and are more likely to move in and out of the labor force. They are less mobile between occupations and less mobile between geographic regions than are men with comparable educational levels. Their economic networks tend to be fewer and less effective and are located in the jobs where opportunities for promotion and rewards for initiatives are fewer than that for men. When we examine the interaction of gender and ethnic origin, it is clear that Jewish Asian-African-origin men are disadvantaged relative to European-American-origin men, but Jewish Asian-African-origin women are not disadvantaged as much relative to European-American-origin women. Women of all ethnic origins in Israel are disadvantaged relative to men. In sum, gender is a more powerful differentiator than is ethnicity in the occupational distribution within the Jewish population of Israel. Put more directly, ethnic disadvantage is less than gender disadvantage in the Israeli labor market (Neuman 1991; Semyonov and Kraus 1983; see also Hartman 1993).

There is also some evidence that suggests an interaction effect of ethnicity and gender. Research has documented that ethnic differences in rates of labor force participation and in the occupational prestige of women reflect differences in the educational, socioeconomic, and related demographic characteristics. There are major ethnic differences in the attitudes toward women working and concerning the balance of work and household responsibilities. These attitudes are likely to have an impact on the priorities assigned to work and to family among ethnic groups in Israel (Hartman 1993).

Even though discrimination on the basis of gender is not legal, there have been no affirmative action policies in Israel. Consequently, there has been no alteration in job recruitment by gender or in job allocation, promotion, and reward. The increase in labor force participation of women also reflects the structure of jobs that are more likely to be part-time for women and linked to family, household, and child care needs. I have already noted that the proportion of women who were part-time workers increased from the 1950s to the late 1990s, when it represented about one out of three women workers in the labor force.

In addition, research has shown that women spend twice as much time in child care as men do and are much more involved in housekeeping, whether or not they are employed outside the home. Working in the formal labor force does not decrease the time women spend on child rearing or on housekeeping (Azmon and Izraeli 1993). As a result, there is a gendered division of labor in the home and at work. Patterns of increased labor force participation of women, combining work and family activities, generate the illusion of gender equality rather than an increasing double burden placed on women. Standards of living rise, outside activities increase, household incomes improve, and there is less pressure to remark on gender inequalities and a decreased sensitivity to gender discrimination. Together, these factors explain the absence of major protests by women about the occupational inequalities between men and women.[4]

Moreover, jobs are often controlled by patronage in Israel, so that networks and connections are often the primary sources of information and control (Danet 1989). In jobs controlled by the state, political considerations (often gender related) are critical. One review of labor force activities of women summarizes occupational gender patterns as follows:

> Women remain virtually absent from positions of influence within all the major economic institutions owned by either the Labor party–dominated Histradut (the Federated Labor Union) or by the government, which together employ the majority of the labor force…. Rather than promoting equal opportunity, current social policy tends to support a system in which the majority of women are on an often-invisible "mommy track." Their place in the occupational structure is paradoxical: their jobs are relatively high status, but their wages are low, and they rarely occupy the top-level positions of power and prestige (Azmon and Izraeli 1993, pp. 4–5).

The critical changes that link labor force with gender roles is the extent to which working outside the home in the formal economy carries over to the home and to other institutions of the society—politics and religion, for example. In this regard, the evidence is clear: Increased labor force participation of women has not equalized the roles of women and men inside the work force or outside of it.

Women and the Military

Like working mothers, women soldiers are often portrayed as symbols of equality in Israel. And like the implications of the examination of the specific jobs that women have in civilian life, a review of studies of women in the military illustrates the ways their distinctive roles are indicators of discrimination. This is particularly the case since military service is often the basis for recruitment into higher-level positions in the civilian labor force. The military is a deeply gendered institution. The careers of men and women in the military are significantly different and have consequences for the status of women in general in the society (Azmon and Izraeli 1993). Indeed, the military institution of Israel and its segregation of women into separate jobs and different career paths is more likely to perpetuate gender inequality than to be a force for change in gender roles.

There are two ways in which the military experiences of women should be viewed as discriminatory. First, and most directly, the kind of responsibilities that women and men have in the military are very different. It is not merely the absence of combat roles for women, but instead, women's responsibilities are almost always subordinate to men and under male control. Promotion and reward in the military are less accessible to women. Second, and more indirectly, experience in the military is often the basis for recruitment for elite managerial and political positions in the civilian labor force. The absence of women in these arenas reduces their ability to use the military (as men do) as a vehicle for job networking and recruitment in civilian life. Thus, in contrast to the gender egalitarian image of the Israeli military, service in the armed forces more often than not reinforces the subordinate and less-powerful status of women in the society.

Military service is compulsory for both Jewish men and women, but, unlike men, women are excluded for reasons of marriage, parenthood, and on religious grounds. In 1990, just over two-thirds of the cohorts of 18-year-old women were conscripted into the military, compared to 56 percent in the mid-1970s. Most of the increase is due to changes in the educational and socioeconomic requirements for conscription (Azmon and Izraeli 1993). The results of a detailed study of the 1954 birth cohort show that almost all of the men (94 percent) served in the Israel Defense Force, but only one-third of the Jewish women of Middle Eastern origin and 57 percent of those of Western origin served. These differences are related in part to the lower educational attainments of women of Middle Eastern origin and the resistance to military service among those who are from more religious families, which are more characteristic of this ethnic origin group. Within each educational attainment subgroup, the percentage of women serving in the Israel Defense Force was higher among Western-origin women than among Middle Eastern origin–women.

What are the effects of schooling and military service on subsequent occupational attainments and social participation of Israeli men and women? A pioneering study of the links between military service and actual occupational attainments over the life course showed the importance of serving in the Israel armed service and the role of military rank in enhancing subsequent occupational prestige in the civilian labor force, net of socioeconomic background and education (Matras, Noam, and Bar-Haim 1984; Matras and Noam 1987). The army experience had a positive effect on the accumulation of human capital, responsibility, and authority in roles; established "connections" and networks; and provided nonfamily (or at least semiautonomous) living experiences. Military service had a significant effect on occupational prestige scores of women but affected jobs closest in time to that service, with a reduced effect over time. Ethnicity remains an important factor in women's occupational prestige (unlike for men), which may reflect the role of work among Western-origin women that is different than that among Middle Eastern–origin women or may indicate their use of "connections" to obtain better jobs.

The argument that women's roles in the military negatively affect later traditional roles or that serving in the army is a liberating experience are, therefore, both exaggerations. The effects of military service are modest at best. Many women reside at home during their military service and are likely to be engaged in gender-segregated clerical roles that are powerless. Family connections are unlikely to be fully severed by being in the Israeli military, and the liberating effects are limited as well.

Taken together, the evidence seems to point to the conclusion that the military experience is more likely to reflect the society than to shape it. Service in the army is not able to help women overcome the more entrenched and powerful effects of differential education by ethnicity and differential family background and experiences. Given the gender-segregated job allocations in the army, the closeness of army personnel to family life (as semiautonomous living), and the army's selectivity, gender-segregated attitudes and traditional roles are likely to be reinforced in this setting.

There is another aspect of the military that relates to the role of women and their place in the household. The reinforcement of traditional gender roles occurs generationally. When sons and daughters begin compulsory military service at age 18, parenting becomes more intense and support roles are expected from the family.[5] As in the care of the elderly, these family-based support systems involve a disproportionate amount of mother's than father's time. Moreover, war and military activities in a conflict situation intensify the salience of primary relationships. The family and, particularly, the role of women within the family are emotional anchors, especially in such family-oriented societies as Israel. In the media and in informal settings, female roles are regularly portrayed during wars as supportive and expressive (Bar-Yosef and Padan-Eisenstark 1993).

Gender, Politics, and Religion

Discrimination against women is not limited to the formal labor force, to their concentration in specific occupations, and to their service in the military. Political and religious institutions are conspicuous in their limited representation of women and their reinforcement of the separate spheres of women's activities. I start with political institutions.

Although women were formally granted equal rights by the Declaration of Israeli Independence, including the right to vote, the number of women in elected positions at all levels is small. The representation of women in the highest elected offices, as members of the Knesset (the Israeli parliament), has always been small and has not increased in recent years. Over the last five decades, less than 10 percent of the members of the Knesset have been women. Even at the local level, less than 10 percent of the political officials are women, although their numbers have increased over the past decades (Azmon and Izraeli 1993, p. 14; see also Azmon 1990). Some research has pointed to the disadvantaged position of women in political power in Israel and the impediments that are gender related, including the fact that political power is largely controlled by men and that women are socialized into family roles (Etzioni-Halevi and Illy 1993). Women have rarely played representative roles at the local level, in party caucuses, and in the power negotiations behind the scenes. Although there have been political parties in Israel that have focused on women's rights, they have been marginal to political power.

One of the spheres in which women are clearly discriminated against is the politics of religion in Israel. In addition to the formal responsibility over all religious rituals and institutions, the Orthodox religious establishment in Israel has always controlled the critical areas of marriage and divorce regulation. Religious institutions and the rabbis that control them have not been responsive to the religious needs of women and have normatively and legally reinforced the subordinate roles of women in their separate spheres. The emphasis on family roles (and indirectly, the priority of family over other roles) by all-male religious hierarchy has institutionalized the disadvantaged and powerless position of women over the rituals of Judaism (prayer services, religious leadership, ritual dietary supervision, and judges in religious courts) and over the role of women in marriage and family life. The religious establishment in its interpretation of Judaism and in its politics reinforces the lower and disadvantaged position of women as independent decision makers and ignores, in large part, their spiritual needs.

The religious establishment in Israel, including the chief rabbis, are political appointments. Religious-based political parties have in the past been important coalition partners in Israel's political system (Arian 1985; Arian and Shamir 1994) and have extracted political control over "personal status"—marriage and the definition of who is Jewish, a critical dimension in a society in which Jewishness has profound political significance—as part of the political exchange and bargaining. The only legitimate Judaism in Israel, supported and sponsored by the government, is Orthodox. This denies formal religious representation to those Jews who are religiously Jewish in the context of other Judaisms. These non-Orthodox Judaisms represent over 80 percent of the Israeli Jewish population.[6] Thus, other Judaisms that have a more egalitarian gender theology and that have been, in other contexts, flexible with regard to the allocation of religious and political nonfamily roles to women are not part of the religious establishment, in either the religious Zionist or the non-Zionist (Agudah) political forms.

The male religious establishment's control over the divorce process has severely alienated a small group of women whose husbands have refused to provide them with a divorce, thus preventing the remarriage of these women. There is no secular or civil marriage in Israel and there is no recognition of divorce that is not a "get," a religious divorce. In traditional Jewish practice, only men had the right to divorce their wives, although religious courts often exercised their power to encourage men to grant a divorce. The *agunah* status (wherein a woman is unwillingly tied to her husband either because he has refused to grant her a divorce or has disappeared voluntarily or otherwise and hence she cannot remarry) symbolizes in dramatic and painful ways gender inequalities in Israel. The number of women in this state of helplessness is relatively small, but it reveals how institutions and their representatives continue to subordinate women's rights to male authority and to the controlling power of the Orthodox religious establishment.

In addition to the politics of religion, which clearly reveals the disadvantaged role of women in Israeli society, women and men have developed different relationships to the rituals and values of Judaism and different conceptions of the religious role: Israeli Jewish women tend to view religion in interpersonal terms, as in helping and caring for others; for men, religion means study and prayer. When women perform religious rituals, it is to help others in distress, the ill or the troubled. When men aid the sick or the poor, they tend to emphasize the more ceremonial aspects of Judaism. Hence, the concept of religion and religiosity mean different things to men and women (see Sered 1993). These differences reflect the separate ways that religion impinges on the lives of men and women. When this gender difference results in differential power and control, the difference is disadvantageous to women.

Families and Power: Abortion and Contraception

The central role of women in families in Israel is clear, and their often disadvantaged status follows from that role. In a subsequent analysis, I detail the familism that characterizes Israeli society and show the changing importance of women in perpetuating that centrality (Chapter 10). Nevertheless, even in the realm of family activity, the role of women tends to be subordinate to men. Changes in fertility in Israel have facilitated the increase in female labor force participation that I previously documented. Among younger cohorts, almost all women have been employed in the formal labor force, and this has been correlated with their decreasing family size (Chapter 11; also Matras 1986). The decrease in family size should facilitate the expansion of women's work in the paid labor force.

In a related way, an examination of the sources of fertility reduction in terms of the means by which couples have planned their family size and the number and timing of births reveals again the more powerless role of women in Israeli society. An examination of contraceptive usage and birth control points to a concentration in the past on coitus interruptus and abortion (Friedlander and Goldscheider 1984). These mechanisms, in large part, place women under the control of men, their husbands, and the medical establishment. Although there is a recent tendency toward greater use of the contraceptive pill for birth control, there remains a continuing pattern of male contraceptive methods or abortion.

Unlike in other societies, abortion is used in Israel among married women as a last resort, when less-efficient contraception has been used and when the pressure to control family size is high. For women who married in the 1940s and were living in Israel in the early 1970s, abortion was used more by those of European origin than by those of Asian-African origin, a continuation of patterns observed in their countries of origin; among cohorts who married in the period from 1965 to 1974, no ethnic differences were evident (Yaffe 1976). It is likely that the religious factor is the major differentiator of abortion patterns, with women from more religious families less likely to have abortions.

Official estimates from 1980s and the 1990s put the number of legal abortions close to 20,000, about one-fourth the number of live births. This appears to be a reduction in the estimated 50,000 to 60,000 abortions in the late 1960s and 1970s, which was equivalent to the number of annual Jewish births. The reduction was likely brought about by the increasing use of more efficient contraception. About two-thirds of the total legal abortions in the 1980s were performed on married women (Sabatello and Yaffe 1988). In 1999, 60 percent of the legal terminations of pregnancy were to married women, and most of those were to women over the age of 30.

What emerges from these scattered data is that the pressure for fertility control results in turning to abortion, even when illegal, as a backup to contraceptive failure. The use of more efficient contraceptive practices and the greater access to modern contraception among Jewish women of European origin results in their lower rates of abortion. In contrast, the lower socioeconomic status of Asian-African-origin Jewish women and their large family size ideals are likely to result in their wanting more children, using contraception less efficiently, having less access to abortions, and aborting less when contraception fails. Contraceptive practices and abortion, for many Israeli women, reinforce their subordinate status to men and their traditional family roles.

Gender Equality in the Kibbutz: Myth and Reality

It is not surprising that women in Israeli society have been in subordinate roles and that they have been dependent on men and the institutions they control. Israeli women share this condition with women around the world. One would have predicted that these inequalities would be more pronounced for women from gender-segregated societies and cultures and that the trajectory of change would be toward more equal gender roles. As I suggested previously, there are some indications that changes are occurring but that institutions, particularly those controlled by men in religion and politics, reinforce the traditional separate spheres of men and women. The emphasis on family centrality and the role of women as guardians of family values constrains the shift toward greater gender equality in the society as a whole.

One would expect that egalitarian gender roles would characterize Kibbutz communities in Israel.[7] Founded on an ideology of equality, with an emphasis on communal responsibilities for family and work, the Kibbutz should be the ideal economic and family setting for more equal gender roles to emerge. And there is some basis for this assessment in the division of labor among Kibbutz members and the shared activities in family and labor.

Yet, it is not surprising that the Kibbutz falls far from the ideal of equality. What is unexpected is that research has documented greater gender occupational segregation in the Kibbutz than in Israel as a whole. This finding contrasts sharply with the expected Kibbutz environment, which should be conducive to occupational equality between men and women, given the deep ideological commitment to equality, high valuation of work, an egalitarian educational system, and collectivization of household work that allows women to develop careers. Although production is not necessarily contributed to equally by gender, equality governs the distribution of income. A striking finding of that research is that occupational segregation on gender grounds is much higher than it is on ethnic grounds—gender occupational segregation is more than double that of ethnic segregation in the Jewish population. The occupational status of women in the Kibbutz is simply inferior to that of women in the rest of Israel (Neuman 1991).

Despite the absence of salaries and income in the Kibbutz, fewer women than men have access to resources. Kibbutz men have more access than women to cars and travel and occupational training. Men are, on the whole, more autonomous economically than women in the Kibbutz and have a wider range of occupational choices. Hence, fewer women acquire the expertise and seniority to become heads of departments or to achieve seniority in positions in the Kibbutz. Like the military and the society as whole, Kibbutz life reinforces aspects of gender inequality (Agassi 1993).

Concluding Observations

In large part, gender inequalities have characterized traditional as well as modern societies for centuries. There are some signs of increased gender equality in Israel, relating to education and increased labor force participation, in formal legal rights and in military service, and in ideological commitments to gender neutrality. Nevertheless, a systematic and careful look at these arenas of social life points to the unmistakable continuation of gender inequalities. There is little evidence in the materials that I have reviewed that indicates that the reduced gender gap in educational attainment levels has been translated directly into occupational and labor force equality. Powerful sources of continued gender discrimination in political, religious, and family institutions result in the disadvantaged status of women in Israel. Indeed, it is likely that these gender-segregated roles are reinforced by the educational system, so that similarity among women and men in the number of years of educational exposure does not necessarily imply similar educational experiences. As in the military, crude measures of exposure to equality in education should not be interpreted as indicators of gender equality.

The aim of the European-based society that formulated the reemergence of the state of Israel was to reorganize the family and work system and the religious and political institutions, in reestablishing Jewish sovereignty. This reorganization was explicitly designed to include greater attention to equality among groups. The inclusion of large numbers of immigrants from gender-segregated societies added a continual challenge to these egalitarian tendencies. Yet, the emergent gender inequalities in Israeli society at the end of the twentieth century were not the simple carryover from the past and from traditional societies outside of Israel, but are Israel-created products. The role of political and religious institutions, as well as the role of the military, in reinforcing and, at a minimum, reflecting inequalities has become a powerful source of gender inequalities among third-generation Israelis.

No less revealing is the occupational segregation of women in Kibbutzim, where control over the distribution of resources and of tasks is collectively managed. There, as elsewhere in Israel, gender patterns are no less segregated (and the evidence suggests even more segregated) and unequal. Whether occupational segregation by gender is a reactionary response to the ideology of equality or a continuing gap between myth and reality, the fact is that nowhere in Israel are there important signs of gender equality in major institutions. Indeed, gender relations in Israel, as well as family processes in general, point to the more traditional basis of Israeli society relative to European and American societies but to a more egalitarian one relative to Third World countries. Again, Israel appears to be straddling the middle, at the crossroads of change, and without a clear direction of development.

Notes

1. There is an increasing social science literature concerning gender issues in Israel, almost always defined in terms of "women's" roles. I draw on some of that research, although many of the questions that I have previously sketched require more systematic and methodologically sophisticated studies than are currently available. For a review and collection of important materials on women in Israel, see Azmon and Izraeli 1993. Important critical assessments of gender inequalities are contained in Hazelton 1977, Rein 1979, and in Swirski and Safir 1991; in Hebrew, see Shamgar-Handelman and Bar-Yosef 1991.

2. For more detailed statistical documentation, see section 22 on education in various issues of the *Statistical Abstract of Israel*. See also Chapter 1, Table 1.1, and Chapter 7, Table 7.2 of this book.

3. I have little information about the character of the informal employment sector. It is likely that for Jewish women the informal sector was in the past a more prominent feature of their work outside the home. It continues to be an important feature of the Arab female population.

4. A similar pattern emerges with regard to ethnic inequalities and the absence of ethnic political protest, since social mobility has characterized all ethnic communities even as the ethnic gap in economic indicators has widened. See the discussion in Chapter 7.

5. This increased parental support is in sharp contrast to the situation in the United States, where significant proportions of young adults leave home at 18 to go to college and to live away from the parental home, thereby increasing autonomy for young adults and reducing parenting responsibilities (Goldscheider and Goldscheider 1993, 1999).

6. On Israeli Judaism see Deshen 1990; Goldscheider and Friedlander 1983; Levy, Levinsohn and Katz 1993; Sobel and Beit-Hallahmi 1991.

7. For a more detailed description of the Kibbutz as a community, see Chapter 6.

9

Inequality and Mortality Decline

The quality of life in society is often revealed by the pattern of death. Societies with high rates of mortality, a heavy concentration of death among infants and children, causes of death that reflect conditions of poor public health and sanitation, and an absence of adequate medical and preventive care are likely to be those where economic development is low, where medical care and access to it are minimal, and where knowledge of disease prevention is limited. Therefore, mortality conditions have often been viewed as indicators of the economic and health contexts of a society and of its quality of life (Goldscheider 1971).

In similar ways, societies in which differential mortality rates characterize subpopulations or regions are likely to have other forms of inequality as well. There are no examples of societies with high mortality levels and systematic differential mortality rates that do not at the same time reflect social and economic inequalities. But the reverse is not necessarily the case: Similar mortality levels do not always imply equality among groups, and high levels of economic development cannot be inferred from low mortality levels. The transfer of death-control technology among countries may obscure inequalities and distort mortality as a measure of development levels.[1] In this chapter, I examine mortality patterns in Israeli society as a whole, with an emphasis on the dramatic reduction in deaths over time and the convergences of mortality differences among population subgroups. I show how changes and fluctuations in death rates offer conspicuous clues about the quality of Israeli life. Using mortality differences as indicators of inequality allows me to specify which types of inequality have characterized the society as a whole.

Mortality levels and differentials reflect how resources in countries are mobilized and used to control the health and welfare of populations. The use and application of resources for the regulation of health and death are, in part, dependent on their availability, but are influenced in powerful ways by the policies and programs that distribute those resources and use them to improve the welfare of people. Into the twenty-first century, extensive technical knowledge about health and death control is available and can be transferred between countries. This knowledge can also be organized to be distributed within a country in a way that increases equality. With the availability of major forms of death control, the ways governments and their institutions deploy resources to improve the quality of life of their populations determine whether mortality levels are low, particularly among infants and children, who are most vulnerable. Public health and medical technology, its development and transfer (internally and internationally)—not economic development alone—have become key factors in the reduction of mortality around the world. Ironically, as public health technology becomes increasingly transferable between places, it is politics, not technology, that emerges as a major source of variation in mortality levels among and within countries.

The links between political and economic development and levels of mortality are manifest in reductions over time in mortality and in the distribution of welfare and health services to the diverse populations in a country. In most pluralistic, Western, more economically developed areas of the world, differences in levels of mortality by social class, economic category, and residence (rural and urban) and among ethnic and racial groups have diminished over time. The greater the variation in mortality among ecological, economic, and racial and ethnic divisions in countries, the more likely that these differences reflect the unequal distribution of resources and the priorities of government investments. Hence, differential mortality rates are reflections of both the inequalities in social life and the values of the political system. In these ways, differential mortality rates are systematic, not random; they are group characteristics and are less likely to be primarily biological or individualistic in origin. Mortality variations are mainly the result of social processes and do not reflect the "tastes" or preferences of populations.

At the most general societal level, mortality rates are an intrinsic part of the population growth process of a country—levels of mortality, together with levels of fertility, shape the "internal" growth of the population (with net immigration rates affecting population size through "external" processes). Therefore, demographers study mortality to analyze the fundamental processes of population change, since the mortality level impinges on population growth and on the structure of the population by age and sex, and affects, and is affected by, the other demographic processes in the population system—fertility and migration rates (see Chapter 1).

In my review of the long-term trends in mortality in Israel, I connect changes in death rates to immigration and political and economic developments since the establishment of the state of Israel. I also examine changes in the distribution of health and medical care reflected by differential rates of death and dying. Because of my examination of the major sources of differential mortality that have characterized Israeli society through most of the twentieth century, I have a basis for assessing the implications of changing mortality rates for population growth and for economic development. Mortality trends and variation offer another context to evaluate the changing inequalities in Israeli society.

Mortality Levels and Changes

I begin by documenting the contemporary mortality pattern in Israel, describing some of the common statistical measures of mortality, particularly those sensitive to the health and welfare of children. What were the patterns of mortality in Israel at the end of the twentieth century? Levels of life expectancy for Israeli society as a whole are comparable to those of the most economically advanced countries of the world. In the late 1990s, life expectancy in Israel was 76 years for Israeli men and 80 years for Israeli women; infant mortality was less than 6.2 deaths per 1,000 births. These levels reflect the widespread availability of medical care and public health services for adults, children, and infants, and an extensive welfare system that protects against the debilitating effects of economic hardship, poverty, and malnutrition.

Most persons who die in Israel do so at older ages, largely from cancer and heart disease. In the late 1990s, there were about 37,000 deaths recorded in Israel annually, a crude death rate of 6.2 deaths per 1,000 population. Most of these deaths were of older persons—78 percent of all deaths in Israel were of persons age 65 or over. In contrast, the percentage of total deaths of persons over age 65 was only 50 percent for the Arab population, reflecting their higher mortality level, their younger age structure, and their higher rates of infant and child deaths. In 1998, 760 children born in Israel died before their first birthdays; over 45 percent of these were Arab infants, disproportionate to their number in the Israeli population (there are 2.5 times as many Jewish children as there are Arab children below age 1).

Improvements in mortality, in general, have been quite dramatic since the 1950s in Israel, particularly among infants and children below age 1. My question is whether mortality levels have decreased for all groups. Have inequalities in death levels among Jews and between Jews and Arabs narrowed with changing levels of mortality? Are there continuing sources of variation in inequality in contemporary Israeli society that would identify groups or areas where differential death rates have been more persistent? Have government policies been supportive, in design and in implementation, of improving the health and welfare of the diverse populations in Israel and thereby narrowing the mortality gap among groups?

The decline in mortality in Palestine and in the state of Israel has been well documented. Life expectancy at birth increased for the Jewish population from about 60 years in the 1930s to 65 years in the 1940s to over 70 years in the late 1950s. By the end of the 1990s, life expectancy was about 78 years, among the highest in the world. Life expectancy among the Moslem population had been 35 to 38 years during the 1920s and 1930s, but it increased to about 50 years during the 1940s (and among Christian Arabs, the increase was from less than 50 years in the 1930s to 60 years in the 1940s). Life expectancy in 1998 was 76 years for the Arab population of Israel.

The infant mortality rate (the number of deaths of infants below age 1 per 1,000 births) is the measure of mortality that tends to be most sensitive to governmental

TABLE 9.1   Infant Mortality of Jews and Moslems in Palestine and Israel,
1925–1998

	Jews	Moslems	Ratio of Moslem to Jewish Deaths
1925	133	173	1.3
1927	117	192	1.6
1930	66	153	2.3
1935	64	148	2.3
1939	54	122	2.3
1946	32	91	2.8
1955–1959	32	61	2.0
1960–1964	25	46	1.8
1965–1969	21	44	2.1
1970–1974	19	40	2.0
1975–1979	15	33	2.2
1980–1984	12	23	1.9
1985–1989	9	17	1.9
1990–1992	8	15	1.9
1993–1995	6	12	2.0
1996–1998	5	10	2.0

Note: Rates are calculated as the number of deaths to infants below the age of 1
year per 1,000 births.
Sources: *Statistical Abstract of Israel,* various years; for the early period, see
Kanev 1957, tables 7 and 9.

policies concerned with mother and child welfare. Data displayed in Table 9.1
show the patterns of infant mortality reduction for both the Jewish and Moslem
sectors, from the 1920s in Palestine to the end of the twentieth century in Israel.
There were dramatic declines for both populations: For Jews there was a systematic
decline, from 133 infants per 1,000 births in 1925 to about 32 deaths per 1,000
births when the state was established and the population was largely European, declining to less than 10 deaths per 1,000 births beginning in the mid-1980s. The
level shifted to around 5 per 1,000 births in the 1996–1998 period. These declines
occurred despite major shifts in the ethnic origin of the Jewish population and the
arrival of a large number of Jewish immigrants from countries characterized by
significantly higher levels of mortality than Israel.

Equally impressive declines in infant mortality may be observed for the
Moslem population in Israel. Starting from a higher level than that of Jews (about
18 percent of all children born to Moslem women in the 1920s did not survive

TABLE 9.2 Infant Mortality Rates per 1,000 Births in Israel, by Religion, 1955–1998

	Total	Jews	Moslems	Christians	Druze
1955–1959	36.5	32.1	60.6	46.1	56.1
1960–1964	29.1	25.3	46.4	42.1	50.4
1965–1969	25.5	20.8	43.8	32.7	43.8
1970–1974	23.5	18.7	40.1	29.6	33.9
1975–1979	18.9	15.0	32.6	20.9	32.1
1980–1984	14.4	11.8	23.0	18.0	22.7
1985–1989	10.9	8.8	17.4	12.1	16.0
1990–1992	9.6	7.7	14.8	8.5	15.8
1994–1996	6.9	5.5	10.9	8.6	8.8
1998–1999	5.8	4.6	8.8	4.8	8.4

Note: The last three annual groupings are estimates.
Source: *Statistical Abstract of Israel,* various years.

their first year), the percentage of Moslem babies not surviving their first year of life decreased to below 10 percent in the mid-1940s, to less than 5 percent in the 1960s, and to 1 percent for the period 1996–1998.[2] A similar reduction in infant mortality characterizes both the Christian and Druze subpopulations, with the Druze pattern closer to the infant (and adult) mortality levels of Moslems and the Christian pattern closer to the patterns of the Jewish population (Table 9.2).

Consistent with these infant mortality rates are the simple data on the number of infants who die before their first birthdays. These numbers reveal that infant deaths impact not only families but also communities and the society as a whole. There has been a decline of 50 percent in the number of infant deaths in Israel as a whole, from 2,000 infant deaths in the 1950s to less than 800 in the late 1990s. The number of Jewish infants who died in their first year of life declined even more sharply, from 1,700 in 1951 to less than 450 in the 1990s. These changes point to the conclusion that deaths in Israel have shifted from being a more common occurrence among the youngest and most vulnerable members of families toward becoming a rare event for infants and a more common pattern among the older age segments of society.

In Israeli society, young adult males have emerged as a new vulnerable age group. They have been exposed to military activities and to wars that have substantially increased their risks of dying. The costs of the Israeli-Arab conflict are reflected in these young adult deaths and in some conspicuous health and disability patterns, as well as in the time spent away from other activities—economic, educational, and family—that active military duty entails. The military obligation in Israel extends beyond the few years of full-time active service for most males (and substantial, if lower, proportions of the unmarried female Jewish population) to include weeks of commitments annually for about 30 years of the life course. The role of politics in shaping the mortality curve by age is nowhere more obvious. As death control from some ages is reduced by the politics of public health and welfare, the increases in deaths to young adults and the costs of increases in widowhood among the young are increased by the politics of war and military conflicts.[3]

The overall dramatic mortality reduction over time reflects the commitment of the government in Israel to provide extensive health and medical care. Mortality levels in Israel are low and reflect well on the general quality of life, the values placed on the health and welfare of children and adults, and the general high level of socioeconomic development and political organization of the society. Nevertheless, it is also clear that the gap between the mortality levels of Jews and Arabs in Israel remains large. Infant mortality data for the 1990s show that rates among Moslems in Israel are about twice as high as that among Jews, despite the major declines in mortality rates in both populations (Table 9.1). The Jewish-Moslem infant mortality gap is greater in the 1990s than it was during the 1920s, when the levels for both populations were much higher. Only during the 1930s and 1940s (based on estimates that are less reliable and for Jewish and Moslem populations that had different characteristics) was the relative gap in infant mortality between these populations higher than in the poststate period. Thus, comparing the current mortality level of each population with its own past reveals impressive mortality declines; comparing long-term infant mortality rates between the Jewish and Moslem populations reveals a continuing health-mortality gap between them that has not decreased over time.

The documentation of the mortality gap between Jews and Arabs, along with mortality reductions over time, raises two broad questions: First, are there other sources of mortality variation that may also indicate social inequalities? Second, what are the structural bases of the inequalities that exist in Israeli society? First, I complete the picture of major mortality variation.

Immigration and Mortality Differentials

Immigration and subsequent ethnic compositional shifts in Israel have had a major impact on mortality trends over time, as well as on the types of differentials in mortality that remain in the second and later generations. Immigrants arrived in Israel from areas characterized by widely varying levels of health and socioeconomic development: Some immigrants came from European countries with low and controlled mortality, but others came from Middle Eastern countries characterized by high, uncontrolled mortality. Moreover, the position of Jews in these societies ranged from middle to lower classes (see Chapter 3).

Hence, there is every reason to expect that immigrants to Israel would be characterized by levels of health and mortality that would reflect the conditions in their countries of origin—in the double sense that Jews came to Israel from areas that had varying health and mortality levels and that the Jewish immigrants from these countries had significantly different socioeconomic backgrounds and exposure to modern medicine than longer-term Jewish residents. These contexts should result in a great diversity in mortality patterns among first-generation immigrants in Israeli society. The further analytic question is directed to the Israeli experience of these immigrant groups: What happened to the mortality levels of these diverse immigrant groups on arrival and subsequently? Do social forces in the society reinforce mortality variations by ethnic origin or do they facilitate their reduction? Have mortality levels converged among second-generation Israelis of different ethnic origins?

The data to answer these questions consistently point to the conclusion that the decline in mortality for all Jewish ethnic groups over time is one of the clearest ethnic demographic convergences in Israel. Research shows that the initial differential mortality by ethnic origin of Jewish immigrants in Israel largely reflected the range of mortality levels among their places of origin. In turn, mortality variation reflected the level of health and social development of these places of origin (the countries themselves and the place of Jews within them). A simple but revealing illustration is immigrant Jews from Yemen. Upon entering Israeli society, Yemenite Jews had rates of mortality that were similar to less-developed countries of the 1950s, with life expectancies of less than 40 years and infant mortality rates that translated into the death of about one-third of the babies during their first year of life. In contrast, the European immigrants to Palestine and to Israel had levels of mortality that were more like the Western mortality model, with average rates of life expectancy of 60 years and infant mortality rates of 3 percent of births when the state of Israel was established (Bachi 1977; Peritz 1986)

With the improvement in the level of health and its extension to the variety of ethnic immigrant groups in the country, there was an almost immediate decline in the mortality levels of Asian and African immigrants. Upon entry into Israeli society, they were exposed to new and better health conditions. Life expectancy rates calculated from vital statistics in Israel show that the rates for the Middle Eastern–origin Jewish population was 35 to 40 years in 1948; in the late 1990s, life expectancy of Jews in Israel was 78 years, with almost no variation by ethnic origin. The beginning of the mortality decline was almost immediate upon arrival and fully affected the first generation of immigrants of all origins. To the extent that mortality levels were the only indicator of immigrant integration, one would conclude that the integration of Jews from countries with diverse mortality levels and with varying socioeconomic backgrounds was in the direction of the rapid reduction of the mortality gap among ethnic groups.

Although data in Table 9.1 show patterns of infant mortality declines among the Jewish populations of Israel, more detailed analyses of infant mortality

(Zadka 1989) indicate that the downward trend includes fluctuations, particularly an increase in mortality following mass immigration. But during the several years subsequent to mass immigration, the infant mortality rates of immigrants from Middle Eastern countries declined and converged toward the level of mortality characteristic of the European-origin population, even as their mortality levels also declined. Similar analysis shows the changing patterns of the infant mortality rate by cause of death: Very sharp declines may be observed in the infant mortality rate due to gastrointestinal causes and infectious disease from 1950s to the 1980s, again moving toward the Western pattern of cause of death among all ethnic immigrant groups in Israel. Thus, while initial differential high mortality levels among immigrant groups have been documented, mortality declined within a relatively short period of time for them and their children.

The decline in mortality and the convergence process among Jewish ethnic groups can, in large part, be attributed to changes in the basic patterns of the health infrastructure, the control over environmental conditions, and the increased access to health resources among all the immigrant origin groups. These changes were part of the development of an entitlement system associated with an emerging welfare state in Israel, which resulted in the spread of health clinics and medical personnel, maximizing the accessibility of these resources to the Jewish population. Health and welfare institutions were developing in the society as a whole; they were distributed among communities and in neighborhoods where immigrant Jews settled, in an attempt to integrate them into the new society and to increase their health and welfare (see Doron and Kramer 1991 on Israel's welfare system).

Since the initial ethnic differences in mortality reflected conditions in the migrants' countries of origin, the observed ethnic inequalities in mortality were not an Israeli-created product. Instead, mortality and health patterns were the consequence of the "baggage" that immigrants brought with them—their own characteristics and their societal origins. The explanation of residual mortality variation in Israel cannot be assessed simply as the product of a system of inequality relative to the ideal of perfect equality. More appropriately, the residual ethnic mortality differences should be contrasted with what the alternative mortality rates would have been had there been no system of entitlement and no attempt to reduce the health-welfare gap among immigrant groups from diverse places of origin. Even though it is likely that ethnic mortality differences would have declined over several decades, the speed of the decline and the clear-cut trend toward ethnic mortality convergences can only be understood as a political (in the sense of policy) attempt to build the society on the basis of health and welfare accessible to all Jews, regardless of ethnic origin and timing of immigration.

One implication of this argument is that there is no evidence of institutional discrimination in health care against immigrant Jews or against those of a particular ethnic origin that extends beyond socioeconomic factors.[4] Had there been institutional sources of discrimination in this area of social life, ethnic mortality differences would have been sharper, the declines of mortality levels among the less-advantaged Middle Eastern–origin population would have been slower, and convergences with the dominant European-origin population would have taken significantly longer. To the extent, therefore, that there are pockets of higher mortality among Israeli Jews that are ethnically based, the source of the ethnic difference should be explored as a secondary consequence of socioeconomic or geographic patterns associated with ethnic origin. This inference about Jewish ethnic differences in mortality contrasts with the case for Arab-Israelis, for whom I have documented that the mortality gap between them and the Jewish population has remained (see later discussion and also Chapter 4).

The system of entitlements that was designed to overcome the liability of ethnic origin for the Jewish immigrant population and to provide equal health treatment to all persons in Israel is not perfect. Two types of contemporary differences in mortality can be examined with recent research data that isolate some of the sources of contemporary variation in Israel: areal and socioeconomic differences in mortality.[5] On these bases, contemporary ethnic differentials in mortality can be assessed.

Areal and Socioeconomic Variation

Changes in areal differences in mortality are associated with the impact of the location of health services and medical personnel on the health and welfare of the population. Indirectly, location variation in mortality reflects the role of resources—occupation, education, and money—to purchase access to health care to reduce mortality gaps. Part of the contemporary ethnic differential in mortality may be reflected in the concentration of disadvantaged groups in selected locations in the country (see the discussion in Chapters 5 and 6).

Overall, there seems to be a general convergence in areal mortality differences over time. One can selectively examine some broadly defined urban places and a few areas that are located geographically and socially on the periphery of Israeli society (Table 9.3). In 1961, there was a difference of 11 years in life expectancy by area: from 64 years of age of death in Dimona to 75 years in Giv'atayim and Qiryat Motzkin. Following an increase in life expectancy for all towns in the period from 1961 to 1983, the areal variation in mortality diminished significantly, although some small differences remained. There was almost no difference in life expectancy among the three largest cities, Haifa, Tel Aviv, and Jerusalem, in both time periods. The life expectancy in Be'er Sheva', another large city in Israel lagged behind that of the previous three, reflecting this city's larger share of the population from Middle Eastern countries and their lower level of socioeconomic and health developments. For all places, there have been improvements in health and an increase in life expectancy over time.

TABLE 9.3 Life Expectancy in Israel by Town, 1961 and 1983

Town	1961	1983
Dimona	64	73
Qiryat Shemona	68	72
Ramla	71	73
Qiryat Cat	69	74
Giv'atayim	75	78
Nazerat Illit	69	73
Qiryat Bialik	74	76
Qiryat Motzkin	75	75
Tel Aviv	73	75
Jerusalem	72	76
Haifa	72	76
Be'er Sheva'	70	73

Source: Adapted from Friedlander et al. 1990, Appendix table A.

The early areal variation in general levels of mortality in Israel in 1960 had moved toward lower levels by the 1980s, as all areas had experienced improved health care. A similar picture emerges when one examines infant mortality rates by district. There was a range of infant mortality rates, from 35 deaths per 1,000 births in Ramla in 1960 to 21 deaths per 1,000 births in Ashkelon. By 1980 the range had diminished to between 11 deaths per 1,000 births in Ramla and 15 deaths per 1,000 births in Ashkelon (see Table 9.4). An even smaller range in infant mortality rates characterized areas in the late 1990s.

Residual areal differences reflect conditions in specific places and the differential distribution of resources of populations, as well as the fluctuations associated with small numbers of infant deaths. More-distant development towns have fewer means of access to health services and are less able to purchase them. Disadvantaged populations in development towns (see Chapter 6) and those more distant from the main population resource centers, therefore, are likely to be characterized by lower levels of health. It is likely that there is some health and mortality variation among neighborhoods in the larger urban areas, although systematic evidence is not available to confirm this. Populations living in areas of poorer economic circumstances are less likely to have equal access to medical care or to receive equal care than populations in areas with better socioeconomic resources. Some areas have fewer public health institutions and, often, the facilities they do have are of lower quality. Populations located in these poorer areas have not been as successful economically and are more likely to be of Middle Eastern rather than of European origin. In these ways, ethnic variation in health care and in mortality levels in cities seems to be primarily a reflection of economic and geographic circumstances and the overlap of ethnic origin and residential concentration.

TABLE 9.4 Infant Mortality Rates in Israel by Type of Locality and by District,
1960, 1980, and 1996–1998

| | *Infant Mortality (per 1,000 births)* | | |
	1960	*1980*	*1996–1998*
All Areas	27	12	6.2
Types of locality			
Large urban areas	25	12	6.6
Other towns	26	13	4.8
Villages	34	12	7.0[a]
Moshavim	33	12	5.2
Kibbutzim	17	6	3.4
Districts (select)			
Zefat	23	11	6.3
Kimeret	32	11	7.6
Yizrael	29	13	8.5
Akko	31	12	7.4
Hadera	25	12	7.6
Sharon	34	12	5.4
Petah Tiqwa	28	12	3.3
Ramla	35	11	4.7
Rehovot	28	10	3.7
Ashkelon	21	15	5.3
Cities			
Tel Aviv	24	12	4.8
Jerusalem	27	12	7.0
Haifa	25	11	6.4
Be'er Sheva'	33	14	8.4

[a] Estimate.
Source: *Statistical Abstract of Israel,* various years.

It is difficult to know how much of these areal differentials in mortality simply reflect socioeconomic variation, without more precise data than are currently available. At the level of individual characteristics, there is evidence of a small but persistent relationship between socioeconomic status and mortality. Data collected by Israel's Central Bureau of Statistics have indicated a link between infants' deaths and births and the occupations of their fathers and the education of their mothers. These data have been used to estimate the social class connections to infant mortality of the Jewish population (Zadka 1989). These results (summarized in Table

9.5) show that there are clear patterns of mortality variation by the father's occupation, despite the decline in mortality levels for all three occupational rankings. Fathers categorized in lower-level occupations were characterized by infant mortality rates 60 percent higher than fathers in higher-level occupations. Although the infant mortality rates of the children of fathers in higher- as well as in lower-level occupations declined during this period, the range remained substantial. No long-term data are available to show whether the gap in infant mortality rates between more-educated and less-educated mothers has been narrowing, but it clearly was substantial around 1980. The risks of having an infant death is 2.5 times higher for women with no education than it is for women with 13 or more years of education.

Contemporary Ethnic Differences

What do these mortality differences by areas and by social class imply for contemporary, second-generation, and later ethnic Jewish differences? Preliminary analysis of combined ethnic and socioeconomic variation in mortality based on the linkage of census (1983) and mortality records (1983–1986) shows that differential mortality levels (and also official causes of death) by ethnic origin in Israel remain: African-origin Jews have higher mortality (and from causes of death that are more directly controllable) than those of European or Asian origin (Eisenbach et al. 1989). Part of these ethnic differences reflect variations in socioeconomic level between these populations. Standard mortality ratios by education and ethnic origin, along with three categories of cause of death, confirm the inverse relationship between educational level and death rates that appear by age, sex, and ethnic origin, as well as by cause of death; differential mortality rates by ethnic origin narrow considerably when educational level is controlled. There are no final data on the residual ethnic variation controlling for education, age, and sex, but based on cumulative research, one should expect it to be minimal.

An examination of specific ethnic group differences in mortality (Peritz 1986) sharpens the analysis and points to the fact that North African Jews in Israel (the largest and most economically disadvantaged immigrant population in economic terms in the mid-1980s) had a distinctly higher mortality rate than Jews from Europe or Asia; the foreign born had higher levels than the Israeli born. These patterns characterize both men and women among those born in Libya, Morocco, Tunisia, and Algeria. One must recognize the importance of socioeconomic factors in accounting for these findings, but the details by cause of death suggest that other factors may also be at work that are not only economic. Some have suggested that cultural factors appear to be operative, but these are not yet understood and have rarely been measured directly. Clearly, there are areal and socioeconomic factors that operate jointly to affect ethnic mortality differentials, and they are more important for the second and later generations than for the immigrant generation. There is no systematic evidence available that significantly

TABLE 9.5 Infant Mortality Rates of the Jewish Population of Israel by Father's
Occupation, 1960 and 1980, and by Mother's Education, 1977–1980

	Infant Mortality (per 1,000 births)	
Father's Occupation	1960	1980
High-level Professional, managers, administrators	18	10
Middle-level Merchants, sales, skilled workers	24	12
Low-level Unskilled workers and services	25	16
Mother's years of education	1977–1980	
0	25	
1–4	19	
5–8	17	
9–10	14	
11–12	11	
13+	10	

Source: Zadka 1989.

higher mortality levels characterize Jewish Asian- or African-origin populations
of the second generation that are not in large part accounted for by socioeconomic factors and geographic concentration.

Few systematic studies disentangle the socioeconomic, locational (i.e., availability
and accessibility of quality medical and health care), and "cultural" or ethnic factors
associated with disease resistance and with nutrition or other health practices that
have been associated with various ethnic communities in places of origin. Cultural
sources of variation are very likely to decline with the second generation and with
greater exposure to Israeli society. The general processes of welfare entitlement, at
least among the Jewish population groups, and the overall access Jews have to health
services mitigate against long-term cultural traditions affecting adult mortality,
beyond social class and locational factors. There is also no evidence that policies in
Israel with regard to health access, infrastructure, and location were based on
considerations designed to advantage one sector of the Jewish population (e.g.,
those of European origin rather than those of Middle Eastern origin).

What about the Jewish-Arab mortality gap? Are there any indications that the
political and socioeconomic disadvantages of the Arab-Israeli population are associated with higher mortality levels? There is evidence that location—in particular,

the high level of Arab residential segregation—is associated with lower government investments in the economic and health infrastructure of the Arab community (Al Haj and Rosenfeld 1990; see also Chapters 4 and 5). These structural features are likely to be the key to understanding the continuing mortality gaps between Jews and Arabs in Israel.

What about socioeconomic factors among Israeli Arabs? Recent research has attempted to examine the relative importance of socioeconomic factors in Arab and Jewish mortality, linking individual death record data with the socioeconomic characteristics of the areas. This is a particularly promising avenue of research on mortality, since rich areal data are collected and are available, as are vital statistics data by area. Although the links between areal and individual data always suffer from the methodological limitations of the "ecological fallacy" (i.e., attributing group characteristics to individuals), the extent of bias is largely a function of the degree of overlap among characteristics. At least for the examination of Jewish and Arab mortality differentials, the areal approach is relatively unbiased.

Results of recent areal analyses connecting mortality and standard of living for Arabs and Jews in Israel are revealing (Anson 1992; see also Friedlander et al. 1990). They show the expected positive association between standard of living and life expectancy for the total Israeli population. But this correlation is not characteristic of all subpopulations in Israel. Using a series of areal indicators— including economic measures, quality of housing, labor force, and consumer goods—life expectancy levels were calculated for both the Jewish and Arab populations, separately for men and women (Anson). The most intriguing findings of this exercise show that life expectancy among Jews increases as standards of living improve—that is, the better the economic living conditions, the lower the rate of mortality. Among Arab males, however, life expectancy declines somewhat as standards of living rise; for Arab women, there is no relationship between life expectancy and measures of standards of living. In short, the relationship between standard of living and life expectancy is positive for Jews and negative or nonexistent for Arabs.[6] These findings point to the health and welfare costs of the areal concentration of the Arab population. Residential segregation of Arabs from Jewish populations is a form of structural discrimination that results in these different levels of mortality. The data suggest that mortality differences between Jewish and Arab populations are unlikely to converge as socioeconomic differences between the populations decrease. There are other factors that need to be considered, probably those specifically associated with the lower niche that the Arab population occupies within the stratification system in Israel. Combined with the evidence on the sustained infant and adult mortality gap between Jews and Arabs, these detailed areal data point to the need to consider more directly the areal segregation of the Arab population in Israel as a key manifestation of the structural inequalities between Jews and Arabs (see Chapters 4 and 5).

Concluding Observations

One can derive several conclusions and inferences from this broad overview of mortality trends and variation in Israeli society:

1. The major declines in mortality in Israel reflect the concerted policies of bringing public health practices and medical care to the wide range of persons who were populating Israeli society. These policies were extremely successful in the process of nation-building, particularly when judged by how swift and how extensively mortality declined.

2. The mortality reductions affected all groups, but not equally or instantaneously, since groups of immigrants brought with them differential health practices and exposures to disease from countries of origin. They also brought with them different resources that provided initial access to the emerging and burdened health system in the early period of mass immigration. The national health and welfare system that was developing led to the rapid reduction of mortality of those whose mortality levels were high by Western standards, whose resources were not sufficient to purchase medical care, and whose living circumstances were less conducive to the prevention of illness. As a result, the wide discrepancies in infant, child, and adult mortality that characterized the society at the early stages of its development have diminished.

3. Contemporary cross-sectional differences in the mortality patterns of the Jewish population tend to be locational and contextual and, to some extent, socioeconomic. Hence, these differences in mortality levels are unlikely to be the direct effects of discriminatory inequalities of the first order but are the indirect effects of geographic and social class characteristics of groups, which have consequences for mortality variation. The overlap of ethnicity and location (and, to a lesser extent, socioeconomic status) appears to be salient for an understanding of ethnic differences in mortality among Jews.

4. The two patterns for Jewish Israelis—ethnic convergences and minimum residual differences that are not socioeconomic and locational—are not characteristic of the Arab-Jewish comparison. Moslems and Druze in Israel continue to have significantly higher levels of infant and adult mortality and have less access to health systems, quality health care, and prevention than do Israeli Jews. The higher Arab than Jewish mortality and morbidity rates reflect the costs of locational constraints (i.e., segregation). Arab mortality levels do not improve systematically with improvement of their socioeconomic environment. Hence, the analysis of Arab-Israeli mortality cannot be understood in the same framework used to understand mortality changes among Jewish ethnic groups. The Jewish-Arab mortality gap has remained wide, and the socioeconomic environment has a different impact on Jewish and Arab populations in Israel.

5. Finally, the continuing differential mortality patterns between Jews and Arabs have consequences for differences in population growth. The higher Moslem than Jewish mortality in the past has led to much more rapid differential population growth among Jews than would have occurred had mortality levels been similar. The transition from high to low mortality levels and the mortality convergences among ethnic groups have removed mortality from being a major factor in the different demographic profiles of ethnic populations in Israel.

Mortality changes over time in Israel have resulted in its classification as among the most demographically developed countries of the world. This is surprising only because Israel has incorporated within its population a wide range of Jewish immigrants from diverse countries of origin, many of them from areas characterized as places of high mortality. The low level of mortality among European-origin Jews is expected, given their origins; the low mortality characteristic of Israel as a whole when it was established is also not particularly striking, given that 85 percent of the Jewish population at that time originated from European countries. What is surprising is the rapid mortality reduction among immigrants from high mortality areas. They were integrated demographically upon arrival in Israel and their mortality levels declined rapidly and dramatically. It is likely that, within a relatively short period of time, the immigrants from Ethiopia who arrived in Israel in the 1990s with higher levels of morbidity and relatively low levels of life expectancy compared to the Israeli population, will begin to approach the long life expectancy and low levels of infant mortality characteristic of the rest of Israel's population.

Although some differential mortality patterns remain in the Jewish population of Israel, they are relatively minor and revolve around levels that are genuinely low, comparatively and historically. To the extent that one examines the efficacy of policy, it becomes clear that the health and welfare system in Israel along with its entitlements, has had a major positive impact toward an equalization of health and welfare among the various segments of the Israeli Jewish population.

At the same time, it is likely that the geographic separation of Arabs in Israel resulted in their higher levels of infant and adult mortality. Government policy was designed to bring about a demographic transformation for all the citizens of the state and to provide equal access to health and welfare for all segments. But other policies were designed for a variety of political and social objectives that have affected the health and mortality patterns of Arab Israelis. As a result, mortality levels of Arabs in Israel have not been reduced to the same extent as the Jewish levels, and the mortality gap between these populations has remained significant. Had there been no policy to bring modern health care to Arab Israelis, the levels of infant and adult mortality would have been much higher; had there been equal treatment of Arabs and Jews and greater residential integration and fuller availability of health services, differential mortality between Jews and Arabs would have diminished even more quickly.

Mortality reduction has improved the quality of Israeli life, and death has become a rare event, concentrated among older persons. Casualties among young adults in the armed forces, however, remain a powerful symbol in Israel and have directly affected a significant number of Israeli families and neighborhoods. War and continuous army service take their toll on the lives of Jews. Among the younger adult population, the major causes of death are war-related or involve accidents on the road.

The significance of mortality reduction on population growth is straightforward. Its importance extends to family structure, fertility, and migration. In particular, reductions in mortality are likely to be among the factors that have influenced fertility changes in Israel, as survivorship of infants has placed an economic burden on large families. In turn, the reduction in fertility may have increased the likelihood of survivorship of children and women. The influence of mortality on family patterns, on relationships between parents and children, and on the norms associated with the household roles of men, women, and children require extensive study. The impact of mortality on the structure of households and their changing composition requires analysis. My review has suggested the influence of residential concentration on the health and welfare of the various subpopulations in Israel. I now turn my attention to family and fertility patterns, which are linked to the changing contexts of ethnicity and demography in Israeli society.

Notes

1. The relationship between mortality levels and economic development is a classic illustration of asymmetry. All areas with high levels of development have low mortality levels, but all areas of low mortality do not have high levels of development. The key to the paradox is the transferability of public health and technology between areas and its direct impact on mortality.

2. These overall data for Moslems in the Palestine and Israeli periods are conservative estimates because of the high rate of out-migration of the Moslem middle classes from Palestine around 1948 and the retention in Israel of the less-advantaged Moslem population. See the discussion of these selective out-migration patterns in Chapter 4. For somewhat different estimates of the general pattern of decline during the early period, see Bachi 1977; Friedlander, Eisenbach, and Goldscheider 1979.

3. This pattern of warfare and its association with public health and welfare, of course, is not limited to Israeli society. Other societies facing long-term military conflicts have the same mortality curve increase at the prime military ages. There is also a striking similarity to African Americans in their late teens and twenties in the United States, who are involved in a different kind of conflict that results in their higher death rates and the different age curve of their mortality, compared to that of whites.

4. This lack of evidence of institutional discrimination against Jews of different ethnic groups does not mean that there are no differences in the quality of health care or in health care attitudes and practices. Instead, it is argued that these ethnic differences do not result in mortality differences that extend beyond socioeconomic and locational factors. Concerning general health patterns in Israel, see Shuval 1992.

5. Individually based differences, such as gender variation in mortality, are more difficult to assess in societal terms. I examined gender inequality in Chapter 8.

6. Even a casual examination of infant mortality rates by area points in the same direction. There is a considerable areal variation in Arab infant mortality rates in Israel, with Arab rates higher in rural areas. In contrast, there is almost no systematic areal variation in infant mortality among Jews. Indeed, rural Jewish populations tend to have the lowest infant mortality rates. Areal variation, in this case, reflects both differential availability of medical and health services and differential access to areas nearby that have such services.

PART FIVE

Family Formation and Generational Continuities

10

Marriage, Family, and Intermarriage

Families are the building blocks of social organization. In obvious ways, families reproduce and socialize the next generation in the values and lifestyles of the community. They are sources of both comfort and conflict, of generational continuity and change, of financial support and the transmission of values; and they are the basis of the social and economic networks that adults share. Family life places the next generation in adult roles, educates children about assuming responsibilities in the community, and fosters family and socially-related obligations. Families provide support and networks that are economic and political, as well as social and personal.

The formation of new families is among the most significant transitions young adults make in becoming fuller members of their community. These transitions are marked by ceremonies and rituals, providing public and social recognition of new families in the community. Newly separated from families of origin and independent of the constraints of parents and their household, new families are linked to the past and form family-based connections. These transitions may be viewed as linkages among families in which new relationships develop for the couple, for their parents and relatives, for broader family networks, and, in turn, for the community. Because these linkages are often economic and social, they redefine the integration of the individuals within the community. In these ways, family patterns reflect the broader societies of which they are a part and shape those societies as new generations develop and new families are formed.

Like families elsewhere, Israeli families are characterized by family transitions that are consistent with the changing contexts of society. The mixture of persons in Israel from very different societies, with concomitantly different family backgrounds, sets up the basis for family transformations consistent with these new social, economic, political, and cultural contexts. The radical societal changes that Israel has experienced since the 1950s, along with the integration of immigrants from diverse countries of origin and the continuing differentiation in Israel of ethnic communities, raise two questions about family change and continuity. First, how

195

have social, economic, and demographic changes influenced Israeli family patterns? Second, how are family changes linked to the integration of ethnic groups and the convergences among those coming from diverse families of origin?

The family life course from birth to death is experienced very differently by persons of different social and cultural backgrounds who are exposed to a rapidly changing society. The dramatic shifts in mortality and the fertility changes experienced by Israeli society imply that more adults in Israel grow up with surviving parents and grandparents, with the possibility of more extensive generational relationships, vertically and horizontally. It has been estimated, for example, that the probability that a 60-year-old Arab-Israeli woman has a living mother increased by 50 percent because of changed fertility and mortality conditions between 1960 and 1980 (Shmueli 1985, as cited by Matras 1986). The reduction in fertility results in fewer siblings and smaller families, placing greater individual responsibilities on children to care for the older generation and creating a very different milieu in the parental household. Given the same general investments, smaller families mean more attention to individual children, and, at the same time, there are fewer years in which the household contains parents and children.

These changes also place strains on marriages. The reduction in mortality implies the joint survival of couples. Marriages under low mortality conditions have the potential of lasting more years and involving more intensive relationships, which in turn may lead to strains and possible dissolution. The shorter span of the life course when there are young children living in the household is likely to have an impact on the family and the economic roles of men and women. As the state replaces some of the care and social responsibilities for older and less-healthy persons in the society, the welfare system also replaces some family responsibility for the education and socialization of children. With the extension of life, the reduction of family size, and the myriad structural changes that ensue, critical questions emerge: What happens to family values? Do these radical social and demographic changes carry with them the cost of greater emphasis on the individual to the detriment of the family? Do the benefits accompanying structural changes in the extension of life and the reduction of family size outweigh the costs to the family?

Family roles do not only impact on children but on adults and their decisions about whether, when, and whom to marry. In some ways, marriage is often the step toward independence from family of origin but also is likely to be the basis of forming new family linkages, with both the family of origin and the spouse's family. The timing of marriage is linked to education and work roles and to other sources of independence. Who one marries is important as it relates to connections to family extension and to networks for the couple as well as for their children. A focus on independence from family and on family extensions connects to broader issues of communities and their cohesiveness.

There are two revolutions confronting the family at the end of the twentieth century (Goldscheider and Waite 1991). The first is internal to the family and involves a change in gender roles, increasing the participation of women in the paid labor force outside of the home and challenging the traditional separation of

TABLE 10.1 Percentage of Israel's Population That Is Single, by Age, Sex, and Religion, 1997

Age	Total Male	Female	Jews Male	Female	Moslems Male	Female	Christians Male	Female
15–19	99	96	99	98	99	85	99	97
20–24	87	67	90	73	77	43	93	63
25–29	48	29	52	31	35	23	60	25
30–34	19	13	21	12	11	16	24	16
35–39	9	8	11	8	5	13	10	13
60–64	3	4	3	3	2	6	6	13
65+	3	3	3	3	2	5	6	15

Note: For Moslems and Christians the 60–64 age category covers ages 55–64.
Source: *Statistical Abstract of Israel 2000,* table 2.19.

male and female activities. The second revolution involves reductions in family living and increases in living alone and in settings where individual worth and dignity are not associated with family roles. These revolutions are complex and have not been examined fully for Israeli society. My review in this chapter assesses changes in the marriage regime and its alternatives as expressed in living arrangements, with a focus on issues of ethnic intermarriage.[1]

To begin to address family changes and continuities, I outline the family processes that have occurred in Israeli society as a whole and among its major communities, review changes in the extent and timing of family formation, and examine marriage and intermarriage between persons of different ethnic origins. In the process, I provide a firmer answer to the question of how familistic Israelis are and how important family connections are in the changes that have enveloped the society over time. My focus, therefore, is on families, not on populations, and I investigate how families are formed and what their relationship is to other events in the life course (marriages, divorces, and remarriages). Marriage across ethnic boundaries informs us about the integration of families and the family networks that are established and reinforced, as well about the relative assimilation of ethnic groups.

Family Formation: Extent and Timing

At what age do Israeli men and women start new families? Are there major ethnic differences in these family formation patterns among Jews and between Jews and Arabs? The data in Table 10.1 are organized to show the percentage of single people

TABLE 10.2 Percentage of Israel's Jewish Population That Is Single, by Age
and Sex, Selected Years, 1961–1997

| | Female | | | | Male | | | |
Age	1961	1972	1983	1997	1961	1972	1983	1997
20–24	34	47	53	73	74	77	83	90
25–29	9	16	18	31	28	28	35	52
30–34	4	6	10	12	11	9	11	21
60–64	3	2	2	3	2	3	3	3

Source: *Statistical Abstract of Israel,* various years.

for various age groups, for men and women, for the total society, and for Jews,
Moslems, and Christians in Israel. These data portray almost universal exposure
to marriage. Almost 90 percent of the women and 81 percent of the men in Israel
have been married by ages 30 to 34, and most by ages 25 to 29. Men marry at later
ages than women, but almost everyone (98 percent of the population) has been
married at least once during their lifetimes. Marriage is thus the normative life
course experience in Israel, with but minor exceptions.[2]

When the data are reviewed in a life-course perspective, they display the
movement from almost universal singlehood in the 15-to–19 age group to almost universal marriage by later adulthood. Marriage rates increase slowly
among those ages 20 to 24, more for women than for men, toward a gradual
equalization of levels among men and women. There is little teenage marriage
among all groups in Israel, except among Moslem women; but fully 85 percent of
Moslem women ages 15 to 19 have not yet married. By ages 20 to 24, 43 percent
of the Moslem women were single compared to 73 percent of Jewish women.
While over half the Jewish Israeli men were single at ages 25 to 29, only one-third
of the Moslem men were still single.

Have these patterns changed very much over time? The evidence supports the
conclusion that family formation patterns have changed substantially toward the
later timing of marriage, but they have changed little in terms of eventual family
formation (Table 10.2). During three and one-half decades of major demographic change (1961–1997), the proportion of young Jewish adults ages 20 to 24
who are single has increased. In 1961, 34 percent of the women and 74 percent of
the men in their early twenties were still single; by 1997 the proportions had increased to 73 percent of the women and 90 percent of the men. The postponement of marriage has been more dramatic for women than for men and, hence,
the gender gap in singlehood has narrowed considerably: from a 40-percentage-

TABLE 10.3 Median Age of Israeli Brides and Grooms, by Religion, 1952–1998

	Jews		*Moslems*		*Christians*		*Druze*	
	Brides	*Grooms*	*Brides*	*Grooms*	*Brides*	*Grooms*	*Brides*	*Grooms*
1952	21.9	26.9	–	–	–	–	–	–
1960	21.7	25.7	–	–	–	–	–	–
1970	21.6	24.4	19.4	24.3	21.5	27.5	19.0	22.7
1975	21.7	24.5	19.3	23.6	21.1	27.1	18.7	22.8
1980	22.3	25.3	19.5	23.7	21.5	27.0	18.2	21.6
1985	23.0	26.2	19.8	23.9	22.4	27.5	18.6	22.3
1991	23.5	26.6	20.0	24.6	22.3	27.8	19.2	24.0
1998	24.4	27.0	20.3	25.1	23.0	28.2	20.3	25.0

Sources: *Statistical Abstract of Israel 1992*; and *Statistical Abstract of Israel 2000*, table 3.5.

point difference between men and women among those in their early twenties in 1961 to a 17-percentage-point difference 36 years later.

An increase in the proportion of single people also characterized those ages 25 to 29, more than tripling for women between 1961 and 1997 and nearly doubling among men (from 28 percent to 52 percent). Again, the greater change among women reduced the gender gap from a level three times higher among men than women in 1961 to about 1.5 times as high in 1997. These changes over time for the Jewish population are consistent with the increase in schooling and military obligations, both extending young adult dependency on parents further into adulthood. Nevertheless among those ages 30 to 34 in the late 1990s, 88 percent of the Jewish women and 79 percent of the Jewish men in Israel have been married.

These patterns of singlehood are reflected in the changing median age at marriage, which has increased among Jewish women and Jewish men since 1970, as Israelis participated in the baby and marriage booms characteristic of Western societies.[3] The age gap between Jewish brides and grooms at the time of marriage remained in the late 1990s, reduced in half from the five-year age gap in 1952 (Table 10.3). The fluctuations in ages at marriage over the long term partly reflect ethnic compositional changes in the Jewish population. Over time, social and economic factors in Israel have affected populations from all ethnic origins, toward a new "Israeli" pattern of marriage timing. Ethnic differences in the timing of marriage have been narrowed considerably in the last decades within the Jewish population.

The age of marriage among Moslem Israelis has also moved toward later ages on average, for both women and men, although more slowly and at earlier ages than among Jews. Christian Arab women marry on average much later than do Moslems; Christian men marry significantly later than either Moslem or Jewish men. The pattern of Druze women and men is very similar to Israeli Moslems: There is about a four-year gap between the average age of marriage of Jewish and Druze brides and between Jewish and Moslem brides. There is a five-year age gap between brides and grooms of the three non-Jewish Israeli groups, twice as high as the age gap between Jewish brides and grooms.

Familism: Family Structure, Divorce, and Living Arrangements

Taken together, data on the extent and timing of marriage suggest the normative condition of marriage and, indirectly, the family centeredness of Israeli society. Clearly, new families are being formed in Israel almost universally, even as the timing of marriage is changing. As marriage timing extends later into the adult life course, there is an increased potential for dependence on parents for a longer period of time and an increase in time available for living in a nonfamily context. The evidence points to the centrality of family formation as a critical adult transition for most persons. To some extent, getting married may be viewed as one indicator of the value placed on families. There are other indicators that support this assessment. Two additional indicators are reviewed below: the changing level of divorce and the extent of nonfamily living arrangements.

Divorce

Although the divorce rate in Israel is relatively low by United States standards, an increase in divorce is unmistakable. The number of divorces has increased in Israel since the mid-1950s, from about 2,100 per year then to 3,100 in the mid-1970s, and to over 10,000 in 1999. The increasing numbers reveal the spread of the divorce experience among larger numbers of persons but do not indicate the relative rate per population. A calculation of crude divorce rates per 1,000 population shows an increase from 1.0 to 1.7 per 1,000 over the five-decade period to 1999. There have been increases from 1961 to 1997 in the divorce rate among Jewish men and women ages 15 to 49: from 5.4 to 11.0 divorces per 1,000 married men, and from 5.1 to 10.7 per 1,000 married women. Since the early 1970s, the rate of divorce among Moslem men and women has more than doubled (Table 10.4). The number of divorces among non-Moslem Arabs in Israel is very low. Thus, although divorce is increasing in Israel, the low level further supports the argument of the continued family centeredness of Israeli society.

Familism as measured by rates of divorce is further documented in the statistics that focus on the proportion ever divorced within the first ten years of marriage. Of those married in Israel in the 1960s, for example, about 8 percent

TABLE 10.4 Divorce Rates in Israel by Religion and Gender, 1961–1997				
	Jews		*Moslems*	
	Men	Women	Men	Women
1961	5.4	5.1	–	–
1972	5.6	5.1	3.4	3.0
1983	8.5	8.0	6.9	6.4
1991	8.7	8.4	5.7	5.3
1997	11.0	10.7	7.6	7.4

Note: The divorce rate is calculated as the number of persons divorcing per 1,000 married, by gender. The figures are for the population ages 15 to 49.

Sources: *Statistical Abstract of Israel 1993*, table 3.10.; and *Statistical Abstract of Israel 2000*, table 3.8.

divorced during the first 10 years of marriage; for those married in the 1970s, about 10 percent divorced within the first 10 years; for those married in the 1980s, almost 12 percent have been divorced in their first 10 years of marriage. In their detail, these data point to the fact that close to 90 percent of those married in Israel remained married to the same person for the first 10 years of married life and with relatively small increases over time. For the several cohorts where 20-year data are available—that is, those married in the 1960s and 1970s who can be traced for two decades—the level of divorce has remained low: 14 to 16 percent were ever divorced. In other words, about 85 percent of the Jews who were married in Israel remained married to the same spouse for at least 20 years.

In addition to the small increase, there have been some changes in the characteristics of those who have divorced. From the 1960s to the 1990s, there was a decrease in divorces among those married for short durations—21 percent of those divorced in the 1960s did so within their first year of marriage, compared to 10 percent in 1989; less than 10 percent of those divorced in the 1960s did so after 20 years of marriage, compared to 20 percent of those who were divorced in 1989. The divorced in 1960 were more likely to be childless (56 percent) than those who were divorced in 1989 (32 percent). Concomitantly, divorces in 1989 were more likely than in the 1960s to involve children in the family (30 percent of all divorces in 1989 involved couples with two or more children, compared to 19 percent in 1960s). So, contemporary divorce in Israel is more likely to occur with longer duration after marriage and among those who are more likely to have had children, both affecting a larger network of family members.[4]

Living Arrangements

Two indicators of strong family ties—the high level of marriage and low rates of divorce—are consistent with an assessment of living arrangement patterns in Israel. Most unmarried persons live in family settings, with marriage marking the transition from one family setting to the next, and with the incorporation of a widowed parent into a family-based household. The extension of life and the increase in age at marriage have not resulted in large proportions of people living independently. Compared to the United States and to other Western countries, there has not been a conspicuous growth of nonfamily living in Israel.[5]

There has been a slow increase in the proportion of households containing only one person, but the extent of living alone has remained at a relatively low level from 1960 to 1999 (Table 10.5). Only 10 percent of the Jewish households in 1960 were one-person households, increasing to 17 percent in 40 years. There has been no increase among Arabs. Clearly, the level of nonfamily living is well below that of the United States or Western European countries (where it is about 25 percent of all households) but above that of many other parts of the world (see Gold-scheider and Goldscheider 1989, 1993). In the early 1970s, most unmarried adults in Israel lived with their families until they were married, and marriage was the major passage to independence. At the other end of the life course, there were over half a million persons over age 65 living in households in 1999. Of these, 75 percent of Israeli Jews were living with others; 85 percent of the Arab population were living with others.

Research has shown that there is some ethnic variation in living arrangements in Israel. Moslems were least likely to live in nonfamily households, Jews of Asian and African origins were next, and those of European-American origins were most likely to live in nonfamily households. This ethnic pattern does not appear to be the result of education, life cycle, or the marital status factors that differentiate these communities. There were no generational differences within the ethnic categories, suggesting the length of stay or experience in Israeli society had little effect on this dimension of ethnic differences in family and kinship ties. Differences among ethnic categories are therefore not due to differences in economic resources or life-cycle factors that differentiate these communities (Goldscheider and Fisher 1989); they are consistent with ethnic differences in familism and the association of living alone with greater independence and individualism.

A detailed look at the proportion living alone by age points to the minor ethnic variations among older persons living in nonfamily settings. The major ethnic difference appears among young adults: Israelis of Western origin are more likely than those of Middle Eastern origin to live alone, and few Arab young adults live independently before they marry. Together with data on the extent and timing of marriage, these patterns of living arrangements reinforce the conclusion that marriage is the normative path out of the parental home, even with the delay in marriage over time.

TABLE 10.5 Proportion of Households in Israel with One Person, by Religion, 1960–1999

	Total	Jews	Arabs
1960	10	10	9
1965	11	11	9
1970	12	13	7
1975	13	14	6
1980	14	15	5
1985	15	16	6
1990	15	17	5
1995	16	17	6
1999	17	19	7

Sources: *Statistical Abstract of Israel 1993,* table 2.29; *Statistical Abstract of Israel 2000,* table 2.27.

Families and Assimilation: Ethnic Families and Intermarriages

Israeli society is family centered, as evidenced by the fact that most marry and few dissolve their marriages. Residential independence is tied to marriage, and few people live outside of family contexts. The familistic context of Israeli society implies the importance of family-based networks for social and economic activities. One source of these family networks is the ties that are formed within communities through marriage. An examination of changes over time in who marries whom in Israel helps us to understand the family connections associated with marriage choices and, in particular, changes in the extent of marriages within ethnic communities.

Intermarriage across ethnic lines may be understood in terms of two interrelated themes. First, and most obviously, marrying across ethnic communities reflects the assimilation and integration of populations of different ethnic origins. Isolated ethnic communities that do not have social contacts with each other are unlikely to experience high rates of intermarriage. A second theme emphasizes the linkages through marriage of two different extended families. Interethnic marriage may be viewed as the breakdown of the ethnic family based on networks and an increase in broader community and national linkages. Increasing levels of interethnic marriages imply greater independence and autonomy of couples from their family origins. This family orientation emphasizes that individual choice is dominant in interethnic marriages and that the centrality of family networks is replaced by broader communal ties and national allegiances. Intermarriage rates have often been interpreted as a prime indicator of the breakdown of the family, or the "primordial" control over individual decision making toward the maximization of personal choice.

Intermarriage rates among ethnic groups counterbalances tendencies toward ethnic particularism and the reinforcement of ethnic communities. Marriage patterns are structural dimensions of social life that most clearly and directly appear to be linked to ethnic continuity. Who marries whom is, first, a question of individual choice and family relationships. In turn, it is also a question of broader communal networks and linkages. The incidence and disposition of interethnic and intra-ethnic marriages reflects and affects ethnic continuity. In a system of choices, persons who interact are likely to develop a relationship that may result in marriage. Hence, the greater the isolation of ethnic groups, the greater the barriers to social interaction across ethnic groups and the lower likelihood that interethnic marriages will occur. The higher the rate of interethnic marriages, the more likely that the family networks of ethnic groups will be reduced, leading generationally to further interethnic marriages. Indeed, intermarriage has often been viewed as the quintessential indicator of ethnic assimilation; at the group level, it is associated with the path to the ethnic melting pot.

By implication, ethnic communities are not able to sustain social and cultural continuity in the face of high levels of interethnic marriage. By the third or fourth generation of ethnic intermarriages, the identity and the culture, the in-group interaction and the networks, have become so mixed that ethnic origin no longer is salient.

Although the power of intermarriage to dilute and diminish ethnicity is clear, we should be cautious about overinterpreting intermarriage rates and their changes over time. Several points need to be stressed from the beginning as this review and analysis unfolds. First, individuals can move into and out of ethnic communities, reducing the salience of ethnicity for them as individuals, even as the community as a whole retains a core committed to ethnic continuity. Intermarriage rates may increase and, as a result, the intermarried may leave both communities, and ethnic continuities may be retained on a narrower basis. Since ethnicity is a constructed category that is not the simple "objective" fact of birthplace, boundaries between ethnic categories are permeable. Indeed, the selective out-marriage of those who are more marginal to the ethnic group may result in a core remnant of ethnic group members who are even more ethnically committed. Although it may seem counterintuitive, intermarriage may actually strengthen ethnic communities over time, if those who leave are the most marginal ethnically and if those who remain are core sources of social and cultural continuity.

A second caution relates to the assumption that the intermarriage rate itself is an indicator of the total assimilation of groups (as seen by Gordon 1963 and others who have used his assimilation typology). The key question left unspecified is how the children of interethnically married persons view themselves and how they are viewed by the various communities with which they identify. If children of the intermarried identify themselves in terms of the ethnic group of one of their parents, then ethnic identity of one group is not diminished. Thus, if the children of Irish and Italian intermarriages in the United States identify themselves as Irish, then interethnic marriage has not necessarily diminished Irish ethnicity, at least demographically. Whether it would dilute the context of "Irish-Americanness" is a complex question that requires some specification of the meaning of ethnicity. Clearly, it is an oversimplification to infer ethnic quality from rates of interethnic marriages.

There is, of course, the possibility that interethnic marriage would result in strengthening neither origin group but, instead, result in the formation of a new ethnic group—broader than the original groups but containing some of the elements of both. Some interethnic marriages in Israel have resulted in the formation (and perhaps the reinforcement) of new ethnic divisions among Jews, the result of some types of marriages and not others. Marriages between Jews of Russian and Argentine origins in Israel or between those of Yemenite and Moroccan origins would fit the newly formed categories of "European-American" and of "Asian-African" that have emerged (see Chapter 2).

A third caution is the assumption that increases in the rate of intermarriage means the growth of individual choice over family preferences. The emphasis on choices that individuals make often excludes consideration of the constraints about the options available. Often there are limits on the availability of potential spouses within the market of eligibles. The selection of spouses from an ethnic group is based first and foremost on availability. If there are potential spouses to choose from, then spouses can be selected from a different ethnic origin, if they are defined within the field of eligibles. To the extent that markets of eligibles contract and expand with waves of immigration and with the age-gender-marital status composition of specific ethnic communities, marriage markets are likely to change rapidly. For example, if there are very few immigrants from Venezuela in Israel of the appropriate age, gender, and marital status, the choice of a Venezuelan marriage partner will be severely constrained, unless the field of eligibles is expanded to include a wider range of potential partners from other Latin American countries or from other ethnic origins. The interethnic marriage issue, then, is not only whether young adults "choose" persons from other ethnic origins but whether there are persons available from similar origins to select from.

Another option for those who cannot find a spouse within their own ethnic group and who do not widen the range of eligibles is to remain unmarried. That choice would be more revolutionary in a family-centered society and would have extensive implications for family and ethnic continuity, demographically and socially. If judged by the marriage patterns in Israel, this more radical alternative (nonmarriage) has been selected by few. Indeed, Israelis faced with a narrowing market of potential spouses of their own ethnic origins have almost always chosen to expand the pool of eligibles to include those of other ethnic origins.[6] This ethnic-marital choice has been reinforced by the Zionist Israeli ideology that challenges the legitimacy of ethnic origins among the Israeli born (see Chapter 2). Israel is among a small number of societies in which marriages between those of different ethnic origins is actively encouraged by the national ideology (see Rosen

1982). Interethnic marriage in Israel may be viewed under some circumstances as a trade-off between familism and ethnic continuity. In the clash between the values placed on ethnic community (with marriage market constraints) and family formation, the overwhelming majority of Israelis appear to select family values. Interethnic marriage cannot simply be viewed in this context as reflecting the value of national integration versus the salience of ethnic continuity.[7]

These four cautions in interpreting increasing intermarriage rates—the looseness of boundaries among ethnic groups over the life course, the need for the children of mixed ethnic origins to identify ethnically, the formation of new ethnic groups that incorporate more than one specific ethnic origin group, and the structural constraints on choices—need to be taken into account in interpreting interethnic marriage patterns in Israel.

A general review of the evidence in Israel suggests two conclusions: First, interethnic marriages have increased over time; and second, higher interethnic marriage rates among Jews do not, in and of themselves, imply the demise of ethnic communities. These conclusions parallel those I reached in my analysis of ethnic convergences in other areas of social life. Convergences in family and demographic processes do not necessarily imply the assimilation of ethnic groups on community and residential dimensions or the demise of all forms of ethnic continuities. In the Israeli context, interethnic marriages do not indicate total ethnic group assimilation, although they are consistent with the redefinition of Jewish ethnicity.

The Increase in Ethnic Marriages

I review some of the fundamental facts of interethnic marriages in Israel, starting with the long-term changing level. Overall rates of ethnic out-marriages show clear increases over time: By the end of the 1980s, about 20 percent of the Jewish marriages in Israel were between those of different ethnic origins. The level has remained relatively steady over the past several years. Census data on first- and second-generation couples married in Israel who were in their first marriage (Eisenbach 1989a) show an increase in intermarriage by marriage cohort; interethnic marriages increased from 8 percent in the 1949 to 1953 period to 22 percent in the 1979 to 1983 period. In part, this increase reflected changes in the composition of the population—the increase in the proportion of Asian-Africans in the marriageable age group from about 36 percent in the early 1950s to about 62 percent in the 1980s. This compositional shift accounts for increases (from the 1960s to the 1980s) in the proportion marrying out among European-Americans (from 16 percent to 32 percent). The proportions marrying out remained at a rather steady level among Asian-Africans (about 16 percent). In the 1949 to 1953 marriage cohort, 80 percent of women of African origin married men from Africa; 81 percent of Asian women married men from Asia; and 95 percent of European women married European men. In the cohort 1979 to 1983, these figures were 59 percent, 57 percent, and 73 percent, respectively (Eisenbach, table A.2)

Viewed another way, the proportion out-married of those married in Israel (defined dichotomously as Asian-African and European-American) was 5 percent until 1945, increasing to 9 percent from 1946 to 1955, to 13 percent from 1956 to 1961, to 18 percent from 1964 to 1973, and to 21 percent from 1974 to 1983 (Schmelz et al. 1990). In each cohort, and for both husbands and wives, the Israeli born have a higher ethnic out-marriage rate than the foreign born. However, there is a great deal of specific country-of-origin variation in the extent of ethnic homogamy. Thus, for those marrying in the period from 1974 to 1983, higher rates of in-marriage characterize Jews from Yemen, India, Morocco, and the USSR, compared to Turkey, Egypt, Germany, and Austria. These differences reflect the size of the marriage market and the recency of immigration, as well as the strength of the communal-ethnic ties and cultural-family relationships that have characterized some groups (Goldscheider 1983; Schmelz et al.).

An interesting exploration of these patterns of ethnic homogamy can be organized by examining data on the ethnic origins of Israeli couples in 1999. Data in Table 10.6 reveal some of the critical interethnic household combinations, using broad continent-of-origin definitions of ethnicity. Six out of ten of the women whose continent of origin was Africa were living in 1999 with men whose continent of origin was Africa as well. Defining homogamy in these terms, Asian homogamy was 61 percent, European was 81 percent, and American homogamy was 42 percent. In this context, the majority of Israel's population lived in homogamous households in 1999. When households had interethnic couples, the combinations were more likely than not to be the adjacent ethnic group. Thus, for example, while 63 percent of African-origin women were living in households with African-origin men, an additional 17 percent were living with husbands from Asian origins. Taking together, the category Asian-African accounts for 80 percent of the homogamous households; 83 percent of the European-American households are homogamous. Part of the difficulty with these data is the category "Israel" as a continent of origin where ancestry or ethnic origin has not been specified. Thus, while 42 percent of the American-origin households are homogamous, adding European-origin households increases the homogamy to 68 percent. Of the women not in European-American homogamously defined households, 13 percent are in households with third generation "Israeli" men. It is likely that the overwhelming majority of these are from European origins. Eliminating the ethnically unspecified Israel category increases the proportion of the homogamously married among American women to 79 percent.

The major conclusion from these data is a clear pattern of ethnic homogamy, redefined by broad continents of origin rather than specific countries and recategorized into Israeli-defined groups. What about changes over time? We have few bases of comparison in Israel, although research in general shows a modest increase in interethnic marriages but the retention of broadly ethnic homogamy. This perspective gains support by comparing the total to the bottom panel of Table 10.6. All the specific continent-of-origin homogamous households have declined. Comparing the total with those who were married since 1983 (and living in Israel in 1999), the African homogamous households declined from 63 to 56 percent; the Asian from 61 to 45 percent and the European from 81 to 69 percent. Declines may be noted even when households are grouped into combined ethnic categories (from 80 percent to 75 percent for Asian-African households; from 83 percent to 72 percent for European-American households). Again the decline in homogamous households is evident, with the retention of homogamy for broad ethnic groups in Israel.

Intermarriage and Educational Trade-offs

The increasing level of intermarriage across ethnic groups directs our attention to the question of the characteristics of those who marry within their own ethnic group compared to those who out-marry. One of the most fascinating results of recent analyses of interethnic marriages in Israel is the educational selectivity of the intermarried among different ethnic origin groups. These ethnic-education trade-offs are quite complex, so a simplified illustration might help.

Let us assume that 100 Israeli-born persons of Western origin marry Israelis of Middle Eastern origins. Further, let us assume that these Western-origin Jews are less educated than the Western-origin Jews who marry within their own origin group and that those of Middle Eastern origin who out-marry are more educated than those of Middle Eastern origins who marry within their own origin group. The resultant pattern at the group level is that those who marry within their own ethnic group (both the Western and the Middle Eastern groups) will reinforce the distinctive educational characteristics of their ethnic origins because of the intermarriage-educational trade-offs that have occurred.

Since it is the more educated who marry out of the Middle Eastern group and the less educated who marry out of the Western-origin group, the former group becomes less educated and the latter group has enhanced its educational advantage. In this scenario, intermarriage has reinforced the overlap of ethnic origins and education and, hence, has enhanced the distinctiveness of both groups. As a result of these patterns, interethnic marriage rates may be lower rather than higher in the next generation, since the remaining ethnic origin groups have become more, not less, distinctive through intermarriage.

The key question in this scenario is the ethnic identity of those who marry out of their ethnic origin group and that of their children. In part, it seems reasonable to expect that, given the ethnic choices, many of those who can identify with the higher-prestige group or with the better-educated group will do so. The patterns

TABLE 10.6   Percentage of Couples in Households in Israel by Ethnic Origin
of Each Partner by Date of Marriage, 1999

Man's Ethnic Origin	Woman's Ethnic Origin				
	African	Asian	European	American	Israeli
Total	100	100	100	100	100
African	63	16	5	12	13
Asian	17	61	6	6	16
European	14	16	81	27	32
American	1	1	2	42	4
Israeli (ENS)[a]	6	7	6	12	36
Married after 1983					
Total	100	100	100	100	100
African	56	24	9	17	14
Asian	19	45	8	6	16
European	15	18	69	24	27
American	2	1	3	33	4
Israeli (ENS)[a]	8	12	12	20	40

[a]ENS = Ethnicity not specified.

Source: *Statistical Yearbook of Israel 2000,* table 2.38.

of ethnic distinctiveness would be enhanced if the children of mixed ethnic origins who are more educated identify with the Western-origin group, and if the children of the less-educated mixed-origin ethnic group identify with the Middle Eastern group. They and their children may form a "mixed" ethnic generation and, as a result, might establish fewer ethnic family ties. But the range of possibilities is substantial, given the multiple bases of identity and the range of factors (characteristics of individuals, couples, and extended families) that will shape their choices over their life cycles.

This exercise is much too simplified and static. A fuller model would add other important social and economic characteristics (for example, gender—whether it is the more-educated Middle Eastern women who marry the less-educated Western-origin men, trading education for the status of the ethnic group; or whether there are other characteristics such as occupation, residence, age, and family ties that separate the interethnically married from the intra-ethnically married). Such a model would have to include the generational and life-course dimensions and the family networks that would influence how ethnicity will emerge among these couples and their children. Suffice it to indicate at this point that the notion that intermarriage between those from different ethnic origins results in an ethnic melting pot is grossly oversimplified, without taking into account these trade-offs. And, unfortunately, the available evidence is weakest when intergenerational questions are raised.

Even with weak evidence, there is a reasonable case to be made that some ethnic intermarriages in Israel result in the strengthening of ethnic communities. Children of mixed ethnic origin can primarily select the ethnic group of one of the parents, adopt neutrality with regard to ethnic origin, remain committed to both ethnic sides of the family, or vary ethnic identity with context and with changes over the life cycle. These choices mean that only if ethnicity loses its salience in the family and community senses can we expect ethnic intermarriages to result in the reduced significance of ethnic origins generationally. There are indications at the community and socioeconomic levels that such a diminution of ethnic salience is unlikely, at least for the next generation in Israel.

What does the limited evidence reveal about these trade-offs? The most significant finding is that interethnic marriages are higher among the Middle Eastern–origin ethnic populations with higher educational levels, but are higher among Western-origin groups with lower educational levels. The proportion marrying-out in the Middle Eastern–origin group increases with education, and it declines with education in the Western-origin group (Table 10.7). Almost one-third of the men of Middle Eastern origin, with more than a high school education, who married in Israel in the 1973 to 1983 period married women of different ethnic origins, compared to 14 percent of those who graduated from high school and 9 percent of those with less that 8 years of schooling. In contrast, 19 percent of the most-educated men of Western origin in this cohort married women of different ethnic origins, compared to 40 percent of the least-educated men. The same positive association of education with out-marriage among Israelis of Middle Eastern origin and a negative association among those of Western origins characterizes women (Eisenbach 1992; Schmelz et al. 1990).

The different patterns by ethnic origin reflect the marriage-market distribution of these groups by education—there is a higher concentration of more-educated people among Israelis of Western origin than among those of Middle Eastern origin. When more-educated Middle Eastern young adults interact with similarly educated persons, the latter are more likely to be of Western origin; when less-educated Western-origin Jews interact with less-educated persons, the latter are more likely to be of Middle Eastern origin. Marriage can be considered a means of establishing economic networks. For example, a less-educated Israeli man of Eastern European origins who marries a Moroccan woman may, in the process, obtain assistance in opening up a gasoline station—"passing," as it were, into the Middle Eastern–origin group for economic advantage. Whatever the determinants of these economic-ethnic trade-offs, interethnic marriages will likely increase the salience of ethnicity in the next generation by increasing, not reducing, the socioeconomic distinctiveness of ethnic divisions in Israel.

TABLE 10.7 Percentage of Israelis Marrying Within Their Ethnic Origin
Groups, by Period of Marriage, Years of Education, and Gender

	Married 1973–1983			Married 1979–1983		
	0–8	9–12	13+	0–8	9–12	13+
Husbands						
African	92	79	57	79	70	50
Asian	93	82	70	77	63	46
European	78	87	93	65	75	89
Wives						
African	84	71	44	73	65	56
Asian	87	73	49	80	65	51
European	89	92	93	61	77	86

Source: Eisenbach 1989a, table A.3.

Viewed in this way, the decision to marry someone of a different ethnic origin may imply that the range of choices has been constrained and that there are gains in the ethnic trade-offs. One manifestation of the changing market is reflected in the very strong imbalances in the age and sex structure by ethnic origin. Estimates based on the 1983 census by ethnic origin show that both Western- and Middle Eastern–origin groups have been affected by a marriage "squeeze" (defined as a contracting number of potential eligible spouses based largely on the age, sex, and marital status distributions of ethnic origin populations); the Western-origin group experienced a sharper imbalance than did other ethnic populations. Despite significant interethnic differences in their marriage markets, both ethnic groups have very similar proportions remaining single, suggesting that nonmarriage is not a normatively acceptable option to the marriage squeeze in the family-centered context of Israeli society. During the marriage squeeze, and especially at its climax, there was a sharp decline in the proportion of Asian-African-origin women marrying European-American-origin men and a sharp increase in the proportion of women of European-American origin marrying men of Asian-African origin (Ben-Moshe 1989).

The structural forces that constrain marriage markets are not limited to Jewish marriage regimes but can affect any population that experiences disruptions over time.[8] Pressure within the Moslem Israeli marriage market has also occurred; this, too, has not been resolved through nonmarriage or through access to the Jewish Israeli market. The squeeze is the result of the declining fertility regime among

Moslems and the decline in infant mortality, combined with the average difference in the ages at marriage of brides and grooms. Thus, among Moslems in 1983, there were 1,323 women ages 20 to 24 for every 1,000 males ages 25 to 29. The same type of comparison in 1972 showed 1,070 women to 1,000 men. This marriage-market squeeze resulted in changes in the age gap between grooms and brides, in the postponement of marriage, in the slight increase in nonmarriage among a few (particularly of more-educated young women), and in the opening of marriage markets to include Arab non-Moslems and Moslems from other countries or from the administered territories. Later marriage among Moslem women and the changes in the age gap between marriage partners both relate to this marriage squeeze (Eisenbach 1989).

Intermarriage and Ethnicity

The increase in ethnic intermarriage in Israel has often been interpreted both in the context of the emergence of independent families and as the basis of ethnic assimilation. It has been argued that ethnic intermarriage

> Reflects the erosion of the marriage regime wherein the newlywed couple is an extension of the family of orientation or the community of orientation. The newlywed couple in Israel, today much more than in the past, represents a new family unit, relatively independent of its family traditions. No less important, the decline of place-of-origin endogamy also reflects the erosion of ethnicity as a central axis of social organization in the Jewish population (Matras 1986, pp. 32, 38).

Others have made a similar argument that "the high rates of ethnic intermarriage reflects ethnic convergences and at the same time contributes to further integration in the future" (Peres and Katz 1991, p. 30).

In addition to the usual data on increasing rates of interethnic marriages, these arguments are bolstered by longitudinal evidence (presented in Matras 1986, table 11) concerning the place of residence of parents and siblings of a 1954 cohort of Jewish women. These data show that 41 percent of these women lived in a different place from their parents, and 55 percent lived in a place different from at least one of their siblings; 31 percent of their husbands lived in a place different from their parents, and 34 percent lived in a place different from their husband's siblings. This evidence is interpreted as revealing the significant distances separating the generations, and separating siblings from each other, and indicating the extent of social-geographic distance among Israel's Jewish families.

These arguments do not take into account that immigration was disruptive of family dependence for many, as the state became the basis of economic support and welfare. Some of the immigrants to Israel did not come from extended families because they originated from communities that were characterized by family independence and nuclear family structure; others came to Israel without their extended family networks. Some early European immigrants rejected their family of origin as they sought to establish new patterns of community based on nationalistic criteria. And many of both the Western- and the Middle Eastern–origin immigrants have used their family networks and ties in contemporary Israel to facilitate their advances in jobs, in schooling, as well as in marriage. So the contrasts of contemporary nuclear family structure with the traditional family extension of the past tend to be exaggerated, as does an emphasis on the lack of family ties among young Israeli-born couples. Until we study the ethnic "orientations" of the interethnically married and their children to determine their degree of selective ethnic attachments and identification, the family and assimilation implications of ethnic intermarriages are not likely to be known.[9]

Using a special file that linked records from the 1995 and the 1983 censuses of Israel, Barbara Okun has explored for the first time the marriage behavior of persons of mixed ethnic ancestries. She finds that persons of mixed ethnic ancestry are less ethnically endogamous than other groups, which contributes to ethnic blending and to the blurring of ethnic boundaries. Using a complex statistical model examining educational marriage trade-offs, she suggests that ethnic distinctiveness is reinforced in these marriages. In particular, marriage patterns of those of mixed ancestry increase the association between low socioeconomic status and Asian-African identity (Okun 2001).

Similarly, the evidence on residential location differences among siblings and between the generations does not necessarily imply the breakdown of ethnic or family ties. The same data show that fully 60 percent of the women and almost 70 percent of their husbands live in the same geographic place as their parents; those who do not may have developed other forms of family contact. In Israel, distances among places are small, and personal ties, family contacts, and family and economic networks are maintained without neighborhood closeness.

Some supportive evidence among high-school students in Israel reinforces the notion of specific ethnic origin preferences among those who will marry in the next generation. Israeli-born Jewish young adults of Israeli-born parents raised with egalitarian and liberal attitudes toward ethnicity express very ethnic-based attitudes about their own ethnic preferences in spouse selection and have fairly strong negative views about specific ethnic origins. Those of Middle Eastern origin are more likely to view others of Middle Eastern origin (not necessarily of their specific country of origin but the Israeli constructed category of "Oriental") as preferable potential spouses and partners over "Europeans," or Westerners (Shahar 1991).

In the longer run, ethnic origin may diminish significantly as a basis for social, cultural, economic, and political cleavages among Jews in Israel. However, there is every basis for arguing the continuing salience of ethnicity in the next generations because of the overlap of ethnic residential patterns and education and occupation patterns with ethnic origin, along with implications for socialization and politics. Ethnicity in Israel is not simply the reflection of closeness to cultural roots; it is the lack of socioeconomic equalization among groups that has characterized Jewish ethnic subpopulations. Family and economic networks have served to reinforce family ties and ethnic communities based on family ties. The shape ethnicity will take in the long term will depend in large part on the continuing overlap of ethnicity and social class, residence, and culture in the next generation.

My assessment of intermarriage follows from the structural argument about communities. On one hand, demographic convergences in mortality and in some family processes occurred among Jewish ethnic populations. Ethnic differences that primarily reflected past origins diminished as Israeli institutions and Israeli contexts shaped immigrant groups and their children. Institutions, such as the army and the system of ethnically integrated schooling, operated to reinforce national allegiances and collectively shared culture. On the other hand, family centrality helped sustain ethnic continuity and reinforced ethnic communities based on residential patterns. The role of the educational system and occupational networks in sustaining or reducing ethnic communities has already been documented (Chapter 7).

Ethnic communities are not simply extensions of past ethnic origins but are based on new Israeli-created constructions, moving beyond the meanings of ethnicity in places of origin. Hence, the key question in understanding intermarriage patterns is whether they signal the retention or the loss of community. The currently stable rates of intermarriage and the educational and ethnic trade-offs, along with uncertainty of how children of mixed ethnic origins will select their own ethnic communities over their life courses, point to the continuous salience of ethnicity for several generations.

What does the generational emphasis imply for an understanding of family connections in Israel? Intermarriage among Jews is marriage between Jews (and their families) across ethnic origin boundaries. The ethnic options are available to the next generation of the interethnically married and may help to solve the ethnic origin dilemma of these children. Their generational choices are to select an ethnic origin of one of the parents or retain the combined mixture of Western and Middle Eastern origins. The latter combination is possible, since the selection does not have to be permanent and can change in context—in the synagogue one could be of "Iraqi" ethnicity because that is the father's origin, and at home one could be of "Polish" ethnicity because the home is the mother's domain.

The second generation of mixed ethnic origins could become "just" Israeli and treat ethnicity as irrelevant. Those of mixed origins might select this option while retaining some relationship to grandparents or other extended relatives who are ethnically identified. The mixed third generation is most likely to respond to a question about their ethnic identity by identifying themselves as "Israeli," but that may not be sufficiently clear as a basis for networking or for identity in all circumstances, even though it solves the confusion of the moment. Networks based on ethnicity are not simply the result of the social psychology of personal identity. The option of individuals identifying themselves only as "Israeli" is most likely to occur when ethnicity at the group level loses its family and social class importance.

I have been surprised by the revolutions in family patterns in Israel—not because of the changes that have occurred but because of the continuities in family centrality despite major changes. Family has remained normative for almost everyone in Israel. Radical demographic and social changes have not moved persons toward nonfamilies, either nonmarriage or extensive nonfamily living arrangements. Delayed marriage, which is responsive to the social, economic, educational, and political contexts among all ethnic origin groups in Israeli society, becomes marriage postponed but not foregone. Changes both in the proportion married and in the age at which persons marry reveal important ethnic convergences and join the converging ethnic differences in other areas as powerful indications of some forms of the national integration of ethnic groups.

Changes in Israeli society would lead us to expect sharper increases in nonfamily living and in the centrality of the family in the life course of young adults than that observed. Similarly, divorce rates have increased but remain low, and remarriages tend to follow where there are options available. Other family changes are less likely to result in the demise of this powerful institution. Family connections must serve economic needs, provide comfort and support of children and grandchildren, and provide social and political connections in order to be sustained in the face of the major demographic and social upheavals Israel has experienced. It is the structural connections to families, not the "value" placed on the family, that have shaped these types of family continuities. Family continuities in Israel are the basis of continuities in ethnic communities. Ethnicity and family issues revolve around generations and around the transmission of community and culture, of rights and obligations, and of continuity and social networks. Together families and ethnicity provide the building blocks for the next generation of Israeli families.

Notes

1. A related theme is changes in the roles of men and women, reviewed in Chapter 8 in the context of inequality.

2. That marriage is normal for everyone in Israel is somewhat less true for Christians than for others, as 6 percent of the men and 15 percent of the women age 65 and over have never married, reflecting in part involvement in institutions requiring religious celibacy.

3. Age-at-marriage data for women and men are from the registry of marriages and therefore do not take into account the whole population, i.e., those that do not marry. Hence, these data complement but do not substitute for the population-based data.

4. Divorces are available in Israel, but the religious establishment controls the procedures of divorce and the granting of formal divorce decrees. There is no civil divorce in Israel as there are no civil marriages.

5. For a review and an analysis of American data among young adults and older persons see Goldscheider and Goldscheider 1993 and 1999 and the references cited therein.

6. The marriage market for Jews in Israel has never included the Arab populations. Arabs in Israel are not acceptable as spouses for Jewish Israelis (and vice versa), on political and institutional grounds as well as for religious considerations from the perspective of

both communities. The small number of Jewish-Arab couples in Israel tend to live on the margins of both communities. Intermarriages across "religious" national lines are not legally permitted in Israel without religious conversion.

7. Many of the first social studies of Israeli society treated intermarriage between ethnic groups as one of the powerful indicators of national integration, and scholars expected this form of ethnic assimilation to occur by the third generation. See for example, Bachi 1977; Bar-Yosef 1971; Ben-David 1970; Eisenstadt 1954, 1969.

8. It is well known that marriage-market squeezes are normal, not exceptional, in periods when cohort fertility patterns change or when migration is selective by age and sex. The issues that need to be isolated are the severity of the impact on the market of eligibles, the normative options available, and how persons differentially respond to these altered circumstances.

9. One in-depth study of thirty interethnically married couples in Jerusalem, along with their children, concluded that intermarriage did not foster widespread integration, noting that the selectivity of those who out-marry is less likely to leave the residual nonintermarrying population more homogeneous. No firm conclusions could be drawn about the ethnic identity of the children of these couples, but a strong implication of that discussion is that the "ethnic neighborhood," or more broadly the ethnic context plus some of the socioeconomic characteristics of parents and children, would determine the ethnic identity of the children of mixed ethnic parents. Clearly, interethnic marriage did not result in the automatic loss of all ethnic identity for those couples. See the insightful discussion in Rosen 1982.

11

The Transition to Small Family Size: The Fertility Revolution and Ethnic Convergences

One of the revolutions associated with the modernization of Western societies has been the transition from large to small family size. This transition has been linked to the decreasing value of children as farm laborers, to the changing role of women, and to the increasing investment parents make in their children and the higher costs of raising them. It has also been related to the greater ability of couples to implement their reproductive decisions. Indeed, the revolutionary changes in fertility levels are one manifestation of the increasing range of choices that accompanies modernization and the higher value placed on individual rather than family goals (Goldscheider 1992c). Changes in the number of children families have and, cumulatively, the fertility levels of communities are therefore central to understanding the development of societies and their ethnic diversity. An examination of fertility levels in Israel provides insight into the linkages among our three themes of population, nation-building, and ethnicity.

Fertility levels, in conjunction with mortality, are primary sources of population growth; with the decline in mortality in Israel, fertility levels have shaped rates of overall population growth and have become sources of differential ethnic population growth rates. Given the importance of population growth for economic planning and development, governments have often fostered policies to enhance fertility control and to provide maternal and child welfare services to emphasize the quality of life of children over the number of children. Fertility control policies in Israel have often clashed with pronatalist Zionist ideologies and Israeli norms, which valued the increase of Jewish population through diverse means— primarily by way of immigration but also through sustained large family size (see the historical review in Friedlander and Goldscheider 1979).

Powerful linkages between immigration and the differential fertility of ethnic origin populations raise questions about the demographic assimilation of groups among Jews and between Jews and Arabs as well. Through the combined effects of immigration and differential fertility, the ethnic composition of Israel has been transformed. Generational continuity of ethnic communities is dependent on intra-ethnic marriages and childbearing. The study of the transmission to smaller family size is therefore of importance for its demographic relevance, for what it implies about individual gender and family roles, and for the structure and composition of communities over time. Because of the links between family size, generational replacement, and social mobility, the decline in fertility level has been used as a prime demographic indicator of the advantage (or continuing disadvantage) of subpopulations and of the relative integration of immigrant groups from different fertility backgrounds.

In this chapter, I link fertility changes to both development processes and ethnic communities in Israel, addressing the analytic questions of the diverse timing of fertility declines and fertility convergences among ethnic groups. Similar to other countries, Israel has experienced fertility reductions over time and the transition to small family size; fertility changes have occurred in more compressed time periods in Israel than elsewhere and without direct government intervention. Moreover, significant fertility variation has characterized major ethnic subgroups in Israel in the past and is likely to continue to have implications for social, economic, political, and demographic processes into the next decades.

Changing Fertility Patterns over Time

I start with the basic description of fertility changes in Israel, noting their complexity and diverse pattern and answering the question, What have been the major changes in fertility and family size in Israel? A careful and detailed look at fertility patterns in Israel since the 1950s reveals several major revolutions, not one simple pattern. The fertility level of Israelis of European-American origins has fluctuated, though it has remained near lower levels, with slight increases over time. In contrast, there has been a steady decline in Christian-Arab fertility levels over more than a half-century and a significant reduction in the Moslem-Israeli fertility level since the 1970s. Major fertility reductions have characterized Jewish immigrants from Asian and African countries and their Israeli-born children, dropping by 50 percent from the 1950s to the 1980s.

Thus, the first fertility pattern that emerges clearly is a reduction in family size over time, fluctuating around low levels of controlled fertility in the new millennium. Data in Table 11.1 show a decline in the crude birth rate among Jews from 34 per 1,000 population in the 1920s to below 30 per 1,000 in the mid-1950s, to around 20 per 1,000 starting in the late 1980s and continuing through the end of the twentieth century. This rather steady overall decline was, in fact, much sharper than what may appear at first glance, since the decline incorporates immigrant Jewish families

TABLE 11.1   Crude Birth Rates of Jews and Moslems in Palestine and Israel, 1925–1999 (births per 1,000 population)

| | Crude Birth Rates | |
	Jews	*Moslems*
1925–1929	34	51
1930–1934	32	54
1935–1939	27	47
1946	30	54
1950–1954	31	52
1955–1959	26	46
1960–1964	23	52
1965–1969	23	51
1970–1974	24	50
1975–1979	24	45
1980–1984	22	37
1985–1989	21	35
1990–1994	19	37
1995–1999	19	37

Sources: *Statistical Abstract of Israel*, various years; estimates for the earlier periods from Kanev 1957, tables 7 and 9.

arriving in the 1950s from Middle Eastern countries, who were characterized by higher fertility than that of the European-origin Jewish population in Israel.

A second pattern evident in these data is the consistently higher levels of fertility among Moslems than among Jews throughout these seven decades. The Moslem fertility level, overall, has also been high relative to world fertility levels, although its current level is among the lowest of Arab populations in the Middle East. The crude birth rate of Moslems in Palestine was over 50 per 1,000 population in the 1920s, and it continued to fluctuate at high levels until the mid-1970s, when a noticeable decline in Moslem fertility began. The Moslem crude birth rate in Israel in the 1990s averaged 37 per 1,000 population, a level characteristic of the Jewish population in Palestine in the 1920s and comparable to many countries in Asia and Africa.

The declining fertility over time and the higher Moslem than Jewish fertility level raise the question of the changing gap between these populations in Israel. The crude birth rate gap between Jews and Moslems in Palestine and in Israel increased significantly until the end of the 1960s, and from an 18-point gap (per 1,000) to a 26-point gap in the early 1970s. The increasing differences between Moslem and Jewish birth rates reflected the relative stability of the Moslem level and sharp declines in the crude birth rate among Jews. Since the mid-1970s, the gap between these populations has narrowed considerably as the crude birth rate among Moslems declined and the Jewish rate declined only slightly during the same period.

These three patterns—general fertility rate declines, higher Moslem than Jewish fertility levels, and the changing fertility gap between those two populations—are derived from simple measures, relating births to total Jewish and Moslem populations rather than to women in their childbearing period. A more refined measure of fertility (and one that has more intuitive meaning) is the total fertility rate: the cumulative age-specific pattern of births to women in the childbearing ages.[1] Changes in these rates over time and in other direct fertility measures (Table 11.2) reveal clearly the overall decline of one child per woman among Israeli families from the mid-1950s until the 1980s, from a total fertility rate of 4 children per woman until 1970 to 3 children per woman during the two decades of the 1980s and the 1990s. This decline was quite pronounced among women with higher numbers of births. The proportion of women with 5 or more births declined in Israel from about 25 percent before 1970 to about 15 percent in the 1990s.

These measures of changing fertility levels over time reinforce the conclusions derived from the crude birth rate data and add details and refinements. For the Jewish population as a whole, there was a decline of 1 child per woman on average (from 3.6 to 2.7 children) during the period from 1955 to the 1990s; the proportion of Jewish women having 5 or more births fell by half, from 24 percent in 1960 to 13 percent in the 1990s (the percentage actually dipped below 10 percent in the 1980s). Impressive fertility shifts occurred among ethnic groups in the Jewish population. Among Israeli Jews born in Asian and African countries, the total fertility rate dropped steadily and dramatically in 40 years—from a total fertility rate of 5.7 children per woman in 1955 to 3.2 in the 1990s. The fertility level of European-American-origin women has been lower and declined only modestly, from 2.6 children per woman in 1955 to 2.3 in the 1990s, having increased to 2.8 children during the 1970s and 1980s.

Detailed data by age (lower panel of Table 11.2) show sharp fertility declines among young Jewish women below age 19 and from ages 20 to 24, particularly for the Asian-African-born Jewish population. During the 1980s and 1990s, there was an increase in the fertility level of European-American-born women ages 40 to 44. In contrast, fertility rates for older Asian-African-born women declined significantly: from 50 to 15 births per 1,000 women ages 40 to 44 between 1950s and 1980s, and from 16 to 2.7 births per 1,000 women ages 45 to 49 between the 1950s and the 1990s. As a result of the sharp decline among Asian-African-born women and the slight increase among the European-American-born, the fertility gap between these populations has narrowed considerably and fluctuates around low levels. Fertility convergences among Jewish women of different ethnic origins (and with different fertility histories) have occurred in Israel, even as women of Asian and African origin have retained a somewhat higher level. Convergences mean narrower gaps over time, not necessarily the full closure of differential fertility among all groups.

Associated with these convergences in the actual fertility of these populations were parallel convergences in fertility norms. The growing consensus among

TABLE 11.2 Selected Measures of Fertility Levels in Israel, by Religion and Ethnicity, 1955–1998

	1955	1960	1965	1970	1975	1980	1985	1990	1995	1998
	Total Fertility Rates									
Total	4.03	3.95	3.99	3.97	3.68	3.14	3.12	3.02	2.88	2.98
Jews	3.64	3.49	3.47	3.41	3.21	2.76	2.85	2.69	2.56	2.67
European-American born										
	2.63	2.38	2.60	2.84	2.82	2.76	2.79	2.31	2.20	2.29
Asian-African born										
	5.68	5.10	4.58	4.07	3.77	3.04	3.21	3.09	3.25	3.20
Moslem	7.96	9.31	9.87	8.95	7.75	5.98	4.86	4.70	4.69	4.76
Christian	4.85	4.61	4.74	3.62	3.35	2.66	2.12	2.57	1.81	2.62
Druze	6.58	7.88	7.61	7.46	6.85	6.09	4.47	4.05	3.51	3.10
	Proportion with Five or More Live Births									
Total	23	29	27	22	17	15	14	16	16	16
Jews	19	24	21	15	10	8	9	12	13	13
Moslem	49	50	51	50	45	40	32	28	26	24
Christian	39	40	33	25	19	16	9	7	5	6

Age-Specific Fertility Rates

	1955–1959	1965–1969	1975–1979	1985–1989	1990–1994	1995–1996
Jews						
European-American born						
<Age 19	43.4	33.3	58.3	34.0	24.1	20.5
20–24	168.1	172.0	166.3	135.6	112.2	100.8
40–44	8.4	5.5	6.8	10.7	9.7	10.8
45–49	0.8	0.5	0.2	0.7	0.7	0.5
Asian-African born						
<Age 19	89.3	61.0	47.6	38.8	46.5	33.6
20–24	289.9	234.4	202.1	163.4	153.4	143.5
40–44	50.2	33.2	17.5	15.1	18.7	21.9
45–49	15.8	8.7	1.9	1.2	2.6	2.8
Moslem						
<Age 19	119.6	113.8	91.8	53.9	56.6	58.0
20–24	375.8	383.9	334.0	236.9	244.5	248.2
40–44	107.8	154.9	90.0	47.4	41.2	37.3
45–49	41.1	55.8	20.6	5.8	4.5	3.7
Christian						
<Age 19	58.7	45.5	30.3	18.0	15.9	18.6
20–24	227.9	224.7	189.5	154.4	134.0	129.7
40–44	29.8	29.6	15.8	7.6	7.3	8.2
45–49	5.5	4.4	1.3	0.6	1.6	–

Source: *Statistical Abstract of Israel*, various years.
Note: These measures are defined in the text.

Jewish Israelis is to have a family size of about 3 children, close to 1 child more than the average family size ideals of persons in most developed countries. In the mid-1970s, young Jewish couples of both ethnic groups revealed a close fit between their expressed family size norms and their actual behavior—they were having the number of children they wanted and planning their families to attain their family size goals. The decline in Asian-African fertility levels was accompanied by a downward adjustment in these women's fertility norms (Table 11.3).

Although not strictly comparable, measures of family size norms in the late 1980s continued to show that desired and ideal family size was higher for younger cohorts of Asian-African Jewish women than for European-American women by about half a child (Schmelz et al. 1990, table 42). A nationwide survey in the late 1980s revealed that Middle Eastern–origin Jewish women desired 3.7 children on average and Western-origin women desired 3.2 children. The "ideal" number of children was even higher: 4.4 children among the Middle Eastern women and 4.0 children among the Western women.[2]

Fertility Transitions, Immigration, and Jewish Cohorts

The fertility changes that I have described direct attention to the reasons underlying these changes and to the factors that need to be taken into account for their explanation. What accounts for the fertility level decline in Israel, its pace, and the reduction of the ethnic fertility gap? What are the causes of the increase in fertility levels among some groups in Israel, and what explains the overall higher level, virtually unique among economically developed countries? What were the mechanisms that resulted in these patterns of fertility change, and what have been the roles of government policy and the "cultural" or social contexts that shaped these patterns? How are changes in marriage, contraception, and abortion linked to these fertility changes? Research addressing these issues provides the basis for understanding the connections between fertility and sociodemographic, economic, and political changes and the changing roles of women and families in the Jewish population.[3]

The country of origin of immigrants, as I have noted, is associated with their particular socioeconomic backgrounds. Duration of residence in Israel is an indicator of exposure to the society, particularly for the second generation. I have already documented the immediate response of immigrants to the new health services and conditions in Israel, which resulted in increasing life expectancy during the first several years of exposure to Israeli society (see Chapter 9). Results of a series of retrospective cohort studies show the effect of immigration on the changing fertility patterns of immigrants of different socioeconomic origins. I begin with European immigrants.

European-origin groups have had, and continue to have, low levels of fertility. Jewish immigrants from European countries arriving before the establishment of the state had, on average, 2.3 children over several cohorts, with no fertility differences among people from different places of origin within Europe. Jewish immigrants from Europe who arrived after the establishment of the state had even

TABLE 11.3 Ideal Family Size in Israel, by Religion, Ethnic Origin, and
Marriage Cohort

Religion and Ethnic Origin	Total	Before 1955	1955–1964	1964–1974
		Average Ideal Family Size		
Jewish women				
Eastern European born	3.5	3.6	3.5	3.5
Western European born	3.8	3.9	3.8	3.8
Israel born				
European origin	3.8	4.2	3.6	3.8
Asian born	4.9	5.4	4.7	4.2
African born	5.6	6.5	5.4	4.9
Israel born				
Asian-African origin	4.0	5.4	4.3	4.2
Arab women				
Christian-urban	5.0	5.8	5.1	4.2
Christian-rural	5.6	6.5	5.7	4.4
Moslem-urban	6.1	7.5	6.3	4.8
Moslem-rural	6.9	8.3	7.0	5.3

Source: Goldscheider and Friedlander 1986, tables 1, 3, and 4.

lower fertility levels, reflecting the effects of the extremely harsh circumstances of World War II on women's reproductive patterns. Recent cohorts of European-origin groups in Israel have experienced about a 10 percent upswing in fertility (a mini–baby boom), averaging around 2.5 children per married woman. The small increase in fertility characterized all European-origin groups and has resulted in higher levels than that in Western industrialized countries.

Immigration from Asian countries was concentrated in the earlier periods of nation-building. Immigrants from North African countries arrived later and were spread over a large number of years (see Chapter 3). Initial levels of fertility among both groups were high—about 6.5 births among those who married in the 1930s (most of whom were married and had children before immigrating to Israel), declining to an average of 3 children among marriage cohorts of the 1950s (most of whom were married and having children in Israel). Fertility levels were almost halved between cohorts 25 years apart, and large family size has been replaced by medium-to-small families. Jewish immigrants from North African countries had higher levels of initial fertility than did Asian immigrants, about 7.5 children per woman. Sharp and early fertility reductions took place for these immigrants upon exposure to Israeli society. These reductions occurred quite soon after arrival in Israel and converged with the patterns for Asian immigrants.

The fertility level differences between Asian and African immigrants and among specific country-of-origin groups within these populations reflect differences in the timing of immigration and length of exposure to Israeli society, not cultural differences among groups. As length of exposure to Israeli society increased, these country-of-origin differences in fertility disappeared. Fertility convergences in Israel have occurred within and between Jewish ethnic groups. Israeli-born Jews of Western origin have somewhat higher fertility than their parents' generation; the second generation of Middle Eastern origin have lower fertility than their parents' generation. Cohort fertility patterns are thus converging between Israelis of Western and of Middle Eastern origins.

One puzzling feature of these changes is that the fertility convergences of the second and later generations of Israelis have stabilized at higher levels when compared to Western countries generally. Explanations for these higher fertility levels relate to specific economic and military conditions in Israel. The economic conditions in Israel have improved considerably for the Jewish population in the post-1967 period, following the Six Day War. Because of the improvements, births, which had been delayed or postponed due to the socioeconomic hardships of earlier periods (among the children of European immigrants) increased, as did the desire for a third child. But why should the Israeli born want and have 3 and not 2 children on average? It may reflect what demographers have referred to as an "insurance" effect, motivated by Israel's flow of military casualties (Friedlander and Goldscheider 1978). This means that people decide on an additional child as insurance against the risk that war or military action will result in the premature death of one child. Higher fertility levels may thus be a result of the willingness of Israeli Jewish families to allocate more resources, compared to those in Western countries, toward raising a somewhat large family. The economic circumstances of the late 1960s and 1970s transformed that potential into childbearing. This would account for the fertility increase among all Jewish ethnic groups (and none of the Arab populations) and their fertility convergences.

Other explanations emphasize the familistic orientation of Israeli society and the continuing segregated roles of Israeli women. Unlike in some Western industrialized nations, the employment of women in Israel does not seem to conflict with their family size goals, nor does it lead to their increased autonomy and status within the family (see my discussion in Chapters 8 and 10; Kupinsky 1992). The greater familism in Israeli society is thus associated with higher fertility levels in Israel than in Western countries.

Contemporary Jewish Fertility Differentials

Clearly, the contemporary Israeli pattern involves fluctuations around low fertility levels, and there is no indication of a return to larger family size. It is too soon

TABLE 11.4 Number of Children Born to Israeli Women, by Selected Towns, 1961 and 1983

	Number of Children Born to Women Age 25–29	
Town	1961	1983
Dimona	4.0	3.3
Qiryat Shemona	4.1	3.1
Ramla	3.6	2.8
Qiryat Gat	3.8	2.9
Giv'atayim	1.9	2.1
Nazerat Illit	2.1	2.4
Qiryat Bialik	2.2	2.3
Qiryat Motzkin	2.0	2.3
Tel Aviv	2.3	2.2
Jerusalem	3.1	2.6
Haifa	2.1	2.2
Be'er Sheva'	3.7	2.6

Source: Adapted from Friedlander et al. 1990, Appendix table A.

to answer fully the questions of total ethnic convergences in family size, since the third generation of Israelis of Western and of Middle Eastern origins have not completed their family formation patterns. More interesting, but less fully documented, are the unfolding fertility patterns among the recent immigrant groups from the former Soviet Union, who have had very low fertility, and immigrants from Ethiopia, who have had higher fertility and mortality. How these groups will develop in Israel will be the social demographic stories of the twenty-first century.

Findings about contemporary fertility variation in Israel parallels the discussion of mortality convergences in Israel (Chapter 9). I noted that areal differences in mortality in Israel have diminished over time; indeed, most differences have disappeared. These differences are particularly significant, given the overlap of ethnicity, resources, and regional concentration. Family size data estimated for women ages 25 to 29 by area (Table 11.4) show that there was a substantial range among areas in 1961, from around 2 children per woman for largely Western-origin Jewish settlements (such as Giv'atayim and Haifa) to 4 children per woman among those living in development towns (such as Dimona or Qiryat Shemona), areas largely populated by Middle Eastern immigrants and their children. All of these areas experienced a downward trend over time toward the two-child family. Areas characterized by an average of 4 children in the 1960s moved toward 3 children in the 1980s; several places that were characterized by families with 2 children in the

1960s increased to 2.3 in the 1980s. Families in Be'er Sheva', among the largest urban places, were reduced in size from 3.7 to 2.6 children, reflecting the fertility reductions of their Asian-African-origin population. Jerusalem retained a higher level of fertility than other urban places, reflecting the impact of its larger religious subpopulations. (see data in Friedlander et al. 1990). As a result of these changes, the general variance in fertility differences among places in 1961 declined significantly by 1983. In the late 1990s, the Jewish population living in Jerusalem, in small-sized places below 10,000, and in selected rural areas have retained somewhat higher fertility. This is likely to be connected to the religious composition of these places.

Some additional insights into the fertility level of recent cohorts can be obtained from the results of a survey of Jewish married women (ages 22 to 39) living in urban communities in Israel, which was carried out in the late 1980s (Kupinsky 1992). These data show that educational attainment continues to negatively affect family size patterns, but the importance of education has declined among recent cohorts. The convergence in ethnic group differences that was documented in the 1970s has continued apace. With increased levels of education among all Jewish ethnic groups, fertility differentials are converging and are likely to converge even further. Indeed, ethnic origin differences in fertility levels tend to be minimal in the most recent marriage cohorts. As length of exposure to the norms and values of Israeli society and to the institutions that shape the lives of those married and educated in Israel increases, fertility patterns lose their ethnic distinctiveness (Eisenbach 1992). The convergence in ethnic fertility has often been attributed to the changes and improvements in the level of schooling, the negative association between number of children and investment in children, the increase in interethnic marriages, and a likely convergence of human capital endowments (Ben-Porath 1986).

Religiosity is a major factor that continues to differentiate the fertility levels of young Jewish families in Israel. Parallel to earlier findings (Goldscheider and Friedlander 1986), recent research has shown a direct relationship between religiosity among Jews and levels of fertility. Using four self-enumerated categories, from secular to ultra-Orthodox (*haredi*), research shows that the higher the level of religious commitments, the higher the fertility, even controlling for educational level. Indeed, fertility differences by religiosity are pronounced among the more educated, since there is no relationship between years of education and fertility among the more religious (Kupinsky 1992). These results are reinforced by systematic ecological analyses, showing the convergences of most fertility differences by ethnic origin and the decline to around 2 children on average, except in areas where religious Jews are residentially concentrated. The fertility levels of families living in those areas raises the average fertility level for the Jewish population as a whole (Friedlander and Feldman 1993).

Not unrelated are the linkages between the attitudes toward the roles of women and fertility.[4] It is not surprising that women who think that childbearing and child rearing are the most important thing in a woman's life are likely to have significantly larger families than women who express less traditional gender-segregated roles. As a composite, the evidence suggests that women have lower fertility norms and behavior if they (1) have higher levels of education, (2) were raised by parents of Western origin, (3) are secular in orientation, (4) have a consistent work pattern outside the home, (5) share housework responsibilities, (6) have higher family incomes and better jobs, and (7) are less positive toward the centrality of childbearing in their lives. Religiosity is the most important factor when all of these variables are examined jointly (Kupinsky 1992).

It is unlikely that religiosity in Judaism implies the simple connection between theology and fertility, since there is neither a known, clear theology in Judaism on family size nor a clear-cut prohibition on the use of all forms of contraception (Friedlander and Goldscheider 1984; Goldscheider 1971; Goldscheider and Fried-lander 1986). In Israel, as elsewhere (Goldscheider and Mosher 1991), religiosity implies a commitment to traditional family and gender roles, and particularly to the family and childbearing roles of women. For the more religious in Israel, the role of women is adjunct to family and childbearing, and not equal to men (see Chapter 8). Gender segregation and inequality are likely to result in higher fertility norms and larger families, not simply because of prohibitions on the use of contraception and specific norms about birth control, but rather because of more general norms and values—and the structures that sustain them—about women's roles and family centrality (see Chapters 8 and 10). Religiosity is linked to values about family and the role of women that are less responsive to changes in socioeconomic contexts.[5]

The similar experiences of Israeli young adults and their shared communications in a variety of settings are likely to result in the growing similarity of their family building and family size patterns. Commonalities in terms of women's roles, the army, and educational experiences; the smallness of the country; and the national welfare entitlement system yield some uniform family formation patterns and shared generational family size goals. Access to information about controlling family size among the diverse segments of the population influences ethnic fertility convergences over time and helps to explain the family size decline converging toward a new Israeli norm. Familism, gender-role segregation, and traditional pressures from both Judaism and secular Zionism result in levels of fertility higher than in Western countries in general.

Moslem and Christian Fertility Changes in Israel

The crude birth rate data (Table 11.1) documented the slowness of the Moslem fertility reduction and the changes that began to occur in the 1970s. More detailed data show important variations between the fertility of Moslems and Christians in Israel (Table 11.2). Fertility levels among Moslems fell from a high of over 9 children per woman on average in the 1960s to 4.7 children per woman in the 1990s; 50 percent of the Moslem women had 5 or more births through the 1970s, declining by 50 percent in the late 1990s. Moslem fertility levels continue to be significantly higher than that among Jews, but have clearly moved toward lower levels in recent generations. Processes of Moslem-Jewish fertility convergences are therefore clearly evident.

The Arab population in Israel is clearly not homogeneous in terms of fertility processes. Both the level of fertility and the pace of its reduction differentiate Christian from Moslem Israelis; both populations are different in pace and level from the Jewish ethnic patterns that we described. Nevertheless, convergence toward small family size has become ubiquitous among all groups. The Christian- Arab fertility levels are more comparable to the Jewish levels (indeed, their fertility levels have often been below the overall Jewish levels in the 1980s and 1990s). The fertility decline has been more steady among the Christian population, and there are indications that it began among the urban and more-educated women as early as the marriage cohort of the 1920s (see Friedlander et al. 1979). In 1998, the total fertility rate among Arab Christians was 2.6 children per woman (lower than among Asian and African Jewish immigrants, higher than among European-Americans and slightly below the overall Jewish level of 2.7) compared to 4.8 per woman among Moslems and 3.1 per woman among Druze. Very sharp declines in childbearing among younger Christian Arab women may be noted, as well as the stopping of childbearing at higher parities.

These patterns help shape two important questions. First, what factors were involved in the reduction of Christian Arab fertility and were they the same as that identified for Jewish Israelis? Second, what accounts for the timing of the Moslem Israeli fertility decline, both the delay up to the 1970s and the subsequent reduction? Research has attempted to resolve these questions and provides insights into the nature of Arab communities in Israel. I start with a more detailed look at the fertility data for these two subpopulations.

The fertility transition was slower and later than mortality changes among the Moslem population in Israel (see Eisenbach 1986) and later than among Christian- Arab Israelis (see Friedlander et al. 1979). After 30 years of marriage, Moslem women who married before 1935 had 8.1 children, those married in 1940 had 9.1 children, and the cohort that married between 1944 and 1948 had 9.4 children. Ideal family size by marriage cohort (as viewed in the 1970s) documented the changing attitudinal and normative expectations of Arab women (Goldscheider and Friedlander 1986). Christian women who were married before 1955 had an ideal family size of about 6 children, but the cohort married in the post-1967 period had an average ideal family size of 4 children. Moslem women of the older cohort had an ideal family size of about 8 children, declining among those married in the 1970s to 5 children. In contrast to the Jewish pattern, most of the Moslem women controlled family size after long marriage durations, using contraception for stopping childbearing but not for the spacing of births. In the period since 1975, fertility reductions occurred even among Moslem women at shorter marriage durations and have included all socioeconomic segments of the

Arab population, even the less educated (Eisenbach 1989). The total fertility rate for the 1990s (4.7) is similar to the number of children considered ideal by the cohorts of Moslem women married in the late 1960s and early 1970s.

The general factors associated with lower Arab fertility patterns include the continuing declines and low levels of mortality (life expectancy increased to about 73 for both sexes; infant mortality declined from 60 deaths per 1,000 births at the end of the 1950s, to 41 deaths per 1,000 births in 1975, to 15 in 1989, and to 9 in 1999—see Chapter 9). In addition, there has been a continuing increase in the educational attainment of Moslem women: Those who benefited from the mandatory education act in Israel reached their childbearing period only in the 1970s. Thus, among those women who were married between 1974 and 1978, only 8 percent had 9 or more years of education, compared to 31 percent among those who married from 1979 to 1983. The labor force pattern of Israeli Moslems has also changed. The formal participation of Moslem women in the paid labor force remains lower than Christian and Jewish women—but the more-educated Moslem women (13 years or more of schooling) participate in the labor force as much as the Christian Arab women (see Eisenbach 1989).

Other factors influencing Moslem fertility connect Moslem families to the communities in which they live. There has been a shift in the kind of male employment, tied to the economic "integration" of Arabs in the Jewish economy (Chapter 4). Moslem Israelis have left agriculture and commute to jobs in the Jewish sector (in 1983 only 7 percent of Moslem men worked in agriculture, compared to 18 percent in 1972 and 35 percent in 1961; fully half of the Moslem men worked outside their residential areas in the 1980s). The proportion of men working in white-collar jobs was 14 percent in 1983, double that of a decade earlier. Part, but not all, of the move toward white-collar jobs was facilitated by the entrance into Israel of Arab day laborers from the administered territories, pushing the Israeli Moslems upward socioeconomically. Standards of living have increased in real terms: Between 1972 and 1983, the income of Moslem laborers in cities has increased by 50 percent, a 5 percent per capita increase per year. Consumption has increased as well (Eisenbach 1989; see also Chapter 7).

Increases in the standard of living and in education, along with the benefits from the welfare state and the increase in the opportunity structure, suggest that the power of the extended family and the *Hamula* has declined,[6] particularly among younger couples whose economic futures are less under the control of their extended families. Thus, from the point of view of the Arab community, fertility is a feature of intergenerational family and economic connections and is an important reflection of the ways Arab-Israeli communities are organized. Changes in the decade beginning in the 1970s, put pressures on this connection and, combined with socioeconomic increases, led to the beginning of the transition to small family size.

Examining fertility by type of settlement and by education shows, for example, the significantly higher fertility level among rural Moslems compared to urban

Moslems, particularly at older ages. Data in Table 11.5 show the significant variation in childbearing by educational level. Although the numbers of Moslem women, as of the 1983 census, who attained 13 or more years of education at the three periods of marriage duration was small, the numbers are increasing and their fertility patterns are clear. After 20 to 24 years of marriage, Moslem women with 11 or more years of education had about 5 children, 3 children fewer than women with little or no education. After a decade of marriage, the more-educated Moslem had 4 children, but the less-educated women had over 5 children, on average.

Have state policies been involved in the changing pattern of Arab fertility? The state has provided the opportunity to increase the educational level of the population; the provision of social security organized at the national level has increased the expectations for higher levels of living. Moreover, the state supports families through subsidies and tax benefits; welfare payments through the national insurance system may, in the early years, have prevented an earlier and even sharper fertility decline (see Friedlander et al. 1979). The shift toward smaller families in conjunction with economic trends has steadily eroded the control that the *Hamula* exercised over women and the value of children and large family size. These changes have broken the powerful linkage between place of residence, *Hamula*, and fertility (Al Haj 1987).

There has been a slight increase in the average age that Moslem women marry, from 19.7 years in 1960 to 20.6 in the 1980s and 1990s. In the period from 1964 to 1968, 34 percent of those who married were under age 18, compared to 18 percent among those married from 1979 to 1983. It is estimated that about one-third of the decline in the fertility of Moslem women between 1972 and 1983 can be accounted for by the decline in early marriage (Eisenbach 1989). The relationship between education of women and their age at marriage is U-shaped among Moslems. Both the least educated and the most educated marry later, in part because of the arranged marriage system wherein women with education are less desirable spouses and women with more education are more likely to delay marriage until after school and some work experience. Thus, when the average age of marriage of Moslem women was 20.6 years, it was 21.7 for those with 0 to 4 years of education and 22.8 years for those with 13 or more years of schooling. Later age at marriage characterizes the Moslem population in the recent period and for each of the levels of education (Eisenbach 1989; see also our earlier discussion in Chapter 10 and the data in Table 10.3). The declining Moslem fertility among the younger generation has occurred primarily through the use of contraception controlling births within marriage.

Changes in marriage and in the control of fertility within marriage are clearly linked to the major demographic and socioeconomic transitions that have characterized the Moslem- Israeli population in the last three decades, and these changes gained momentum in the 1970s and 1980s. Large family size contradicts the emerging tastes associated with higher standards of living and increased education.

TABLE 11.5 Average Number of Births to Moslem Women in Israel in Their First Marriage, by Number of Years of Education and Duration of Marriage, 1983

Years of Education	Years of Marriage		
	10–14	*15–19*	*20–24*
	Number of Births		
0–4	5.4	7.0	8.2
5–8	5.0	6.4	7.3
9–10	4.6	6.0	6.3
11–12	4.3	5.3	5.2
13+	3.5	4.3	4.7

Source: Adapted from Eisenbach 1989, table 11.

The importance of higher Arab than Jewish fertility for differential population growth is unmistakable. The emerging ethnic convergence in fertility levels indicates the end of the sharp fertility gap that has characterized these populations for a century. High fertility rates reflect the traditional family roles of Moslem women, their segregation, lower status, and less power in the society. High fertility has been costly for Arab women and families; it has affected the availability of socioeconomic opportunities for the next generation. In large part, the traditional role of Arab women has almost always been treated as one of the determinants of sustained high fertility levels. The argument has been that unless the status of women changes to nonchildbearing roles, there is little likelihood of a significant change in fertility rates. As a result of this perspective, the theoretical challenge became to understand why the role of Arab-Israeli women did not change with the first indication of economic development and why large family size was reinforced by the absence of migration and by state welfare policies (Friedlander et al. 1979).

But gender and family roles are also the consequences of the size of families. Large family size reinforces the traditional ties of women to households and families and enhances their segregated roles. It takes sustained economic, political, and social demographic changes to break the cycle so that women (and men) are able to move toward the small family size model. Often this sustained break comes with migration (or immigration), when the family is no longer the source of economic reward and family members become less dependent on traditional economic supports. The break between family and economic resources is often facilitated by geographic and social mobility. In the case of Moslem Israelis, the state reinforced the family and economic connection as it sustained a dependency of Arab Israelis on the Jewish economic sector. The absence of Arab geographic mobility resulted in higher levels of dependency at a time when economic and social characteristics would have led to the expectation of greater mobility. Only after sustained changes could the cycle be broken. The longer-term disadvantages of high fertility levels for mobility is clearly emerging for Israeli Arabs, and the role of large family size in sustaining the family-oriented roles of women is clearly weakening.

The Nature and Impact of Fertility Policies

There is no reason to postulate (as some have in the past—see Bachi 1977 and the extensive evaluation in Friedlander and Goldscheider 1979) that Israel will face a demographic "crisis" from the differential population growth implications of the low fertility levels of Jewish Israelis and the high fertility levels of Arab Israelis. The differential fertility of Jews and Arabs does not translate into differential population growth rates that result in a "demographic threat" from Arab Israelis or from zero population growth among the Jewish population. The higher-than-average level of Jewish fertility (even not taking into account the powerful and continuous demographic role of Jewish immigration to Israel) and the declining rate of Moslem fertility (even not taking into account their low proportion of the total population) makes the Israeli concern over a demographic crisis unrealistic. Indeed, the continual fears expressed about the potential "decline" in Jewish population in Israel is a demographic myth, reinforced by the lower fertility level of Jews in communities outside of Israel and by the threat that is invoked by the Holocaust (see Chapter 4).

Without an empirical basis to identify a problem, it is difficult to consider seriously fertility-stimulating policies. Nevertheless, there is a demographic center attached to the prime minister's office in Israel that has, over the years, espoused policies to increase Jewish fertility in Israel. Myths are often powerful when they are reinforced by a broader ideology, regardless of the evidence about the reality. A central tenet of Zionism is the need to "repopulate" the Jewish nation state and rebuild it culturally as the center of world Jewry since, it is postulated, Jewish communities outside of the state are not likely to survive demographically and culturally. On these grounds, the higher fertility level of the Israeli-Arab population and the lower-than-average Jewish fertility level in communities outside of Israel reinforce these myths of Jewish demographic crisis in Israel.

I have noted the role of policy and, more broadly, of the state both in the discussion of the decline of Jewish fertility levels and in the pattern of Moslem fertility. Here, I review more systematically the specification of fertility policies and their importance in the transition to small family size in Israel. Fertility policies in the Israeli context have in the past been pronatalist in ideology and have been addressed to the Jewish population. (Friedlander and Goldscheider 1979, 1984).[7] Official fertility policies have never been effectively implemented and have had marginal impact or no impact on increasing fertility levels. Indeed, as I have reviewed, the major feature of fertility in Israel has been its remarkable decline, particularly among Middle Eastern immigrants and their children. This transition from the larger to the small family occurred without direct government intervention and primarily through the use of nonmechanical contraceptive means, withdrawal, abortion—not always legal—and delayed marriage. No fertility policy has been designed for the Arab population in Israel, although it has been influenced indirectly by health and welfare entitlement programs designed for the Jewish population. Modern contraception has become more readily available from the public health clinics that serve the majority of Israel's population, Jewish and Arab.

Given the heterogeneity of Israel's population and the fertility levels characteristic of the various communities, religious and ethnic, a comprehensive fertility policy would have to be differential. By this I mean that policy measures directed at reducing fertility for some communities (e.g., rural Moslems) would not be applicable to others (e.g., Israelis of European origin) (see Goldscheider and Friedlander 1986). If, for ideological or political reasons, the state of Israel wants to increase the fertility level of the Jewish population as part of a grander Zionist design to increase the population of Jews, such pronatalism would hardly be appropriate for Israeli Arabs. It is difficult to construct a national pronatalist policy that does not apply to all the various segments of the population that is not at the same time coercive or discriminatory. The tensions between the democratic base of Israeli society and its ethnic particularism are clearly reflected in these concerns.

There are fertility policies that are direct in that they are specific to fertility issues; other policies have primarily socioeconomic or welfare goals that have important, albeit indirect, consequences for families and fertility. Policies relate to both the normative climate of reproduction and the provision of efficient means of fertility control. Data on fertility norms collected in the mid-1970s and reinforced by survey data in the 1980s point unmistakably to the normative changes that have already occurred for the high-fertility populations of Israel. The difficult task of restructuring norms toward smaller family size has already occurred, in large part as a result of the transformations in socioeconomics, families, and women's roles.

The provision of a full panoply of contraceptive information and family planning strategies will reduce the reliance on abortion as a last resort for unplanned late births and the reliance on less-effective birth control methods. Unlike in other countries, a significant proportion of abortions in Israel are obtained by married women with several children. The introduction of new contraceptives would provide women with greater autonomy and control over their lives and would reduce their dependency on male-controlled contraceptives. Current contraceptive patterns often result in the use of inefficient contraception and in unplanned pregnancy (among older as well as younger women). The provision of contraceptives to all communities would enhance the greater demographic equality among religious and ethnic communities. Policies that expand these family planning services can rely on the existing public health institutions and mother-child clinics, which have already played an important role in bringing medical care to the population and which have reduced significantly the differential accessibility of that care to the more economically disadvantaged sectors.

The major reasons that a more equitable policy of family planning information and access has not been implemented are related to the coincidence of political-family-ideological-religious interests. The religious and socially conservative argument emphasizes the traditional sanctity and importance of the family, the retention of traditional roles for women within the family, and the role of sexual activity limited to marriage. Normally, these forces would be on the decline in a modernizing country that is governed by a secular polity. Two features upset these processes in Israel. First, religious institutions and political parties have played an important part in recent years in coalition politics. The price of the religion and politics connection has been the disproportionate power of religious institutions in reinforcing limited contraceptive access. In turn, this connection has been reinforced by the Zionist ideological commitment (among some but not all secular Zionists) to increase the Jewish population of the state, either through immigration of Jews from outside of Israel or through the retention of larger family size. The external conditions of the Arab-Israel conflict and the concern expressed by some Israeli policymakers about the large Moslem populations that surround the state of Israel or the growing Palestinian population living in the West Bank further strengthen this ideological concern about Jewish population size.

So Israel has not and is unlikely to adopt a policy that more democratically educates the population in the planning of family size and in the use of efficient contraception. This does not mean that fertility will increase or that contraception will not be used. Instead, it means that the pressure to limit family size, derived from economic, housing, employment, and lifestyle contexts, will more often than not result in limiting childbearing through later marriage, abortion, and less-effective means of birth control. It means, as well, that those who can afford to purchase birth control information and obtain family planning materials and contraceptives on the private market will do so. The absence of a more democratic policy will reinforce the existing social class and, in turn, the ethnic and religious gaps that exist in Israel's population. No less important, and often overlooked, is the impact of these patterns for the perpetuation of inequalities in women's roles and the lack of control women are likely to continue to have over their family and social status. These are high costs indeed for a democratic society.

Concluding Observations

What are some general features of fertility that can be learned from the specifics of the Israeli case? What implications do these fertility patterns have for the society? I suggest the following: The first general lesson to be learned from studying fertility patterns in Israel is the importance of the variety of transitions. Some populations have experienced fertility decline, baby boom, and recovery, but there have been continuous declines in fertility for other populations; the pace of fertility change has varied among the various groups in Israel. An examination of national data on fertility levels would have neutralized these variations and would have led to a chaos of explanations, since the ethnic compositional shifts of the society as a whole have been enormous. Communities defined in real terms of ethnic origin or religious divisions are the more appropriate unit for fertility analysis.

When social scientists have carried out fertility studies, they have often gone to the other extreme and have focused on the characteristics of individuals (usually women) in studying family size behavior and norms. For example, there is a long research tradition of studying the labor force participation of women or their ethnic origins as a basis for understanding fertility.

A second lesson derived from my analysis of fertility in Israel is the importance of family, in the context of roles of women and the connection of the family to the community. The key linkages have been those that connect family processes to the economy and that emphasize social class and political and family networks. A focus on family and household units is the most direct way of approximating the links between the individual and the community. Limiting fertility studies to women often misses family and community connections.

The classic theoretical framework for examining fertility change focuses on the "intermediate" and "proximate" determinants of fertility—factors that influence fertility through marriage, contraception, and abortion. After those are clarified, we turn to the background social and economic determinants that affect fertility through these proximate determinants. That framework is useful in separating immediate and background effects, but often does not specify the mechanism that links the social to the intermediate variables. So it has been argued in the past that economic changes (such as those associated with urbanization and industrialization) and the changing roles of women are among the important factors related to the decline of fertility. We have less often specified the mechanism that links one set of changes to others. On the one hand, studies have demonstrated the different ways in which family and economic changes have brought about pressure to reduce family size for communities faced with different circumstances. The response of Christian Arabs has been to delay marriage; withdrawal and abortion have been used efficiently among Asian- and African-origin Jews; increased use of contraceptive pills have characterized young Israelis. The important point is that there have been a variety of responses to the pressures to reduce family size.

On the other hand, the state has played an important role in the process of fertility reduction, but not in the sense of direct birth control or antinatal family planning policies. Instead, Israel has developed an extensive welfare entitlement system, along with health and educational programs, that has had important, indirect effects on providing incentives to reduce family size. These incentives in the past have had the reverse effect on the Arab population, slowing the pace of fertility reduction by relieving the pressures from the family. This is all the more remarkable (and ironic) since the formal policy of the government and the official ideology was pronatalist for the Jewish population (which witnessed the most impressive voluntary decline in fertility recorded); they were unintentionally pronatalist for the Arab population. The state can have a powerful role in altering fertility patterns, even when policies are not fertility specific and regardless of the policy's "intention."

One of the most conspicuous lessons that one can derive from studying Israeli fertility patterns is that changes in fertility are connected to other issues of demographic importance. Clearly, the relationship of fertility to immigration is well documented and, along with the decline in mortality, lies at the heart of issues of demographic assimilation. But it is less well appreciated how migration and location have shaped fertility responses. The residential stability (nonmigration) of the Moslem-Israeli population, the selective migration of the Middle Eastern–origin population, and the links between migration and schooling, jobs, and generational continuity are powerful in the migration family–fertility connection.

In the end, the analysis points us in the direction of community, focusing on family and gender roles, migration, social class, and the use and distribution of resources. Ethnic convergences in both fertility and mortality patterns raise the broader question of demographic and related forms of ethnic assimilation. In particular, the demographic assimilation of Jewish ethnic groups in Israel does not necessarily imply the broader pattern of total ethnic assimilation. A similar conclusion emerges from the understanding of changes in the Israeli-Arab community, where I documented the powerful effects of their continuing geographic concentration and segregation. These ethnic-related patterns appear as ethnic distinctiveness in the context of assimilation in some, but not all, dimensions of social life, and in the context of the continuing importance of family and ethnic networks in fostering generational continuity at the community level.

Ethnic continuity confronts the question of national community developments in Israel. Indeed, the ideological and political question raised in the late nineteenth and early twentieth centuries of the role of ethnic communities in the development of the nation-state is again raised by Israeli patterns, as it is being addressed by other multicultural and pluralistic societies around the world. The "Jewish question" raised by Karl Marx in 1843 about the place of the Jewish minority in the emergent nationalism and capitalism of Europe has become Israel's ethnic question. The place of Jewish and Arab ethnic groups in Israel's changing society becomes the question in the beginning of the twentieth-first century.

Notes

1. The total fertility rate of a given year indicates the average number of births per woman if all women were to live through their childbearing years and have births at the same rate as women of those ages who actually gave birth in that year. It is an artificial con-

struct that may be viewed as an estimate of eventual family size over the life course, derived from cross-sectional, age-specific patterns. It is particularly unreliable as an estimate of actual family size when age-specific fertility patterns are changing.

2. Since these data do not standardize for education and other factors that differentiate these groups, the ethnic gap appears greater. There is every likelihood that most, if not all, of these differences are accounted for by social class and related economic factors.

3. These questions and the detailed data to examine them form the basis of research that appears in Friedlander and Goldscheider 1978, and Friedlander, Eisenbach, and Goldscheider 1979, 1980. We draw on past research for the retrospective reconstruction of cohort ethnic changes in fertility, adding in more recent data for the 1980s and 1990s.

4. These questions have rarely, if ever, been asked of men, although men and women increasingly share in the decisions about childbearing and child rearing.

5. The efficient use of contraceptives, abortion, and the timing of marriage are more likely to be the result of fertility norms and behavior rather than their cause. Hence, my attention focuses on the factors affecting fertility, without concern at this point about the proximate or intermediate mechanisms that have been used to convert family size norms into fertility behavior.

6. *Hamula* are patrilineal descent groups that involve kin rights and obligations and that establish kinship relationships. See Al Haj 1987; Rosenfeld 1968; and Chapter 4.

7. Official pronouncements and ideological exhortations to the Jewish population about "internal" immigration—having more children—have been associated most prominently with Israel's first prime minister, David Ben-Gurion. He was quoted as saying, "Any Jewish woman who, as far as it depends on her, does not bring into the world at least four healthy children is shirking her duty to the nation, like a soldier who evades military service. . . . Every family (should) have at least four sons and daughters, the more the better" (Rein 1979, p. 65; see also the discussion in Friedlander and Goldscheider 1979).

PART SIX

Diasporas, Dependencies, and Ethnic Continuities

12

The Jewish Diaspora and Palestine: Ethnicity and Nation-Building in the State of Israel

My primary focus has been on the formation of Israeli society and its development. I have identified some of the central threads of its demographic, economic, political, and cultural transformations and have explored the changing significance of ethnicity, community, and family. In the process, I have analyzed the impact of Israeli-created conditions and the changing importance of group experiences prior to arrival in Israel concerning issues of social inequality and group assimilation.

Yet, internal developments do not occur in an international or regional vacuum. As a new state, Israel has political and economic linkages to countries and people in and out of the region. As a Jewish state, it has important social and cultural relationships with Jewish communities around the world, those that represent potential sources of immigration and that are primarily sources of social, political, and economic support, as well as those that have received significant numbers of Israeli emigrants and visitors. Ethnic divisions among Jews in Israel are strongly influenced by events occurring outside the state. As a state with a significant Arab minority population that is under its administrative control and a state that occupies a territory that has been claimed by some former residents, Israel has been centrally positioned in the aspirations of Palestinians for political autonomy.[1]

My goal in this chapter is to review some of the externals to enhance the understanding of internal developments in Israel's changing society. I focus on three questions. First, what is the relationship between Jewish communities outside of the state of Israel to developments in Israeli society? I shall refer to this as the "Jewish diaspora" question. Second, what has been the relationship of the state of Israel to the territories it administers (referred to as Judea and Samaria, or the

West Bank, or Palestine by persons of different political-ideological orientations)? I shall refer to this as the "Palestinian" question. Third, what are the prospects for Jewish ethnic assimilation in Israel, and what is the role of the Arab or Palestinian citizens living in the state in the context of both the Palestinian and Jewish diaspora questions. I shall refer to this as the "ethnic-national" question. I identify how these three sets of "external" considerations have conditioned developments in the state and, in particular, how they have influenced the linkages among population, ethnicity, and nation-building.[2]

The Jewish Diaspora and Israeli Society

The background for understanding the emergence of the state includes the links between Israel and what it defines as the *golah*, or the Jewish diaspora, that is, Jewish communities outside the state. Most directly, these links are important because these Jewish communities have been sources of immigrants to Israel. Hence, they have had a powerful influence on the changing population growth and ethnic composition of Israel. Moreover, these Jewish communities have been Israel's financial and political backbone, supporting domestic programs and providing important aid for defense purposes and political legitimacy in the international arena. Jews outside of Israel have been partners in formulating the intellectual and ideological basis of Israeli society and have provided the political rationale for its reemergence. What occurs in outside Jewish communities has important consequences for developments in the state; what happens in Israel has implications for Jewish communities outside Israel. Although a systematic analysis of the impact of Israeli society on outside Jewish communities moves this work beyond its focus, some aspects of the organization and functioning of Israeli society are conditioned by the relationship of the "center" of Israel to its defined Jewish "periphery."[3]

Three brief examples illustrate some of the more obvious interdependencies between Israel and Jewish communities outside of Israel. First, changing immigration rates and shifts in the composition of immigrant streams to Israel have been strongly influenced by changes in the number of potential Jewish immigrants in communities around the world. The size of particular Jewish communities and the pool of potential Jewish immigrants have varied since the 1950s, in part in relation to the rate of immigration to Israel. The end of Jewish emigration from Yemen or Iraq can only be understood against the background of the demographic demise of those Jewish communities. The commitment of American Jews to remain in the United States has a major impact on the relationships between Israel and the American Jewish community and the U.S. government. Shifts in the cohesion of the Soviet Union and its breakup, along with implications of these changes for the Jewish population living there, were the most immediate cause of the large-scale immigration of Russian Jews to Israel in the 1990s, as was the shifting immigration policy of the United States government about accepting Russian immigrants. Thus, an examination of the impact of the timing and rate of Jewish immigration from various countries of origin to Israel must be understood in the context of these Jewish communities.

A second example relates to the ways that events in Israel affect Jewish communities in the world. The 1967 Six Day War between Israel and its Arab neighbors had a major impact on economic and political developments within the state and deeply affected the relationship of Israeli Jews to Palestinians and to the Arab populations of the region. The effect of the war extended well beyond the border of the state, increasing the financial and political support to Israel by Jewish communities around the world and more firmly anchoring their ethnic identities in Israel's development. As the very survival of Israel was perceived to be threatened, the post-Holocaust generation of Jews outside Israel responded in a variety of ways to link itself to the future of the Jewish state. After 1967, Israel symbolized the political "redemption" of the Jewish people and redirected issues around its role in the continuity of Jewish communities. These developments, in turn, led to new and more conspicuous dependencies between Israel and Jewish communities, often involving the exchange of Jewish "ethnic" identity for financial and political support.

A third illustration relates to the continuous terrorist attacks directed at Jews in Israel. These have always generated political responses and concerns among Jews outside Israel; attacks on Jewish communities in North and South America, in Europe, and in Asia and Africa have, in turn, generated responses from the Israeli government. Israel views itself as the guardian of the Jewish people; Jewish communities outside Israel are defined as part of the history and culture of Israeli Jews. An attack on Jews anywhere is treated as an attack on Jews everywhere, promoting a mutual, unwritten pact of normative responsibilities and obligations. Often this takes the form of political action; at times, economic exchanges or military actions are generated as well, reinforcing the bonds between Israel and Jewish communities around the world.

These simple illustrations can be multiplied. My major point is that there are important linkages between internal developments in Israel and Jewish communities outside Israel that require analysis if the goal is to understand the dynamics of Israel's changing society.

Who Is Jewish in Israel and in the Jewish Diaspora?

Since Israel defines itself as the center of the Jewish people, an elementary question about the "ethnic" relationships between Israeli and non-Israeli Jews is, Who is included as a member of the Jewish people? The sociological response for voluntary communities is that membership is by self-definition, along with the normative consensus of the community. Political criteria (such as citizenship) or some other formal status (such as temporary resident status) are used for states.[4] The definitional question of Who is a Jew? in the state of Israel symbolizes the connections,

244 12. The Jewish Diaspora and Palestine

and the gap, between the two largest Jewish communities in the world: that of Israel and the United States.[5]

The definition of who is to be included in the category "Jewish" falls under the Law of Return in the state of Israel (the law that grants every Jew in the world the right to immigrate to Israel and thereby become a citizen of the state). The state formally grants citizenship rights to all those who are Jewish by religious and legal (*halachic*) criteria, because of birth to a Jewish mother or conversion to Judaism by a recognized Orthodox rabbi. At the end of the twentieth century, having one grandparent who was defined as Jewish allowed for the entry into Israel under the Law of Return. But the Rabbinate is unlikely to recognize such a person as Jewish for purposes of marriage. Occasionally, these formal definitions are problematic. Discussion about the criteria used to define Jewishness in Israel often occurs in the context of coalition politics involving "religious" political parties that exercise power over the definition at the junctures of political transitions (that is, citizenship in the context of immigration) or life-course transitions (that is, at birth, induction into military service, marriage, divorce, and death). Israeli Jews are rarely affected by these coalition bargaining tactics, and the issue is marginal to their lives, except as it reveals the political nature of Israeli Judaism. In contrast, when these tactics are enforced and publicly debated in Israel, the vast majority of Jews living in the United States become concerned. Israelis are perplexed as to why American and other Jews outside Israel are so concerned about these political maneuverings. An understanding of why the latter is the case and why American Jews have been concerned over the definitional question help to clarify the linkages and conflicts between Israeli and non-Israeli Jews.

The issue of defining who is Jewish is not new historically nor is it particular to the state of Israel. All societies struggle with defining membership and citizenship. In Israel, the definition has been decided by Israel's parliament, the Knesset, on "religious" grounds and has been implemented by the Jewish religious authorities of the state, that is, by Orthodox rabbis and their institutions. The paradox is that American Jews are concerned about the legalities of citizenship in a Jewish country thousands of miles away that the majority have not visited and in which most have no intention of applying for such citizenship and are unlikely to test whether they would ever fit those criteria. American Jews who are most likely to immigrate to Israel would be defined as Jewish in the overwhelming majority of cases.

To understand this elementary issue from the point of view of Israeli society, we can unravel the Israeli view of the core issue of Jewish life in the aftermath of European modernization: the integration and assimilation of Jews in modern, secular, open pluralistic societies. In its most simple form, the Israeli argument about the assimilation of diaspora Jews is as follows. In modern, open pluralistic societies, for example in America, Jews are assimilating. Assimilation, they argue, means the erosion of Jewish life in the process of becoming like non-Jews. Intermarriage is the most conspicuous indicator of such erosions, because when Jews intermarry with non-Jews, they are distancing themselves from their "traditional" roots, rejecting their Jewishness and their Judaism together with their links to the Jewish people, community, history, and culture. Such intermarriages are unlikely to occur in Israel (in large part because of the boundaries between Jews and Arabs); "assimilation," therefore, is only a problem when Jews are a minority community. Since American Jews are assimilating, the Israelis argue, it is particularly unclear why they should be concerned about the way Jews are being defined in the state of Israel. Assimilating Jews should be particularly indifferent to formal issues about the Judaism of the Jews. Why should American Jews care about the way rabbis, from another culture and with very different values from theirs, jockey for political power and make legal and political pronouncements that are irrelevant to their lives and their Jewishness? Shouldn't Jewish Americans, who are committed to American political values of separation of church and state (not necessarily Jewish or Israeli political values), be indifferent to religious-political parties in Israel?

The answer to these questions relates to changes in Judaism in the process of modernization. Over the past century, Jews have become less-observant religiously, their institutions have become secular, and their Judaism has been re-formed. At the same time that traditional religious practices and institutions were declining, new ways of expressing Judaism were emerging and new forms of Jewishness were substituting for religion. Just as secular Zionists developed new ideological and cultural Jewish expressions, rejecting the traditional Judaism and the "diaspora" Jewish culture of the past, so American Jews found news ways to express their Jewishness and Judaism. They redefined their religious commitments into new denominational forms and developed new Jewish institutions and ideologies.

These expressions of Jewishness took shape through secular-based social and communal institutions, emphasizing Jewish peoplehood and American versions of Zionism. As American Jews became less religiously and ritually observant, moving away from Orthodox toward Conservative and Reform Judaisms, the state of Israel became a major basis of communal consensus, reinforcing Jewish continuity as part of ethnic activities, in other words, Jewish peoplehood. Thus, religious changes did not imply the end of their commitments as Jews within their families and their communities or as part of the Jewish people everywhere and over time. "Ethnic" Jewishness, and especially its Israel-centered component, emerged to replace the Judaisms of ritual and belief.

Most American Jews, then, define Israel as a very important part of their lives and central to the education of their children. Substantial proportions of American Jews have visited Israel, have relatives and friends living in Israel, and financially contribute to Israeli-related projects. Israel's survival is bound up with the ethnic lives of American Jews since they consider themselves part of the Jewish people. The state of Israel has become a psychological anchor for many American Jews and is the sociocultural foundation of their Jewishness and a source of communal cohesion. American Jewish identity is defined by its pro-Israelism. How Jewishness is defined in Israel, therefore, seriously matters to most Jewish Americans.

The centrality of Israel in the Jewishness of American Jews is one side of the story; Americanness is the other side of Jewishness. Clearly, Jews living in the United States have assimilated, changing and adapting to the society in which they live. However, assimilation and integration have not, by and large, led to the loss of community. After decades of integration into American society, the Jewish community has powerful anchors of social, religious, and family life (see Gold-scheider 1986a, 1986b). Family communal, political, economic, and associational networks are the key indicators of ethnic continuity in Jewish communities as it is in the Jewish state. Most American and Israeli Jews would not be very Jewish if re-ligious observances were the only criteria (on the religiosity of Israeli Jews, see Deshen 1990; Goldscheider and Friedlander 1983; Levy, Levinsohn, and Katz 1993; Sobel and Beit-Hallahmi 1991).

Although there have been increases in the rates of intermarriage between Jews and non-Jews in the United States, there is no simple association between inter-marriage and alienation from the Jewish community. The relative rates of genera-tional continuity of the intermarried in the Jewish community (i.e., how many children raised in households where one or more persons was not born Jewish re-main Jewish as they form their own families) have changed over the past decade as the levels of intermarriage and conversions have increased and as the levels of acceptance of the intermarried in the community have increased.[6] In many inter-marriages, the Jewish partner remains attached to the Jewish community through family, friends, and organizational ties; often the non-Jewish-born spouse becomes attached to the Jewish community, as do many of the children of the intermar-ried. Most of their friends are Jewish, many support Israel, and most identify themselves as Jews. Some proportion formally convert to Judaism; many are con-verted by religious procedures under the direction of Orthodox and Conservative rabbis, but more are converted to Judaism by Reform rabbis using nontraditional religious criteria.

Taken together, the research evidence shows that the intermarried, certainly the formally converted (by whatever denomination and by whatever criteria) cannot be written off as lost to the Jewish community. Their families, rabbis, and Jewish organizations have not excluded them and they have not excluded themselves. Can a citizenship law in the state of Israel write them off as Jewish people without creating concern among the intermarried, their families, their rabbis, their com-munity, and their institutions?

The increasing rate of intermarriage means erosion of the Jewish community primarily through the prism of the segregated Orthodox who reject the Jewishness of non-Orthodox Jews and from the perspective of Israeli Jews who reject the possi-bility of Jewish continuity in the diaspora. High intermarriage rates mean that the wide networks of Jews are affected by the intermarriage issue and that these net-works are larger than the percentage who are currently intermarrying. There is hardly a Jewish household in America that has not experienced the taste of inter-marriage among family members, neighbors, or friends. Even American Jews who have not been affected directly by intermarriage are concerned about the political resolution of a formal "Who is a Jew?" question in the state of Israel. American Jews are concerned when the secular Israeli Jewish government declares that their Jewish friends, neighbors, and family are not "Jewish" when these people are defined by the interest of coalition politics and political bargaining in Israel.

These issues come to a head when large numbers of temporary non-Jewish immigrants are working in Israel (well over 100,000 at the end of the 1990s). These workers are in large part replacing the Palestinians who are blocked from working in Israel because of the Palestinian-Israeli conflict. They add to the significant number of non-Jewish immigrants from the former Soviet Union who have joined family members who are Jewish and have been granted the rights of citizenship. An estimated half of the immigrants from the former Soviet Union entering Israel in 2000 and in 2001 have been defined as not Jewish by Orthodox religious criteria. These two groups of immigrants, the temporary foreign workers and the non-Jewish immigrants, are again raising the Jewish and the Zionist questions in the state of Israel.

Even though immigration is not part of the agenda of most American Jews, their identity as Jews is intertwined in complex and profound ways with their associations with Israel. At the same time, about 85 percent of American Jews reject Orthodox Judaism as their form of religious expression, and most have developed religious alternatives; their legitimacy as Jews is unquestioned in America. Although, in large part, they have rejected the version of Zionism that insists on their immigration as the only legitimate solution to the Jewish condition in the diaspora, they have developed alternative versions of Zionism that allow them to have strong bonds to the state of Israel. Pro-Israelism has been their commitment without the ideological imperative of immigration or the rejection of the continuation of American Jewish life (see Cohen 1983; Leibman and Cohen 1990).

American Jews are comfortable as Jews where they live and display their Jewishness openly and legitimately. Anchoring their Jewish identity in the Jewish state, which calls into question their legitimacy as Jews, their children's legitimacy, and that of their religious leaders, becomes untenable. For some time, Orthodox rabbis have called into question the Jewishness of those who have become Jews by choice or who practice their Judaism differently from theirs. American Jews have, in large part, ignored these Orthodox rabbis and have been indifferent to their values. Orthodox Judaism in Israel, in its political form, has become more intolerant of Jewish diversity, at the same time that American Jews have embraced pluralism in Judaism. By recognizing only one of the several variants of Judaism, Israel calls into question the ethnic legitimacy of the overwhelming majority of American Jews. The recognition that the American Jewish community is a viable and concerned Jewish- and Israeli-oriented community raises fundamental questions about the premises of some forms of Zionism. Israeli Jews, therefore, have difficulty understanding the Jewishness of Jews outside the state of Israel.

The United States and Israel represent different strategies of Jewish survival in the modern world. The state of Israel is a major source of Jewish culture, experience, identity, and history for American Jews, since it is their link to Jewish peoplehood, the quintessential form of political ethnicity. Israel is not their "national origin" in the geographic sense. In its constructed ideological form, Israel is no less powerful as a symbol of ethnicity for Jewish communities. For many Israeli Jews, the American Jewish community is the paradigm of erosion and decay and the lack of Jewish viability and continuity, yet a source of potential immigration.

Gaps Between Jewries: Are Relationships Changing?

The different constructions by Israeli politics and American Jewries of "Who is a Jew" reveal broader political and cultural differences between these communities. American Jews view their Jewishness in the context of individual choices and communal consent; Israeli Jews have a major political component attached to their assigned status. How have these relationships changed over time? Have Jews inside and outside of Israel moved closer or further apart? The "peoplehood" paradigm has a component that emphasizes "oneness" across contexts, which has been emphasized by both Israeli and non-Israeli Jewish institutions. It is symbolized by the public relations slogan "We are one," used by national and international Jewish organizations. There is some basis for this view in the long history of Jews and in Judaism, often in response to how others define Jews as part of one people and as being distinctive.[7] Only in the past century have Jews formulated a separation of Judaism and Jewishness—that being religious and being part of the Jewish community are not necessarily the same, although the integration of religious and ethnic forms continues to be the defining quality of community and cultural forms of Jewishness.

Oneness does not necessarily imply similarities in every cultural and communal sphere; obligations and responsibilities do not mean uniformity of identity and singularity of goals and objectives or sameness of values. Indeed, there are increasing indications that Israeli Jews and Jews in communities outside Israel are moving apart from each other. Although the state of Israel has become the center of Jewish peoplehood, large, cohesive, and powerful Jewish communities have emerged in modern pluralistic societies. These are legitimate and accepted ethnic-religious communities, with long-term roots in these societies, as well as strong linkages to Israel. Whereas most of the Jews outside of Israel are committed to the state, in their view and in their behavior they are not in "exile" or in diaspora. Their home is where they live, where they expect to continue living, and where they are raising the next generation to live. Mutual dependencies have developed between Israel and the Jewish communities outside Israel. These dependencies have changed over time as these communities have responded to each other and as technology has brought geographically spread persons into new forms of communication to exchange ideas, cultures, and people. The exchanges have flowed in both directions.

In the past, there were major commonalities of background and experience between Israeli and American Jews. Both groups were heavily influenced by their European origins, and many Jews were raised in families where Yiddish was spoken and were rooted in Yiddish culture. Many struggled with second-generation status; in other words, they were raised by parents who were not native to the country in which they were living. Many shared the cultural and social disruptions of secularization and assimilation; the struggles of economic depression, war and Holocaust in Europe; and the rebuilding of the lives of Jewish refugees. They shared in the most tangible and dramatic ways the establishment and the rebuilding of the state of Israel. Jews in both Israeli and non-Israeli Jewish communities had limited exposure to formal Jewish education, rejected traditional Jewish ritual observances as reflections of their discarded past, and developed ethnic-national Jewish rituals as substitutes. Israeli Jews became less traditional by becoming attached nationally to their new country; American Jews became less traditionally oriented by becoming American. In short, there was a shared sense of origins, experiences, and objectives in the past, although each group was living in a different society and building a new community with an appropriate set of institutions.

New generations have emerged in Israel and in the United States that are more distant from Europe and from the commonalities of language. For them, the European Holocaust is history, and immigration origins are far away, as are the struggles of pioneering in Israel and upward generational mobility in the United States. The different experiences of Israel and the United States as societies have shaped the lives, lifestyles, institutions, and values of the people of these communities. Not only have past commonalities declined but also new gaps have emerged. A key example is the role of women in both societies. American Jewish women have been in the forefront of social changes in their increasing independence from traditional gender roles and family relationships. Their high levels of education, career orientations, small family size, and high aspirations for themselves and their children have been truly revolutionary. Many American men have shared and adjusted to these changes in the workplace and in families. In contrast, Israeli men and women tend to have much more traditional segregated family and social roles. Family relationships are more patriarchal, work patterns for women are less tied to careers, and Israeli women lack the autonomy of American women. So this particular gap, with its implications for work and family, has grown in recent years.

A second related shift involves the growing demographic, political, and cultural importance of Asian-African-origin Jews in Israel. This compositional change has created new gaps at the leadership and community levels between Israelis of non-European origin and American Jews. Language barriers have increased and limited communication occurs between these communities. Diverse social class backgrounds and lifestyles exacerbate these differences. Jews in the United States have become concentrated in high-level educational, occupational, and income categories. College-educated, white-collar professionals are exceptional among Israeli Jews, and particularly among women. So, social class, ethnicity, and gender differences reinforce gaps between Jews in Israel and the United States.

Religion is the most serious manifestation of the gap between Israel and Jewish communities external to Israel. Judaism has been highly politicized in Israel, with control over religious institutions exercised by one segment of Judaism (the Orthodox). Religious leaders of Israel and of communities outside Israel have so little in common that there is virtually no communication between them. Although the Jewish populations in both societies have similar levels of secularization, the gap in religious leadership is total.[8] Add in the religious role of women in American Judaisms and one sees that there is a stark contrast between the dominance of American Reform and Conservative rabbis (men and women) as religious leaders outside Israel and the general lack of legitimacy of non-Orthodox rabbis in Israel.

The commitment of American Jews to the separation of religion and politics contrasts sharply with the clear interrelationship of religion and politics in Israel, with the long-standing power of religious-political parties, and with the conspicuous intervention of religious leaders in Israeli politics. Religious pluralism characterizes Jewish communities outside Israel, and multiple expressions of Judaism are normatively accepted and valued; only one Judaism, Orthodoxy, is defined as legitimate in Israeli society, although there are two chief rabbis defined along ethnic lines. Israel and its leaders are not committed to ethnic or religious pluralism in the same way that is characteristic of American Jewry. The trajectories of changes in these two communities are moving in the direction of straining the relationships between them, not in closing the gap. As each is moving through its own developments, each is moving away from the other. In the short run, at least for another generation, differences between Jews in Israel and elsewhere are likely to be accentuated, despite increasing flows of money, culture, and people between these communities.

The Palestinian Diaspora

How have the external conflicts with Arab Palestinians reshaped and affected the changes within the state? How have they influenced the way Israeli society relates to its Arab minority and to the broader Arab-Israeli conflict? What is the situation of the Palestinians who are residents of the areas that have been administered and occupied by the state of Israel since the 1967 war? Through the end of the 1970s, these territories were referred to officially as administered territories and incorporated the West Bank and Gaza (the latter and Jericho came under Palestinian administration in mid-1994). They became officially known by their Biblical names, Judea, Samaria, and Gaza—reflecting the ascendancy of the Likud government in 1977 and its more nationalistic policies with regard to these territories. The political symbolism of this name switch is of profound importance in understanding the relationship of the Israeli government to these areas,[9] which encompassed around 180,000 Jewish settlers and over 2 million Arab Palestinians at the end of the twentieth century.

The administration of these territories since 1967 has influenced population, development, and ethnicity in Israel through the territories' impact on the economy, their connection to the Israeli Arab community, and their influence on stratification and inequalities in Israeli society.

The Israeli government has never officially incorporated into Israel the Arab Palestinian population living in these territories, except for East Jerusalem in 1967. The political rights of citizenship accorded to Arab Israelis were not extended to those living in the West Bank and Gaza. The incorporation of the large Arab population within "Greater Israel" would have threatened the demographic dominance of the Jewish population. In the 1970s and 1980s, a series of demographic projections showed clearly that the differential growth rates of Israel's population and the Arab-Palestinian population under its administrative control would result in a declining Jewish proportion and would entail the risk of losing a Jewish majority in a little over a generation (see Friedlander and Goldscheider 1974, 1979, 1984). Ironically, some of the most nationalistic among the Israeli Jewish population argue for the incorporation of the Palestinian population. If they were successful, the demographic result would be the emergence of an Arab-Palestinian demographic majority. Hence, the more extreme among the Israeli nationalists instead argued for the incorporation of the administered land within the state, without integrating the Palestinian population.

These early demographic scenarios were not designed to project what would happen but what would be the demographic consequences if there were no policies to deal with the future of these areas. Indeed, the alternatives to returning control over the administered territories to the Palestinians ranged from the development of a quasi-colonial relationship between Israel and the Palestinian population under its administration (which in part occurred) to the evacuation of the Arab population, to be replaced by Israeli residents (which has occurred only marginally). The notion of a combined Israeli-Palestinian state shared between Jewish and Arab-Palestinian populations was not acceptable to either side of the conflict. Such a state would require a radical transformation of the institutions, values, and symbols that mark Israel as a Jewish state.

The size of the Arab population of these territories is somewhat in dispute, since there are different estimates depending on how Palestinians are defined and by which officials.[10] Data in Table 12.1 display some of the basic demographic patterns over the two decades beginning in 1970. There was a substantial growth in the population of the West Bank and Gaza, increasing to over 1.6 million persons from less than 1 million in 1970, and growing at a rate that would double the population every generation. The estimates for 2000, obtained from the Palestinian Central Bureau of Statistics, are likely to incorporate many nonresident Palestinians and those living in territories not identical to that covered by the Central Bureau of Statistics at early points in time. Although not accurate, the comparisons over time reveal a tendency toward very high population growth rates with the attendant consequences. With the return of Gaza and its population to Palestinian control in 1994, over 2 million Palestinians are likely to have remained under Israeli administration (in addition to the Israeli-Arab population—see Chapter 4). The birth rate remains quite high, as are death rates, and the potential for continuing rapid growth is high as a result.

Indicators of health conditions and health infrastructure reveal the poor and disadvantaged economic conditions of Arab Palestinians in the administered areas, relative to Israeli society as a whole and to the Arab-Israeli population. Additional data on the possession of durable goods among households reveal the increases over time of basic items such as stoves and refrigerators and the continuing low levels in the 1990s of items of communication—that is, telephones, bicycles, and cars.

The administration of these territories by Israel involves political control and the presence or involvement of government agencies such as health, education, agricultural regulation, and administrative justice. This administration implies that economic decisions are more likely to serve the interests of the Israeli economy and that investments in local control are minimal. Local Palestinian residents have not been part of the political process that has shaped these economic policies. Domestic needs and local economic development have been secondary to the needs of the Israeli government, including the recruitment of labor to work in Israel and the flow of Israeli goods into the territories. Thus, agricultural developments in the West Bank have been realigned to produce crops that are not competitive with the Israeli agricultural markets, and prices have been regulated.

Similar control is exercised by Israel over water drawn from the West Bank into Israel. Israel has also controlled some land areas in the West Bank and Gaza for Jewish settlers, introduced Israeli firms to set up industry in the areas through financial incentives, and established export connections to Jordan and other Arab countries through the West Bank. At the same time, the territories have become markets for Israeli goods. Thus, "Israeli policies have blatantly steered the territories toward a state of dependency on Israel. . . . The economies of the West Bank and the Gaza still lack indigenous and financial institutions necessary for setting up development programs and channeling savings and investments into various economic sectors" (Gharaibeh 1985, p. 137).

The occupational patterns of men in these territories are revealing. There are few persons employed in white-collar jobs (less than 10 percent) and the overwhelming majority (over 7 out of 10 of the employed males) are skilled and unskilled workers in industry. A significant proportion of these people work in the state of Israel, commuting on a daily basis. In 1992, 38 percent of the employed males living in the West Bank and Gaza were working in the construction industry. Three-fourths of Arab Palestinians commuting to Israel were working in the construction industry (*Statistical Abstract of Israel 1993*, table 27.22). Data show

TABLE 12.1 Selected Population, Health, and Economic Indicators of the Arab Population in the Territories Administered by Israel, 1970–2000

	1970	1975	1980	1985	1990	2000[a]
Population size (in thousands)						
Total	978	1,101	1,181	1,343	1,600	2,895
West Bank	608	675	724	816	957	1,873
Gaza	370	426	457	527	643	1,022
Crude birth rate (births per 1,000 population)						
West Bank	44	45	42	41	47	41
Gaza	42	51	48	45	55	45
Infant mortality rate (deaths to children under age 1 per 1,000 births)						
West Bank	37	38	28	25	22	26
Gaza	86	69	43	33	26	30
Percentage born in medical facilities						
West Bank	15	30	40	56	53	–
Gaza	10	21	29	47	–	–
		1972	1975	1980	1987	
GNP per capita (current prices)						
West Bank		410	836	1,334	2,090	
Gaza		268	605	878	1,486	
		1981	1974	1985	1992	
Running water (%)						
West Bank		24	45	62	79	
Gaza		14	51	75	93	

Note: The data are official Israeli estimates for the Arab population in the areas of Judea and Samaria (West Bank) and Gaza.

[a] The data on population size for 2000 must be considered an overestimate or defined as part of a larger territory than previous estimates.

Sources: 1988–1989, Jerusalem, April, 1989; *Statistical Abstract of Israel,* various years; compare the data presented in *Palestinian Bureau of Statistics 1994.* For the year 2000, information was selected from the Web site of the Palestinian Central Bureau of Statistics (PCBS.org).

the decrease in the number and the proportion of Jews in the construction industry as the number of Arabs from the administered territories in that industry increased. Between 1975 and 1987, the number and proportion of Israeli Arabs working in the construction industry remained relatively the same, but the number and percentage of Arabs from the administered territories in this industry increased significantly. By 1987, about one-third of those employed in construction in Israel were Jews (down from 52 percent), 42 percent were Arabs from the administered territories (up from 29 percent), and 22 percent were Israeli Arabs.

Looking at the employers, the evidence identifies the Jewish role in construction in particular and in the stratification picture in general. Although the number of Jews in construction declined and the number of Arabs from the territories increased significantly, the proportion of employers remained overwhelmingly Jewish. About 80 percent of the employers in 1975 were Jewish, as were 76 percent in 1987. These patterns of employment changed in the years 2000 and 2001, as less daily commuting to the state of Israel was permitted and violence between Israelis and Palestinians became daily occurrences. The Palestinian workers from the territories were replaced by temporary guest workers from a wide range of countries.

A final socioeconomic and cultural indicator of the Palestinian population in the West Bank and Gaza relates to the dramatic increase in the level of formal education between the 1970s and the 1990s. In 1970, about half of the population had no formal education; 65 percent of the women had none. By the early 1990s, the proportion with no education declined to 20 percent overall and to about 30 percent of the women. The educational level is rapidly changing among the younger generation. In 1992, for example, over 90 percent of the Palestinian teenage boys and girls had some formal education, and about 70 percent of those ages 15 to 17 had some high school education (*Statistical Abstract of Israel 1993*, table 27.41). Whether these education levels will be translated into commensurate jobs remains the challenge of the next decades. In the mid-1990s, the local economic infrastructure and development had not kept pace with the new educational levels.

Clearly, the political control exercised by Israel over these territories has resulted in an economic dependency, as reflected by the occupational and industrial characteristics of the Palestinians as well as by indicators of the balance of trade and economic flows between Israel and the administered territories. The identity of the Israeli-Arab population has been influenced, sharpened, and challenged in a variety of ways by the links between Israel and the Arab Palestinians in the territories. First and foremost, Arab Israelis became linked to Arab Palestinians in the West Bank and in Gaza in their national aspirations. The links have heightened their sensitivities to the value of ethnic networks and their own national origins and have confronted them with the choice between identifying as Arab Israelis or as displaced Palestinians. The connections between Arab Israelis and Arab Palestinians after 1967 have also sharpened the distinctiveness of the former as Israeli citizens. Arab

Israelis are caught in the middle. They are beneficiaries of the system created to control and protect them as a minority and as citizens of the state of Israel, and yet they are viewed as disloyal Palestinians by their Arab-Palestinian cousins. Although Arab Israelis identify as Palestinians in some contexts, they have been living as citizens in Israel for generations. Lacking the structural opportunities to integrate residentially and regionally with Jewish Israelis, they are a minority with rights and entitlements as citizens of the state. Their identity may be challenged and conflicted, but they do not always identify fully with the aspirations of the Palestinians in the territories (see Smooha 1991; Smooha and Hanf 1992).

Since 1967, the Arab-Israeli population has been pushed up in the social and economic hierarchy in Israel, ahead of the noncitizen Palestinians (but remaining below Jewish Israelis). They have relinquished part of the lowest paid positions and unskilled work to Palestinian day workers and have been mobile in the Israeli social class system. In 2000–2001, the Palestinians in the West Bank and Gaza were no longer part of the social class hierarchy within the state. Even though Arab Israelis live and work and go to school in Israel and have access to the goods and welfare of Israeli society, they are connected ethnically to Palestinians. The linkages between Israel and the territories since 1967 has reinforced and legitimated the minority status of its Arab-Israeli population.

Previously I noted the role of over 180,000 Jewish-Israeli settlers in the territories, their Zionist nationalistic aspirations, and the dilemma they face in the emergence of Palestinian autonomy there (Chapter 6). Almost all Jews living in these areas view themselves as Israelis living under Israeli auspices. They are committed to the legitimate rights of Israeli Jews to live in these areas for nationalist, security, and religious reasons. The majority are concentrated in a few select areas that are located around Jerusalem and that are within easy access to Tel Aviv. These areas are most likely to be retained as Israeli outposts for at least another generation. There are other settlements that are more scattered and isolated and cannot sustain themselves as dormitory suburbs without support from the Israeli government. These are less likely to remain under Israeli control in the next period of time and are very unlikely to expand in Israeli-Jewish population. The Jewish population in these territories administered by Israel are segregated ethnically and religiously from the Palestinian population.

When Peace Arrives

Some Israelis view giving up land as a violation of a fundamental ideological principle; others are more willing to consider trading territory for a process that would lead to peace. Palestinian control over land occupied by Israel for a quarter of a century is countered by arguments over who has the "right" to the land (divine or political) and by the Israeli concern that terrorism and uncontrollable conflict, not peaceful neighborly relations, will result from Palestinian autonomy and statehood. Fear and distrust have often been replaced by hatred and by Israeli suppression of Palestinian self-determination. This may be slowly changing, but it is a long process that requires unfolding and has been frozen since the second *intifada*, uprising, of the Palestinian population beginning in 2000.

In the 1990s, the world's international situation had altered, particularly with the collapse of the Soviet regime and its diminished influence in the Middle East, with the changing role of the Persian Gulf states, and with the increasing ethnic-national identity of the Palestinians. Israelis and Palestinians had been talking to one another, yet terrorism continued. Syria and Israel had been more open to negotiating control over the Golan Heights. Russia was overwhelmed with its own national and regional economic problems and was less involved in power politics with the United States. It is clear that Israel will give up territory (how much and when is not clear) and that the Palestinians will have increasing control over their own autonomous political unit in the West Bank, parallel to the developing institutions and infrastructure in Gaza. There is likely to be a gradual end to the Israeli military presence in the West Bank and diminished control over local Palestinian institutions (health, education, welfare, and economic). The indicators all point to processes that will result in new relationships between Israelis and Palestinians. But, as in the past, these forward patterns toward peaceful resolution have been placed in serious jeopardy by terrorism and mistrust, by actions and reactions, by armed struggle and resistance.

In the late 1930s and 1940s, when faced with a similar dilemma, the Jewish government in Palestine, under the leadership of Ben-Gurion, opted for people over land and accepted the idea of the partition of the land of Israel. It was a decision reached not without considerable pain and internal conflict. Faced with a similar choice, the leadership in Israel at the end of the twentieth century reached similar conclusions. The costs of continuing with occupation and violence were too high, development and peace were too important for the internal development in Israeli society, and the toll in the quality of life in Israel and in the administered territories was too high to justify the continuation of the status quo. The dependency of both populations on other nations and on outside support is too great for either side to only follow its ideological imperatives. The cost in human life and hatred between neighbors is not measurable.

Ethnicity and Nationalism: Are Ethnic Groups Transitional?

To review the impact of Jewish and Palestinian diasporas on Israeli society, in general, and on ethnic divisions in Israel, in particular, I turn to one of the key questions raised in the beginning of this excursion into understanding Israel's changing society: What is the relationship between nation-building and ethnic stratification? Specifically, what are the contexts in Israel that exacerbate the ethnic division of labor, and when do these forms of ethnic stratification and inequality diminish? How has ethnic stratification in Israel changed in the context of the external developments in the Jewish and Palestinian diasporas? In the process of understanding these issues, I shall attempt to clarify the conflict between ethnic pluralism and nationalism in the formation of new states.

I have already identified some of the major ethnic divisions in Israeli society, those that divide Jews from each other and those that separate Jews from Arabs. I have documented the spheres of convergences and divergences among these groups and the basic differences in community institutions that have emerged to reinforce ethnic inequalities. I have shown how the divisions between Jews and Arabs are different from the internal divisions among Jews, although they share some basic similarities. What can one infer from this understanding of the sources of these differences about the relative permanence of these divisions and whether Jewish and Arab ethnicity in Israel is transitional? We have documented ethnic convergences in some processes (e.g., fertility, family, and mortality) and continued ethnic distinctiveness in others (e.g., residential concentration and socioeconomic measures). Have these patterns resulted in the declining significance ·of ethnicity and of ethnic communities? If ethnic communities are continuous features of Israel's emerging pluralism, how is national integration affected? In short, does ethnic continuity conflict with national Israeli integration?

It is clear that the earlier entry into Israel's society of European immigrants and their socioeconomic and demographic backgrounds facilitated their relatively successful socioeconomic mobility and their access to power, resources, and opportunity. European immigrants could take advantage of their connections to the European-dominated society and economy that they found established as the state was developing. Burdened by larger families, higher mortality and morbidity, and fewer resources than Jews from Western societies, Asian and African immigrants arrived in Israel later in time, with a higher level of dependency on sociopolitical institutions. They came from less-developed societies, with fewer urban skills and less-powerful economic networks, and they were therefore less able to compete with European-origin groups in Israel. The timing of immigration and the cultural differences between groups reinforced these structural background factors that divided Israeli Jews.

The differential timing of immigration and the changing ethnic composition of immigrant streams created the contexts of residential concentration among Jews. Ethnic residential patterns, more so than the legacy of social and cultural origins, shape what ethnicity continues to mean in the process of nation-building in Israel. Residential concentration forged from political and economic considerations has become the key process marking off Israeli-born Jews from each other as it has been the demographic foundation of the continuing Jewish-Arab distinctiveness.

New Israeli patterns have emerged among Jews that are neither fully "Western" nor "Middle Eastern." Although ethnic cultural differences remain salient and distance from the immigrant generation continues to be an important factor in understanding social change, the structural features in Israel—particularly residential segregation and its implication for access to opportunity—are critical in retaining ethnic distinctiveness. Ethnic residential concentration is linked to educational opportunities and, in turn, to jobs; it is likely to relate to intra-ethnic marriages and a reinforced sense of ethnic self-identity, pride, and culture, connecting ethnic origins and families into networks of relationships. These separate patterns are almost total between Jews and Arabs and characterize significant segments of third-generation Jews when examined by the two broad Jewish ethnic categories: Western and Middle Eastern.

In my review of the political and demographic contexts of Israeli society, it has become clear that some ethnic demographic differences diminish in importance and that ethnic convergences occur over time. Ethnic convergences seem to result when differences are primarily the result of the background of immigrants and are largely the legacy of the past. Thus, for example, family size and family structure differences among ethnic groups have diminished with each passing generation, as mortality differences disappeared among the foreign-born first generation. In contrast, ethnic communities remain salient when the sources of ethnic differences are embedded in the society of destination as a result of the timing of immigration and the ethnic and economic selectivity of immigrant streams or because of emerging residential segregation, occupational concentration, or economic niches that flow from political and economic considerations. These structural features are, in turn, legitimated by cultural expressions and values.

Ethnic residential concentration among Jews and between Jews and Arabs reinforces the overlap of ethnicity and socioeconomic factors through the impact of locational factors on access to educational and economic opportunities. Together, residential and socioeconomic concentrations shape the continuing salience of ethnic distinctiveness in Israel. When groups are integrated residentially, ethnic differences become marginal in their social, economic, and political importance; where residential segregation in Israel has persisted, it has become the primary engine of ethnic persistence and inequality. Although ethnic segregation is associated at times with poverty and lower socioeconomic status, it also implies supportive and family networks that shape the lives of many Israelis. Local institutions serve as further bases for ethnic continuity. These include ethnic family networks, economic networks that are ethnically based and some local institutions—synagogues, community centers, political interests, health clinics, and leisure-time and cultural activities (sports and music, for example)—that are concentrated among particular ethnic groups. Jewish ethnic continuities persist despite government policies and ideological orientations to deny the salience of ethnicity.

The Arab-Jewish distinction is driven by these same processes of economic concentration, residential segregation, and institutional separateness. It also reflects the political legacy of the broader Arab-Israeli conflict, the role of Palestinians in their quest for national identity, and the importance of Jewishness in the political shape of Israeli society and its symbols. The ethnic identity of Arab-Israelis can never be fully Israeli as long as being Israeli involves a clear and unmistakable Jewish cultural component, Jewish historical constructions, and dominant Jewish symbols.[11] The economic integration of Israeli Arabs makes their distinctiveness sharper and their powerlessness obvious and does not increase their social integration. Conferring political rights and welfare entitlements cannot erase the effects of their Palestinian identity and their minority status in Israel. The Arab population of Israel is likely to struggle with the conflicts of their identity for another generation and with their unequal access to opportunities as citizens of the state.

These arguments suggest that convergences among ethnic groups in some aspects of social life do not necessarily provide clues about total ethnic assimilation. Increasing similarities in family structure or educational levels among Jews from different ethnic origins are an inadequate basis for concluding that assimilation is proceeding to eliminate ethnic communities. Ethnic communities have been redefined away from specific countries of origin toward an amalgamation of broader ethnic groups that represent new forms of ethnic differentiation. The diminished significance of Polish, Romanian, Algerian, and Tunisian ethnicity, for example, does not preclude a recombination into new ethnic categories that are specific to Israel's society and have importance as "European" and "Asian-African" Israeli communities. New ethnic divisions mark Jews off from each other and have ethnic significance only in the context of Israeli society. The conspicuous structural differences among Jews negate the "melting pot" response to the economic and demographic integration of ethnic populations. The resultant ethnic divisions do not imply that individuals do not move between ethnic groups or into a third ethnically neutral Israeli group. The fluidity of boundaries does not imply their absence. Ethnicity may continue to be a characteristic of populations, although it may not be an ascribed feature of each person's identity.

By the standards of ethnic assimilation, in Israel and in other pluralistic societies, the Arab-Israeli distinctiveness is embedded in the social and demographic structure of the society, its values, and its political culture (Goldscheider 1991). Jewish and Arab residential segregation in Israel and the resultant distinctiveness and disadvantage of Israeli Arabs are unlikely to be resolved without major internal changes in the society, its institutions, values, and political system. Barring such fundamental changes in the Jewish state of Israel, the residential segregation of Arab Israelis will continue, and the consequences for socioeconomic inequalities will persist. Only local control over institutions and the development of local opportunities for socioeconomic mobility in Arab-Israeli communities can reduce their disadvantaged status. How Israeli Arabs will be linked to autonomous Palestinian areas and Arab states remains unclear.

The social, political, and economic structure of Israeli society will continue to reflect the fundamentals of its demography. At both the societal and the community levels, Israel's demographic patterns may be viewed as a microcosm of general population patterns in Western and Third World countries. In their detail, these patterns reflect the historical legacy of Israel's formation as a new state in the post–World War II era, the distinctive demographic patterns that have characterized its development from the turn of the century in Palestine, and the influence of demographic, social, political, and cultural events around the world at the end of the twentieth century. Indeed, Israel is an extraordinary illustration of the dynamic interplay among population processes, nation-building, and ethnicity.[12]

These are initial answers to the consequences of demographic changes for ethnic communities in the context of nation-building in Israel. My orientation in thinking through the broader questions of the conditions under which ethnic communities retain their salience and of the contexts that facilitate ethnic assimilation, particularly under a regime of some demographic convergence, is to emphasize ethnic networks and ethnic institutions in the context of residential concentration. Clearly, and for different reasons, neither the Jewish diaspora nor the Palestinian diaspora is about to join the state and the society. As the twenty-first century begins, it is clear that these relationships, whatever their particular nuance, will be different from those of the past.

Notes

1. The area under Israel's administrative control included the West Bank and its population, since Gaza and Jericho came under Palestinian administration in summer 1994. The territory under Israel's administration encompassed over 1 million Arab-Palestinian residents at the end of 1994. The ongoing peace process between Israel and the Palestinians is likely to result in further administrative, political, and demographic changes over the next several years; Israel's administration of Palestinians is significantly different in 2002 than a decade or two earlier. The peace treaties and economic relations with Egypt and Jordan and the changing relationships with Syria will also alter Israel's regional development. For a review of the Arab-Israel conflict, see Goldscheider 2001b.

2. There are broader areas of international relations and foreign policy between Israel and various industrialized nations in Europe and America, as well as between Third World countries and Israel. There is also an extensive literature on the Israel-Arab conflict, the Palestinian question, and the relationship of Israel to neighboring Arab states—Jordan, Egypt, Syria, and Lebanon—and other states in the region. These issues and their vast literatures address themes that extend beyond the purview of this book. I present a modest and narrow view of these issues that focuses on the major themes I have emphasized throughout.

3. A revealing illustration of how important (ideologically and nationally) Jewish communities outside Israel are to the state is the annual inclusion of data in the official *Statistical Abstract of Israel* on the "Jewish Population in the World and in Israel." These statistical data begin with the Jewish population of the world in 1882 and continue until the latest year. They include estimates of Jewish population size in the world and the percentage of Jews living in Israel. I know of no other country's statistical yearbook that includes historical and comparative materials that would parallel this statistical table. See, for example, the *Statistical Abstract of Israel 2000*, no. 51, table 2.3.

4. In the United States, the category "Jewish" therefore, includes those who define themselves as Jewish and are defined by others as Jewish. It is a voluntary status in most Western countries. In some countries, the designation "Jewish" may be more formally noted on personal documents and, more often than not, has been the basis of discrimination and distinctiveness. Jews in Israel are automatically entitled to citizenship and are provided with a for-

mal document indicating Jewishness by religion and nationality. In marginal cases in Israel, mostly among antireligionists, requests have been made to be declared Jewish by nationality (and not by religion). A small number of Jews claim that they are Jewish by religion but not by nationality (e.g., some antinational, ultra-Orthodox residents). But for the overwhelming majority of Israeli Jews, the differences between religious and national definitions of Jewishness is a distinction without significance.

5. I use the United States as an example to simplify the discussion. Although there are some obvious differences, there are also major similarities. For a comparative view, see Goldscheider and Zuckerman 1984.

6. Data on the marriage and ethnic continuity of the children and grandchildren of those currently intermarried, as they grow up and have families of their own, are not available. The need to study generational transmission of ethnicity among the intermarried was also noted in connection with interethnic marriages in Israel (see Chapter 10).

7. For a very different view of issues of unity and diversity, drawing from a theological (and an Orthodox Judaic) view, see Sacks 1993. A thoroughly pessimistic view is presented by historian and Zionist David Vital (1990). I disagree with Sacks regarding the centrality of his conception of Judaism in what ought to be the "oneness" of the Jewish people. Vital misunderstands the transformation among American Jews and their power as an ethnic community and exaggerates the importance of secular nationalism in Jewish peoplehood.

8. The religious leadership of Jewish communities outside Israel has much more in common and is more likely to interact with the secular-political leadership of Israel than with the formal representatives of the religious establishment. Although some American Jewish young adults (and their parents) would place Hasidic or ultra-Orthodox Jews lower in their preference ranking for a "potential" spouse than non-Jews, ultra-Orthodox Jews are not likely to think of Conservative or Reform Jews as Jewish at all. In the view of ultra-Orthodox Jews in Israel, a Reform rabbi is not only not a rabbi but questionable as a Jew, and certainly not an acceptable "match" for a spouse. A Reform rabbi who is female is too exotic a creature for ultra-Orthodox Jews to think about!

9. As "administered territories" these areas could be negotiated about and exchanged; they were political entities under political control of the victor in a military battle. No long-term possession or control was implied, since there was a clear recognition that control was "administrative" not ideological. In sharp contrast, "Judea, Samaria, and Gaza" are Biblical names, reflecting the historic Judaic connection of these areas that were recaptured and repossessed after a long hiatus. The control is political and firmly anchored in history, religion, and legitimacy. The concept "administered territories" implies that the territory of others is administered; territory that is named by its Hebrew-Judaic origins is part of the gift of God to the Jewish people. Therefore, the switch in emphasis after 1977 was more than a name change of these parcels of land.

10. I use the official estimates of the Israel Bureau of Statistics. Whether the de jure or the de facto population is counted becomes one basis for the different estimates. For alternatives, see Abu-Lughod 1983, Peretz 1986, Roy 1986, and population estimates published annually by the Central Bureau of Statistics in Israel. A different set of estimates is reviewed and presented in Palestinian Bureau of Statistics 1994. See its web site (PCBS.org) and the web site of Central Bureau of Statistics of Israel (CBS.gov.il) for the latest statistical information.

11. Arab Israelis cannot seriously relate to the Israel "national" anthem, which refers to the 2,000-year longing for Jewish statehood for the Jewish people—"To be a free people in our land, the land of Zion, Jerusalem." National events and their symbols are infused with

Judaic, religious distinctiveness (e.g., national-religious holidays such as Passover and Israeli Independence Day), and Jewish historical meaning (e.g., the Holocaust) and are annual reminders of the distinctive status of Arab Israelis.

12. For comparative case studies on nation-building, population, and ethnicity, see those reported in Goldscheider 1995.

References

Abu-Lughod, Janet. 1983. "The Demographic Consequences of the Occupation," in N. Aruru (ed.), *Occupation: Israel over Palestine*. Belmont, Mass.: Arab-American Graduates.

Agassi, Judith. 1993. "Theories of Gender Inequality; Lessons from the Israeli Kibbutz," in Yael Azmon and Dafna Izraeli (eds.), *Women in Israel*. New Brunswick, N.J.: Transaction Publishers.

Alba, Richard. 1990. *Ethnic Identity: The Transformation of White America*. New Haven: Yale University Press.

Al Haj, Majid. 1985. "Ethnic Relations in an Arab Town in Israel," chapter 6 in Alex Weingrod (ed.), *Studies in Israeli Ethnicity*. New York: Gordon and Breach.

_____. 1987. *Social Changes and Family Process: Arab Communities in Shefar A'm*. Boulder: Westview Press.

_____. 1992. "Soviet Immigration as Viewed by Jews and Arabs: Divided Attitudes in a Divided Country," in Calvin Goldscheider (ed.), *Population and Social Change in Israel*. Boulder: Westview Press.

_____. 1995. *Education Empowerment and Control: The Case of the Arabs in Israel*. Albany: State University of New York Press.

Al Haj, Majid, and Elazar Leshem. 2000. *Immigrants from the Former Soviet Union in Israel: Ten Years Later*. Haifa: The Center for Multiculturalism and Educational Research.

Al Haj, Majid, and Henry Rosenfeld. 1990. *Arab Local Government in Israel*. Boulder: Westview Press.

Alonso, William. 1987. "Introduction: Population North and South," in *Population in an Interacting World*. Cambridge: Harvard University Press.

Amir, S. 1986. "Educational Structure and Wage Differentials in the Labor Force in the 1970's," chapter 6 in Yoram Ben-Porath (ed.), *The Israeli Economy*. Cambridge: Harvard University Press.

Anson, Jon. 1992. "Mortality, Ethnicity, and Standard of Living: A Minority Group Effect?" in Calvin Goldscheider (ed.), *Population and Social Change in Israel*. Boulder: Westview Press.

Aran, Gideon. 1990. "From Religious Zionism to Zionist Religion: The Roots of Gush Emunim," in Calvin Goldscheider and Jacob Neusner (eds.), *Social Foundations of Judaism*. Englewood Cliffs, N.J.: Prentice-Hall.

Arian, Asher. 1985. *Politics in Israel: The Second Generation*. New York: Chatham House.

Arian, Asher, and Michal Shamir. 1994. *The Elections in Israel, 1992*. Albany: State University of New York Press.

Avineri, Shlomo. 1981. *The Making of Modern Zionism: The Intellectual Origins of the Jewish State*. London: Weidenfeld and Nicholson.

Avruch, Kevin. 1981. *American Immigrants in Israel*. Chicago: University of Chicago Press.

Azmon, Yael. 1990. "Women and Politics: The Case of Israel." *Women and Politics* 10: 43–57.

Azmon, Yael, and Dafna Izraeli, eds. 1993. *Women in Israel*. New Brunswick, N.J.: Transaction Publishers.

Bachi, Roberto. 1977. *Population of Israel*. Jerusalem: Institute of Contemporary Jewry, The Hebrew University.

Bar-Gal, Yoram. 1986. "Arab Penetration and Settlement in Nazareth Ilit," pp. 51–64 in Arnon Sofer (ed.), *Residential and Internal Migration Patterns Among the Arabs of Israel*. Monograph series on the Middle East No.4. Haifa: University of Haifa, the Jewish-Arab Center.

Bar-Yosef, Rivka. 1971. "Absorption Versus Modernization," in Rueven Kahana and S. Koppelshtein (eds.), *Israeli Society, 1967–1973*. Jerusalem: Academon Press.

Bar-Yosef, Rivka, and D. Padan-Eisenstark. 1993. "Role Systems Under Stress: Sex Roles in War," in Yael Azmon and Dafna Izraeli (eds.), *Women in Israel*. New Brunswick, N.J.: Transaction Publishers.

Bean, Frank, and Marta Tienda. 1989. *The Hispanic Population of the United States*. New York: Russell Sage Foundation.

Ben-Artzi, Yosi, and M. Shoshani. 1986. "The Arabs of Haifa, 1972–1983: Demographic and Spatial Changes," pp. 33–50 in Arnon Sofer (ed.), *Residential and Internal Migration Patterns Among the Arabs of Israel*. Monograph series on the Middle East No.4. Haifa: University of Haifa, the Jewish-Arab Center.

Ben-David, Joseph. 1970. "Ethnic Differences of Social Change?" in Shmuel N. Eisenstadt, Rivka Bar Yosef, and Chaim Adler (eds.), *Integration and Development in Israel*. New York: Praeger Publishers.

Ben-Moshe, Eliahu. 1989. "Marriage Squeeze and Marriage Patterns in Israel," pp. 87–96 in Uziel O. Schmelz and Sergio Dellapergola (eds.), *Papers in Jewish Demography: 1985*. Jewish Population Studies 19. Institute of Contemporary Jewry. Jerusalem: The Hebrew University.

———. 1989a. Internal Migration Processes in Israel: Demographic, Ethnic and Social Aspects. Ph.D. diss., The Hebrew University, Jerusalem.

Ben-Porath, Yoram, ed. 1986. *The Israeli Economy*. Cambridge: Harvard University Press.

Ben-Porath, Yoram. 1986a. "Diversity in Population and in the Labor Force," in *The Israeli Economy*. Cambridge: Harvard University Press.

———. 1986b. "The Entwined Growth of Population and Product, 1922–1982," in *The Israeli Economy*. Cambridge: Harvard University Press.

Ben-Rafael, Eliezer. 1986. "The Changing Experience, Power and Prestige of Ethnic Groups in Israel: The Case of the Moroccans," vol. 5 of Peter Medding (ed.), *Israel: State and Society, 1948–1988*. Jerusalem: Studies in Contemporary Jewry, Institute of Contemporary Jewry.

Ben-Yehuda, Nachman. 1989. "The Social Meaning of Alternative Systems: Some Exploratory Notes," pp. 152–164 in Baruch Kimmerling (ed.), *The Israeli State and Society: Boundaries and Frontiers*. Albany: State University of New York Press.

Berelson, Bernard. 1979. "Foreword," in Dov Friedlander and Calvin Goldscheider, *The Population of Israel*. New York: Columbia University Press.

Berglas, Eitan. 1986. "Defense and the Economy," chapter 8 in Yoram Ben-Porath (ed.), *The Israeli Economy*. Cambridge: Harvard University Press.

Berler, Alexander. 1970. *New Towns in Israel*. Jerusalem: Israel Universities Press.

Bernstein, D. 1993. "Economic Growth and Female Labour: The Case of Israel," *The Sociological Review* 31(2): 263–292.

Blalock, Herbert. 1967. *Toward a Theory of Minority-Group Relations.* New York: John Wiley.

Blauner, Robert. 1989. *Black Lives, White Lives: Three Decades of Race Relations in America.* Berkeley: University of California Press.

Cohen, Erik. 1977. "The City in Zionist Ideology." *Jerusalem Quarterly* 4:126–155.

Cohen, Steve. 1983. *American Modernity and Jewish Identity.* New York: Tavistock Publishers.

Danet, Brenda. 1989. *Pulling Strings: Biculturalism in Israel Bureaucracy.* Albany: State University of New York Press.

Dashefsky, Arnold, et al. 1992. *Americans Abroad: A Comparative Study of Emigrants from the United States.* New York: Plenum Press.

Dellapergola, Sergio. 1986. "Aliya and Other Jewish Migrations: Toward an Integrated Perspective," in Uziel O. Schmelz and Gad Natan (eds.), *Studies in the Population of Israel.* Jerusalem: Magnes Press.

———. 1993. "Demographic Changes in the State of Israel in the Early 1990's," Jerusalem: Center for Social Policy Research.

Demeny, Paul, and Goeffrey McNicoll, eds. 1998. *The Reader in Population and Development.* New York: St. Martin's Press.

Deshen, Shlomo. 1990. "The Social Foundation of Israeli Judaism," pp. 212–239 in Calvin Goldscheider and Jacob Neusner (eds.), *Social Foundations of Judaism.* Englewood Cliffs, N.J.: Prentice-Hall.

Doron, Abraham, and Ralph Kramer. 1991. *The Welfare State in Israel.* Boulder: Westview Press.

Eisenbach, Zvi. 1986. "Family Planning Among the Muslim Population of Israel," pp. 1–14 in Uziel O. Schmelz and Gad Natan (eds.), *Studies in the Population of Israel.* Jerusalem: Magnes Press.

———. 1989. "Changes in the Fertility of Moslem Women in Israel in Recent Years," *HaMizrach Hahadash*, pp. 86–102.

———. 1989a. "Marriage and Fertility in the Process of Integration: Intermarriage Among Immigrant Groups in Israel." Paper prepared for the IUSSP 21st International Population Conference, New Delhi, India, September.

———. 1992. "Marriage and Fertility in the Process of Integration: Intermarriage Among Origin Groups in Israel," in Calvin Goldscheider (ed.), *Population and Social Change in Israel.* Boulder: Westview Press.

Eisenbach, Zvi, Y. Hayat, P. Tzedakah, A. Reiss. 1989. "The Inequality of Death: Socioeconomic Differentials in Israel 1983–1986." Paper presented at the Association of Israeli Epidemiology.

Eisenstadt, Shmuel. 1954. *The Absorption of Immigrants.* London: Routledge and Paul.

———. 1969. "The Absorption of Immigrants, the Blending of Exiles, and the Problems of the Transformation of Israeli Society," in *The Integration of Immigrants from Different Countries of Origins in Israeli Society.* Jerusalem: Magnes Press.

———. 1985. *The Transformation of Israeli Society.* Boulder: Westview Press.

Etzioni-Halevi, Eva, and A. Illy. 1993. "Women in Legislatures: Israel in a Comparative Perspective," in Yael Azmon and Dafna Izraeli (eds.), *Women in Israel.* New Brunswick, N.J.: Transaction Publishers.

Farley, Reynolds, and William Allen. 1987. *The Color Line and the Quality Life in America.* New York: Russell Sage Foundation.

Friedlander, Dov. 1969. "Demographic Responses and Population Change." *Demography* 6:359–382.

Friedlander, Dov, Eliahu Ben-Moshe, and Yona Schellekens. 1989. "Regional Demographic Changes in Israel." *Machon Yerushalayem L'Heker Yisrael*, Jerusalem.

Friedlander, Dov, Eliahu Ben-Moshe, Yona Schellekens, and Carole Feldman. 1990. "Socioeconomic Change, Demographic Processes, and Population Aging in Israel's Cities and Towns: Implications for Welfare Policies." The Jerusalem Institute for Israel Studies, Research Studies No. 37.

Friedlander, Dov, Zvi Eisenbach, Eliahu Ben-Moshe, Ahmad Hleihel, Shlom T. Luniavski, Lion Elmakis and Dan Ben Hur. 1998. "Changes in the Educational Attainments in Israel Since the Fifties: Effects of Religion, Origin and Family Characteristics." Working paper, Central Bureau of Statistics, Jerusalem.

Friedlander, Dov, Zvi Eisenbach, Eliahu Ben-Moshe, Ahmad Hleihel, Shlom. T. Luniavski, Lion Elmakis and Dan Ben Hur. 2000. "Matched Census Results of Education in Israel Since the Fifties: Effects of Origin and Selected Characteristics, Jews and Arabs." Working paper, The Hebrew University, Department of Population Studies, Jerusalem.

Friedlander, Dov, Zvi Eisenbach, and Calvin Goldscheider. 1979. "Modernization Patterns and Fertility Change: The Arab Populations of Israel and the Israel-Administered Territories." *Population Studies* 33:239–254.

_____. 1980. "Family Size Limitation and Birth Spacing: The Fertility Transition of African and Asian Immigrants in Israel." *Population and Development Review* 6 (December):581–593.

Friedlander, Dov, and Carole Feldman. 1993. "The Modern Shift to Below-Replacement Fertility: Has Israel's Population Joined the Process?" *Population Studies* 47:295–306.

Friedlander, Dov, and Calvin Goldscheider. 1974. "Peace and the Demographic Future of Israel." *Journal of Conflicts Resolution* 18:486–501.

_____. 1978. "Immigration, Social Change and Cohort Fertility in Israel." *Population Studies* 32:299–317.

_____. 1979. *The Population of Israel*. New York: Columbia University Press.

_____. 1984. "Israel's Population: The Challenge of Pluralism." *Population Bulletin, Population Reference Bureau* 39(2).

Gharaibeh, Fawzi A. 1985. *The Economics of the West Bank and the Gaza Strip*. Boulder: Westview Press.

Ginor, Fanny. 1986. Chapter 11 in Yoram Ben-Porath (ed.), *The Israeli Economy*. Cambridge: Harvard University Press.

Gitelman, Zvi. 1995. *Immigration and Identity: The Resettlement and Impact of Soviet Immigrants on Israeli Politics and Society*. Los Angeles: Wilstein Institute of Jewish Policy Studies.

Glazer, Nathan. 1983. *Ethnic Dilemmas 1964–1982*. Cambridge: Harvard University Press.

Glazer, Nathan, and Daniel Moynihan, eds. 1975. *Ethnicity: Theory and Experience*. Cambridge: Harvard University Press.

Goldberg, Harvey. 1977. "Introduction: Culture and Ethnicity in the Study of Israeli Society." *Ethnic Groups* 1:163–186.

Goldscheider, Calvin. 1971. *Population, Modernization, and Social Structure*. Boston: Little, Brown and Co.

_____. 1974. "The Future of American Aliya," in Marshall Sklare (ed.), *The Sociology of the American Jew*. New York: Behrman House.

———. 1983. "The Demography of Asian and African Jews in Israel," in Joseph B. Maier and Chaim I. Waxman (eds.), *Ethnicity, Identity, and History*. New Brunswick, N.J.: Transaction Books.

———. 1986. "Family Changes and Variation Among Israeli Ethnic Groups," in Steve M. Cohen and Paula Hyman (eds.), *The Jewish Family: Myths and Reality*. New York: Holmes and Meier.

———. 1986a. *Jewish Continuity and Changes: Emerging Patterns in America*. Bloomington: Indiana University Press.

———. 1986b. *The American Jewish Community*. Atlanta: Scholars Press.

———. 1990. "Israel," in William J. Serow, Charles Nam, David Sly, and Robert Weller (eds.), *Handbook on International Migration*. New York: Greenwood Press.

———. 1991. "The Embeddedness of the Arab-Jewish Conflict in the State of Israel: Demographic and Sociological Perspectives," pp. 111–132 in Bernard Reich and Gershon Kieval (eds.), *Israeli Politics in the 1990's*. New York: Greenwood Press.

———. 1991a. "Census Monographs on Ethnicity," *Demography* 28:661–666.

———, ed. 1992a. *Population and Social Change in Israel*. Boulder: Westview Press.

———. 1992b. "Demographic Transformations in Israel: Emerging Themes in Comparative Context," in *Population and Social Change in Israel*. Boulder: Westview Press.

———, ed. 1992c. *Fertility Transitions, Family Structure, and Population Policy*. Boulder: Westview Press.

———, ed. 1995. *Population, Nation-Building, and Ethnicity*. Boulder: Westview Press.

———. 2001a. "Ethnic Categorization in Censuses: Comparative Observations from Israel, Canada, and the United States," in David Kertzer and Dominique Arel (eds.), *Census and Identity*. Cambridge: Cambridge University Press.

———. 2001b. *The Arab-Israeli Conflict*. Westport, Conn.: Greenwood Press.

———. 2002. *Studying the Jewish Future*. Seattle: University of Washington Press.

Goldscheider, Calvin, and Ann Dill. 1991. "Linkages Between Health and Ethnic/Racial Differentiation: Methodological and Conceptual Considerations." Paper presented at the annual meeting of the American Sociological Association, August.

Goldscheider, Calvin, and Dov Friedlander. 1983. "Religiosity Patterns in Israel." *American Jewish Yearbook* 83:3–39.

———. 1986. "Reproductive Norms in Israel," pp. 15–35 in Uziel O. Schmelz and Gad Natan (eds.), *Studies in the Population of Israel in Honor of Roberto Bachi*. Jerusalem: Magnes Press.

Goldscheider, Calvin, and Frances Kobrin. 1980. "Ethnic Continuity and the Process of Self Employment." *Ethnicity* 7:256–278.

Goldscheider, Calvin, and William Mosher. 1991. "Patterns of Contraceptive Use in the United States: The Importance of Religious Factors." *Studies in Family Planning* 22:102–115.

Goldscheider, Calvin, and Jacob Neusner, eds. 1990. *Social Foundations of Judaism*. Englewood Cliffs, N.J.: Prentice-Hall.

Goldscheider, Calvin, and Alan Zuckerman. 1984. *The Transformation of the Jews*. Chicago: University of Chicago Press.

Goldscheider, Frances, and Zara Fisher. 1989. "Household Structure and Living Alone in Israel," in Frances Goldscheider and Calvin Goldscheider (eds.), *Ethnicity and the New Family Economy: Living Arrangements and Intergenerational Financial Flows*. Boulder: Westview Press.

Goldscheider, Frances, and Calvin Goldscheider. 1989. *Ethnicity and the New Family Economy: Living Arrangements and Intergenerational Financial Flows*. Boulder: Westview Press.

_____. 1994. "Leaving and Returning Home in 20th Century America." Population Reference Bureau, vol. 48 (March).

_____. 1999. *The Changing Transition to Adulthood: Leaving and Returning Home*. Thousand Oaks, Calif.: Sage Publications.

Goldscheider, Frances, and Linda Waite. 1991. *New Families, No Families? The Transformation of the American Home*. Berkeley: University of California Press.

Gonen, Amiram. 1985. "The Changing Ethnic Geography of Israeli Cities," in Alex Weingrod (ed.), *Studies in Israeli Ethnicity*. New York: Gordon and Breach.

_____. 1993. "Under-Representation of Ashkenazic Jews in Certain Israeli Towns," pp. 266–273 in Uziel O. Schmelz and Sergio Dellapergola (eds.), *Papers in Jewish Demography: 1989*. The Hartman Institute of Contemporary Jewry, Jerusalem: The Hebrew University.

Gordon, Milton. 1963. *Assimilation in American Life*. New York: Oxford University Press.

Grossman, David. 1993. *Sleeping on a Wire: Conversations with Palestinians in Israel*. New York: Farrar, Straus, and Giroux.

Halevi, Nadav. 1986. "Perspectives on the Balance of Payments," in Yoram Ben-Porath (ed.), *The Israeli Economy*. Cambridge: Harvard University Press.

Halpern, Ben. 1961. *The Idea of the Jewish State*. Cambridge: Harvard University Press.

Hartman, Harriet. 1993. "Economic and Familial Roles of Women in Israel," in Yael Azmon and Dafna Izraeli (eds.), *Women in Israel*. New Brunswick, N.J.: Transaction Publishers.

Hazelton, Lesley. 1977. *Israeli Women: The Reality Behind the Myths*. New York: Simon and Schuster.

Heilman, Samuel. 1992. *Defenders of the Faith: Inside Ultra-Orthodox Jewry*. New York: Schocken.

Hertzberg, Arthur. 1960. *The Zionist Idea*. New York: Meridian Books.

Hofman, John. 1988. *Arab Jewish Relations in Israel*. Bristol, Ind.: Wyndham Hall Press.

Horowitz, Dan, and Moshe Lissak. 1978. *Origins of the Israeli Polity: Palestine Under the Mandate*. Chicago: University of Chicago Press.

_____. 1989a. "The State of Israel at Forty," vol. 5 of Peter Medding (ed.), *Israel: State and Society, 1948–1988*. Jerusalem: Studies in Contemporary Jewry, Institute of Contemporary Jewry

_____. 1989b. *Trouble in Utopia: The Overburdened Polity of Israel*. Albany: State University of New York Press.

Inbar, Michael, and Chaim Adler. 1977. *Ethnic Integration in Israel*. New Brunswick, N.J.: Transaction Books.

Israeli Central Bureau of Statistics. *Statistical Abstract of Israel*. Various issues.

Kanev, Itzhak. 1957. *Population and Society in Israel and in the World*. Jerusalem: The Bialik Institute.

Katz, Elihu. 1974. "Culture and Communication in Israel: The Transformation of Tradition." *Jewish Journal of Sociology* (June): 5–22.

Kellerman, Aharon. 1993. *Society and Settlement: Jewish Land of Israel in the Twentieth Century*. Albany: State of New York Press.

Keysar, Ariela. 1990. Demographic Processes in the Kibbutzim of Israel. Ph.D. diss., The Hebrew University, Jerusalem.

Kimmerling, Baruch, ed. 1989. *The Israeli State and Society: Boundaries and Frontiers*. Albany: State University of New York Press.

Kimmerling, Baruch, and Joel Migdal. 1993. *Palestinians: The Making of a People*. New York: Free Press.

Kirschenbaum, Avi. 1992. "Migration and Urbanization: Patterns of Population Redistribution and Urban Growth," in Calvin Goldscheider (ed.), *Population and Social Change in Israel*. Boulder: Westview Press.

Klaff, Vivian. 1977. "Residence and Integration in Israel: A Mosaic of Segregated Groups." *Ethnicity* 4:103–121.

Klayman, Maxwell. 1970. *The Moshav in Israel: A Case Study of Institution-Building for Agricultural Development*. New York: Praeger Publishers.

Kraus, Vered, and Robert Hodge. 1990. *Promises in the Promised Land: Mobility and Inequality*. Westport, Conn.: Greenwood Press.

Krausz, Ernest. 1983. *Studies on the Kibbutz*. New Brunswick, N.J.: Transaction Books.

Kupinsky, Shlomo. 1992. "Jewish Fertility Patterns: Norms, Differentials, and Policy Implications," in Calvin Goldscheider (ed.), *Population and Social Change in Israel*. Boulder: Westview Press.

Lamdany, Ruben. 1982. *Emigration from Israel*. Discussion Paper No. 8208, The Maurice Falk Institute for Economic Research in Israel, Jerusalem.

Leshem, Elazar, and Moshe Sicron. 1999. "The Absorption of Soviet Immigrants in Israel," pp. 448–552 in *American Jewish Yearbook, 1999*. New York: American Jewish Committee.

Levy, Shlomit, Hannah Levinsohn, and Elihu Katz. 1993. *Beliefs, Observances and Social Interaction Among Israeli Jews*. Jerusalem: The Louis Guttman Institute of Applied Social Research.

Lewin-Epstein, Noah, and Moshe Semyonov. 1986. "Ethnic Group Mobility in Israel's Labor Market." *American Sociological Review* 51:342–351.

_____. 1992. "Local Labor Markets, Ethnic Segregation and Income Inequality." *Social Forces* 70:1101–1119.

_____. 1993. *The Arab Minority in Israel's Economy: Patterns of Ethnic Inequality*. Boulder: Westview Press.

Lieberson, Stanley. 1980. *A Piece of the Pie: Black and White Immigrants Since 1880*. Berkeley: University of California Press.

Lieberson, Stanley, and Mary Waters. 1988. *From Many Strands: Ethnic and Racial Groups in Contemporary America*. New York: Russell Sage Foundation.

Liebman, Charles, and Steve Cohen. 1990. *Two Worlds of Judaism: The Israeli and American Experiences*. New Haven: Yale University Press.

Liebman, Charles, and Eliezer Don-Yehiya. 1983. *Civil Religion in Israel*. Berkeley: University of California Press.

Light, Ivan, and Edna Bonacich. 1988. *Immigrant Entrepreneurs: Koreans in Los Angeles, 1965–1982*. Los Angeles: University of California Press.

Lipshitz, Gabriel. 1991. "Immigration and Internal Migration as a Mechanism of Polarization and Dispersion of Population and Development: The Israeli Case." *Economic Development and Cultural Changes*, pp. 391–408.

Lustig, Ian. 1988. *For the Land and the Lord: Jewish Fundamentalism in Israel*. New York: Council on Foreign Relations.

Mandel, Neville. 1976. *The Arabs and Zionism Before World War I*. Berkeley: University of California Press.

Massey, Douglas. 1990. "American Apartheid: Segregation and the Making of the Under-class." *American Journal of Sociology* 96:329–357.

Massey, Douglas, and Nancy Denton. 1993. *American Apartheid: Segregation and the Making of the Underclass.* Cambridge: Harvard University Press.

Matras, Judah. 1973. "Israel's New Frontier: The Urban Periphery," in Michael Curtis and Maurice Chertoff (eds.), *Israel: Social Structure and Change.* New Brunswick, N.J.: Transaction Books.

————. 1977. *Introduction to Population: A Sociological Approach.* Englewood, N.J.: Prentice-Hall.

————. 1985. "Intergenerational Social Mobility and Ethnic Organization in the Jewish Population of Israel," in Alex Weingrod (ed.), *Studies in Israeli Ethnicity.* New York: Gordon and Breach.

————. 1986. "Demographic Trends in the Population of Israel: Implications for Changing Patterns of Dependency." Discussion paper, 127–186. Brookdale Institute of Gerontology and Adult Human Development, Jerusalem.

Matras, Judah, and Gila Noam. 1987. "Schooling and Military Service: Their Effects on Israeli Women's Attainments and Social Participation in Early Adulthood." *Israel Social Science Research* 5:29–43.

Matras, Judah, Gila Noam, and M. Bar-Haim. 1984. "Israeli-Educated Men: Transition to Adulthood." Brookdale, Jerusalem. Mimeographed.

Medding, Peter, ed. 1989. *Israel: State and Society, 1948–1988.* Jerusalem: Studies in Contemporary Jewry, Institute of Contemporary Jewry.

Moore, Dalia. 1993. "Relative Deprivation in the Labor Market," in Yael Azmon and Dafna Izraeli (eds.), *Women in Israel.* New Brunswick, N.J.: Transaction Publishers.

Morag-Talmon, Pnina. 1989. "The Integration Process of Eastern Jews in Israeli Society, 1948–1988," vol. 5 of Peter Medding (ed.), *Israel: State and Society, 1948–1988.* Jerusalem: Studies in Contemporary Jewry, Institute of Contemporary Jewry.

Nahon, Yaacov. 1987. "Dfusei Hitrahavot Hahaskalah Umivneh Hahizdomnuit Hataasukatit: Hammemad HaAdati" (Types of Educational Expansion and the Structure of Occupational Opportunities: The Ethnic Dimension). Machon Yerushalyim L'hekar Yisrael (Research Studies No. 25, Jerusalem Institute for Israel Research).

————. 1989. "Self-Employed Workers: The Ethnic Dimension." Research Studies No. 30, Jerusalem Institute for Israel Research.

Near, Henry. 1992. *The Kibbutz Movement: A History.* Vol. 1, *Origins and Growth, 1909–1939, The Littman Library.* New York: Oxford University Press.

Neuman, Shoshana. 1991. "Occupational Segregation in Israel: The Gender-Ethnicity Interaction." Bar Ilan University, Israel. Mimeographed.

Okun, Barbara. 2001. "Marriage Patterns Among Jews of Mixed Ancestry in Israel: The Fading Centrality of Ethnicity." Paper presented at the annual meeting of the Population Association of America, Washington, D.C., March.

Palestine Bureau of Statistics. 1994. "Demography of the Palestinian Population in the West Bank and Gaza Strip." *Current Status Report Series*, No. 1, Ramallah, West Bank.

Peres, Yochanan, and Ruth Katz. 1991. "The Family in Israel: Change and Continuity," in Lea Shamgar-Handelman and Rivka Bar-Yosef (eds.), *Families in Israel.* Jerusalem: Academon, The Hebrew University.

Peretz, Don. 1986. *West Bank: History, Politics, Society, and Economy.* Boulder: Westview Press.

Peritz, Eric. 1986. "Mortality of African Born Jews in Israel," pp. 229–242 in Uziel O. Schmelz and Gad Natan (eds.), *Studies in the Population of Israel.* Jerusalem: Magnes Press.

Peritz, Eric, and M. Baras, eds. 1992. *Studies in the Fertility of Israel.* Jerusalem: The Institute of Contemporary Jewry, The Hebrew University.

Plessner, Yakir. 1994. *The Political Economy of Israel: From Ideology to Stagnation.* Albany: State University of New York Press.

Portes, Alejandro, and Ruben Rumbaut. 1990. *Immigrant America: A Portrait.* Berkeley: University of California Press.

Rabie, Mohamed. 1988. *The Politics of Foreign Aid: U.S. Foreign Assistance and Aid to Israel.* New York: Praeger Publishers.

Rayman, Paula. 1981. *The Kibbutz Community and Nation Building.* Princeton: Princeton University Press.

Rein, Natalie. 1979. *Daughters of Rachel: Women in Israel.* London: Penguin Books.

Rosen, Sherry. 1982. "Intermarriage and the 'Blending of Exiles' in Israel." *Race and Ethnic Relations* 3:79–102.

Rosenfeld, Henry. 1968. "The Contradictions Between Property, Kinship, and Power, as Reflected in the Marriage System of an Arab Village," pp. 247–260 in John Peristiany (ed.), *Contributions to Mediterranean Society.* The Hague: Mouton and Co.

Roy, Sara. 1986. *The Gaza Strip Survey.* Boulder: Westview Press.

Sabatello, Eitan F., and Nurith Yaffe. 1988. "Israel," pp. 263–278 in Paul Saachdev (ed.), *International Handbook on Abortion.* Westport, Conn.: Greenwood Press.

Sacks, Jonathan. 1993. *One People? Tradition, Modernity, and Jewish Unity.* London: The Littman Library of Jewish Civilization.

Schmelz, Uziel O., Sergio Dellapergola, and Uri Avner. 1990. "Ethnic Differences Among Israeli Jews: A New Look." *American Jewish Yearbook* 90:3–204.

Seliktar, Ofira. 1984. "Ethnic Stratification and Foreign Policy in Israel." *The Middle East Journal* 38:34–50.

Semyonov, Moshe. 1988. "Bi-Ethnic Labor Markets, Mono-Ethnic Labor Markets, Socio-economic Inequality." *American Sociological Review* 53:256–266.

Semyonov, Moshe, and Yinon Cohen. 1990. "Ethnic Discrimination and the Income of Majority Group Workers." *American Sociological Review* 55:107–114.

Semyonov, Moshe, and Vered Kraus. 1983. "Gender, Ethnicity and Income Inequality: The Israeli Experience." *International Journal of Comparative Sociology* 24:257–272.

Semyonov, Moshe, and Noah Lewin-Epstein. 1987. *Hewers of Wood and Drawers of Water: Non-Citizen Arabs in the Israeli Labor Market.* Ithaca: ILR Press.

Semyonov, Moshe, and Andrea Tyree. 1981. "Community Segregation and the Costs of Ethnic Subordination." *Social Forces* 59:649–666.

Sered, Susan. 1993. "Ritual Mortality and Gender: The Religious Lives of Oriental Jewish Women in Jerusalem," in Yael Azmon and Dafna Izraeli (eds.), *Women in Israel.* New Brunswick, N.J.: Transaction Publishers.

Shahar, Rena. 1991. "Attitudes Towards Interethnic Marriages Among Israeli Youngsters," in Lea Shamgar-Handelman and Rivka Bar-Yosef (eds.), *Families in Israel.* Jerusalem: Academon, The Hebrew University.

Shamgar-Handelman, Lea, and Rivka Bar-Yosef (eds.). 1991. *Families in Israel.* Jerusalem: Academon, The Hebrew University.

Shavit, Yossi. 1984. "Tracking and Ethnicity in Israel Secondary Education." *American Sociological Review* 49:210–220.

_____. 1989. "Tracking and the Educational Spirit: Arab and Jewish Educational Expansion." *Comparative Education Review* 33:216–231.

_____. 1990. "Segregation Tracking and Educational Attainment of Minorities: Arabs and Oriental Jews in Israel." *American Sociological Review* 55:115–126.

_____. 1993. "From Peasantry to Proletariat: Changes in the Educational Stratification of Arabs in Israel," chapter 14 in Yossi Shavit and Hans-Peter Blossfeld (eds.), *Persistent Inequality: Changing Educational Attainment in Thirteen Countries.* Boulder: Westview Press.

Shavit, Yossi, and Vered Kraus. 1990. "Educational Transitions in Israel: A Test of the Industrialization and Credentialism Hypotheses." *Sociology of Education* 63:133–141.

Shenhav, Yehouda, and Y. Haberfeld. 1993. "Scientists in Organizations: Discrimination Processes in an Internal Labor Market," in Yael Azmon and Dafna Izraeli (eds.), *Women in Israel.* New Brunswick, N.J.: Transaction Publishers.

Shmueli, A. 1985. "The Demography of Kinship in Israel, 1960–1980." Discussion paper 116–185, Brookdale, Jerusalem.

Shuval, Judith. 1992. *Social Dimensions of Health: The Israel Experience.* New York: Praeger Publishers.

Sicron, Moshe. 1957. *Immigration to Israel, 1948–1953.* Israel: Statistical Supplement, Central Bureau of Statistics.

Smooha, Sammy. 1978. *Israel: Pluralism or Conflict.* Los Angeles: University of California Press.

_____. 1983. "The Tolerance of the Jewish Majority in Israel of the Arab Minority: Comparative Perspectives," pp. 91–107 in Aluf Hareven (ed.), *Is It Really Difficult to Be an Israeli?* Jerusalem: The Van Leer Jerusalem Foundation.

_____. 1987. "Jewish and Arab Ethnocentrism in Israel." *Ethnic and Racial Studies* 10:1–26.

_____. 1989. *Arabs and Jews in Israel.* Vol. 1. Boulder: Westview Press.

_____. 1990. "Minority Status in an Ethnic Democracy: The Status of the Arab Minority in Israel." *Ethnic and Racial Studies* 13:389–413.

_____. 1991. *Arabs and Jews in Israel.* Vol. 2. Boulder: Westview Press.

Smooha, Sammy, and Theodor Hanf. 1992. "The Diverse Modes of Conflict-Regulation in Deeply Divided Societies." *International Journal of Comparative Sociology* 33:26–47.

Smooha, Sammy, and Vered Kraus. 1985. "Ethnicity as a Factor in Status Attainment in Israel." *Research in Social Stratification and Mobility* 4:51–76.

Snipp, C. Matthew. 1989. *American Indians: The First of This Land.* New York: Russell Sage Foundation.

Sobel, Zvi. 1986. *Migrants from the Promised Land.* New Brunswick, N.J.: Transaction Books.

Sobel, Zvi, and Benjamin Beit-Hallahmi. 1991. *Tradition, Innovation, Conflict: Jewishness and Judaism in Contemporary Israel.* Albany: State University of New York Press.

Spilerman, Seymour, and Jack Habib. 1976. "Development Towns in Israel: The Role of the Community in Creating Ethnic Disparities in Labor Force Characteristics." *American Journal of Sociology* 81:781–812.

Spiro, Melford. 1979. *Gender and Culture: Kibbutz Women Revisited.* Durham, N.C.: Duke University Press.

Steinberg, Stephen. 1981. *The Ethnic Myth.* Boston: Beacon Press.

Swirski, Barbara, and Marilyn Safir (eds.). 1991. *Calling the Equality Bluff: Women in Israel.* New York: Pergamon.

Talmon-Garber, Yonina. 1972. *Family and Community in the Kibbutz.* Cambridge: Harvard University Press.

Toren, Nina. 1993. "The Status of Women in Academia," in Yael Azmon and Dafna Izraeli (eds.), *Women in Israel.* New Brunswick, N.J.: Transaction Publishers.

Toren, Nina, and Vered Kraus. 1987. "The Effects of Minority Size on Women's Position in Academia." *Social Forces* 65:1090–1100.

Vital, David. 1975. *The Origins of Zionism.* New York: Oxford University Press.

_____. 1982. *Zionism: The Formative Years.* New York: Oxford University Press.

_____. 1987. *Zionism: The Crucial Years.* New York: Oxford University Press.

_____. 1990. *The Future of the Jew: A People at the Crossroads?* Cambridge: Harvard University Press.

Waldinger, Roger, Howard Aldrich, and Robin Ward. 1990. *Ethnic Entrepreneurs.* Sage Series on Race and Ethnic Relations. Beverly Hills, Calif.: Sage Press.

Watkins, Susan. 1990. *Nation Building and Population.* Princeton: Princeton University Press.

Waxman, Chaim. 1989. *American Aliyah: Portrait of an Innovative Migration Movement.* Detroit: Wayne State University Press.

_____. 1991. "The Israeli-Jewish Presence in the Territories: Historical and Cultural Roots," pp. 95–110 in Bernard Reich and Gershon Kieval (eds.), *Israeli Politics in the 1990's.* New York: Greenwood Press.

Weintraub, Dov, et al. 1971. *Immigrants and Social Change: Agricultural Settlement of New Immigrants in Israel.* Manchester, England: Manchester University Press.

Weintraub, Dov, and Vered Kraus. 1982. "Social Differentiation and Locality of Residence: Spatial Distribution, Composition and Stratification in Israel." *Megamot* 27:367–381.

Weintraub, Dov, Moshe Lissak, and Yael Azmon. 1969. *Moshava, Kibbutz, and Moshav: Patterns of Jewish Rural Settlement and Development in Palestine.* Ithaca: Cornell University Press.

Wilson, William Julius. 1987. *The Truly Disadvantaged.* Chicago: University of Chicago Press.

Yaffe, Nurith. 1976. "On Contraception and Abortion in Israel." Department of Demography, The Hebrew University. Mimeographed.

Yuchtman-Yaar, Ephraim. 1986. "Differences in Ethnic Patterns of Socioeconomic Achievement in Israel: A Neglected Aspect of Structural Inequality." *Megamot* 19:393–412.

Zadka, Pinina. 1989. "Infant Mortality of the Jewish Population in Israel: Trends over Two Decades," pp. 219–228 in Uziel O. Schmelz and Sergio Dellapergola (eds.), *Papers in Jewish Demography: 1985.* Jewish Population Studies 19, Institute of Contemporary Jewry. Jerusalem: The Hebrew University.

Zureik, Elia. 1979. *The Palestinians in Israel: A Study of Internal Colonialism.* London: Routledge and Paul.

Index